P9-AFX-644

The THEBAID

Johns Hopkins
New Translations
from Antiquity

Publius Papinius Statius

The THEBAID

Seven against Thebes

Translated with an Introduction
by Charles Stanley Ross

The Johns Hopkins University Press
Baltimore and London

Printed in the United States of America on acid-free paper
9 8 7 6 5 4 3 2 1

The Johns Hopkins University Press
2715 North Charles Street
Baltimore, Maryland 21218-4363
www.press.jhu.edu

Library of Congress Cataloging-in-Publication Data

Statius, P. Papinius (Publius Papinius)
[Thebais. English]
The Thebaid : seven against Thebes / Publius Papinius Statius ; translated with an introduction by Charles Stanley Ross.
p. cm.
Includes bibliographical references (p.).
ISBN 0-8018-6908-0 (acid-free paper)
1. Seven against Thebes (Greek mythology)—Poetry. 2. Epic poetry, Latin—Translations into English. 3. Polyneices (Greek mythology)—Poetry. 4. Eteocles (Greek mythology)—Poetry. 5. Sibling rivalry—Poetry. 6. Thebes (Greece)—Poetry. I. Ross, Charles Stanley. II. Title.
PA6697.E5T5 2004
871′.01—dc22 2004008928

A catalog record for this book is available from the British Library.

Now for the bare-pick'd bone of majesty
Doth dogged war bristle his angry crest.

Shakespeare, *King John* 4.3.148–49

I do not scruple to prefer Statius to Virgil; his images are strongly conceived, and clearly painted, and the force of his language, while it makes the reader feel, proves that the author felt himself.

Robert Southey, preface to *Joan of Arc* (1798)

Contents

Introduction ix

The THEBAID

1 Exile 1
2 Ambush 27
3 Omens 54
4 Thirst 82
5 Women of Lemnos 114
6 Funeral Games 141
7 Earth Opens 175
8 Savage Hunger 204
9 Tide and Time 232
10 Sacrifices 264
11 Piety 298
12 Clemency 326

Notes 355
Selected Proper Names 377
Selected Annotated Bibliography 381
Acknowledgments 385

Introduction

Publius Papinius Statius lived from approximately A.D. 45 to 96. He was favored by the emperor Domitian, during a reign that degenerated into despotism. Although Rome was still pagan, Statius composed his epic in a period of religious fervor, within a few years of the Christian Gospels, the letters of Saint Paul, and the Midrash commentators. Like other writers on religious issues, Statius constantly questions the relationship between violence and divinity, but he differs in his decision to use the form of narrative poetry in the epic style as a vehicle for his thought. His work was ranked with that of Homer and Virgil throughout the Middle Ages and the Renaissance. Statius appears as a Christian in Dante's *Purgatory*, and he stands as a pillar of poetry in Chaucer's *The House of Fame*. Many critical editions of the *Thebaid* (pronounced THEE-bah-id or The-BAI-id) date from the early seventeenth century, a period of religious war and strife in Europe.

Contributing scenes of terminal destruction to the vocabulary of Western literature, Statius writes of the spectacular deaths of six of the seven heroes who wage war against Thebes: Amphiaraus, Tydeus, Hippomedon, Parthenopaeus, Capaneus, and Polynices. The powerful impact of reading how Tydeus spends his last moments alive gnawing the severed head of his enemy prompted Dante to describe Ugolino chewing the skull of Archbishop Ruggieri in canto 32 of the *Inferno*. Statius is also known for illustrating a key stage in the decline of myth and the rise of allegory, as C. S. Lewis pointed out in *The Allegory of Love*. Boccaccio, for example, used the *Thebaid*, with its figure of Clemency, its House of Mars and House of Sleep, as a model for his influential *Teseida*. Boccaccio's story, in which two men fight for the favors not of a city but a woman, in turn was the source of Chaucer's *Knight's Tale*, one of whose themes is the inability of social bonds to forestall violence.

The conditions of society often determine its aesthetics, and it is interesting to look in the past for changes in critical sensibility. A fifteenth-century Irish translator found in the *Thebaid* a prescient understanding of the forces that threaten civilization. When all ideologies are unmasked, no one's identity is safe, except the barbarian's. Irish culture had reached such a point in 1487, when the violence of social disintegration gave birth to a translation in Gaelic. That work begins by rehearsing a series of local murders, and it is not hard to imagine the translator seeking understanding in Statius for the violence around him. The Irish *Togail na Tebe* incorporated into its text the fifth-century Latin commentary by Placidius Lactantius that had appeared in the first printed editions, and it was influenced by the medieval tradition of chivalric romance. Thus, at the beginning of the speech where Oedipus curses his sons, the translator—to explain otherwise elliptical references to Thebes's history—has Oedipus duel Laius at the crossroads because neither man would stoop to give his name. Such readings are creative and intense. A modern translation may reveal something equally compelling.

Statius's *Thebaid* relates the strife of two brothers, Polynices and Eteocles, the sons of Oedipus, who struggle for control of an ancient Greek city. The myth of the founding of Thebes comes earlier, how armed soldiers sprang up from the furrows Cadmus plowed, creating discord and civil war. The story of Antigone comes after, the subject of Sophocles' tragedy about a woman caught between the law of men—Creon's decree that she not be allowed to bury her brother Polynices—and a higher morality, which demands that she tend her brother's body. Statius's subject, however, is neither the raw force that underlies civility nor the moral blindness of human lives but rather the sad horror and inevitability of conflict. The *Thebaid* is not about society as it develops—the emergence of civilization, order, and language as they overpower brute violence and political chaos—but the stress lines of the modern: the return of repressed violence and the fragmentation of culture. There is, it seems, such a thing as too much success, as well as too much failure, whether in Rome two thousand years ago or today. Even unopposed power may be uneducated, unsteady, liable to new problems but old emotions. Humans are self-destructive; anger comes easily.

Writing in a rhetorical style that stressed the emotions, Statius says that his "*task is to give length to lives*" (4.33; line numbers refer to the Latin text), and to do so he postpones the mutual slaughter of Polynices and Eteocles until almost the end of the poem. He replays, in his own style, many motifs that he drew from Virgil's *Aeneid*. In that earlier Roman epic, the goddess Juno tries to delay the founding of Rome but her efforts are thwarted by fate. Nonetheless, Virgil is always economical; his story moves forward briskly. Statius, by contrast, prefers to linger. The provocation that drives the Argives to war occupies the *Thebaid* for three books. Some years then pass before the beginning of book 4, where Statius first catalogs the forces of the seven against Thebes and almost at once inserts the most pronounced digression in the poem: Bacchus, the god of wine, causes a drought that impedes the Argive advance on his hometown. The tactic Bacchus announces—"meanwhile I will use fraud to weave delay" (4.677)—resembles Statius's own technique, for Statius relishes the story of Hypsipyle, who first leads the Argives to water, then recounts the saga of Lemnos (book 5), where the women slaughtered their men. The death of Archemorus requires lengthy funeral games (book 6) before the war can be resumed.

The story that follows these delays is somewhat similar to the plot of the film *The Magnificent Seven:* a sequence of assaults by seven heroes, each with a unique personality. Most of the heroes die; there is a final battle, and then an outside intervention. Like the *Thebaid,* Hollywood's postwar epic seems to represent history's winners. Seven American cowboys ride into Mexico to free a small town from bandits. The good guys succeed, yet they are oddly troubled by their profession: they long to hang up their guns and find stability, a family, a place to settle. The film imitates, often very closely, *The Seven Samurai,* made in 1954 by Akira Kurosawa. The Japanese film maker, like Statius, understood what it meant to live in the wake of the grim victories that established an imperial state. It is so easy to go awry.

We too move hesitantly into the future, the new world order, and it may be that Statius's art of passion, delay, and extension provides some form of guidance. His poetry combines horror and grace, war and romantic variety. Its sheer intensity still speaks to us, if we listen. This new translation seeks to give Statius a modern voice in clear, unstilted, and rhythmic American verse. Statius's lines conjure a vision we see with our ears, a set of themes and notes unlike anything else but, at the same time, oddly familiar. Strange, dark, and nervous, the poem creates a continual contemporaneity. "But here, at present, now" (1.15): the poet's triadic affirmation insists on the relevance of this epic of Thebes to our own political consciousness.

Statius's Life

Statius's epic strongly influenced Western literature before anyone knew much about its author. Medieval writers inferred Statius's personality from the *Thebaid,* from an unfinished poem on the youth of Achilles called the *Achilleid,* and from scattered comments, such as one by the satirist Juvenal, who said Statius was penurious. Early in the fifteenth century the Italian humanist Poggio Bracciolini discovered a manuscript of occasional poems and personal reflections titled the *Silvae.* (The name means "raw pieces," sticks or wood; Ben Jonson would similarly title his collection of lyrics *Timber.*) An edition appeared in 1494. The master of horror and fraternal strife, the creator of screeching furies and raging warriors, turns out to have been a congenial professional writer, ready to provide poems to order for a wealthy society. He wrote in praise of his contemporary Lucan, for example, whose story of the civil war between Pompey and Caesar rivaled Statius's epic during the Middle Ages and Renaissance. He composed wedding pieces, called epithalamions, and his rhetorical style sometimes reminds one of Milton's *L'Allegro* ("hence, Cares"). He mentions his passion for singing of Thebes and his thoughts about how to end his poem (3.2.29). He several times refers to the myth of Palaemon that so oddly recurs in the *Thebaid*. The *Silvae* suggests that Statius propitiated the god to protect his friends at sea.

Besides showing us a somewhat superstitious but cultured poet at home with the works of Ovid, Virgil, Lucretius, Valerius Flaccus, and various forms of poetry, the *Silvae* provides us a glimpse of Roman life among the well-heeled. A poem about a villa at Tibur mentions grottoes and marbles, quiet shades, buildings, and pools. In a poem thanking Domitian for an estate where Statius can escape the summer heat, a thunderstorm interrupts a picnic and the revelers retreat to a small shrine dedicated to Hercules. Slave girls parade through the emperor's games. Dante may have had it right when he reversed Juvenal and made Statius a prodigal. Everywhere we see the wealth of Rome, the vast reach of the empire, and its trade in gold, jewels, marble, exotic foods, wild animals, woods, cloth, and wines. Aqueducts carry water to the capital; fortresses protect its frontiers. Statius loved hot baths.

Sexual morality seems to have been variously prescribed in first-century Rome. The *Silvae* several times praises Parthenopaeus, one of the seven against Thebes, whose name refers to his feminine features. One poem celebrates the emperor's dedicating a minion's blond tresses to the god Asclepius (3.4). Statius compliments Domitian for passing a law forbidding the creation of eunuchs. Elsewhere he reproaches his wife for despairing at his plan to retire to his native Naples: Vesuvius, he says, has not destroyed everything in the region. He celebrates his wife's fidelity, although she still loves her first husband and misses her daughter. He recalls how she kissed him when he won the Alban wreath for poetry and consoled him when he lost a poetic contest by the Capitol. She shared the long labor of his *Thebaid*.

Throughout his minor poetry Statius shows an artist's sensitivity. He appreciates architecture, sculpture, literature, and beauty. Years after the death of his father, he thanks him for guiding his epic in the footsteps of the ancient bards (*priscorum vatum*). He admits to polishing his *Thebaid* endlessly (4.7). Perhaps his most charming poem is a little ode to sleep. Wracked with insomnia, he asks not for a shower of drowsiness but only a touch of the tip of Sleep's wand.

Critics contend about the extent to which the *Thebaid* reflects Statius's views on contemporary politics. During the first century Rome was ruled by those whom Edward Gibbon in *The Decline and Fall of the Roman Empire* called the iron emperors, despots such as Tiberius (A.D. 14–37), the almost insane Caligula (37–41), and Nero (54–68). Four pretenders struggled for power in 68–69, after Nero died, ending a line that traced itself back to Julius Caesar. They represented, in turn, the power of the Spanish legions, the imperial household in Rome, the army of the Rhine, and the armies of the Danube and Middle East. The winner was Titus Flavius Vespasian (70–79). He had two sons, Titus (79–81), who captured Jerusalem in 70 and later completed the construction of Rome's Colisseum, which his father had begun, and Domitian (81–96). Despite hints of rivalry between the brothers, Statius's audience, like that of today, would have been unsure whether Statius meant to mirror contemporary politics in his epic. It may be that Statius both courted and avoided relevance. As John Henderson argues, the Romans could hardly *not* read into the *Thebaid* the story of Vespasian and his two sons, whose troubled reigns followed the civil wars led by Galba, Otho, and Vitellius: "Myth was always a vehicle of civic thought, otherwise our reading of Latin would be dead" (p. 221).

My own view is that emotions, customs, and attitudes, rather than specific events, connect Thebes to contemporary Rome. Quintillian advised poets not to be *too* obvious, but the passions of the *Thebaid* are real enough, despite—or because of—its mythic plot. For example, in a lament for the death of his son, whom Statius had adopted as an infant, he remarks that his own name was the first word his son spoke. He gives the same blessing to Hypsipyle in the *Thebaid,* who made the mother of Archemorus jealous because it was Hypsipyle, the nurse, who experienced the baby's first motions. Where Virgil salutes the birth of a child in his celebrated fourth eclogue, Statius mourns for the death of children by means of a rhetorical style that everywhere strives to put troubles at arm's length. A poem in the *Silvae* about someone else's dead son mentions Palaemon, whom Ino drowned, and Opheltes, the baby torn by a serpent as he lay in the grass of Lerna (cf. *Silvae* 2.1 and *Thebaid* 5.588–604).

Besides touching on intimate emotions, the story of Thebes shows how a belief in destiny allows people to accept their misfortunes. In his essay "On Fate" Ralph Waldo Emerson defines destiny as the minister who executes in this world what God has foreseen. Citing Chaucer's *Knight's Tale* (which begins with a Latin quotation from the *Thebaid*), Emerson claims that a heroic belief in fate makes people free. Statius anticipates this thought. Six of the seven against Thebes are doomed to die and know it, once Amphiaraus reads the auguries and Tiresias foresees the future in the flames of hell. The war is fated to fail, yet no one alters his actions. Each champion perseveres in the enterprise that dooms him. Statius is regularly accused of not constructing a sound plot. Tasso and Boileau and Pope said he should have started *in medias res,* and the second half of the poem strains to overcome sequential deaths by fortune, drowning, lightning, and misjudgment. Yet the linearity of the *Thebaid*, like the theme of delay, challenges fate. Statius's heroes exemplify what Emerson called the "impulse of choosing and acting in the soul." They celebrate favorable omens and ignore signs of disaster (the point of the funeral games in book 6). Human hatred may never die; men may be fools to read the future; the Argive heroes perish in a questionable cause but, as Statius tells the story, they die freely.

Statius himself died at the very beginning of Rome's greatest century, the era of the golden emperors Nerva, Trajan, Hadrian, Antoninus Pius, and Marcus Aurelius, which lasted from 96 to 180. During this period Rome finally renounced its pretensions to territories beyond the Euphrates. Given the good fortune of Statius's poem, it is possible to believe that its generally pacifist but heroic tenor found appreciation in the age that followed his death.

Statius and Virgil

Although Homer's *Iliad* is the source of most of the features of the Western epic, from catalogs of armies to divine interventions, Statius openly admired Virgil's *Aeneid* and often developed elements of his Roman predecessor's plot, even when these derived from Homer. The theme of delay, for example, arguably goes back to Achilles' anger at Agamemnon that both delays the hero's return to war against the Trojans and provides the unity that Aristotle so much admired in Homer's poem. In Virgil's hands a similar delay occurs as Juno prevents the Trojan refugees from finding their destined homeland. Statius eliminates the Odyssean element of Virgil's epic; his armies do not wander the Mediterranean in ships, but he does imitate Virgil's reprise of the theme of delay when, after the Trojans land in the right place, Juno calls on the demonic forces of the underworld to postpone their settlement in Latium. Just as Allecto rouses the hounds of Ascanius against Silvia's pet stag in *Aeneid* 7, Tisiphone maddens the sacred tigers of Bacchus (*Thebaid* 7.579). But where Virgil is concise and confines Allecto to a single episode, Statius spreads the role of Tisiphone throughout the poem. She hears Oedipus's call in the first book, lifts her serpent tresses from the waters of Cocytus, and enters the upper world, where she remains until the end of the story.

Also in contrast to Virgil, Statius extends the motivation for the war beyond the underworld to Jupiter's anger and his design to punish mankind. Virgil makes Jupiter a figure of serenity whose purpose is not to provoke strife but to mirror the justness of Aeneas, which contrasts with the angry passions of Dido, just as Jupiter contrasts with his wife. As A. J.

Gossage argues, when comparing Virgil and Statius, Virgil's figures of Jupiter and Aeneas represent the

> Roman genius for organization and order over the forces of destruction, war and civil conflict. The Jupiter of the *Thebaid* who punishes men for their crimes is a moral castigator far removed, despite his basic serenity, from Virgil's Jupiter; moreover, since he too is angry, there is no great contrast with Juno, who, in any case, is not a powerful enough character to make a balance or contrast possible. The inner tension of the *Thebaid* is a more complex matter. Angry passions appear in both Argos and Thebes; the main conflict is between two men who, with their supporters, are both driven on by *furor*. Besides this there is an effective contrast between the uncontrolled violence of men like Polynices, Tydeus and Capaneus and the efforts of Adrastus and Amphiaraus to calm them; this contrast is emphasized and typified by the clash between Tisiphone and Pietas. The pattern of human relationships in the *Thebaid,* therefore, is not, as in the *Aeneid,* simply and clearly reflected in the relationships of the gods. (p. 81)

If Statius altered Jupiter, he also developed ideas that made readers like Dante believe that Virgil, who died in 19 B.C., was a Christian before the fact. Like Virgil, as Gossage points out, Statius describes the terrors of approaching war, families searching for dead relatives on the battlefield, and mothers lamenting lost sons. He understood the sufferings of the innocent involved in the conflicts of their rulers and, as usual, expanded what Virgil touched. The expedition of Hopleus and Dymas to recover the bodies of their leaders, Tydeus and Parthanopaeus, imitates Virgil's story of Nisus and Euryalus, and Statius adds other examples of *pietas,* which Gossage defines as "the close ties of duty and affection among members of a family," including the self-sacrifice of Menoeceus to save Thebes and the "mission of the Argive women, and in particular Argia, the widow of Polynices, to recover the bodies of their menfolk slain at Thebes and give them burial" (p. 73).

In another alteration of Virgil, Statius expands the death of Lausus, known for his personal beauty, into a lengthy portrait of Parthenopaeus, the youngest of the Argive captains. He shows him running nude in the funeral games of book 6 (itself an imitation of *Aeneid* 5); gives him, like Lausus, a tunic woven for him by his mother; and has his enemies accuse him of attempting deeds beyond his strength. Michael C. J. Putnam has argued that by killing Lausus, who dies protecting his father Mezentius, Aeneas fails to respond to the virtue of *pietas,* supposedly his personal strength, when he sees it in others. In the *Thebaid,* Parthenopaeus is killed not so much by a single warrior as by an accumulation of obstacles. Here, too, Statius expands a single element in Virgil's poem, projecting Aeneas's moral failing onto the entire Argive cause.

Sometimes Statius pays homage to Virgil by successfully giving prominence to his predecessor's details. He moves Virgil's opening sea storm into the mountains and forests of Greece; both scenes show, as Gossage notes, an exile in distress, the mirroring of human frenzy in the agitations of nature, and deceptive calm when the storms end. Later in the poem Hypsipyle's narration of the Lemnian massacre begins with lines that recall Aeneas's beginning of his tale of the fall of Troy. Both narrators recoil in horror from what they have to say: "Although the main details of the story are quite different, there are other Virgilian reminiscences, such as the approach of the fleet, the false security before the massacre, Hypsipyle's sudden alarm for the safety of her father, and the escape itself, through the unfrequented places of the city" (p. 85). The story of Coroebus and the monster in the *Thebaid* derives from Evander's account of Cacus and Hercules in Virgil's seventh book, as both are "introduced during an entertainment as an explanation for religious observances" (pp. 86–87). Finally, Adrastus is based on Virgil's Latinus, the leader of a community whose peace is interrupted. Both men try to calm the ardor of younger heroes and flee when their efforts fail.

The Influence of the *Thebaid*

Statius's envoy tells us that even before its completion his *Thebaid* was taught in Italy's schoolrooms and the young memorized verses. It was the last successful epic written in Rome. Like other literary works, its survival depended on the senatorial class, which paid for the copying and editing of texts. The Roman families that maintained polytheism until the fifth century would likely have seen their values mirrored in the exploits of Statius's great heroes. But the frank unfairness of the gods, particularly Apollo, would also have played into the interests of the new church as it sought to overcome the beliefs of the rural populations, irrespective of the gentry.

The allegorist's task of explaining away the rude husk of the poem fell to Fabius Planciades Fulgentius, who may have lived in the fifth or sixth century or as late as the twelfth. He turns the war against Thebes into a spiritual war for the soul of man. His imaginative reading is worth reviewing as an antidote to the dismissal of Statius that occupied the antiallegorical interval of criticism that lasted from roughly the English Civil War to World War II (1640–1940). During this period Statius was condemned because he did not leap through the neoclassical hoop of the unities. Critics said the *Thebaid* lost track of its narrative line. It repeated figurative devices, usually animal similes. Its moralizing was thought to be sometimes sincere but sometimes perfunctory. Most agreed that Statius was less than Virgil. Alexander Pope condemned Statius's catalogs of armies as merely imitative and said that Statius destroyed the unity of his action by including funeral games for Archemorus. Others regarded Statius's gods as pale imitations of Homer's originals. The result was that Statius's message was lost for several centuries.

Fulgentius believed that Statius's story of Thebes taught people how to develop sound habits of life. This allegorical reading is no more extraordinary than Fulgentius's analysis of the *Aeneid,* which discovers the progress of a human's life in Virgil's first six books, from the pangs of childbirth in the storm that blows Aeneas into Dido's kingdom to the figuration of death in Aeneas's descent to the underworld. In Fulgentius's commentary, Thebes is the soul inhabited by virtues and ruled by Laius, or sacred light, and Jocasta, or Joy. Oedipus, or licentiousness, extinguishes the light, and his birth defiles the purity of Joy. The chorus in Aeschylus's *Seven against Thebes* says Eteocles means "full of glory" and Polynices' name means "full of strife." For Fulgentius, by contrast, the sons of Oedipus are greed and lust. Greed destroys morals (*ethos*) and lust is the conqueror (*nichos*) of many. Eteocles rules Thebes because greed easily suppresses the lustful man, who goes in exile to the Greeks, just as licentious men, who waste their wealth, flee to worldly wisdom.

Although Fulgentius is guilty of false etymologies (his ability to comprehend Greek does not withstand scrutiny), he has alertly and with some sensitivity read the poem he explicates. He is wrong to claim that Adrastus derives his name from *adrios,* Greek for *profunditas,* but he is correct about the suitability of that theme to the king of Argos. In a similar way Fulgentius identifies Adrastus's daughter Argia with foreknowledge, since *argeos* in Greek is *providentia,* as in the name Argus, the monster with a hundred eyes. Fulgentius is wrong again, but the allegory he derives is cleverly constructed. In this scheme of things, Polynices marries foreknowledge, the daughter of philosophy, and at the end of a year, emboldened by worldly wisdom, he seeks to regain the rule of Thebes from his brother. When Eteocles refuses, seven kings pledge to support Polynices. They are the seven liberal arts, for they guide and support all branches of learning, and they are subject to Adrastus because he represents philosophy. (Fulgentius forgets that Adrastus is one of Statius's seven against Thebes, but then, Greek authors were never exact. Aeschylus lists an Eteoclus instead of Adrastus among the seven. Homer mentions the expedition of the seven against Thebes as an adventure that occurs in the generation before the events of the *Iliad,* but neither he nor Greek tragedy offers a consistent account of the heroes' personalities or deaths.)

Writing from a Christian perspective Fulgentius explains that the Argives grow thirsty because they lack the wellspring of faith: to drink of worldly knowledge does not lessen thirst but increases it. Hypsipyle is the love of Isis, the chief goddess of Egypt—that is, Idolatry, which leads to its stream all who strain after worldly knowledge. A serpent kills Archemorus because the foster child of idolatry is death. Naturally the serpent is the devil. It is appropriate that the Greeks console Lycurgus, the child's father, because worldly knowledge consoles those who die in their sins. They bury Archemorus with honor because, says Fulgentius, "the followers of idolatry, who as they sleep in death are enveloped in the praise of men and the vainglory of earth, are at least in the vulgar view buried with pomp and circumstance" (p. 242).

Fulgentius had a ready eye for details and for questions raised by the text. The story proceeds as those who grasp at philosophy fight against greed, but unsuccessfully, because men choose what is worthless or they esteem vain knowledge. Adrastus survives because philosophy may lead others to ruin but does not die itself. The poem ends when the royal widows, who represent human feelings, make their appeal to Theseus, or God, who liberates Thebes, the soul, by overcoming pride with humility. Although Fulgentius comments that the rest of the story is worthless, he developed a powerful reading of the poem that helps explain the despair that characterizes Statius's representation of human affairs.

Fulgentius did not leave a strong textual tradition from which we might deduce his influence, although his method of reading, which can be found in Macrobius, was common enough. By contrast the comments of Lactantius Placidus (who cites and therefore postdates Boethius) are fairly unimaginative but offered grammatical and mythological guidance, if not to the Middle Ages, from which only four manuscripts derive, then to Renaissance readers who benefited from more than twenty editions of the *Thebaid* that included Lactantius's extensive sets of glosses.

Statius became popular in the early Middle Ages as the role of the classics grew in medieval education. In 1086 Americo di Gâlinaux listed Statius in his *Ars lectoria* along with Terence, Virgil, Ovid, Sallust, Lucan, Juvenal, and Persius. An eleventh-century anthology that once belonged to Saint Augustine in Canterbury includes the laments of Eurydice for her dead son Opheltes. Twelfth-century monastic libraries list 61 *Thebaids*, compared with 80 *Aeneids*, 34 *Metamorphoses,* and 113 copies of Lucan's epic.

Sometime in the later twelfth century the *Thebaid* was translated into

French octosyllabics and turned into a chivalric romance, probably for an audience of nobles and clerics, perhaps for the Plantagenet court of Henry II and Eleanor of Aquitaine. The story begins with the history of Oedipus, turns the ancient Greeks into jousting knights, and includes a final episode featuring an attempt to betray Thebes. The extended version of the Oedipus story blurs Statius's theme of fraternal strife, while the theme of betrayal illustrates the obsession with loyalty that characterizes early French epics, including *Le chanson de Roland,* whose author probably knew Statius. Written by a Christian, the French version of Statius's poem omits the gods and so excludes Apollo's vengeance and Adrastus's prayer.

Le roman de Thèbes is really a story of a social order gone awry, where sons disobey their fathers and women do not know their place. Furious at his brother's marriage, Eteocles would rather let himself be hanged than hand over his kingdom. Eight days before his term is due, he holds a private council where he reveals a treacherous plot to kill his brother. Tydeus, when ambushed, fights "like Roland." The Argive heroes join Adrastus because of the treacherous attack on Tydeus, not from any sense of a civil war or fraternal strife. Eteocles had wronged each of them in some way.

Oblivious to the theme of fate, the translator can find no excuse for what even modern readers might feel is a flaw in Statius's story, the way Hypsipyle leaves behind Lycurgus's baby when she leads the Argives to water in book 4. Driven not by destiny but by the ethos of a French nobleman, Eteocles offers Polynices a fief, to be held from him. The Argives reject this proposal as an insult. The author then has them hold a tournament near Thebes to replace the funeral games in Statius's poem. He turns the augur Amphiaraus into an archbishop and decorates the chariot that carries him to the underworld with symbols of the liberal arts, such as rhetoric, music, and astronomy. The translator, who may have been Anglo-Norman, also gives Eteocles a set of exotic associates: a girlfriend named Galatea, whom he abandons; a Jewish adviser named Salaciel; and an English supporter named Goodrich. Theseus intervenes in the end, not to maintain the custom of burial or relieve the suffering of the Argive widows, but because Creon breaks his word by failing to acknowledge his lordship and pay tribute.

During the thirteenth and fourteenth centuries *Le roman de Thèbes* was redacted into prose (*Roman de Edipus* and *Hystoire de Thebes*) and later into verse. As Robert R. Edwards notes in his edition of John Lydgate's *The Siege of Thebes,* universal histories like the *Histoire ancienne jusqu'à César* (ca. 1208–13), which begin with the creation of the world and connect pagan, Jewish, and Christian history, take the story of Thebes as a warning against cyclic violence. Lydgate himself was a Lancastrian propagandist for Henry

V, who died in 1421 or 1422, soon after Lydgate composed *The Siege of Thebes*. The Monk of Bury, as Lydgate is known, makes Tydeus a model of knightly virtues, perhaps even a portrait of the famous victor of Agincourt. Tydeus does not eat anyone in Lydgate's version, and he is less passionate than Statius's creation, at one point refusing to seduce the daughter of Lycurgus, who nurses him back to health in her father's garden. When Shakespeare dramatized the strife between Henry V's surviving brother Humphrey, duke of Gloucester, and John, duke of Bedford, he gave the short but powerful limbs of Tydeus to Talbot, England's fiercest warrior (*1 Henry VI* 2.3.22).

Statius's influence on Renaissance English literature is most vividly felt in Edmund Spenser's *Faerie Queene,* where each book is composed of twelve cantos on the model Statius first copied from Virgil. A Cambridge graduate and educated in the classics, Spenser must have regarded Statius as a master of horror. At the end of the first canto of the *Faerie Queene,* Archimago rouses a false dream from hell to give Red Crosse a nightmare, just as the shade of Laius infects the sleep of Eteocles (*Thebaid* 2.94–119). It is a very odd way to start an epic, unless the model is not the abstract ideal of an action that should begin in the middle of things, but the actual practice of a master like Statius (whose own inspiration was probably Agamemnon's dream at the beginning of book 3 of the *Iliad*). As Archimago works his magic—"A bold bad man, that dar'd to call by name / Great Gorgon, Prince of darknesse and dead night, / At which Cocytus quakes, and Styx is put to flight" (*Fairie Queene* 1.1.37)—he invokes the same infernal power that Tiresias dares not name in the fourth book of the *Thebaid.* (A scribal error in the commentary of Lactantius turned the unnamed *demiurge* into Demogorgon, an overseer of demons and fairies who appears in Boccaccio's *Genealogy of the Gods,* Boiardo's *Orlando innamorato* [2.13.26–29], and then Spenser's romance epic.)

Spenser knew Statius directly, but he also knew the romance traditions Statius inspired, including the work of Ariosto and Tasso. The brawl between Britomart and other knights in a pigsty outside the house of Malbecco (*Fairie Queene* 2.9) ultimately derives from Statius's description of Polynices battling Tydeus for shelter on Adrastus's porch (*Thebaid* 1.408–27). Their brawl, I would argue, gave rise to the custom of the castle motif in medieval French and Renaissance Italian romances, since the two Greeks fight for lodging in a context that raises fundamental questions of justice, as later knights will do (see my *Custom of the Castle from Malory to Macbeth* [Berkeley: University of California Press, 1997]).

There is no evidence that Shakespeare read the *Thebaid,* but like Spenser he knew the traditions it spawned. The Gloucester subplot of Shakespeare's *King Lear* derives from Statius by way of Philip Sidney's *Arcadia* (1590), which includes a story about two rival brothers and their blinded father (bk. 2, chap. 10). In the *Defense of Poetry* Sidney says that the story of Polynices and Eteocles is about ambition, a word he may have gleaned from Euripides' *Phoenician Women*. In that play Jocasta asks Eteocles why he pursues Ambition, the worst of gods, instead of Equality. George Gascoigne, whom Sidney knew, translated Euripides' play from an Italian version by Ludovico Dolce, but we may suspect that Sidney read Statius directly because a soldier who works for one of the rival brothers is named Tydeus.

Whether or not Shakespeare read Statius, at least some in his audience associated the Gloucester subplot with the story of Thebes. John Webster's *The White Devil*, first performed in 1612, openly imitates *King Lear* and also recalls Polynices and Eteocles. Bracciano raves madly in his bed and seeks to dispute with the devil, just as Lear wants to talk philosophy with mad Tom. Webster's Flamineo, like Shakespeare's Edgar, counsels patience. Marcello then compares Flamineo and himself with "the two slaughtered sons of Oedipus, / The very flames of our affection / Shall turn two ways" (5.1.198). The details of the battling flames and Oedipal madness indicate that Webster had Statius in mind, not Greek drama.

Shakespeare also knew the reputation of Theseus, and in *A Midsummer Night's Dream* he consciously set the Athenian leader in a *Thebaid*-like context of conflicting customs and fraternal strife. Classical Greek drama had already made Theseus a figure of redemption who resolved the nightmare of social disorder that ancient Athenians projected onto Thebes. In Euripides' *Suppliant Women*, Adrastus (not Argia) appeals to Theseus. The Athenian leader berates the Argive king for arrogance and for stupidly marrying his daughters to foreigners, thereby muddying the clear waters of his house. He also accuses Adrastus of ignoring the prophecies that predicted doom for his expedition against Thebes and for being led astray by young men who want war without realizing its consequences because they want to lead armies, acquire power, or win wealth. Although Theseus at first refuses to help, blaming Adrastus for his poor judgment, eventually he yields to the entreaties of the Chorus in order to uphold his reputation as a punisher of wrongdoing. He believes that all Greece is affected by Creon's violation of the custom of burial, whose purpose, he believes, is to encourage men to go to war.

Shakespeare turns the figure whom Fulgentius said represented God, the man who delivers mercy to the Argive women and ensures the proper burial of the dead, into an overly cerebral observer of young lovers. At first he sternly upholds the custom of Athens that Hermia must marry according to her father's wishes. Eventually he comes to his senses and lets the dreams of the young lovers come true. Often at odds, Demetrius and Lysander and Hermia and Helena are latter-day versions of Oedipus's sons. Their love stories trace back to Boccaccio's *Teseida,* the fourteenth-century romance that turned Statius's story of two brothers who compete for a kingdom into a medieval tale of two knights who joust for the affections of a lady.

Like Shakespeare, Chaucer seems to have read Statius for the most part indirectly. He based his *Knight's Tale* on the *Teseida,* where he would have read Boccaccio's *chiodi,* or keys, to the poem, which retell Statius's epic. Chaucer invokes the fury Tisiphone in the first and fourth books of the *Troilus,* but makes the fury sad herself, not the source of terror in others as she is in the *Thebaid.* He also shows Cressida reading the story of Thebes, but she seems to read the French romance version, not the Latin original in twelve books. Nonetheless critics have suggested a deep affinity between the poets. Some argue that Chaucer found a model for Cressida's suffering as a woman among the widows depicted in the *Thebaid.* Others point out that Pandarus may raise the issue of what text Cressida reads to make her feel uneducated and vulnerable. He wants to remind his niece of her lack of education and so make her susceptible to his suggestions that she take Troilus as a lover and protector. Among those who detect a strong Statian influence Lee Patterson argues that Thebes represents cyclic disorder in *The Knight's Tale.* He contrasts the recursive violence that Chaucer associated with Theban myths (as when the incest of Oedipus replays the fate of Cadmus's earthborn soldiers) with the linear but limited plot of Christian causality, which obscures the role of chance and is ultimately grounded in human will. According to Patterson, Chaucer responded to the way Statius asserts the value of virtue and piety and the hints he gives of a happier afterlife. Nonetheless Chaucer's reading of Statius seems not to have been as direct as Dante's.

Statius's presence in English literature has always been more precarious than in Italy. In his *Convivium* Dante exalts Argia and Deipyle as models of virtue, and he included all of Statius's major figures in his *Divine Comedy.* The first great elaboration of an episode from Statius's poem occurs when Dante recalls Capaneus in *Inferno* 14, where he empties him of heroism and makes him a figure of impiety. Later he puts Tiresias's daughter Manto among the seers of the fourth *bolgia* (*Inferno* 20.52). Dante encounters Statius in Purgatory on the fifth terrace, among the avaricious and the prodigal, almost as part of a divine plan. He watches Statius approach Virgil as Statius himself might expect a future poet, steeped in his works, to meet and admire his own shade (*Purgatorio* 21). Less clear is why, in *Pur-*

gatorio 25, Statius explains the reason that souls survive the body after death. The early commentator Pietro di Dante suggested that where Dante saw Virgil as the model of rational philosophy, he regarded Statius as someone suitable for giving examples from moral philosophy.

In general the role of Statius expresses Dante's view that Latin poetry provided a providential vision to guide the might of the Roman Empire toward Christianity (cf. the words of Justinian in *Paradiso* 6.92–93). The figure of Statius passes through the flames at the entrance of the Earthly Paradise with Dante and Virgil and is present when Dante awakens (*Purgatorio* 27.47, 114). For a similar reason Dante turns to Statius and Virgil after listening to Matilda (28.145–46); then, after a long silence, we see Statius follow Beatrice's chariot, accompanied by Matilda and the pilgrim (32.29). At *Purgatorio* 33.134–35 Beatrice invites Statius to accompany her procession. Statius then accompanies Dante until the end of the canticle, and by the beginning of the *Paradiso* he has been assumed into heaven on his own account and dwells among the blessed.

Given the way Dante promoted Statius, it is not surprising that the *Thebaid* continued to exert an influence on later Italian writers. Giovanni Boccaccio owned a twelfth-century manuscript (Biblioteca Medicea-Laurenziana, MS Plut. 38.6) and sought out Lactantius's commentary and another copy of the poem. Matteo Maria Boiardo knew the first printed edition of the *Teseida* (1475), which included a commentary by Pier Andrea dei Bassi. Boiardo reprises Boccaccio's theme in his *Orlando innamorato,* where the cousins Rinaldo and Orlando vie for the love of Angelica. In contrast to Dante, for whom Statius is a deeply meaningful figure, Boiardo, fully aware of how Boccaccio rewrote the *Thebaid,* catches Statius's lightness, sense of humor, and ironic distance from his subject. For example, Boiardo's Algerian warrior Rodamonte makes fun of fortunetellers just as Capaneus does in the *Thebaid.* In Boiardo's epic the ancient king of Garamanta warns against war, thereby provoking the skepticism of Rodamonte:

> Laughing his hardest, Rodamonte
> heard the old man's prophetic words.
> But when he saw him mute and silent,
> in a loud, booming voice he said,
> "It is all right while we are here
> to prophesy all you desire.
>
> "But after we have crossed the sea
> and ruined France with sword and fire,
> don't come to me to make predictions—

I'll be the prophet over there!
To these men you can threaten harm
but not to me; I don't believe you.
Your foolish brain and lots of wine
make you hear Allah in your mind!"

Many men laughed, who gladly heard
that haughty cavalier's response.
(*Orlando innamorato* 2.1.60–61)

In the *Thebaid,* Boiardo's source, the narrator addresses Amphiaraus, then Capaneus similarly mocks the augur for predicting disaster for the Argives.

He stood before your gates, Amphiaraus,
among the mob of rabble and its leaders,
and yelled, "What kind of cowardice is this,
o Argives, and you blood-related Greeks?
Do we, so many people armed in iron,
hang here before a common person's doorway,
a single citizen's, when we are ready
and willing? I won't wait while some pale virgin
utters her warning riddles for Apollo—
if he exists, if he is not a rumor
or something for the timid to believe—
secluded deep within his crazy cavern,
beneath the hollow peak of Cirrha, moaning!
My god is my own strength, this sword I hold!
Now let that timid priest, that fraud, emerge—
or I will demonstrate the power of birds!"

The rabble howled with joy . . . (3.606–18)

Like Boiardo, Ludovico Ariosto, the most popular poet of Renaissance Italy, borrowed several motifs from Statius's epic and, at the same time, learned how Statius absorbed his precursors. In his *Orlando furioso* (1516), Doralice complains that Mandricardo fights Ruggiero over a trivial item, the insignia of an eagle, not because he loves her but because he is naturally ferocious and always looking for an excuse to fight (3.34). Her complaint is based on Argia's attempt to delay Polynices from leaving for Thebes (*Thebaid* 2.332–63), which in turn recalls a bedroom conversation between Amata and Turnus (*Aeneid* 12.54) and its Homeric source, the conversational exchange between Andromache and Hector in the *Iliad,* which this translation mimics through the filter of Shakespeare's version (*Troilus and Cressida* 5.3.1).

In the absence of much academic commentary, poets who admired Statius have often been his best critics. For example, Ariosto responded to Statius's sympathy for suffering. He based the Cretan women of the Guido Selvaggio episode (*Orlando furioso* 20.5–61) on the women of Lemnos in Statius, and the prayers and laments of women during the siege of Paris recall the way the Argive women pray to Juno (*Thebaid* 10.49), a scene, Ariosto knew, that Boiardo also drew on (*Orlando innamorato* 1.7.4). From Statius later writers learned to put passion into their allegorical personifications. Ariosto's Saint Michael is sent to find Silence and Discord, and the source is in the pagan epic, a mixture of Iris and Mercury, messengers of Juno and Jupiter respectively. Iris visits the cave of Sleep in the Ovid's *Metamorphoses* (11.585) and, more important for Ariosto, in the *Thebaid* (10.80), where the Italian poet found abstractions like Laziness and Silence who inhabit the court; moreover the mission is similar, to put a band of soldiers to sleep and make them helpless victims. Michael's second visit to Discord (*Orlando furioso* 27.35) derives from Mercury's trip to the house of Mars (*Thebaid* 7.5). Ariosto would have been aware that Virgil's Juno gives one of the Erynnis, Aletto, a similar mission (*Aeneid* 7.339).

The death of Parthanopaeus was a model for that of Ariosto's Dardinello, Almonte's young son, whom Rinaldo kills; the simile at *Orlando furioso* 18.151 comes from *Thebaid* 7.670–74. Night quickly ends the siege of Paris in *Orlando furioso* 18.161, just as Jupiter accelerates evening after the death of Parthenopaeus (*Thebaid*. 10.1–4). The Christians remain outside Paris and besiege the besiegers, just as the Thebans do. (Contrast *Iliad* 7.435–41.)

Ariosto's most extensive borrowing comes in the episode of Cloridano and Medoro (*Orlando furioso* 18.165–19.15), a version of Statius's Hopleus and Dymas, which Statius in turn openly modeled on Virgil's Nisus and Euryalus (*Aeneid* 9.300–597). But where Virgil tells the story of two men who lose themselves and each other as they slaughter sleeping enemies at night, Ariosto and Statius tell a story of two very close friends who wander through the aftermath of battle in search of the bodies of their commanders. Ariosto must have noticed how Statius set up a comparison between two soldiers who search for their lords' bodies (10.347–448) and Antigone and Argia, who later look for Polynices (12.111–463). Medoro's prayer to the moon comes from Statius. Ariosto's Dymas, like Statius's Argia, also prays to the moon.

Over the centuries scores of poets modeled compositions on the *Aeneid* and tried to compete with Virgil. Statius was the best of these myriad competitors in the epic vein, on a par with Lucan, Tasso, and Milton. He is sometimes baroque, as when he makes Neptune's horses behave like waves in book 2 ("First their hooves / scrape up the sand, but then they disappear / into the sea, like fish," *Thebaid* 2.46–47), but he is often movingly spiritual. Such poetry flourished in the seventeenth century. Milton's deepest debt to Statius was similar to Dante's. His religious verses, such as the heartfelt prayers of Adam and Eve or the narrator's meditation on his blindness and circumstances, evoke Statius at his most hymnal, as when Adrastus prays to Apollo, Tydeus praises Athena, Tiresias evokes the spirits of hell, the earth swallows Amphiaraus, or the Argive women flock to the altar of Clemency in Athens.

For English readers Milton may be the best witness to Statius's powers of poetry. *Paradise Lost* directly borrows two images from Statius's book of gloom, the visible darkness of hell's "livid flames" (1.182; cf. *Styx livida, Thebaid* 1.57) and Adam's reaction to Eve's having eaten the forbidden fruit. In the *Thebaid* Bacchus drops his garlands when he sees the Argive army threaten his home city of Thebes: "his hand released his thyrsis; / his garlands and his curls fell out of place; / his horn of plenty dropped unblemished grapes" (*Thebaid* 7.58). Adam is similarly stunned:

On th' other side, Adam, soon as he heard
The fatal Trespass done by Eve, amaz'd,
Astonied stood and Blank, while horror chill
Ran through his veins, and all his joints relax'd;
From his slack hand the Garland wreath'd for *Eve*
Down dropp'd, and all the faded Roses shed:
Speechless he stood and pale . . .
(*Paradise Lost* 9.888–95)

Milton also would have known that one of Statius's favorite tropes is the uncertainty topos. Milton adopts the topos at the beginning of *Paradise Lost,* when, uncertain where the Holy Ghost of inspiration may dwell, he invokes him "on the secret top / of *Oreb,* or of *Sinai* . . . *Sion* Hill . . . and *Siloa's* Brook" (1.7–11). Statius also uses it to offer possible explanations for things he cannot know, such as why the flights of birds foretell the future:

What is
the cause that makes the miracle? What gives
winged birds this power? Is it that the founder
of heaven's upper halls weaves wondrous patterns
throughout vast Chaos? or because winged birds
have been transformed from human origins

by metamorphoses? or is the truth
more easily obtained because birds fly
in heaven's purer air, removed from sin,
and rarely land on earth? (3.482–88)

Another version of the uncertainty topos occurs when Adrastus invokes Apollo on "Lycia's / snow-covered mountains or Patara's thorns" or Castalia or Thymbra or on Mount Cynthus (*Thebaid* 1.696–702).

Statius and His Poem

Statius was a recognized role model for poets, and his story of the Theban war taught a moral lesson, despite its horrors. Paolo Orosius, a fifth-century Christian historian, regarded the mutual murder of Polynices and Eteocles as a revolting crime. The husk of the story hid a kernel of truth, however, for the medieval commentator Fulgentius, who interpreted the Theban war as an allegorical battle for the soul of man. In the *Purgatory* Dante not only has Statius express his admiration for the *Aeneid,* which he often imitates, but the later Roman poet claims to have learned Christian doctrine from Virgil's earlier poem. For such commentators Statius's subject matter illustrated the failings of the pagan world, yet beneath the poem's sordid exterior readers could detect a glimmer of truth. Nor were early readers far wrong, for Statius seems to have recognized the implications and complexities of his theme.

The *Thebaid* explores fraternal strife in ways that go beyond a simple battle between two brothers for political power. Statius's epic delays until late in book 11 the final confrontation of Polynices and Eteocles. It then continues beyond the death of the brothers, as the twelfth book tells how Theseus leads an Athenian army against Creon. Before this resolution, however, the poem provides a rich cast of characters whose relations allusively comment on the meaning of brotherhood and the sources of strife. The Argive, Theban, and Lemnian women, the Furies, the deaths of the great heroes that culminate several books, the epigrammatic demise of incidental characters, the blackening of Apollo's reputation, the flights of birds, the incest of Oedipus, the interference of the gods, and echoes of Virgil contribute to a broad exploration of the poem's central theme.

Statius redefines the problem of warring brothers even as he begins his poem with the words *fraternas acies.* According to Quintillian's *Instituto Oratorio* 10.1.48, the first words of an epic poem should state its main theme as concisely as possible. Homer starts with the wrath of Achilles, Virgil with the man forced to fight (*arma virumque*). A translation should probably start with Statius's precise words, but this one does not because of the difficulty of presenting to a modern audience an allusion to the fountain of Pierus and a call to the muses, which follows a few lines later. They sound artificial. Even to Statius they were probably archaic, rhetorical devices. To make them work, a translation must give life to deadened tropes. Pierus is a mountain sacred to the muses. Creative heat, Pierian heat, Statius says, cuts into his thoughts. English usage allows us to say that something fires us, that someone or something takes fire. Therefore a modern translation may well begin with an image of the poet and then move to the epic theme. "My mind takes Pierian fire. Fraternal strife/ unfolds."

Statius immediately lists all the elements of fraternal strife that account for the Theban war. The first cause is hatred, a human emotion that bedevils the best efforts of society to control it. The second, more specific cause is political, an agreement between the sons of Oedipus to alternate reigns once they find their mutual hatred makes it impossible to rule Thebes together. They plan to alternate their time in office, each one to take over in successive years. The final cause of strife is neither the human condition nor a misguided pact, but a curse on Thebes that makes bad things inevitable. In a few lines Statius creates the narrative persona of a man in despair and establishes the moral turpitude (*sontes*) of Thebes that grips the sons of Oedipus.

> My mind takes Pierian fire. Fraternal strife
> unfolds: unholy hatred, alternating reigns,
> the criminality of Thebes. (1.1–3)

For Statius, the causes of war go beyond human agency. Thebes cannot escape its history, most of which was familiar to Roman readers from the second, third, and fourth books of Ovid's *Metamorphoses*. Sexual violence and paternal tyranny characterize the Theban story from the beginning. Jove, disguised as a white bull, carried Europa away from her native country of Sidon, near Tyre (hence Sidonian and Tyrian are synonyms for Theban). Europa's father, Agenor, commanded his son Cadmus to recover Europa or not come home. Cadmus's mission was doomed to failure, since a mortal could not hope to uncover the secrets of the gods. Instructed by Apollo's oracle, Cadmus settles where he is led by an unyoked heifer. The land is named Boeotia (from the word for cow). But Apollo's guidance proves duplicitous, and Cadmus's founding of Thebes is flawed when he slays a serpent sacred to Mars. He sows the dragon's teeth, and armed soldiers grow from the soil. These warriors then murder each other and are reabsorbed by the earth. The meaning of the myth is that Thebes is founded in civil war and cursed with violence. Eventually Mars punishes Cadmus and his wife by turning them into serpents.

Thebes was founded in dissension, but the ruling family nonetheless gloried in its past, which is why Statius mentions that Amphion, a king of Thebes, built the city's walls by the sound of his lyre (*Thebaid* 1.9–10). The lyre's tune represents the harmony, or central authority, that overcomes dissension. Five earthborn men survived the founding civil war and became the ancestors of the noble families of Thebes. Cadmus had to recognize them because he had no male heirs. To highlight the problems of power sharing and succession that will be the theme of his story of the sons of Oedipus, Statius often refers to the four daughters of Cadmus in his poem.

Two daughters are mentioned in the opening lines of the *Thebaid* as Statius gives us a glimpse of the troubled royal history of Thebes. One of them, Semele, died when Jove appeared to her in his full glory, but not before she gave birth to Bacchus. Later Pentheus—son of Echion, one of the Sparti, or sown men—resisted the attempt of Bacchus to bring his revels into the city, as in Euripides' *Bacchae* ("What was the source/of Bacchus' hostile rage against his homeland?" *Thebaid* 1.11). At Juno's request, the fury Tisiphone poisoned the minds of Athamas and his wife Ino, another daughter of Cadmus. Athamas killed their son while hunting ("What did fierce Juno do? At whom did maddened/Athamas bend his bow?" 1.12–13). Ino leaped into the sea with her child Melicerto, and Neptune transformed them into deities, Leucothea (spelled Leucothoë elsewhere) and Palaemon ("Why did the mighty/Ionian not terrify the mother/who leaped into that ocean with Palaemon?" 1.13–14). The curse on Thebes continued through the life of Oedipus, but Statius properly limits himself to a single topic:

> But here, at present, now I will permit
> the groans of Cadmus to elapse, with his
> prosperity. I will set my song this limit:
> the horrors of the house of Oedipus.
>
> (1.15–17)

In the repeating structure of the myth, the incest of Oedipus with Jocasta reenacts the return of the dragon warriors to mother earth. Oedipus is unable to escape this pattern of reversion. He kills his father and curses his sons, as his own father exiled him.

Polynices and Eteocles are born into this endless cycle of illicit eroticism and violence, but their struggles may also be seen as part of a divine plan. Brothers acting in concord can combine to overcome their father and all he represents. The Bible has various expressions for a son's desire to replace his father: a yearning to build heavenward, for a blessing or a mantle, to enter the presence of God, or to be God. The Old Testament deity scatters nations that would imitate him by aspiring to heaven in the story of the Tower of Babel. Since brothers must be divided, Cain slays Abel; Noah's sons contend, as do Jacob's. The *Thebaid* similarly sustains patriarchy. Both Oedipus and Creon outlive their sons, and the sole survivor among the Argives is King Adrastus, the oldest.

In the Theban story the gathering of heroes who support Polynices never bickers among itself, making its members all the more dangerous, not only to Thebes but to the divinities who refuse to allow Thebes to be defeated. Capaneus openly scorns auguries, and all of the heroes vie to be godlike. They exhibit pride, not just in the feats of arms that characterize their Homeric *aristeiai* (episodes in which a lone hero performs outstanding deeds), but in their superhuman prowess. Amphiaraus, who shows outstanding foreknowledge, must be sent away from heaven, to the underworld. Tydeus reveals exceptional anger: his cannibalism offends even his patron goddess. Hippomedon has an unusual relationship with the elements. Parthenopaeus, blessed with youthful beauty, seems dangerously unaware of his physical limitations. Each of these personalities threatens Olympus and must be thwarted. Apollo buries Amphiaraus; Minerva abandons Tydeus; a river god destroys Hippomedon; Jupiter hurls a lightning bolt at Capaneus as he scales the towers of Thebes; and Diana allows Parthenopaeus, the son of her follower Atalanta, to overreach his powers. Whereas Lucan, who was only five years older than Statius, rejected the *aristeia* as well as the Homeric gods when he wrote his epic of civil war (*cognatas acies*), Statius used the clash between human heroes and the deities to broaden the import of the similar but more mythic theme of fraternal strife.

Statius's style and ability to transcend his subject matter help explain why Dante could characterize Statius as a Christian. The twin flames of Ulysses and Diomedes (*Inferno* 26) derive from the funeral pyre of Polynices and Eteocles, where contending flames show that the brothers' hatred continues even after death (*Thebaid* 12.429–46). The Roman epic also provided rare thrills, such as the pure horror of Tisiphone's head full of hissing snakes or the circling landscape that surrounds hell's flaming rivers at the beginning of book 2, where an unknown Dantean ghost steps forth to voice his envy that a soul is allowed to leave the underworld. The very tercet-like character of Statius's lines may have influenced Dante's choice of a three-line verse form. Statius's basic unit is not the verse paragraph, as in

Milton, or Virgilian hemistiches, but frequently sections of four or five lines, roughly the equivalent of two three-line sections of *terza rima*.

Reflecting the times in which he wrote, Statius weakened the Homeric gods, whose imaginative vitality is usurped in his poem by allegorical figures such as Piety, Clemency, Virtue, and Nature. As C. S. Lewis argued, Mars is no longer a mythic figure of varied passions but merely an accident in a substance. He raves and nothing more. Minerva represents the mind of Tydeus. Apollo is practically degenerate. In an inset story typical of the digressions that Statius uses to delay his plot, King Adrastus tells his visitors why the Argives worship this troubled deity. The god once raped a woman. Her father, feeling her shame, cast her out, and she died. To avenge the woman whom he himself had violated, Apollo created a baby-eating monster that spun out of control until a hero named Coroebus killed it. (This murderous underwater monster that walks the earth might have influenced the author of *Beowulf*.) As the first book ends Adrastus praises Apollo in one of the most religiously inspired paeans in all of poetry, but he seems not to recognize that the god he hymns is a cruel tyrant. By contrast, the allegorical figure of Virtue operates like grace in Menoeceus, whose sacrifice is required to save Thebes. The final crusade of Theseus, prompted by the Argive widows, is a holy war under the banner of Nature to restore Pietas. For such reasons, Dante could persuade his readers to accept the otherwise implausible notion that the Silver Age Roman poet had converted.

Statius's story of fraternal strife includes two other elements suited to a monotheistic myth. If the core of biblical monotheism is the protection of the Hebrew father, its motive is often scarcity. Polynices and Eteocles do not battle for wealth, Statius comments. Instead "they fought to win a kingdom that had nothing" (1.151). Roland Barthes noticed in his analysis of a similar theme in Racine's work that even where nothing is at stake, brothers are "always enemies because they are quarreling over the inheritance of a father who is not quite dead and who returns to punish them." Eteocles clings to his kingdom in part because he is jealous that Polynices marries well; he enlists a home guard of loyal retainers to sustain his local identity. The Thebans several times recite the history of their founding because group members tell stories about themselves to exclude others. The truth Statius elicits is that memories are constructions. We never know which brother, if either, has right on his side. Polynices flees Thebes in storm and paranoia, turning the innocent eyes and noises of forest creatures into awful threats. Eteocles dreams that he wakes bathed in blood from his grandfather's slit throat. It is not clear that either brother recovers his equilibrium. Even Jupiter claims he cannot control Fate. He is said to be the weaver of the stars (*sator astrorum, Thebaid* 3.218), a figure who encompasses the expanses of heavens toward which Statius several times gestures in the poem. But Jupiter also presides over a Theban world of scarcity and disordered memory. The *Thebaid* hints at monotheism not only because Statius may have glimpsed divine truth, as the Middle Ages believed, but because of what is implied when a father weakens the power of his sons by setting them at odds.

Gender and Sexuality in the *Thebaid*

On the surface Statius's epic is remarkably abstemious about sex. The *Thebaid* seems suspicious of physical love, even in marriage. There are no explicitly erotic scenes, or even much of a love story. Statius follows Virgil in punishing deviations from heterosexual dominance, including amorous passion or anything that interferes with the paternal mission of empire. In the earlier poem Aeneas leaves Dido, who kills herself; the female warrior Camilla does not survive in battle; the intense friendship of Nisus and Euryalus dooms them to die. Statius has no female warriors. His only equivalent for the love story of Dido is the Lemnos episode, where women rise up and slaughter their men, only to be subdued by the Argonauts. And Statius seems to recognize that his Hopleus and Dymas, whom he assigns to retrieve the bodies of their captains, never achieve the suggestive sexuality of the pair of friends whose ruthless but passionate midnight raid in the *Aeneid* shapes up as a shared, private adventure. In the *Thebaid* and also in the *Orlando furioso,* where Ariosto follows Statius more closely than he does Virgil, two men raid at night as a tactical necessity for the public good, not from their own passion.

Cleaving closely to the theme of fraternal strife, Statius is more interested in images of concord and discord than passing moral judgments on sexual behavior. He is no more prurient about men in love than he is overly obsessed with women. His acceptance of human nature allows him to reflect his theme of fraternal strife in multiple images of brothers, sisters, and twins. Some of this work was inherent in the myths he inherited. Thus the first man Polynices meets in exile is Tydeus, who has slain his own brother. The two men then marry sisters, Argia and Deipyle. Oedipus has two daughters, Antigone and Ismene, as well as the two sons (who are also his half brothers). The key to Aeschylus's *Seven against Thebes,* one of Statius's sources, is a soldier's horror at the thought that Eteocles will face Polynices, since brother-murdering pollutes the ground and will not fade. But Statius does not introduce this superstition into his work. Nor does he replay the pairing of champions at each of the seven gates of Thebes.

In Euripides' *Phoenician Women* Polynices briefly recounts how he met Tydeus and their coming to blows over a bed, but Statius's expansion is original. In the *Thebaid* the two men pummel each other as if such physical contact necessarily precedes friendship. Their progress from two men who fight for a doorway to loyal comrades illustrates Barthes's point that love is hard to distinguish from hate because both emotions are openly physical. When Tydeus dies, Polynices laments him as his real brother who has replaced false Eteocles. But their brotherhood is deadly too, because Tydeus refuses to allow Polynices to accept Jocasta's offer to arrange a reconciliation with Eteocles (17.470–563). Fate also contributes, which may explain why Polynices strangely abandons Tydeus body (9.73–85), leaving Hippomedon to defend it against a band of Thebans led by Eteocles.

Throughout the poem images of twins highlight the perils of fraternity. In a passage that deserves to be far more famous than it is, Statius portrays two brothers who die together when Tydeus defends himself against an ambush of fifty soldiers. As the sons of Thespius die, one cradles the drooping neck of his brother in his left hand and upholds his side and body with his right (2.629–43). The romantic poet Robert Southey, in the preface to his epic poem *Joan of Arc* (1798), said that although Statius's subject matter was ill chosen, his poetic images are strongly conceived and clearly painted. The *pietà* the two brothers form is precisely the kind of image we would expect to find in a text that Dante could read as Christian, a piety that contrasts with the hatred of the sons of Oedipus.

Like this image of concordant but dying brothers, Statius's women express the emergence of a new religious ethos and morality in first-century Rome. Just as the Greek pantheon yields to Statius's allegorical but genuinely felt virtues, Aristotle's aristocratic disdain for men who could feel temptation turns into Argia's learning to live with a man who finds it impossible to be good. At first the blushing bride is appalled by Polynices' dreams of war and, like Andromache or even Kate Hotspur, she tries to deflect her husband's need to fight. Eventually she yields and asks her father to support her husband's cause. The years that pass between the end of book 3 and the beginning of book 4 reinforce the gravity of Argia's new position. She is a good person, but she yields to temptation.

Perhaps the most obvious image of an immoral woman is Eriphyle. Again Statius blurs the outlines of a story he inherited, how in exchange for a beautiful but cursed necklace that Argia owns the wife of Amphiaraus convinces her husband to join a war he knows is doomed. The *Thebaid* merely hints at this betrayal, when the narrator tells the origin and fatal effects of the necklace (*Thebaid* 2.267–305), and when Amphiaraus, once the earth swallows him, asks the god of the underworld to save a place for his wife (*Thebaid* 8.120–22). By leaving the role of Eriphyle uncertain, Statius creates a connection between her and Argia, who encourages the war in Thebes despite herself. Both women send their husbands to die, although Eriphyle takes money and knows the expedition is doomed. The role of the women is allegorically figured by the goddess Bellona, who arms Argos at the beginning of book 4, a section of the poem that lingers over the influence of women.

Countering events that conspire to produce war, women tend to derail the progress of the armies. They weep and dispirit the men. In the Theban myth Bacchus, the god of wine, gives women the freedom to dance in the hills under his influence. He reflects the interests of those who are threatened by war. To protect them and his native city, Bacchus dries up the rivers and streams of the Nemean plain, which the Argives must cross. And so the epic catalog of Argive troops that occupies the first portion of book 4 gives way to renewed delay. The resulting digression lasts through books 5 and 6 not because Statius loses track of his poem's unity of action, but because he focuses on the way war disrupts life. Hypsipyle eventually gives the Argives the drink that they crave, but whatever spiritual good water stands for is undercut when a serpent crushes the baby she leaves lying on the plain as she guides the Argives to the hidden stream of Langia. As part of this digression *in medias res,* the Lemnos episode and the funeral games for Opheltes prepare for the end of the poem, where Argia and Antigone enlist the Athenians to ensure the burial of the Argives. Here and elsewhere Statius's concern is not so much for the dead soldiers but for the suffering of the women who survive them. Burial provides closure for the living.

The Lemnos episode enforces the view that women are most vulnerable to war. Love (that is, Venus) leaves the island because the men are obsessed with attacking Thrace (the home of Mars). Filled with Bacchic frenzy, a woman named Polyxo descends from the hills to encourage the women to murder their husbands when they return from war. Even their own valor does the women no good, however, as they are soon forced to accept the rule of the Argonauts, who sail into the island as representatives of an older world of heroes. Women may introduce delay, but they cannot cheat fate. After the funeral games, the Theban war resumes. The later attempts of Jocasta in book 7 and Antigone in book 11 to persuade the brothers to negotiate come to nothing.

Translating Statius

Perhaps because of the uncontrollable violence that dominates Statius's epic, many manuscripts of the *Thebaid* survive from the Middle Ages, and the poem was still popular when printing was invented. Thirteen editions were issued between 1471 and 1500, and then another seven during the sixteenth century, including translations into Italian (1503) and French (1558). During the period of religious war and strife in Europe that covered the first thirty years of the seventeenth century, more than twenty editions were printed. Jean Racine, one of France's greatest poets, based his first play, *Les frères ennemis*, on the story of Thebes. England's Civil War period saw an English translation of the first five books (1648). Statius's reputation was still alive when Alexander Pope was a boy. As a child prodigy he translated the first book into heroic couplets (1712). William L. Lewis achieved the first complete English translation in 1766. During the nineteenth century the Latin text of Statius's work was edited and annotated six times. The Loeb Classical Library published J. L. Mozley's prose translation in 1928 and kept it in print until 2003, when the series switched to a new prose version by D. R. Shackleton Bailey. Oxford University Press published A. D. Melville's verse translation of the *Thebaid* in 1990.

Like its predecessors, the present translation not only seeks to keep alive an ancient classic but to let readers and listeners understand and experience Statius's art. I have tried to find a smooth modern syntax to render the high style, since Statius valued oration and pathos. A diligent reviser of his verses, he was a surprisingly clever writer of epigrams, a talent he uses to enliven his catalogs of troops and the several battles in the poem. He may cut through the chaos of war by writing a series of vignettes:

Dircean Amyntas aimed an arrow at
Phaedimus, son of Iäsus. Alas,
how swift is Fate! for Phaedimus hit ground
even before Amyntas' bow was silent.

Agreus, the Calidonian, removed
Phegeus' now useless right arm from his shoulder:
it gripped his sword and grappled in the dirt.
Acoetas stabbed that arm through scattered weapons:
it terrified him, even unattached.

Dark Acamas struck Iphis, fearsome Hypseus
Argus, and Pheres carved through Abas—these
lay moaning from their different wounds: the rider
Iphis, footsoldier Argus, driver Abas. (8.438–47)

Statius's aim in writing poetry was to impress readers and listeners with his eloquence. Although the Renaissance theorist Giraldi Cinthio said that Statius's work is very rough and far from natural in its verses, Cinthio admitted that Statius had assumed authority over the course of a thousand years. Renaissance Latin poets like Pontano and Sannazaro often borrowed Statius's grammatical constructions and numbers.

Throughout this translation I have relied on clarity to determine what could and could not be brought across the linguistic barrier from Latin to English. The point of my using a regular iambic pentameter line is that it is easy to follow. (The word *iamb* is a Greek term for a two-syllable foot where the stress is on the second syllable; *pent* means five in Greek, and so pentameter refers to five metric feet, or units—in this case, five iambs, which comes to ten syllables per line.) Readers may generally rely on the regular stress on the even syllables to guide pronunciation of the Latin names that add so much to the sonority of Statius's verse, particularly in the catalogs of armies that join with Argos (book 4), Thebes (book 7), and Athens (book 12). The Greek ending -eus has been something of a problem, since it should probably be pronounced as a single syllable but in English is often two syllables, as in Odysseus, Theseus, or Tydeus. Capaneus, a name woefully absent from English literature, considering the vibrancy of his character, is generally stressed on the penultimate syllable in this translation, as it is in Italian. The final e of proper names is usually pronounced. Occasionally a diaeresis indicates separate syllables, as when there might be confusion with a diphthong (e.g., Danaë). The stressed syllables in the following passage appear in small capitals to show the meter:

> NEWS of the WAR brought MEN from CITies IN
> AeTOliA to HIM: it REACHED PyLEnë,
> which SITS on CLIFFS, and PLEUron, WHERE the SISters
> of MEleAger WEEP, and CAlyDON . . . (4.101–4)

The first foot, or iamb, is the exception to the rule that the stress falls on the even syllables. A stress on the first syllable instead of the second gives the line a strong beginning, thereby assisting in the task of defining the verse line as a unit, something with a beginning, middle, and end. The real purpose of rhyme in English verse is not to jingle but to define the end of the line. I have therefore used rhyme whenever available, but also various types of assonance (matching vowel sounds) and consonance (similar consonants). Giving strength to the middle of the line is trickier. The best way is to be sure the line contains a verb, the strongest part of speech, but the middle of the line can also be strengthened by varying the pauses between syntactic units. These variations relieve the metric monotony that is the danger of regular verse stresses. I also try to rely on natural syntactic units, as modern poets do, who use the rhythms of everyday speech to define verse lines.

Some of my methodology derives from a course on Latin composition taught by the late Edward Bassett, who emphasized that Latin translation requires the full resources of English and that what may seem literal is not literal at all in a different idiom. The spelling of proper names generally follows Hill's edition, but occasionally a more familiar form is used (e.g., Ischia for Inarime; Jocasta for Iocasta; Cyclops for the plural Cyclopes, which sounds awkward; Laconia for Lacon; Tyre for Tyros). For the convenience of modern readers I have supplied titles and prefatory summaries for each of the *Thebaid*'s twelve books.

The THEBAID

BOOK 1 Exile

Invocation. Oedipus curses his sons, Eteocles and Polynices, and invokes the fury Tisiphone, who brings civil unrest to Thebes. Jupiter decrees the harsh fate of Argos and Thebes. Juno protests. Mercury descends. Polynices and Tydeus refuse to share one shelter. King Adrastus of Argos and his daughters. The oracle. Apollo's monster and festival in Argos.

My mind takes Pierian fire. Fraternal strife
unfolds: unholy hatred, alternating reigns,
the criminality of Thebes. How far,
O goddesses, should I go? To the beginnings,
in Sidon, of the unholy race? the rape?
the rigor of Agenor's law? to Cadmus,
Agenor's son, who scrutinized the seas?

Events stretch back in time. Should I rehearse 7
the warriors the farmer's plow unearthed,
his fear, unspeakable furrows of dark Mars?
Or, if I follow further: with what song
were Tyrian mountains moved by King Amphion
to form defensive walls? What was the source
of Bacchus' hostile rage against his homeland?
What did fierce Juno do? At whom did maddened
Athamas bend his bow? Why did the mighty
Ionian not terrify the mother
who leaped into that ocean with Palaemon?

But here, at present, now I will permit 15
the groans of Cadmus to elapse, with his
prosperity. I will set my song this limit:
the horrors of the house of Oedipus.

Not yet dare I, inspired, praise Italian
ensigns of war or triumphs of the North,
how twice the Rhine has felt our yoke, how twice
Danube has known our laws; how the conspiring

◆ Dacians descended from their heights, and how
in early manhood Jove averted war.
Nor yet dare I praise you, o glorious
addition to the fame of Latium—timely
successor to your parent's prodigies,
whom Rome would call her own—eternally.

Granted that stars seek narrow paths, that heaven's 24
bright region tempts you, free from strikes of lightning,
the northern winds, and Pleiades; and granted
that he himself, the charioteer of fiery
horses—Apollo—with his radiance
may crown and garland you; or Jupiter
cede you an equal portion of the cosmos:
yet may you be content to govern men,
rule sea and land, and not to seek the stars.

There will be time. Your deeds will be my theme 32
when I am touched by keener Pierian fire.
For now, another subject suits my lyre:
Aonia arms; two tyrants crave the fatal
scepter of office; hatred does not expire
at death—flames strive anew within the pyres—
unburied kings lack graves, reciprocal
slaughter drains cities. Dirce's dark-blue waters
are stained by Lernaean blood, and Thetis trembles
as the Ismenos, which usually streams
along dry banks, brings heaps of dead to sea.

Clio, which demigod is suitable 41
for my beginning? Is it Tydeus,
whose rage is measureless? Could it be he
for whom earth gaped, the bay-leafed seer? I'm pressed
by wild Hippomedon, who turned his enemy,
the river—did it by killing men. The wars
the wild Arcadian waged should prompt laments,
and dreadful Capaneus calls for song.

—◆—◆—◆—

His eyes had seen impieties. His right 46
hand racked them. Oedipus, disgraced, now lies
condemned to endless night, yet he survives.
He favors shadows, deep interiors;
he keeps his household gods from heaven's light,
while days—on constant wing—afflict his mind,
and Dirae—furies of remorse—his heart.

His vacant eyes upturned, the wretch displays 53
his punishment and misery. His blood-
stained hands strike empty depths. Voice hoarse, he prays:

"You gods who govern guilt, the spirits damned 56
to narrow Tartarus! and you, black Styx,
whose shadowy depths I see: acknowledge me!
Favor, perverse Tisiphone, my prayer;
you know my call. If I have ever merited
favor; if when my mother's womb dropped me
you nurtured me, and healed my transfixed feet;
if then I sought my future in the fens
of Cirrha, spread beneath twin summits, when
I could have lived content with Polybus,
◆ and his untruth; if then a man of years,
a king, impeded me where three roads meet
in Phocis, and I split the trembling face 64
of that old fool, while searching for my father;
if you instructed me and gave me skill
◆ to solve the riddle of the wicked Sphinx;
if I knew passion and delirium
and marriage and my mother's moans, and spent
many unmentionable nights, engendering
children for you, as you well know, until
my fingers tore my eyes out in revenge
and dropped them on my mother's prostrate form—
Listen! I want what is worthwhile, the sort
of thing you make your madmen pray you for!

"I have lost sight. I miss the power of rule. 74
My sons leave me unguided, unconsoled,
and suffering. It does not matter how
they were born. They show insolence. They hurt me!

Made lords by my demise, they mock my darkness.
They hate to hear their father whine. Am I
pernicious? And the father of the gods
sees all this and ignores it? You, at least,
offer appropriate revenge. O spin
consummate punishment for my descendants!

"Put on the blood-soaked diadem my reddened 82
fingers tore off—a father's prayer incites you—
then introduce yourself between those brothers.
May war annihilate their bond of kinship!
Queen of the depths of Tartarus, grant me
the wickedness I want to see: young minds,
not slow, will follow. Now, divinity,
appear! You'll recognize my progeny!"

–♦–♦–♦–

He spoke these words, and the cruel goddess turned 88
her hardened gaze his way. By chance she had
let down her hair and sat beside Cocytos—
the inhospitable, infernal river—
to let her serpents drink the sulfur waters.
She started up with meteoric speed
like lightning from the dreary shores and moved
through ghosts across dark plains where shadows swarmed.
The lifeless multitudes made way, afraid
to strike against their mistress, as she sought
the gates of Taenaros, a threshold none
may trespass twice. Day sensed her presence. Night
proffered dark clouds that dimmed his horses' light.

Far off steep Atlas shuddered, and his shoulders 98
shifted the weight of heaven. She emerged
deep in Malea's vale with sudden force
and set out on the road she knew to Thebes.
There was no faster way to travel, nor did she
prefer to be in Tartarus, her home.
A garland of a hundred serpents shaded
her dreadful face. Her eyes, set deep, emitted

an iron light, as when Thessalian magic
reddens the moon's descent through phantom clouds.
She was suffused with spreading pestilence. 105
Corrupt blood puffed her skin. Her black mouth spewed
hot vapors, which spread famine and diseases
and distant drought and epidemic death.
A stiff robe bristled down her back, fastened
by blue points down her breast. (Prosperpina
herself and Atropos design her styles.)
Her mad hands flailed. One waved a funeral flame,
one whipped a living serpent in the air.

She halted where Cithaeron's towering heights 114
and ruined fortress loom. Her dripping tresses
of vibrant serpents seethed and screamed and hissed,
sending her warning to surrounding cities,
from sea to sea, reechoing through Greece.
From high Parnassus to the swift Eurotas
the sound was heard. It hurdled into Oete's
precarious ascents. The Isthmos repulsed—
but barely—swelling waves. Palaemon, who
rode on a dolphin's arching back, was saved
by Ino, who protected her own son.

Headlong the goddess to the palace roof 123
descended and assumed her place, and fog
infected all at once the household gods
of Cadmus. Passion struck the brothers, made
them frantic; their majestic souls went mad.
Pleasure turned sick with envy. Fear bred hate.

The consequence was savage lust for power 127
that could not tolerate successive rule
or revolution of authority,
for it is sweet to be alone and first, but shared
◆ dominion makes companions disagree.
It happens when a farmer leads a pair 131
of chosen oxen from a savage herd
and puts them to the plow. Indignant, they—
whose necks farm implements have not yet pressed

into their brawny shoulders with long toil—
pull in divergent ways with equal force,
stretching and weakening their chains, as they
confound the furrowed soil with wavering rows.
Not otherwise, the stubborn brothers strove.

The two agreed to alternate exile 138
and office year by year. Their unsound law
decreed the end of their good fortune, since
the one who wields the scepter will be pressed
by that rash treaty and his new successor.

Such was fraternal piety; such then 142
the only way to stop dissent, nor would
peace last until a second term begins.

Nor yet, in Thebes, were laquearia— 144
panels of coffered ceilings—rich with gold
and marble from Greek mines whose patterns glow
in atria—immense halls—built to hold
crowds of petitioners; nor yet did kings
sleep undisturbed unless armed guards attended.
No sullen sentries changed watch; no one served
jeweled cups of wine or sullied gold at meals.
The brothers went to war for power alone;
they fought to win a kingdom that had nothing.

Now, when it was uncertain who would rule 152
the waste lands of the narrow Dirce River
and lord it on the lowly throne of Tyre,
undone were civil laws, divine decrees,
morality, and decency. 155

How far
you bitter men, did you intend to take
your violence? What if the zodiac
of heaven felt your criminal attack
from pole to pole?—the path on which the sun
gains prospect as it travels from the East
till it sets westward in Iberia,

touching remote lands with slant influence,
where north winds freeze, or wet south winds blow fire.
What if the wealth of Phrygia and Tyre 161
were massed together, making one empire?
A foul land and cursed walls aroused your hate.
To take the place of Oedipus you paid
with deep distraction!

Lots were cast. The fate 164
of Polynices was, he had to wait
for his preferment.

◆ Now, you savage one, 165
what kind of day was it, when you alone,
free in your palace, knew you were the law,
that others were inferior to you,
and no head rose but yours? And yet, already,
murmuring spread imperceptibly
among Echion commoners. They stood
apart from princes, unattended, and—
as people do—preferred the one whose turn
awaited. One of them—his mind intent
on trouble, base and venomous, loathe to bend
to uncontrollable authority—
found words to speak: "Does our Ogygian 173
community deserve this fate? this cruel
vicissitude? this constant change in those
whom we must fear? By alternating rule,
the sharers toy with our town's destiny.
They leave us to the whims of fortune. Am
I to comply with exiles who take turns?
Mighty Creator! Lord of gods and men,
is this what you and your companions want:
that the old curse of Thebes continue? It
started when Cadmus—on command—pursued
the massive, beautiful Sidonian bull
across the sea to where he founded, in
Boeotian fields, an exile's realm. There earth
◆ opened, and battle lines of brothers grew
and fought, bequeathing their posterity

a legacy, a warning. Watch him, stiff 186
with pride, his face stern; he stares, menacing.
His power grows dangerous, now that his brother
has been removed. His look spells danger. His
disdain oppresses everyone. Will he
ever return to private life? By contrast,
his brother flatters those who ask for favors.
He speaks urbanely. What is fair, he wants.
And why not? He has company—we're it:
a worthless bunch. Ripe for catastrophe. Ready
to follow anyone. Now one commands,
while one forewarns, just like contrary winds—
first freezing Boreas, then cloudy Eurus.
They lash the sails. The fortune of our ship
wavers between them. Trapped by fear—to move
in two directions—it's intolerable!"

–♦–♦–♦–

But now by Jove's command, a gathering— 197
a council of selected gods—convened
within the halls of whirling heaven, in
the deep empyrean. Its distance is
the same from everything: the houses of
the sunrise and the sunset, equally
from dry land and seas spread beneath the skies.
Jove entered, upright—and the deities 201
trembled as he approached, although his gaze
was calm. He took his seat: a throne of stars.
No one dared move, till he himself, the father,
waved a calm hand, permitting everyone
to sit. And now a crowd of demigods 205
and Rivers (relatives of soaring clouds)
and Winds (whose terror quiets them)
filled the gilt hall. Its arched roof radiated
the majesty of many gods; its heights
glowed with a mighty splendor; and its doors
were luminous, their light mysterious.

One called for silence. Heaven hushed, and then 211
from his preeminence, Jove spoke with words

of sacred weight: immutable the fate
that followed his address.

"Terrestrial
offenses—human ingenuity
no Dirae of remorse can mollify—
these I denounce! How far am I supposed
to go to punish criminals? I'm tired
of hurling lightning in a rage: long use
wears out the Cyclops' arms; Aeolian
anvils lose fire. I have already let
◆ the horses of the sun draw Phaëthon
off course, his chariot ignite the air,
his ashes scorch the earth. What must I do 222
further? My brother, Neptune, even you
signaled permission with your trident to
let oceans overwhelm forbidden shores.
Now I descend to discipline a pair 224
of houses my own blood produced: one branch
settled in Argos, home of Perseus'
grandfather; one, Aonia—in Thebes.
Their hearts remain the same in everything.
Who can forget the slaughter Cadmus caused,
how the Eumenides were called to war
from deepest hell, the evil joy and zeal
◆ of savage women who roam forests, or
the crimes against the gods that they conceal?
All day, all night would not enable me 231
to name the customs wicked people keep.
A shameless heir ascends his father's bed
and stains his mother's innocence—seeking
entrance to his own origin. The man
is horrible, but gave a permanent
atonement to the gods: he threw away
the light of day. No longer does he feed
on upper air. But then, much worse, his sons
trample his fallen eyes. Perverse old man! 240
Now what you prayed for will occur. You and
your blindness earn you the revenge that Jove
can offer. I pronounce this cause of war:
the fatal wedding, when Adrastus turns

father-in-law. The Argive race deserves
punishment, for I still feel, in my heart's
secret recess, how Tantalus deceived
the gods when he prepared his savage feast."

All-powerful, the father spoke. His words, 248
however, wounded Juno. Her heart burned
with unexpected rage, and she returned
her answer, thus:

"Of all the gods, you are
the most ingenuous, that you bring war
to me. Why me? You know that I support
Argos with men and wealth. The Cyclops built
her citadel; there, great Phoroneus ruled
a kingdom of wide fame. You, with no shame,
murdered—there as he slept—the one who watched
your cow; you turned to gold to penetrate
the walls. I overlook your secret rapes,
but I detest the town where you displayed
yourself in public places, openly 256
thundering your adultery, flinging
the lightning bolts that should be mine. Let Thebes
pay. Why should Argos be your enemy?

"If you resent our sacred marriage, then 260
why not demolish old Mycenae or
◆ Samos? Or level Sparta? anywhere
festival blood and ample incense warm
the altars of your wife. Sweeter to you
◆ the prayers and smoke of Mareotic Copts,
loud wails, the sound of bronze along the Nile.

"If it's the case that men must expiate 266
their father's crimes, and this new sentiment
obsesses you, then search eternity:
how far back must you follow to amend
the madness of the world or rectify
the spirit of the age? Start in the place
◆ where mazy Alpheos seeks Arethusa,
driven by waves to his Sicilian love

across the sea. You do not seem ashamed
that the Arcadians have set your shrine 273
on ground unsanctified or that the steeds
of Oenomaus better suit the stalls
of Thrace beneath Mount Haemus than
they do that king's war chariot, for still
his daughter's suitors lie unburied, mangled
and torn by those man-eating animals,
their bodies stiff. Yet you are gratified
to have the honor of a temple there. You like
baleful Mount Ida, Crete, where people lie
and say you're nothing but a dead soul. Why
envy my habitation in the land
of Tantalus, where sons of yours reside?
Pity them. Turn aside war's violence.
So many faithless cities better serve
your purpose than the one that must endure
your feuding progeny."

Jove heard the words 282
of Juno, her reproaches mixed with prayers,
and he responded not unpleasantly,
although his meaning stung: "To tell the truth,
I never thought that you would tolerate
anything I considered suitable
for Argos. I know Bacchus and Dione
can make long speeches in defense of Thebes,
but they defer to my authority.
By Styx, my brother's dreaded lake, I swear 290
I will not change what I have said—my word
is irrevocable and firm. And so,
Cyllenian Mercury, my son: take wing
on lifting airs. Be diligent. Outspeed
the currents of the southern wind. Descend
where darkness reigns. Say to your uncle,
'Let ancient Laius, murdered by his son, 295
ascend to upper air! The law of hell
forbids his passing to the further shore
of Lethe yet.' And carry my decree
to his ill-omened grandson: 'Banishment
has brought your brother strength, and friends

in Argos lend him confidence. You, then,
may keep your brother distant from your court
and contradict his claim to rule in turn.'
He'd do this anyway—and lay the grounds
for enmity. The rest I shall arrange."

◆ His father spoke. Atlas's grandson appeared 303
and quickly bound winged sandals on his feet.
A cap concealed his hair. His glow dimmed stars.
In his right hand he held the slender wand
he uses to induce and banish sleep
or send dead souls to deep, dark Tartarus
or, on occasion, bring dead shades to life.
Down he leapt, upright; by the air sustained
that instant, flying on the vast sublime
and traced a mighty down-gyre through the clouds.

–◆–◆–◆–

Meanwhile, the exiled son of Oedipus 312
furtively wandered from his former home
along the wastelands of Aonia,
already ill-disposed toward the realm
that should be his. The long year made him groan.
The signs moved slowly by which time is told.

One thought obsessed the man: that he might see 316
his brother driven out, brought low, and Thebes
and its possessions his to own—alone.
He'd trade eternity for that one day.

He grudged and sulked, as if this loss delayed 320
his flight, but soon his royal pride upswelled,
and his imagination set himself
upon the throne—his brother down, deposed.
His thoughts swung from anxiety to hope; 322
his mood was altered by his endless longing.

Whether Erinys—the avenging spirit— 324
led him, or Fortune showed the way, or steadfast

Atropos lured him there, he chose to go,
undaunted, to Danaan fields, to Argos—
the town of Inachus, beside Mycenae,
a place of dark where sunlight disappears.
He left behind the cave that echoed with 328
Ogygia's shrieks and mournful cries, the hills
rich with the blood of Bacchic revelries.
From there he skirted shores on which extend
the pleasant plains that lie beside Cithaeron,
whose languid mountainsides decline toward water.
He climbed a rocky road and left behind
♦ the rocky, infamous Scironic cliffs,
♦ the rural realm where Scylla cut the king
her father's purple lock, and pleasant Corinth.
From one field he could hear two different seas.

And now the rising moon, Titania, 336
sailed through the wide expanse, conveyed above
the silent world where Phoebus served his term.
Her moisture-bringing two-horsed chariot
scattered thin frost across the lower air.
Now herds and birds fell silent. Swaying sleep 339
bent down from heaven, bringing misery
of life the solace of oblivion
and respite from anxiety and greed.

But it was stormy, dark. No red night sky 342
promised a day of sunshine. No long rays
of brilliant twilight streaked through thin, high clouds.
Blackness and night veiled heaven, impenetrable
to flame; the dark more dense the nearer earth.
♦ Stiff Aeolus, the wind, rebounded in
his bolted fortress cavern; raucous sounds
announced the coming of cold storms; gales howled,
cut at right angles, clashed, and—when the doors
were severed from their hinges—sought the pole.
They strove to win a portion of the sky.

Auster, the hot south wind, accumulated 350
the largest mass of night, unwound long scrolls

of clouds, and poured out rain that Boreas,
the north wind, turned to hail. His breath blew cold.
The air caught fire; the lightning never tolled.

In Nemea and on Arcadia's 355
tall peaks that bound the groves of Taenaros
it poured so that the Inachus ran high
and ice swells made the Erasinus rise.
Rivers that had been dirt paths now defied
their banks as Lerna's ancient poison stirred
and from the bottom of the lake upswirled.

Dashed were the sacred groves. The hurricane 361
tore ancient limbs off trees. Lycaean glades—
summer retreats the sun had never seen—
no longer lay concealed in mountain shades.

The traveler pressed on, although he watched 364
rocks fly from broken peaks and disappear,
and listened, equally amazed, afraid,
to streams in spate, rain-swollen, sweep away
sheepfolds and shepherd's huts: nor did he slow,
although distracted and uncertain where
the road led through black silence, wasted fields,
while in the night, imagining his fear,
he felt his brother here, and here, and here!

Just as a sailor, caught on winter seas, 370
looks for the tardy Wagon of Boötes
or kindly moonlight to reveal his way
but stands resourceless, uninformed, when sea
and sky combine in storm, and he expects
at any moment that his ship's high prow
will run on sunken rocks or sea-sprayed cliffs
in shallows or in whirlpools—deadly deeps—
then, even so, the hero, he of Thebes, 376
wandered through opaque forests full of trees
and thrust the cold boss of his mighty shield
before him, driving beasts from dreadful lairs;
his forward-leaning chest tore thickets (fear

and melancholy gloom impelled his soul)
◆ until the turrets of Larissa leaped
to view. Their light shone over Argive roofs
and poured down sloping walls. His hope aroused,
he flew in that direction—on his left, on high
Prosymna, Juno's temple; over here,
the Lake of Lerna, whose black fens had been
disfigured by the flames of Hercules.
He reached the open portals and went in.

He saw, at once, the royal entry way. 386
Limbs stiff from wind and weather, there he lay,
leaning against the posts of unknown doors,
and beckoned tender sleep to that hard floor.

–◆–◆–◆–

There ruled a king, Adrastus. He had passed 390
most of his peaceful life and now grew old.
Rich in forefathers, he'd inherited,
on either side, the blood of Jupiter.
He had no children of the stronger sex,
yet he was blessed with daughters, who, to him,
were pledges of prosperity and strength.
To him had Phoebus sung of destiny. 395
(What had been thought an evil prophecy
would soon reveal itself.) The god foretold
one son-in-law would be a bristly boar,
the other one a tawny, yellow lion.

Deep in the heart a parent's worries grow.
O Amphiaraus, seer of future things, 398
what had been hidden from you by Apollo
Adrastus could not guess, nor could you know.

It chanced Olenian Tydeus had departed 401
that very night from ancient Calydon.
◆ His guilt and horror at his brother's death
drove him, exhausted, as he wore his way
through haunts of savage beasts, till burdened by

the same north wind and wet, his back infused
with frost, rain pouring from his face and beard,
he found a shelter partly occupied.

Just here, chance brought both men to bloody fight; 408
they would not share one roof to fend off night.
A little they delayed, exchanging threats,
but doing so, grew vexed. Each stood erect,
uncovered his bare shoulders, then attacked.
The Theban's step was faster, his reach long, 414
and he was fresh in years; but Tydeus had
a soul and heart as large, and greater strength
flowed through his smaller body to his limbs.
They aimed quick jabs head-high, redoubling blows
around the ears and temples, flurries thick
♦ as flights of arrows or Rhipaean hail,
then bent their knees to pummel hollow flanks.

Not otherwise than when the games recur 421
at Pisa, where they honor Jupiter,
and the dust burns with crude, hot sweat of men,
where youthful athletes are made violent
by squabbles in the stands, while, shut outside,
their mothers wait to hear who wins the prize,
just so, these hotheads clashed, and, quick to hate,
had no regard for praise. They sank their nails
deep in the other's face and naked eyes.
Surely—what won't rage do?—they would have bared 428
their side-borne swords, and you, young Theban, would
have fallen—and been better off, mourned by
your brother—had the king, astonished by
the strange commotion in the dark of night
and harsh cries from deep throats, not taken steps.
He did not sleep well, at his time of life,
since age and apprehensions sobered him.
He now proceeded through high, well-lit halls
to his front door and had the bar removed.
He saw cut faces, cheekbones soaked in blood.
A spectacle. "You must be foreigners. 438
No citizens would dare be so uncivil.
What caused this outrage? What implacable

hatred disturbs the peace, the silent night?
Are days too short for you? Is it so hard
to calm sad souls and sleep? But tell me this:
whence come you? on what road? why do you fight?
Your anger tells me you are not base born;
this spilled blood is a sign of noble birth."

He hardly finished. Both men yelled at once, 447
glancing at one another: "O mild king
of Argos, you can see our blood-stained faces!
What use are words?" But their loud clamors drowned
all hope of conversation. Tydeus then
◆ began again: "I left the Acheloian fields 453
and wealthy Calydon, the home of monsters,
to search for solace for my sad misfortunes.
I reached your country in the deep of night.
Who is this man? What right makes him deny me
a shelter from the storm?—because, by chance,
his step brought him here first? Half beast, half man,
the Centaurs share their stables. The Cyclops live
in peace, they say, on Aetna. It's the law
of nature; even savages obey it.
And we can't share a piece of dirt? Whoever 462
you are, I say that you will either be
happy to conquer me or learn my blood
has not grown weak from my distress. I am
the son of Oeneus—no degenerate—
and Mars." 465

"Nor do I lack proud heritage,"
the Theban answered, but he hesitates
to name his father, mindful of his fate.

"Come now," said mild Adrastus, "lay aside 467
your quarrel, whether caused by sudden anger,
virtue, or darkness. Welcome to my house,
both of you. Join your right hands. Pledge your faith.
The gods have not been absent, nor in vain
this strife. Perhaps you will remember it
with pleasure, and how love to come sent forth
this hatred as its harbinger." The end 473

the old man spoke of was not idle, since,
♦ indeed, they say, the loyalty their wounds
produced matched that of wild Pirithoüs
after his war with Theseus or that
of Pylades, who saved Orestes when
the fury named Megaera drove him mad.

Just as when windblown seas grow calm, and sails 478
luff in the last remaining, lingering breeze,
they let the king (for they had suffered) soothe
their hard—now unresisting—hearts. They entered.

–♦–♦–♦–

The king now first had leisure to regard 482
his visitors' demeanor, and he saw,
among their armaments, that one man wore
a lion skin that bristled down his back.
Its shaggy mane hung down his sides. It looked
like the one Hercules, when he was young,
slew in Teumesia, before he killed
♦ and wore the Nemean lion in Cleonae.
♦ The Calydonian boar—an honored hide— 490
with terrible stiff hair and long, curved tusks
was draped around the shoulders of stout Tydeus.
Stunned by an omen of such magnitude
the king stood motionless, acknowledging
divine prevision, portents cavern-given,
Apollo's oracle. His frozen face
concealed his contemplation. Veneration
seized him, and he rejoiced, for he believed
the power of the gods had brought these men
and they would be the son-in-laws ordained
by the ambiguous prediction of
prophet Apollo to appear as beasts.

He stretched his hands, palms upturned, to the stars: 497
"Night, you enfold the labors of the earth
and heavens. You propel the shooting stars
on errant courses. You restore men's souls.
You let tomorrow's sun shine healthful rays 500

on our infirmities; you give me strength.
You bring me understanding when I stray
and seek the truth through error's mazy way,
for you unveil the ancient oracles.
Now guide my hand. Corroborate your omens.
Through the revolving years this house will keep
your memory intact, and two black sheep,
o goddess, will be sacrificed to you,
as Vulcan's flames, splashed with fresh milk, consume
the entrails of our lustral offering.
I hail the truth of cauldrons and deep caves.
Fortune, I feel the presence of the gods!"

He spoke and took the two men by the hand
into an inner hall beneath his roof.
White ash slept on the altars where low flames
still warmed libations, sacred to the gods.
The king commanded hearths be lit anew
and that the banquet recommence. At once,
waiters emerged from nowhere, and a din
rang through the royal residence. Attendants
cushioned the couches; strewed thin, purple lawn
and rustling cloth of gold; or on high walls
hung tapestries; or lifted up by hand
smooth, polished tables where the feast would stand.
Others strung chains of lanterns whose gold light
defeated shadows in the darkened night.
Butchered meat, drained of blood, was slipped on spits
that servants turned, or they filled canisters
with ground-grain cereals and bread. The bustle
and effort pleased Adrastus, who displayed
himself upon on ivory throne, arrayed
with bolsters, royal robes, and cloth of state.

Elsewhere the young men washed their wounds and then 527
reclined at table, and those hurts established
a common bond, and they apologized.
Tydeus forgave, and so did Polynices.

–♦–♦–♦–

Then the king called his daughters' nurse, Acaste. 529
She was the one he trusted to instill
a sense of modesty in them, to keep
his girls intact until with lawful rites
of Venus they were married. Standing silent,
she listened as the old king held her ear.
She carried out Adrastus's commands 533
and led both maidens from their inner room.
They walked before her. They looked wonderful,
like Pallas, clangorous with arms, or like
Diana, with her quiver charges, but
they caused no terror. Facing unknown men,
they showed no impropriety; their cheeks
blushed red and white with shy variety;
their eyes were lowered, and they only saw
their father, whom they held in veneration.

With hunger banished and the tables cleared,
Adrastus asked some servants for his bowl,
the custom of the house of Iäsus.
It was bright gold, engraved with images,
from which the gods' libations had been poured
by Danaus and Phoroneus, former kings.
♦ Cast images in raised-relief displayed 543
the snake-haired Gorgon's severed head whose eyes,
heavy with death, and fainting mouth yet seemed
to move and grow pale in the metal gold,
just as her gilt-winged victor seemed to fly
unsteadily in air. Here Ganymede, 548
the Phrygian hunter, rose on golden wings.
His comrades mourned him, and his hounds grew weary
baying in vain at clouds or chasing shadows.
As Ganymede ascended, Troy receded,
and Gargara (Mount Ida) seemed to sink.

Wine overflowed this bowl as King Adrastus 552
called on the gods of heaven, Phoebus first.
The company, including servants, moved
around Apollo's altar, singing hymns
and crowned with simple branches. Frankincense

smoked from the glowing fires that they renewed
in honor of Apollo's holy day.

The king spoke: "My young visitors, you may 557
wonder what is the origin of our
ritual supplication of the god.
It is not blind religion; rather, we
Argives atone for what we have endured.
♦ If you will hear the story, I'll explain:

♦ "The Python was a serpent born of earth 562
that wreathed its black tail into seven folds
and wrapped its sinuous, prodigious rolls
near Delphi. It crushed oak trees and lay sprawled
by the Castilian spring, where its three tongues
imbibed the nutriments that make black venom.
There, Phoebus killed it. Phoebus tracked it down
and riddled it with arrows. There it died,
stretched on a hundred acres of Cirrhaeus.

"Stained by that slaughter, needing to appease 569
the deity, Apollo undertook
a quest that brought him to the humble roof
where lived our king Crotopus and his daughter.
She verged on womanhood. She had not known
the marriage couch, but she was beautiful
and she maintained the household gods with grace.
She would have been much happier had she
not shared Apollo's furtive love, or known
his secret, Apollonian desire,
for she was ravished by the god beside 575
Nemea's fetid waters. After, when
the moon had filled its orb full twice five times,
her womb produced a son, Latona's grandson,
and he was like a star—he was that handsome.
Yet she feared punishment (the king would blame
his daughter, even though she had been raped),
and so she chose to wander trackless wastes,
and there, among the sheepfolds, secretly
gave up her newborn baby to be raised

and parented by those who roamed the mountains.
The infant, taken in, deserved a bed 582
better than one of grass, a better roof
than one of woven oak. His limbs were wrapped
in arbute bark for warmth, and shepherd's pipes
of hollow reeds persuaded him to sleep
as he lay on the ground beside the sheep.
Nevertheless, his fate would not permit him 586
even this household, for a pack of dogs
attacked him in the meadow where he lay,
open-mouthed, breathing drafts of air. Their rage
was indiscriminate; their bloody maws
ripped him to pieces. This news reached the ears
of his astonished mother, who was torn
by terror of her father and by shame.
Her mad screams filled the house; she bared her breast
and ran to face her father and confess.
Unmoved, he ordered what she too desired
(unspeakable, this punishment): dark death.

"Mindful, too late, of his debauchery, 596
Apollo sought atonement for the slain—
◆ a monster, born deep down in Acheron
where the Eumenides abide. Its face
and breast were of a woman, but a snake
rose from its head and cleaved its iron brow. 600
This foul plague hissed nonstop and walked at night.
It entered chambers, those where women nursed,
and snatched up babies. With its bloody teeth
it gobbled them and fattened on our grief.

"A hero—armed, courageous—named Coroebus 605
could stand no more, so he recruited men
of prowess who sought fame, not length of life.
Out of a gate where two roads parted came
the monster, fresh from recent devastation,
the body of a baby on each hip.
Her hooked hands held their organs in her grip,
and iron nails grew warm in tender hearts.
The soldier blocked her path. Coroebus had
his crowd of men surround their enemy

then drove his heavy sword through her hard heart
and turned its gleaming point to probe her life
in its deep refuge, sending Jupiter's
monster back down to Jupiter's abyss.
It was a joy to go and see, up close, 616
her dead, black eyes and all the excrements—
unspeakable—that poured out from her womb.
Her breast was stained by clots of blood.

"She had
destroyed our spirit. Even as they cheered,
the Argive young looked pale because they'd wept
so many tears. They pounded lifeless limbs
with cudgels (they sought solace for their sorrows—
a useless task) and knocked her pointed fangs
out of her jaws but could not calm their anger.
They say that night birds would not touch her body 624
and hungry packs of dogs went mad, unfed,
while anxious wolves with dry mouths stood and gaped.

"Apollo, in his fury at the fate 627
of his avenger's death, rose up against
the sufferers, and from the shadowed heights
of twin-peaked Mount Parnassus, where he lay,
the savage god of Delos fired a plague
of arrows from his bow. He wasted fields.
He cast a cloak of pestilential fog
over the lofty roofs the Cyclops built.
Our dearest spirits fell. Death sheared the thread 632
of Destiny's three sisters with his sword
and held our city hostage to hell's fiends.
When our king sought the reason and asked why
◆ lightning fell leftward and the dog star Sirius
ruled the entire year, the holy lord
◆ Apollo, known as Paean, sent back word
that those who took his bloody monster's life
must make atonement and be sacrificed.

"Coroebus openly declared himself—
may his soul prosper through long centuries!
He merits life; he did not hide his deeds

or tremble at the thought that death was near!
At Cirrha, at the temple gates, his anger
was sacred, and his words were fierce, roughhewn:

◆" 'I was not sent here, god of Thymbra. I 643
come not as suppliant before your shrine.
I have been driven here by my own sense
of virtue and propriety. Apollo,
I am the one who killed your short-lived horror,
the object of your poison-dripping skies,
black clouds, harsh days—a man unfairly sought.
If heaven now prefers fierce monsters' lives 648
to those of common humans who may die
(expendable)—if gods are that severe,
why should the Argives suffer? It is I,
mighty divinity, and only I,
who owes his life to satisfy the fates.
Or does it do your heart more good to see
the desolation of our town, the light
of flames lit by our dwellers on the land?
Why should I stay your weapons and your hand
by speaking? Mothers wait, the final prayers 656
are said for me, and I do not deserve
your mercy. Seize your quiver; stretch your bow;
let its string sing; destroy this human soul,
but as I die, dispell the infestation
that hangs pale on the Inachus at Argos.'

"Only the brave find Fortune provident— 662
Latona's ardent son was reverent.
Apollo gently granted this reward:
he yielded and he spared his life. The clouds
that showered evil from our skies were banished,
and you, Coroebus, left the gates of Phoebus,
who heard, to your astonishment, your prayer.
Our solemn feast recalls this blest event,
and every year this anniversary
commemorates the temple of Apollo.

"But who are you, whom chance has brought before 668
our altars? If I heard correctly, you're

the right lord of the house of Calydon,
the son of Oeneus, Parthaon's son.
And you—you come from Argos. It's not late;
night offers time to talk. Why not explain?"

At once the Theban hero dropped his gaze 673
and stared down sadly at the earth. He looked
askance at Tydeus on his left. He felt
awkward and long was silent. Then he spoke:
"Religious services are not the place
for you to question me about my race,
my homeland, or the ancient origins
of blood that flows through me: to my chagrin,
the subject does not suit this sacred day.
However, if you care to hear me groan,
my father's line descends from Cadmus; home
is Mars' own Thebes; my mother is Jocasta."

Moved by his guest—he knew of him—Adrastus 681
asked him, "Why do you hide what's known? We've heard
all this, for fame does not avoid the road
around Mycenae. Those who shiver in
the Arctic sun or drink the Ganges or
sail the dark, western ocean know your realm,
its rage, the eyes that saw impieties—
◆ those too who seek the Syrtes' shifting shores.
Forget your father's errors. Sigh no more!
Our blood has also not been scrupulous, 689
yet sins are not transmitted by descent.
Dare to be different. Let your good deeds
redeem your people. But the frozen bear
grows faint; the beam-pole of the Northern Wain
slopes down and back. Pour wine upon the hearth,
and let us sing again, and yet again,
hymns to Latona's son, who has preserved us:

"Our father Phoebus! Either Lycia's
◆ snow-covered mountains or Patara's thorns 696
are your resort, or you for pleasure bathe
your gold hair in Castalia's sacred dew,
or you inhabit Thymbra, in the Troad—

where, it is said, nobody thanked you when
you shouldered building blocks of Phrygian stone. 700
Perhaps you take your pleasure on Mount Cynthus,
whose shades extend across Aegean seas,
there where Latona brought you forth on Delos,
the island with no fixed locality.
Your long bow bends, your long-range arrows rend
your savage enemies. You have been given
eternal youth by parents in the heavens.
You can predict the Parcae's violence,
what pleases Jove, what destiny will send,
which years bring death, who'll suffer war, and when
scepters may change, as comets may portend.
◆ You played the lyre to vanquish Marsyas. 709
You stretched the earthborn Tityus
beside the river Styx. You terrorized
the mighty Python and the Theban mother,
proud victims of your quiver. Avenging you,
gloomy Megaera buried Phlegyas
inside a hollow rock, where he inclines
eternally at table. There he starves,
tormented by a wicked feast, because
his pride and loathing overcame his hunger.

"O guardian of hospitality, 716
attend the right-hand side of Juno's fields;
be present, love us, make us fortunate—
whether, as in the rituals of Persia,
we call you rose-red Titan, or we say
O bountiful Osiris, or you shape
yourself as he who twists the horns of bulls
◆ in Perses' rocky caverns—holy Mithras!"

—◆—◆—◆—

BOOK 2 Ambush

The ghost of Laius. Celebration of Bacchus at Thebes. Eteocles' nightmare. Marriage negotiations in Argos. Weddings of Argia and Deipyle. An evil omen. The fatal necklace of Harmonia. Polynices frets about exile. Tydeus insults Eteocles, who plots an ambush. Two brothers (sons of Ide) die one death. A memorial to Athena.

Now, the winged son of Maia—Mercury—
returned through ice and dark to terminate
his mission for great Jove. Unmoving clouds
impeded progress. Vapors bogged him down.
No gentle zephyrs eased his steps through foul
smoke from the noiseless underworld. Here, Styx
curved round the fields nine times, and there, opposed,
torrents of fire debarred the traveler's road.

A trembling ghost—old Laius—followed slowly, 7
wounded by the unholy sword of one
of his own breed who'd pierced his breath of life
more than hilt-high and first enraged the Furies.
A staff sustained his steps as he proceeded.

Dry thickets, ghost-filled fields, and rusted trees 12
stared in astonishment, and Earth herself
marveled at god and ghost as they returned.

The blue-black bile of envy (even among 14
those shadows who had lost the light) was not
wanting: before the others, there stood one—
ill-willed and sinister—ready to curse
the gods for his distress. His life's last years
had burdened him; he could not stomach joy.

"Walk on!" he cried, "you lucky man, whatever 19
the reason you are called, whether at Jove's
command, or that the great Erinys sends

you to the daylight, or Thessalian witches
are mad to make you leave your secret tomb!
You are about to see a better sight,
the sun death left behind, pure streams and springs
and earth's green fields, but you'll be sadder when
you enter, once again, this shadowed world!"

They were seen, too, by Cerberus—the bane 26
of those who enter hell—who, curled beneath
a hidden threshold, raised his heads and gaped;
his jutting black neck swelled; he would have thrown
the bones that lay along the ground had not
the god, with wand of Lethe, calmed him down
and closed his iron eyes with triple sleep.

There is a cove the Greeks call Taenaros 32
from whose sea sprays the fearful height Malea
lifts skyward till its peak admits no sight.
Its summit stands serene, sublime above
the winds and rain. There weary stars recline.
Its shadow floats at sea, and long lines reach
the deepest waters when day's light declines.

Taenaros curves its coast: its inner bay 43
absorbs the breakers that it dare not face.
Here Neptune steers his weary steeds to harbor,
weak from Aegean whirlpools. First their hooves
scrape up the sand, but then they disappear
into the sea, like fish. It's said pale shadows
follow deserted pathways to this place
and fill infernal Jove's vast halls with death.
If what Arcadian peasants say is true,
shrieks can be heard; the groans of punishment;
crowds of dark figures hurrying; the shouts
and wars of the Eumenides: these sound
till noon; and Death's three-headed watchman howls
and drives the listening farmers from their plows.

This was the place, then, where the winged god, 55
heavy with clouds and soot, found heaven's light.
He wiped the deep-earth's shadow off his face

and drew in breaths of life-restoring air,
then flew in silence over fields and cities
under Arcturus and the demimoon.
Sleep led the steeds of Night, solicitous
before the deity; he yielded him
a portion of the sky to show respect.

The ghost flew lower than the god and gazed 63
down on the hills of Cirrha, on his birthplace,
and Phocis, which his own dead corpse pollutes.
When he reached Thebes, he sighed and stood before
the threshold of his son, the home he'd known.
He lingered, not entering, and Laius grew
uneasy when he saw there, propped against
a lofty column, yokes that had been his,
his blood-stained chariot. He almost turned—
the Thunderer's commands could not restrain him,
nor the Arcadian's wand, whose breath gives life.

◆ That day, it happened, was the Bacchanalia. 71
It was established when the Thunderer's well-known
lightning bolt hastened, tender Euhius, your birth.
Your father carried you to term, so Tyrian
colonists kept a custom, for that reason,
of playing through the night. Indoors and on
the fields they lie at random. Woven garlands
and empty bowls surround them; when it's day,
their breaths exhale the god. Their cymbals play
and drown the sound of bull-skin drums and flutes.

Sensible women, driven to Bacchic frenzy, 79
take pleasure in Cithaeron's trackless groves.
◆ They celebrate like wild Bistonians,
who feast on half-dead cattle chewed by lions
on Rhodope or deep in Ossa's hollows.
Newly drawn milk subdues the taste of blood
and seems, to them, a luxury, unless
◆ the drunken scent of Theban Iacchus
blows over them. Then ecstasy it is
to scatter rocks and wine cups and the blood
of innocent companions in the morning—

to start fresh and resume their festive meals. 89
In such a night as this, the swift Cyllenian
glided through silence to the king of Thebes
and reached the lofty couch where he had thrown
his body, cushioned by Assyrian rugs.
His heart knew nothing of his mortal fate;
he'd had his feast, and now he took his sleep.

Meanwhile, the ghost performed his mission. Not 94
to seem some false night vision, he adopted
the shaded visage, voice, and famous garb
of old Tiresias, the prophet. He
maintained his own gray hair and flowing beard
and pallor, but he feigned the sacred fillets
woven with silver olive leaves. Around
his head he wore these badges of respect.

The apparition held an olive branch 100
and touched the chest of King Eteocles.
He spoke these words to warn him of his fate:

"Sluggard! there is no time for you to sleep,
to lie unmoving here. The night is deep!
Be wary of your brother! Mighty deeds
and serious preparations beckon, yet
you hesitate like some Ionian sailor
when south winds swell the seas and clouds turn black—
he does not think about his ship or how
the ocean twists his rudder!

"Everyone knows
your brother married well, that he enlists
soldiers and seeks the kingdom you deny him.
He plans to spend old age in your high halls!
He is encouraged by an augury 111
come true, that said Adrastus would be his
father-in-law and give an Argive dowry.
Stained by fraternal blood and full of self-
importance, Tydeus joins your brother's cause
and promises long banishment for you.
The father of the gods commiserates, 115

and he has sent me here to say: keep Thebes,
and keep your brother out! He's blinded by
his craving for your kingdom. He would dare
do the same thing. Do not permit a man
who studies your destruction to succeed
in his foul undertaking. He would make
Mycenae mistress over Cadmus' city!"

He spoke, and even as the pale stars dimmed
before the horses of the sun, he threw
aside his olive branch and drew his cloak
open. There's no mistaking the grandfather,
who hovered above his grandson's bed. He bared
his throat—the gash received when he was murdered—
and let blood overflow the sleeping king.

Peace shattered, he awoke from his bad dream.
He shook imagined blood off, terrified
by his grandfather's ghost, but equally
intent to find his brother—like a tiger
who arches when the sounds of hunters reach
her den. She shakes off sleep, prepares for battle,
flexes her jaws, and lets her claws extend
before she rushes out among the hunters
and seizes one, still breathing, in her mouth
to carry back to feed her savage young.
Just so, the Theban tyrant was aroused
and ready to confront his absent brother.

–♦–♦–♦–

And now Aurora left her husband's bed
and cut the frozen shadows of the skies.
She shook her dripping hair and crimsoned as
the sun pursued her—that is, Lucifer,
whose languid steeds move slowly through the heavens
as lingering scarlet flames undo damp mists.
He is the fiery father, he who fills
the world with rays, but who does not allow
sunlight to reach his sister.

Elderly
Adrastus, on this morning, rose not long
before the heroes of the Dirce and
the Achelous rivers left their beds.
The horn of Sleep had poured its plenty on 143
Tydeus and Polynices, weary from
the tempest that had punished them, but scant
slumber had visited the king of Argos,
for in his mind he thought about the gods,
the friendships he'd begun, the sons-in-law
the fates had promised. Having met within
the middle court, they shook hands but then sought
a place inside the palace where they could
keep secrets and express their deepest thoughts.

Adrastus put his proposition first: 151
"Something not undivine—perhaps Apollo—
guided you, excellent young men, through darkness,
through rain and thunder, through the storm and lightning
of Jupiter, to reach my realm and house.
I think that you and every Greek must know
with what devices crowds of suitors seek
my daughters and the right to marry them,
for I have twins, my promise of grandchildren,
who've grown beneath the same stars into women.
Their honor and their virtue may be gauged
by the behavior you saw yesterday
when feasting. You need not believe their father:
they are the objects of proud men with kingdoms
♦ and mighty armies, Spartans and Pharaeans,
great men, too numerous to count. Achaean
mothers in every city hope their sons
will marry them, more than your father Oeneus
considered for alliance or who feared
♦ the Pisan father's chariot. But fate
permits no Spartan sires or sons-in-law
from Elis, for by long decree the cares
attendant on my kingdom and my blood
have been ordained for you. The gods are good! 170
Prophecies please when they bring men of birth

this spirited. This is the prize the hard
night's storm has brought you; this is your reward
for everything you've suffered and endured."

The young men listened, their eyes fixed, regarding 173
each other for long instants to determine
who would permit the other first to speak,
but, bold in every undertaking, Tydeus
began: "Your mind is mellow, therefore you
are sparing in self-praise. Your virtue conquers
whatever Fortune hands you. Who commands 178
more power than Adrastus? Everyone
knows you established law in untamed Argos
after you had been driven from your home
◆ in Sicyon. If only Jupiter
had let the nations bound within the Doric
Isthmos, as well as those beyond her margins,
◆ prosper beneath your rule! Mycenae's crimes 184
would not have dimmed the sun, nor would the savage
◆ battles in Elis have made valleys groan.
How many other kingdoms would have been
spared the Eumenides—the Furies? Theban,
nobody knows this better than yourself.
Therefore, our minds are set and truly willing."

Those were his words, and his companion added: 188
"Would anyone refuse this marriage offer?
It is not often Venus favors exiles
without a country; here our hearts are settled;
our minds no longer linger over sorrows.
Our comfort is no less than that of sailors
who spy a friendly harbor after storms
that batter them. We are delighted that
the omens welcome visitors. We join
to you our fortunes, labors, lives, and fates."

Without delay, the three men rose. The king 197
of Argos added weight to what he'd said
by promising assistance in the future
to reinstate the exiles in their homes.

The happy Argives heard the news, which ran 201
throughout the city, that great men had come
as sons-in-law to wed the well-endowed
young virgins: beautiful Argia and,
deserving no less praise, Deipyle,
Argia's sister. People talked in public
in allied towns and nearby fields, in woodlands
high on Lycaeus and Parthenius,
as they prepared to celebrate their joy.

Rumor, the goddess who confuses things, 205
had reached the lands of Corinth, even Thebes,
over whose walls she spread her wings and rained
down terror: her mad mouth was unrestrained.
To King Eteocles, who heard her ravings,
it felt as if his past night's dream continued:
Rumor told him of friendships, marriages,
alliances, mixed nations—also war.

In Argos, it rained happiness: the day 213
had come, and revelers gained entrance to
the royal palace, where they saw, up close,
spectacular reliefs that illustrated
their history; the bronze art vied with life,
◆ so skillfully was it conceived. It showed 217
the twin-horned Father Inachus himself,
propped on his left against a tilted urn.
He is attended by Iasius,
by peaceful, old Phoroneus, and the image
of Abas, who makes war; Acrisius,
who curses at the Thunderer; Coroebus,
who bears a head upon his naked sword;
and Danaus too, who contemplates great crimes.

A thousand others followed. Commoners 223
streamed through the lofty portals of the palace,
but standing in the first rank were the men
who ranked beside the king in precedence.

Within the hall the altar fires grew warm; 226
the sound of female voices echoed; chaste

matrons of Argos formed a ring around
the queen, and others tended to her daughters.
Some calmed their fears; some offered them advice
to help them act correctly: modesty 230
made them remarkable for how they moved
and gazed—their eyes were lowered—and they blushed
a color suited to their shamefastness.
Sudden nostalgia for their virgin state
came over them, and as they felt their guilt,
tears dewed their honest faces, and their parents,
who knew why they were weeping, were delighted.

They might have been Minerva and Apollo's 236
fierce sister: keen, well armored, wearing their
blond hair upwoven, leading followers
from Cynthus and from Aracynthus. If
the eyes of humans could behold such things,
then you might gaze forever to determine
which one was more resplendent, which displayed
more grace or more of Jupiter; and had
they changed their clothes, the crested helmet
would suit Diana, and the quiver, Pallas.

The Argives strove to celebrate; 244
they wore the gods out with their vows; each house
observed what sacrifice it could prepare:
entrails or slaughtered animals or turf,
but all were heard; the gods rewarded those
who cared, who offered frankincense, who shaded
their doors with branches. Lachesis, however— 249
the Fate who weaves the threads of life—took pleasure
in sudden terror. Minds grew numb. The father's
joy all but vanished, and the day was ruined!

There on the threshold of unwed Minerva 251
(for she esteemed Larissa's fortress in
Argos no less than she did Athens), where
according to the custom of their parents,
young Argive women on the brink of marriage
offered their maiden tresses to atone
for their first time in bed, a great bronze shield,

the spoil of the Arcadian Euhippus,
fell from the tower. It hit those who climbed
the stairs to reach the summit and extinguished
the forward torches, casting darkness over
the light of the processional; what's more,
everyone hesitated as, from far,
an oracle emitted horns of war.

Fearful at first, they turned toward the king 262
refusing to admit what they had heard,
although they knew the omen was disastrous,
and they increased this feeling as they whispered.
No marvel, for, Argia, you were wearing
a most unlucky gift your husband gave you—
the fatal necklace of Harmonia.

The narrative is long, but what is known 267
about this evil thing I shall rehearse
so you will know the power of its curse.
♦ *Vulcan devised this gift as his revenge.*

The former age has handed down the story
♦ that when the lord of Lemnos long endured
the secret passion Mars and Venus shared—
which his complaints could not amend, nor his
avenging chain-link net correct—he crafted
a talisman or charm to grace Harmonia,
their daughter, on her wedding day. The Cyclops, 273
though skilled in greater tasks, began to work,
♦ in friendly rivalry with the Telchines,
a family of famous artisans,
but Vulcan sweated most: he shaped a ring
of emeralds that glittered secret fire
and adamant; on it he etched the figures
of evil fortune and the Gorgon. Ashes
remaining from the lightning bolt last fashioned
on that Sicilian anvil added green
fluorescence to the vipers that slid down
the mane of the Medusa. Vulcan used
♦ the mournful fruit of the Hesperides

and gold, dread gold from Phrixus' golden fleece, 281
and he wove in the strength of different plagues,
the bull-snake taken from Tisiphone's
◆ black forehead, and the force of Venus' cestus.
He shrewdly bathed the whole with lunar foam
and melted pleasing poison through the jewel.

Whose right hand formed the object? It was not 286
the most alluring of the sister graces,
the one named Pasithea, not Fair Form
or Cupid, the Idalian boy, but Grief,
Torment, Dissension, and Distress. Harmonia
felt its effect first in Illyria:
Cadmus, her serpent husband, crawled around;
her own mouth hissed; her prone length furrowed ground.

As soon as Semele had put the poisoned 292
jewels on her neck, deceitful Juno crossed
her threshold. People say the gift belonged
to you as well, unfortunate Jocasta!
Its horror suited you; its beauty made
you feel attractive, pleasing to the man
who shared your bed. There will be other owners,
but now Argia glittered with the necklace,
adorned with that cursed gold that made her sister's
jewelry seem tawdry by comparison.

◆ The wife of one whose death was near (the prophet 299
Amphiaraus) plotted—as she stood
in front of every altar, at each feast—
on secret schemes to make that dread jewel hers.
She did not understand the auguries.
What groans she longed for; o what devastation
the evil woman wanted—and deserved!
But must her husband suffer, whom she lured
to arms, and must her guiltless son go mad?

–◆–◆–◆–

After twelve days of royal banqueting,
after the public celebration finished,

the Ismenian hero turned his thoughts to Thebes: 307
he longed to have a chance to rule that realm.

He thought about the day his brother won
the lots they cast, how he had been deprived
of place in the Echion palace; how he watched
the gods desert him; how his anxious friends
abandoned him; how Fortune fled; how he
remained alone, exposed: Antigone 313
accompanied his first sad steps of exile—
she'd dared that much—but he had left her at
the outset, when his anger was so great
he could not even weep as he withdrew.
He'd taken note of those he'd seen rejoicing
(the close associates of their vile king)
and those who suffered at his banishment.
Each night and every day, hot anger ate
his soul, and crazy indignation, and
that heaviest of mortal sorrows—hope
that has been long delayed. Such was the cloud
of thought that occupied his heart as he
decided to go home, though banned, to Thebes,
back to the town of Cadmus on the Dirce.

After a chief bull loses his loved valley— 323
after the victor orders him to leave
his customary grass, that he may bellow
off in the distance for his captured cow—
his muscles gain fresh vigor during exile;
his mighty neck, engorged with blood, renews;
his chest breaks oaks; his horns and hooves grow strong.
He wants his pasture, seeks his captured herd.
Although the shepherds hardly recognize him,
his vanquisher feels fear when he returns.
So Polynices made his anger keen 331
by silent brooding, but his loyal wife
knew he had secrets and he planned to travel.

She lay in bed and held him in the early 333
pale light of dawn. "When was my lord so shrewdly
tempered?" she said, "or bothered so by exile?

Lovers see all! You lie awake at night,
cry out, and sigh; you never sleep in peace.
How often have I seen tears bathe your face
and touched you with my hand to calm the cares
that make you groan? I am not moved by broken 339
marital obligations, nor the threat
of widowed youth. Our love is young; our bed
has not grown cold since I became a bride.
My love, I must confess: your welfare is
what worries me. Will you pursue your kingdom
unarmed, with no companion? If your brother
denies you, will he let you out of Thebes?
Fame is a skillful analyst of leaders. 345
Fame says he is a proud man, insolent,
a plunderer who showed hostility
even before his year had run its course.
Soothsayers frighten me: they see divine
warnings in flights of birds and vital organs;
night visions trouble me, and I have seen
Juno, for real, in dreams! Where are you going?
There has to be some woman, one whose father
has offered better marriage terms in Thebes!"

This last made Polynices laugh, if briefly: 352
he calmed his wife's soft sorrow, and he held her.
He kissed her mournful cheeks to stop her tears,
in timely fashion. "Free your soul from fear.
Believe me, I will seek advice from men
of merit. Days of peace will follow. Cares
beyond your years should not be your concern.
If the Saturnian father—Jupiter—
should learn of my ill fate, and Justice cast
her gaze down from the heavens and attend
to virtue on this earth, then there may come
a day when you, as queen, will travel through
twin cities to survey your husband's walls."

He spoke, then hurried through the threshold he 363
adored to talk to Tydeus, his companion,
whose loyal breast felt—as his own—his cares
(for so men who have striven will be friends).

He also had to speak to King Adrastus,
their father-in-law. 367

–♦–♦–♦–

They lingered in debate,
then they approved, of many plans proposed,
the best one—best because they would discern
his brother's credibility and learn
if an ambassador might safely journey
to Thebes and back. The man of daring, Tydeus,
at once assumed the task. No less were you,
strongest Aetolian, restrained by tears,
but all the efforts of Deipyle
were vanquished by her father's orders, by
the custom of safe conduct granted envoys,
and by her sister's justified persuasions.

Already he was measuring hard roads 375
through forests and along the coast: the swamp
of Lerna, where the burned-out Hydra warms
those deep, unholy waters; Nemea,
through which few shepherds yet dare play
their songs; the morning side of Ephyres,
where southeast winds touch Corinth; past the port
of Sisyphus, and round the curving bay
Palaemon blessed—Lechaeum—where the shore
is riled by waves. His path took him past Nisus.
O gentle Eleusin, he passed you
on his left side. Teumesian fields received him,
and then he reached the battlements of Thebes,
entered, and there beheld Eteocles, 384
a hard man on a high throne walled by spears
that bristled upright. He breached time and law
and kept the kingdom that he owed his brother
under his savage sway. He sat, prepared
for anything, and griped about the lateness
of this request that he maintain his promise.

Holding an olive branch, which signified 389
his status as an envoy, Tydeus

stood openly before him to explain
the reason for his journey, and, when asked,
he gave his name. But he was rude of speech
and always quick to quarrel, and he mixed
rough words with what he properly should say:

"If you dealt plainly and maintained your promise, 393
you would have sent legations to your brother
after your year was finished. It was right,
it was your turn, to set aside good fortune,
to be content to yield your kingdom, so
your brother, who had wandered endlessly—
who had endured indignities in towns
no one has heard of—could succeed to office.
That is what you agreed. But you—because
you love sweet rule, and power is enticing—
have to be begged. The circle of the stars
has turned through its swift orbit once already,
the mountain leaves have fallen and renewed,
during which time your brother has endured
the bitterness of exile, indigence,
and unknown cities. Now, it is your turn 403
to pass your days in open weather, lay
your body on the cold ground, be submissive
before a strangers' hearth gods while you wander.
It's time to end your revels. Long enough
you've made yourself look rich in gold and purple;
you've mocked your brother's year of poverty.
I'm warning you, now you must learn to live
without the joy of making other men
obey you. Suffer exile. Earn your throne!"

While he was speaking, his opponent smoldered. 410
He felt hot flames consume his silent heart,
just like a snake that nurses constant thirst
in dry shades till its rock moves; then it draws
venom into its scaly neck and jaws.
Its body wracked, it closes in. 415

"Were I
to have suspected, by uncertain signs,

my brother's animosity toward me,
and were his secret hatred not apparent,
your rudeness would suffice to indicate
his mind, which you prefigure, like those men
sent forth to undermine a city's walls
or trumpets that announce a hostile army.
Your militance foreruns his. Had you faced 420
◆ Bistonians with your message, or Geloni—
pale from the lack of sun—you would have been
more sparing in your speech, more reverent
for protocols your mission here demands!

"I would not lay the charge of this offense, 423
this madness of the mind, on one who serves;
what you repeat is what you have been told.
But since your speech has been so full of threats—
you seek my scepter but you offer nothing
to guarantee security or safety
and you are quick to seize your weapon's hilt—
then bear my words to your Argolic master,
although they cannot hope to equal yours:
'Why should I envy your accomplishments?
The lots we cast were just; my years deserve 428
this office and the scepter that I hold—
and long will hold. You own a dowry palace,
the gift of your King Adrastus, your wife's father.
The wealth of Danaus has been heaped before you.
In Argos and along the Lerna, may 432
the auspices be fortunate, and may
you rule supreme. Scruff pastures on the Dirce,
Euboean coasts of little width are ours,
and we who rule do not disdain to say
our father is the miserable Oedipus.
Your noble line will not be traced to Pelops
and Tantalus, for you have married blood
more closely tied to Jupiter. Why bring
a wife accustomed to her father's riches
here, to this house? According to our custom, 439
our sisters must attend her. Mother mourns
incessantly; she lives in filth. The old

man's curses echo loudly from deep shadows
and interfere with our religious rites.

" 'The people are accustomed to my yoke. 442
The commoners and lords would be ashamed
to suffer alterations; they would groan
under uncertain leadership. Short terms
of office are a burden to the state.
It irks men to obey inconstant rule.
Look at the terror and astonishment
my danger breeds among the citizens.

" 'My brother, you would come to Thebes in anger!
Should I abandon men whom you, as king,
are sure to punish? Even if I should,
I know these men: they love me; they think I
deserve support. They won't let me surrender
power . . .' "

                                        But Tydeus could endure no more. 451
He interrupted him. "You *will* surrender!
You will surrender *power!* If iron walls
encircled you, or if Amphion sang
a second song and mounded triple ramparts,
not fire or sword could save you! You will pay
for your impertinence, and you will strike
your crown against the earth before you die.
Our armies will defeat you! You deserve it,
but they are to be pitied whom you tear
away from wives and children, those whose fate
leaves them to die in your unholy war.
You're a fine king! How many funeral pyres 460
will dot Cithaeron's heights, and how much blood
will flow along Ismenos stream? So much
for piety; so much for promises.
But should I be surprised? Let us consider
your origins and Oedipus, your father.
You are his sole true heir. Your bear the stain—
mad man—of his behavior and his crimes.
But I am wasting time. We want our year!"

He screamed these bold words backward from 467
the threshold, and he hurried out. He parted
the instigated multitude just like
the Calydonian boar who guards Diana:
his bristles stiff, his curved tusks slash like lightning
when he is pressured by the Argive army,
which cuts him off by heaping stones and piles
of branches torn from trees along those banks
the river Achelous penetrates.
Now Telamon is on the ground, and he 473
leaves prostrate Ixion and then assails
you also, Meleager. There, at last,
a broad spear strikes him, but he blunts its point
by resolute defense. In such a way
the Calydonian hero ground his teeth
and left the terrified assembly—just
as if they had denied him his own kingdom.
He hurried on his way; he threw aside 478
the olive branch he'd held as suppliant.
Astonished mothers watched him from the ledges
along high roofs; they hurled their insults on
the savage son of Oeneus but were thinking
similar awful thoughts about their king.

Eteocles, their ruler, was not slow 482
to plan his wicked crimes and his deceits.
Enraged, he gave instructions to a chosen
squadron of loyal young men, fit for war,
and now with prayers, now with harsh commands,
he ordered them to undertake a battle
at night—to violate the sacred name
of legate with their silent swords: an ambush.
What is more cowardly for one who rules?

Along a nearby path through underbrush 496
(a hidden track), these young men raced each other:
their shortcut skipped the deep part of the forest.

There is a seat that's suited to their fraud, 498
where far from town, two hills, like evil jaws,
impinge upon the roadway. There a mountain

casts its long shadow, and the leafy slopes
create a sylvan bowl as if, it seemed,
Nature arranged a place fit for deceits
and ambushes, where men might hide behind
downsloping rocks through which the footpath winds.

A plain below held broad, inclining fields 504
and, opposite, a bold protuberance,
the former dwelling of that winged beast
that once confronted Oedipus. She'd perched there,
insolently, with sallow cheeks and pus-
filled eyes, her feathers stiff with human blood,
embracing the remains of men, and clasped
half-eaten bones to her bare chest. Her dreadful
eyes scanned the far horizons to determine
whether a visitor approached to pierce
her riddles. If a traveler came near 511
and dared but failed to guess her secret meaning,
she would not wait to strike but straight would soar:
her talons would extend from leaden hands,
and she would beat her victim with her pinions
and tear him with her teeth. She thus concealed
her secret wiles until undone by one
whose cunning matched her own. Her wings ceased beating,
and from her bloody precipice she fell
and hit harsh rocks that tore her empty belly.

The forest was infected with her horror: cattle 519
refuse to pasture in the nearby fields,
and hungry sheep avoid the tainted grass.
Shadows no longer please the choirs of Dryads,
nor did the Fauns perform their rituals.
From that enchanted grove, even the birds
of bad luck fled. Destined to perish, the squadron
silently marched and circled through the forest.
Men lay their battle armor on the ground
but kept their grips and leaned on upright spears
while waiting for their puissant enemy.

Night veiled the sun beneath her cool, damp mantle 527
and spread her sable shadow on the land,

as Tydeus, drawing closer to the grove,
glimpsed, from a lofty mound, the reddish glint
of shields and crested helmets worn by soldiers.
Their copper armor flickered through the shadows,
reflecting moonlight in between the trees.
He halted at the sight but then advanced.
He kept two steady spears prepared, his hand
positioned on the grip of his sheathed sword.

Tydeus spoke first, not terrified, unhumble: 535
"Who might you be, you men who hide your weapons?"
but no one answered him. The quietness
inspired no confidence; it seemed suspicious;
it did not promise peace. Then suddenly
the leader of the cohort, Chthonius,
unbent his giant arm and flung his spear:
it whirled through darkening air, yet neither Fortune
nor heaven favored his attempt. The weapon
flew and pierced through the cloak of savage boar—
black, bristling leather the Olenian wore
knotted on his left shoulder—and almost
drew blood: its blunted spear tip spared his throat.

Tydeus' blood froze in his heart; his hair stood stiff, 544
his eyes glanced savagely from side to side,
courageous, eager with desire, but pale.
He yet had no idea how many waited.

"Step forward! Meet me in the open! Is 547
your cowardice so great you will not talk?
Alone, myself, I challenge you!"

They did
not hesitate when they heard his defiance.

As soon as he beheld their numbers, saw 549
soldiers emerge from countless shadows—some
descending from the heights, while others climbed
the slopes of valleys, and the plain held many
whose lucent armor lighted all the road—
he sought the steep cliff of the savage Sphinx.

As when the beaters' cries drive animals 556
from their retreats, in his uncertainty
he found the only means to save himself,
tearing his fingernails on pointed stones
that broke off as he scrambled up hard rock
and made himself the master of the ridge.

Fear now was far behind him, and a path 558
lay open for destruction. He upheaved
a boulder from the hill that groaning oxen,
straining their necks, would be hard pressed to drag
when drafted to construct a city wall.
He bent his strength beneath it, seeking 561
to balance that immense projectile—like
◆ the empty wine bowl righteous Pholus lifted
◆ against his enemies, the Lapiths. Death
stared at those looking in astonishment 564
as he stood over them and then released
that weight, which maimed their bodies, hands, and faces
and smashed their iron armor and their weapons.

Four men groaned in one heap beneath that mass 568
of mountain he dislodged, an overture
that terrified the others. These withdrew,
for those who died were not despicable.
The first was Dorylas, whose ardor matched
the strength of kings; then Theron, born of Mars,
who trusted in his earthborn ancestors.
Second to none in managing his horse, 573
◆ but now dead in the field they'd walked was Halys
◆ and Phaedimus, whom Bacchus hated, as
he hated all King Pentheus's descendants.

Their unexpected fortune terrified 576
the cohort; Tydeus saw them scattering,
disorganized, but only had two spears,
still propped against the mountain where he'd left them.
He hurled these to exacerbate their flight, 579
and then he sought the plain, lest weapons strike
his unprotected body. Down he leaped
swiftly to seize a shield that he had seen

rolling away from Theron where he fell.
He took his stand, thrusting the small, round target
before him that his enemy had held.
He blocked his back and head with his own armor.

Meanwhile, the Ogyidae regrouped, closing 585
their ranks, and took position. Tydeus
drew his swift sword—Bistonian, a gift
of war from Oeneus—and he attacked
his opposition equally, wherever
he could, opposing some, while with his sword
he parried flying weapons others hurled.
Now their own numbers hindered them; they fought 590
encumbered by each other's armaments.
They struggled, strengthless; their missed blows hit comrades;
their whole disordered battle line collapsed.

Tydeus, expectant, waited their attack,
small, hard to hit, invincible, unmoved.
♦ Not otherwise, immense Briareus, 596
in Phlegra, where the Getes live, fought the gods,
where he defied—if this may be believed—
Apollo's arrows and the dreadful serpents
♦ of Pallas, and Mars's Pelethronian spear
tipped with sharp iron, and the thunderbolts
♦ that weary Pyracmon produced for Vulcan
when all Olympus spent itself in vain; 600
Briareus sulked—so many hands were idle!
With equal energy the fiery Tydeus
handled his shield, retreated, circled back,
and even as he tore darts from his targe
and armor where they dangled, he rearmed
and cut off those who tried to get away.
His wounds were many, deep, yet none had found
his hidden life; they did not threaten death.

A sword-swing toppled mad Deilochus, 607
who joined his comrades in the underworld:
Phegeus, whose upraised ax announced his threat,
and Gyas and Lycophontes of Thebes—
one of the Dirce, one they call Echion.

Those who escaped now sought each other out 611
and counted heads; their thinned ranks sorrowed them.
Chromis could trace his origin to Cadmus
in Tyre. (Phoenician Dryope
was pregnant when a band of revelers
swept her along and she ignored her womb;
she dragged a bull for Bacchus by its horns,
a mighty labor that induced the birth.)
He was a bold spearman; he'd killed the lion 618
whose skin he wore. He shook a hardwood club,
knotted with spikes, and told his people, "Men,
will one alone go back and boast in Argos
of so much slaughter? He will hardly be
believed when he returns! Companions, are
your hands and weapons worthless? Cydon, Lampus:
is this what we were sent for by our king?"

But a Teumesian shaft of dogwood entered 624
his throat while Chromis spoke; his jaws were no
protection, and his tongue, which shaped new words,
swam loose in waves of blood. He stood until
death glided through his limbs, then, falling, bit
the spear, and he was silent.

Why should I 629
◆ forget to honor you as well, Thespiadae,
and make you famous? Periphas uplifted
his brother's dying body: he was one
whose inborn piety was unsurpassed.
His left hand raised the drooping neck, his right
sustained the body. Sobbing grief emerged 633
from his tight-fitting breastplate. His strapped helmet
could not stop tears and groans, when from behind
a weighty spear transfixed his curving ribs;
it entered through his back and exited
into his brother, binding loving hearts.
Periphas let his eyes, which still could see,
fall closed; his brother watched, for he had life
and strength despite his wounds, and told him, "Sons
of yours will hold you; they will give you kisses!"

They sank beneath a single destiny
whose hope had been to die if either died:
with their right hands they closed each other's eyes.

Tydeus pressed forward, forcing back Menoetus; 644
his legs were trembling, till his spear and shield
undid him; he gave way and fell, and from
the dirt, disgraced, outspread his lifted hands
and pushed the glittering spear point from his throat.

He made this supplication, "By the stars 649
that fall through darkness, by the gods, and by
this night which now belongs to you, have mercy!
Make me your messenger, and I will bring
this devastating news to Thebes and sing
your praises openly—despite the king—
before our terror-stricken public; how
our falling javelins were useless; how
no sword could pierce your breast; how you returned,
the victor, to the friend who longs for you!"

He spoke. The face of Tydeus did not alter. 655
"Your tears are wasted, vain," he told him. "You
promised your prince my head, or I'm mistaken.
It's what he wanted. Now lay down your armor;
take a last look at daylight. Should a coward
care if his life is short? Wars last forever!"

Blood weighed his weapon, even as he spoke, 659
and he withdrew it, then chased beaten soldiers,
bitterly railing, "This is not the night
that comes each second year, according to
your country's custom; you see here no Cadmean
orgies, or Bacchus desecrated by
insatiable mothers. You thought you would wear
the skins of fawns and carry slender wands
like the Bacchantes, while you heard soft airs,
◆ or you would listen to Celaenean pipes
and join disgusting contests warriors shun.
You found here other carnage, other madness.
So few, so cowardly: descend to shadows!"

His voice was thundering, but nonetheless 668
his heart lost force; his limbs were unresponsive
and his blood tired; his lifted hand dealt empty
blows now; his steps were slow; he could not raise
his shield and elbow, weighted down with spoils;
cold sweat dripped down his panting chest, and drops
of gore ran through his hair and burning face.

The smell of death came over him, as when
a lion, who has culled Massylian herds
after their guardian has fled the fields,
stands with his neck and mouth congealed with gore,
sluggish and panting, overwhelmed by carrion;
the slaughter and the blood have slaked his hunger;
his rage declines; he snaps his jaws at nothing;
his long tongue licks away soft bits of fleece.

Carrying trophies, bloody, Tydeus would 682
have entered Thebes to show its prince and people
his unexpected triumph, had not you,
♦ Tritonian maiden, deemed him worth your counsel.

He was still heated, grimy from his exploit,
when she explained: "Born of the blood of proud
Oeneus, o you who have, by our consent—
though we were distant—overcome these Thebans,
be moderate and do not overtrust 689
the favor of the gods. This ought to be
your single wish: that fame attend your deeds.
You have been fortunate. Desist!"

Among
the horrors of the killing one survivor
remained, and not by chance, for he alone,
of many, knew the omens of the air.
The birds did not deceive him. He alone
♦ foresaw this tragedy. His name was Maeon.
The son of Haemon, he was not afraid
to warn his prince, but destiny deprived
his words of credence. Like a man condemned,
his life devoid of meaning, Tydeus sent him

to carry this stern message: "Tell your duke, 697
whoever you may be, Aonian,
this—and Aurora will tomorrow see you
spared by my mercy from the other shadows:
'Pile mounds before your gates. Take down your weapons.
Inspect your walls for signs of ruinous aging.
Draft your best men, and plan to multiply
your crowded battle lines. Look how this grove
smokes from my sword; see how we manage war!' "

He said these words, then he prepared a handsome 704
memorial in honor of Athena
to recollect his bloody massacre.
He mounded bodies lying on the ground
and felt the pleasure of his puissant deeds.

There was an old oak on a small mound in 707
the middle of the flatland; heavy bark
ringed its thick trunk; its branches drooped low; here
he hung smashed swords, pierced armor, leather helmets,
and spears that he had drawn from breathing bodies.

Night and far mountains echoed as he prayed, 713
surrounded by accumulated slain:

"Ferocious goddess, soul and image of
your father Jupiter; great Maid of War,
whose sullen helmet hides a terrible
beauty beneath a Gorgon stained with blood!
The blasts of your stern trumpets equal those
that Mars and spear-equipped Bellona blow.
Favor this votive offering! Behold 719
our slaughter, whether from Pandion's hill
in Athens, or, if you prefer, among
the glad choirs in Aonian Itone,
or as you comb your hair in Libyan
Tritonis' waters, where your chariot,
drawn by a pair of virgin mares, has swept
you in your frenzy: we will dedicate
these mangled limbs to you, these shapeless corpses;
but should it be that I return to my 726

home country, where Parthaon ruled; should warlike
Pleuron accept me back, then I will found
a golden temple on the central hill
inside the city. I will honor you
where you may joy to see Ionian storms
and Achelous—sandy, flowing yellow—
stream past the islands of Echinades
irrupting to the sea. Here I myself
will fashion portraits of my ancestors'
battles and fearful images of kings.
I will hang armor from the cupola:
armor I won when ambushed and, o Pallas,
the armor you will give when Thebes is captured.
A hundred Calydonian votaries 736
shall tend your vestal altars, burn Actaean
torches, and they shall hang chaste olive trees
with purple ribbons intertwined with white.
A priestess of long years devoted to
your secret virtues will maintain your flame.
Diana will permit my rich firstfruits
from works of war and peace to be your gifts."

He walked to friendly Argos when he finished. 743

–♦–♦–♦–

BOOK 3 Omens

Eteocles dreams. Maeon returns, alone. Thebes mourns the slaughter. The horror of Ide. Aletes remembers other Theban disasters. Jove calls for war. Venus intercedes with Mars. Return of Tydeus to Argos. The evil augury of Amphiaraus. Thebes arms. Capaneus mocks the gods. Argia urges her father to allow war.

Meanwhile, the master of Aonia—
the man of treachery, Eteocles—
can't sleep, and still the humid stars must glide
long distances till dawn. Uncertain is
the night, his mind preoccupied; the crime
he ordered torments him, and fear, the worst
augur for one who worries, makes him ponder.

"Why this delay?" he cried—yet he believed 7
the odds were in his favor, Tydeus
an easy target for so many men—
but heart and soul may weigh more than mere numbers.

"Is there an odd road through the realm? Were soldiers 9
sent out from Argos to assist him? Did
rumor about this ambush reach the towns
nearby? Were those I chose too few, or, Father
Gradivus, were they cowards? No, for they
included Chromis, Dorylas, and those
Thespiadae, the match of any who guard
our towers—men capable of taking Argos;
nor do I think that Tydeus traveled here
wearing bronze armor impenetrable to weapons
and thewed like solid adamant. Malingerers!
What obstacle could one man offer, if you fought?"

He suffered waves of anguish, but he blamed 18
himself above all else, for he had failed

to draw his sword and strike when Tydeus spoke
before their conclave: he'd contained his rage
in public; he had plotted, to his shame,
and now was sorry. He was like a sailor
chosen to guide his vessel from Calabria
on the Ionic Sea: no novice to the waves,
he leaves safe harbor when Olenian
starlight in Capricorn, the sign of rain,
shines clear but fools him; then the sudden thunder
of winter weather fills the world, unbolts
the heavens, and Orion tips the poles.
He'd rather be on land, fights to return,
and wails as mighty south winds blow his stern;
he cannot steer; he now sails unknown seas.
Just so, Agenor's heir, headman Eteocles,
mourned Lucifer's late rising, dawn's delay.

–♦–♦–♦–

Then, suddenly, the chariot of Night
altered its course and set, as did the stars,
♦ and mother Tethys drove Hyperion,
the straggling sun, across the eastern seas.
The tortured earth quaked—deadly sign of trouble—
its depth tormented, and Cithaeron heaved
and stirred its ancient snows. Then rooftops rose;
rocks crashed the seven gates—or so it seemed.

The cause was not remote. Through the cold dawn
the son of Haemon, angry at the fates,
disconsolate because his life was spared,
returned. His face was not yet visible,
but even distant tokens indicated
the scope of this disaster. He had shed
all tears but groaned and beat his chest, just like
a ruined shepherd who has quit his pasture
when wind storms and the crescent moon of winter
and unexpected rains have driven him
into the forest with his master's cattle:
at night, ferocious wolves attack; next day

the killing can be seen, and he is frightened
to bring his lord the news of this fresh slaughter;
he wallows in the dirt, and his laments
reecho through the fields; he can't endure
the silence of the stockyard, and he calls
his missing bulls and names them all in order.

When he appeared—this was too horrible— 53
alone, the mothers, crowding just inside
the portals, did not dare ask why no troops,
no sterling lords, surrounded him. They let
out wails, the sound of which was like the last
scream when a city's walls are breached in war,
the sound one hears when vessels sink at sea.

As soon as he received his leave to speak 58
before his hated king, he said, "The savage
Tydeus returns you my sad life, from many.
Whether it was the judgment of the gods,
or Fortune, or, though shameful to admit,
one man's invincible endurance—I
hardly believe it, though I bring the news—
everyone, everyone has fallen: I
could see them in the pale light of the night.
The ghosts of comrades and the evil birds
already gather there from whence I've come.
I earned this cruel indulgence not with tears
or cunning: no, the gods rewarded me
with shameful daylight. Atropos ignored
my preference, and Fate has kept me living
for some time since she closed the doors of death.

"I say—that you may know how prodigal 69
of life my heart is and how little horror
final things hold for me—your war is cursed,
o man of death, and all the omens say so!

"You trample down the law; you are disdainful 72
because your brother has been banished and
you rule, but constant lamentations from
the many houses suffering bereavement

and fifty dead souls flying day and night
will overwhelm you with their ghastly horror—
and I won't be restrained!" 77

The savage king
trembled, enraged, and his glum face was lit
with red blood. At his side his henchmen—one
was Phlegyas, the other Labadacus,
two men not slow to wickedness—prepared
to seize the man by force, but Maeon drew
his sword with bold authority and gazed
now at the tyrant's face, now at his blade:

"You have no right to spill my blood or strike 83
the chest that mighty Tydeus did not pierce.
I go, exultant, following the fate
that warrior denied me, to the shades
where my companions wait. But as for you,
the gods, your brother"—even as he spoke,
◆ he thrust his sword hilt-high and through his side. 88

He fought the pain; he doubled over, struggling—
the cut was deep—and sank, and as he gasped
his last, his blood throbbed from his mouth and from
his wound. The Theban elders' hearts were shaken;
the anxious council murmured, but his wife
and loyal relatives, who even now
rejoiced at his return, took up the corpse
that death disfigured, and they bore it home.

No longer could the flaming anger of 96
unspeakable Eteocles be checked.
He issued a decree against cremation
and to his infamy forbade the peace
of burial among unseeing shades.

Maeon! Despite him you have earned distinction 99
in life and death, and it is right that you
shall never be forgotten, you who dared
to show contempt for kings and sanctify
an ample path for Liberty to walk.

What praise is worthy of your fame? What can
be added to your courage by my chant?
You are a prophet whom the gods adore!
Apollo deemed you worthy of his laurel;
he educated you in things divine—
♦ *and not in vain: Dodona's sacred grove*
♦ *and Cirrha's prophetess delight in puzzling*
petitioners when Phoebus does not answer.

Enter Elysium; walk through those regions, 108
far from the hellish terrors of Avernus!
That space does not admit the men of Thebes
nor are a tyrant's orders valid there.
Your body and your clothes remain untouched
by savage animals, and though you lie
exposed to heaven, you will be preserved
by sacred groves and night birds that revere you.

–♦–♦–♦–

They flooded through the gates—wives dead with fear, 114
children, sick parents—and they crossed the plain,
through barren waste, miserable but eager
to find the objects of their tears, while thousands more
massed side by side to offer solace. Others
sought evidence of just one soldier's deeds
among the many feats performed that night.
They moved in seething swarms, and they lamented. 120
The countryside resounded with their groans.
But when they reached the dreadful cliffs and savage
forest, their groans were greater than before,
and bitter tears flowed faster, as the sight
of blood enraged the mob in all its madness.
A sad sound seemed to rise as from one voice.

Wearing a robe of blood, his breast rent open, 125
violent Sorrow overcame the mothers.
They scrutinized the helmets of the stiffened
corpses as they identified dead bodies.
Wives fell upon their husbands; others tended
men who were not their own. They used their hair

to wipe away the blood; they closed dead eyes,
dropped tears upon deep wounds, or strove to draw
the points of weapons out (a useless labor)
as others tasked themselves to reattach
arms onto bodies and put heads on necks.

–♦–♦–♦–

Now one lost woman, Ide, wandered through 133
the thickets and the dust of empty fields
in search of her lost sons. She was the proud
mother of twins (her boys, now dead), and she
was not unfortunate or to be pitied.
The truth is, she was terrible in sorrow.
Her uncombed hair flew loose, and everywhere
among the armor and the bodies she
begrimed her white hair with the filth of dirt
and raked her angry face. She mourned each corpse
in turn, but did so like a sorceress 140
in Thessaly, whose foul inhabitants
know charms that can revive the dead. She took
pleasure in war, and afterward, at night,
bearing a cedar torch with many knots,
she roamed the fields and rolled the dead through blood
as she chose corpses whom she'd use in tombs
to send prayers to divinities in heaven.
The sad assembly of deceased deplored her:
even the lord of darkest hell condemned her.

Happy are they who lie together in 152
the hollow of a rock, whose lives were lost
on one same day to one same hand, whose bodies
were joined together by a single spear
and by their wounds. When she beheld this sight,
her eyes poured tears profusely.

"These embraces—
is this the sight your mother sees? Do your
lips touch? Did Death's cruel genius bind you two
together in your final hour? Which of your wounds
should I first search, whose face should I first stroke?

"You were your mother's source of strength, her womb's 154
good fortune, and the means by which she thought
to touch the gods, to overcome the glory
of other Theban mothers. Better off
and far more fortunate are married women
whose beds are sterile and whose homes Lucina
spares from the sufferings and shrieks of childbirth.

"My labor brought me sorrow; worse, your deaths 159
have been obscured, because you did not fight
in daylight where your destiny could be
observed and your defeat immortalized—
although it makes your mother miserable.

"You poured your blood in vain; you lie unpraised, 164
obscure in death among so many others.
I have no heart to separate your sad
embrace or break the partnership your strange
death has created. Forward, undivided
and constant brothers, to the final flames.
♦ Mingle your precious ashes in one urn!"

–♦–♦–♦–

Meanwhile, the others mourned no less. Among 169
the scattered dead the wife of Chthonius
was here; here was Astyoche, the mother
of Pentheus. Also, Phaedimus, your children,
your little innocents, discovered their
father was gone; Marpessa tended her betrothed,
named Phylleus, just as the sisters of
blood-covered Acamas sponged off their brother.

Then men with axes lay the forest open 174
and chopped the knotty pines on nearby hills—
hills that had heard men's groans and knew what passed
that night.

♦ Before the pyres, Aletes, the oldest
present, told stories to assuage the grief

of those unfortunates who had convened
to tend the fires and did not want to leave.

"Our people come from Sidon; we have known 179
calamity; fate plays with us for sport.
A prodigy occurred when Cadmus sowed
his seed of iron in Boeotian furrows:
a strange growth, fields that terrorized his farmers.
It was as bad the time indignant Juno
reduced to fiery ash the royal palace
of aging Cadmus, or when Athamas
carried the half-dead body of his son,
Learchus, from the mountain where he'd won
funereal praise and shouted out for joy
because he was insane and in confusion;
when echoes from Phoenician houses rang
out clearly and the madness of exhausted
Agave dissipated, and she feared
the weeping of her women, her companions,
and Thebans moaned. But there has only been 191
a single day whose fate and evil form
compares to this one. That's when the impious
Niobe, daughter of Tantalus, atoned
for her proud words and arrogance. Unnumbered
fallen surrounded her, yet for each body
she lifted from the earth, she found a flame.
That was the state of things, when young and old 195
and grieving mothers exited the city
and raised a cry of sorrow to the gods
for those who died; they pressed around a pair
of funeral pyres at each enormous gate.
I can remember weeping, copying
my parents, since I was too young for sorrow.

"The gods permitted this. Nor did I weep 201
more for Actaeon, whose Molossian hounds
tore him apart when you, Diana, found
him watching from a high and hidden place,
profaning your chaste waters when you changed
that son-in-law of Cadmus to a deer.

◆ "It also was no worse when our cruel queen— 205
named Dirce—was transformed into a lake
(all of a sudden) where her spilled blood lay.

"The Fatal Sisters spun these bitter threads,
occurrences that Jupiter approved,
but here, at present, now, we are deprived
of blameless men, supporters of our city,
so many victims of an evil king.
News of the broken treaty has not reached
Argos, yet we endure the grief of war.
The blood of men and horses will lie thick 210
over the ground, and rivers will run red.
Men in the first green sap of youth will see it.
I only want a pyre to call my own
and burial in my ancestral ground."

These were the old man's words. He then rehearsed 214
the crimes Eteocles committed, and
he listed punishments the man deserved
and said he was a cruel and brutal person.

From whence proceeds this liberty? His age 216
had reached its limit; he had lived his life
and looked to grace late-coming death with fame.

—◆—◆—◆—

The father of the heavens, Jupiter, 218
for long had been observing everything—
the bodies stained with first blood—and he sent
a summons for Gradivus, god of war.
He was destroying Getic towns and killing
the mad Bistonians. He swiftly turned
his horses toward the heavens, and he shook
his weapons—his terrible gold armor, and
his helmet that a bolt of lightning crested,
bright with engraved and terrifying figures.
The pole of heaven thundered, and his shield
reflected blood-red light, as if in envy.
It struck the distant sun, and Jove said, seeing 226

♦ Mars panting from his labors in Sarmatia,
his armor soaking wet and stained by war:

"My son, go as you are, just as you are,
to Argos, your sword dripping, anger like
a cloud surrounding you. Remove the last
restraints. Let those who hate, whom nothing pleases,
love you, and let them vow to you their hands,
their fleeting lives. Eliminate delay!
Trample the treaty! We give you the right
to immolate the gods themselves. End peace!
I have already sown the seeds of war: 235
Tydeus returns with his report of deeds
past measuring, a prince's crimes, the first
beginnings of a vicious fight: the ambush,
the treachery for which his weapons gave
him vengeance. May he be believed and may
you gods who share my blood not let old hatreds
make you participants. But do not pray
to me to change things. Sisters of the dark 242
spindles—the Fates—have made me promises.
Since the beginning of the world this war
has been appointed for this day and for
these people born to battle. Interfere
with me, as I mete sacred punishments
to these inhabitants for old offenses
their ancestors committed, and I swear
by my eternal heaven, by the shrines
where we are worshiped and the rivers of
Elysium, which even I hold sacred,
that I, with my own hand, will level Thebes 248
and raze her lofty walls to their foundations.
The towers of Argos I will overturn,
crumble the city's rooftops underneath,
or cover them with rain, and I will have
them swept away, turned into seaside swamps,
even if Juno should protect their hills
and temples from the turbulence of war."

He spoke, and his commands astonished them. 253
You would have thought them mortal, since

nobody uttered one word as they listened,
not otherwise than as at sea, where winds
have made their peace or where the coasts recline
in unresisting sleep, when summertime
caresses silver leaves, and dying breezes
finger the clouds. Then lakes and ponds subside,
the sun burns rivers dry, and streams run silent.

–◆–◆–◆–

His orders were a joy for Mars, a pleasure; 260
his chariot was hot, and he was eager.
He swung his horses left—but Venus crossed
his path and stood before them undismayed.
The steeds moved back, relaxed their flowing manes,
and moved as if they were her suppliants.
She leaned her breasts against the lofty yoke,
tilted aside her tear-stained face, and spoke:

"My noble lord, are you preparing war 269
for Thebes? Do you intend to kill your own
descendants by the sword? These people are
the children of Harmonia! And what
about our union, made in heaven? What
about my tears? Will you not hesitate
for them, you madman? Is this my reward
for misbehaving? Is this how you pay
me back for my lost shame, my infamy,
◆ the net of Lemnos? As you like it—go! 274
◆ My husband Vulcan is much more compliant,
despite the injuries that anger him.
I only have to ask him: he will sweat
for endless nights at his unceasing forge
to fashion me new ornaments; what's more,
he likes to make me weapons, even yours!

"But you—I might as well attempt to move 280
rocks or a heart of brass as talk to you.
Answer one question for me; tell me this:
why did you let me give our precious daughter
a Theban husband, since her marriage proved

unfortunate despite your certainty
the Tyrians, descendants of a dragon,
men of the race of Jupiter, would be
famous in arms and vigorous in deeds?
I would have rather that my daughter married 286
someone Sithonian or Borean—
or north among your Thracians. Have I not
suffered enough that she, the daughter of
Venus, a goddess, crawls along the ground
and spits out venom in Illyria?
The Tyrians are innocent"—but Mars 291
could not endure her weeping any longer.
His left hand grasped his spear, and he leaped down
from his high chariot without delay.
He hurt her as he clasped her to his shield
while soothing her with amicable speech:

"My sure rest from the wars, my sacred joy, 295
my only peace of mind: to you alone
among the gods and men has it been given
unharmed to face my weapons, to approach
my neighing horses in midslaughter and
to pluck away this sword from my right hand.
Neither the marriage contract of Sidonian
Cadmus nor your dear trust have I forgotten.
Do not take pleasure in false accusations!

"I'd rather sink inside my uncle's lake
or flee pale shadows unarmed, like a mortal,
but now the Fates, the mighty Father's will, 304
command obedience. I'm warned. The skill
of Vulcan was not needed for this mission.
He was not chosen. What excuse would I
have for ignoring Jove or for denying
decrees that he has spoken?—he who has
such strength that I have seen the earth and sky
and oceans tremble, and the gods conceal
themselves when he is speaking—even now!
Be not afraid, my darling, for although
I have no power to alter what must be,
I will be present at the walls of Thebes

when both sides fight, and I will help our people.
You will not be unhappy when you see 314
my fury overwhelm the Argive army
in fields of blood. I am allowed this care;
the Fates do not forbid it." Then he rose
and drove his flaming horses through the air.

The wrath of Jupiter descends to earth 317
with no less swiftness when the godhead walks
◆ the snows of Othrys or the frozen peak
◆ of Ossa in the north and takes in hand
a weapon from the clouds. His lightning bolt
carries the savage message of the god.
It's three-pronged fork sends terror through the heavens;
farmers point with their fingers, while at sea
poor sailors in their ships are overwhelmed.

Meanwhile, returning Tydeus measured back 324
his path through Danaan fields and traced a track
on slopes of green Prosymna. Terrible
to see, his hair was thick with dust, and sweat
and dirt ran down his shoulders through deep wounds.
His eyes were wild and red from lack of sleep;
he thirsted, he breathed hard and sucked his cheeks
but in his mind was conscious of his deeds.
He held himself in high esteem, just like 330
a fighting bull who enters his home pasture
dripping his own and his opponent's blood
that streaks his neck, his dewlaps, and his shoulders.
His strength is puffed with weary pride; he scorns
to look down at his chest, as his opponent
lies in the sand alone and sadly moans.
The sound is soothing to his own raw wounds.

And such a one was Tydeus. Everywhere 336
he traveled through the towns between Asopos
and ancient Argos he ignited hatred
as he retold how he went forth, a legate
sent by the Grecian nations to regain
a kingdom for the exiled Polynices.

It was the Echionian ruler who denied
his rights and answered him with force, at night—
an ambush, men in arms, and treachery.
These were the means by which he kept his treaty!
People believe him readily. The god— 343
Mars, the great warrior—made all seem real,
and Rumor doubled listening people's fears.

–◆–◆–◆–

Father Adrastus had, by chance, convened 345
a council of respected, leading men,
when Tydeus entered. Suddenly he stood
inside the portals, at the great hall's threshold,
and shouted, "Warriors, to arms! To arms! 348
Noble Lernaean chieftain, if you share
the blood of your magnanimous ancestors,
prepare to arm! There is no piety,
no sense of right and wrong among the nations,
and no regard for Jove. It would have been
better to send me as ambassador
among the mad Sarmatians or to one
◆ who waits within Bebrycian woods for murder. 353
I do not blame your orders or regret
my mission: I rejoice—rejoice!—that I
experienced myself the Thebans' crimes.

"It was a war, believe me: it was war! 355
I stood there like a strong tower or a city
of fitted stones. Those chosen for the ambush
were armed with every weapon, but in vain.
I was alone. I did not know the place,
but they could not contain me, even though
they ambushed me at night. They lie in blood,
before their desolated city. Now, 360
father-in-law, now is the time to fight
the enemy, while they are pale with fright
and timid, while they bear their dead, and while
the memory of what I did survives.
I beg you, even though I am exhausted

from making ghosts of fifty warriors
and bear wounds that grow cold and blood that festers,
begin at once!"

The timid Argives cheered.
In front of all of them, his head down, stepped 366
the Cadmean, that hero, and "Can I—
whose life is guilt, one whom the gods detest—
look at your wounds and not wish I were wounded?
Brother, would you have done these things if I
had come home? Were your weapons meant for me?
It is a loathsome thing to cling to life! 370
I let this happen, but I never knew
Eteocles could be so barbarous. . . .

"I am a guest, and it is not my place 372
to bring you trouble. Let the walls of Argos
remain in peace. I know—and what has happened
makes it no easier—how difficult
it is for children, for the country, for
husbands to leave their wives: let no house blame
me for its troubles; let no mothers squint
at me askance with savage eyes! I hold
my throat before you Thebes; to you, my brother—
great Tydeus, most especially to you.
Father-in-law has spoken but, this time,
may not deter me, nor my loving wife:
freely I go, though sure to lose my life."

♦ These were the words by which he tried their hearts. 381
He asked by indirection, roused defiance,
brought tears, let indignation smolder.
Soon all were angry, not just youths but those
whom age had frozen into indolence.
All were one mind, to empty out their homes
and summon men from nearby towns, and go.

The patriarch, however, was well counseled, 386
not unaware of what it takes to govern.
"These things are for the gods, and what must be

remedied, I entreat you, leave to me.
Your brother will not bear his scepter un-
punished by you, but we will not be pushed
to promise war. Welcome the son of Oeneus,
and celebrate the honor blood has brought.
May his great heart find long-sought rest in season.
Let us dispense with sorrow, but not reason."

At once his comrades and his pale wife crowded 394
Tydeus, worn out from battle and from travel.
He was a happy man. He settled in
the middle of the hall and leaned his back
against a mighty column while his wounds
were tended by the Epidauran, Idmon,
who varied his swift knife with warming herbs,
a milder treatment. He was lost in thought,
then he recounted, from its origin, 400
his bitter struggle, how it started, each
event in turn, the place where he was ambushed,
the silence of the night in which he fought.
He told who faced him and how many, then
described the moments of his maximum
exertion and how he preserved one sorry
witness, named Maeon. His retelling stunned
the loyal troops, their chieftains, and his father-
in-law. The Tyrian exile burned in anger.

–◆–◆–◆–

On the steep margin of the western sea 407
the sun had set his flaming horses free
and in the currents of the ocean bathed
their red and yellow rays. The followers
◆ of Nereus, the sea god, and the Hours
relieved him of his reigns and his high crown,
woven of gold, and they released his sweating
horses from harness. Some turned out the team,
for they had earned soft pasture; others leaned
the chariot to rest and raised its beam.

Night. It arrived and calmed the cares of men
and movements of the beasts. It wrapped the heavens
in its black shroud. Calm came to everyone
indeed, but not to you, Labdacian prince
Eteocles, or you, Adrastus, for
deep sleep made Tydeus dream of great achievements.

–♦–♦–♦–

Among night-wandering shades the war god thundered
along Arcadia's borders in his armor,
along the heights of Taenaros, in Nemea's
♦ fields, and in Apollo's town Therapnae.
He agitated hearts and made men want
to enter war at once. Long flowing hair
hung from his crest arranged by Rage and Madness.
His weapon bearer Terror drove his stallions.

But Rumor, wrapped in idle speculation,
attentive to the least sound, flew before
his chariot, blown by the winged steeds' sighs.
She fluttered her impatient, humming plumes.
The driver urged her with his bloody lash
to utter what is true and what is false
even as Mars, the father, poked the goddess
with Scythian spear and struck her back and tresses.
It happened as when on the great Aegean
Neptune drives willing winds he has released
from their Aeolean prison. They precede
his dreadful company. They stir the seas.
The Clouds of Storm, Deep Winter Showers, and Gloom
drone and conglomerate around his reins.
Dark Tempest tears the sand up from the deep.
♦ The islands of the Cyclades are doubtful,
their roots are torn, but they withstand, and Delos,
you are afraid you will be torn and lose
your moorings from Myconos and Gyaros.
You pray for help from your great son, Apollo.

–♦–♦–♦–

Aurora, goddess of the dawn, appeared— 440
her red face shining—for the seventh time
before Adrastus left his inner chamber.
His sons-in-law's ambitions and the war
greatly perplexed the Persean hero's thoughts,
and he could not decide whether to license
a call to arms and start new conflicts that
would shake the commonwealth, or put a brake
to all the anger and resheathe drawn blades.
He mulls tranquillity and peace, the quiet 447
disgrace of doing nothing, and the task
of swaying an unmanageable people from
the wondrous charms of battle. He resolved,
at last, to settle his misdoubts, to know
the minds of prophets and to move the gods
whose sacred rites give foresight to the truth.

It is a craft, a skill, to know the future: 451
Amphiaraus had been given it.
Joining him on his journey was Melampus,
the son of Amythaon: he was old,
but vigorous of mind; he knew Apollo.
It would be hard to say to which one Phoebus
answered more fully, which one's mouth received
more satisfying drafts of Cirrha's waters.

At first they searched the blood and inner organs 456
of animals to understand the gods,
but they were frightened when the mottled hearts
of sheep spelled trouble and their fatal veins
threatened adversity. They then decided
to go seek omens in the open sky.

◆ There is a mountain named Aphesas by 462
Lernaean farmers, which the Argives once
held sacred, and it raises its bold ridgeline
far in the air. They say that there swift Perseus
profaned the skies with his suspended flight—
his rapt steps terrified his mother, who
observed him from a cliff and tried to follow.
Here the two prophets climbed. Gray olive leaves 466

circled their sacred hair, and white-wool fillets
adorned their temples. They chose moistened meadows
where rising sunlight loosens frozen snows.

Amphiaraus, son of Oecleus, prayed 470
the proper god for his propitiation.

"Almighty Jupiter, we do believe
that you give meaning to swift birds, that these
portend your future plans, and that their flights
hide omens—secret causes—in the skies.
♦ Apollo's cave at Cirrha cannot show
the god with greater certainty, nor can
♦ Chaonian leaves that, it is said, reveal
your oracle within Molossis' grove.

"The man for whom you set the birds in motion 476
♦ to make your favor manifest, Dictaean,
is more enriched in mind than he who seeks
♦ the oracle of Ammon in dry sands
♦ or your competitors at Lycia,
♦ the sacred ox along the Nile, or Branchus,
son of Apollo—and as famous as
his father—or nocturnal Pan, for whom
the rustic dwellers of sea-beaten Pisa
♦ listen within Lycaon's shades. What is
the cause that makes this miracle? What gives
winged birds this power? Is it that the founder 483
of heaven's upper halls weaves wondrous patterns
throughout vast Chaos? or because winged birds
have been transformed from human origins
by metamorphoses? or is the truth
more easily obtained because birds fly
in heaven's purer air, removed from sin,
and rarely land on earth? You are permitted 488
to know these things, great source of earth and heaven.
Allow the skies to prophesy for us
the origins and outcome of the wars.
Is strife the fate of Argos? Do the stern 491

Parcae decree that our Lernaean spears
will open up the gates of Thebes? If so,
give us the sign of thunder on our left
and then let every bird in heaven warble
their welcome songs and secret messages.
If not, if you prohibit victory,
contrive a way to give us pause; obscure
the skies with bird wings on our right." 496

He spoke,
then settled on the brow of that high cliff
where he invoked both known and unknown gods,
holding communion with the infinite
universe of innumerable shadows.

They carefully divided up the sky 500
and studied it at length and let their eyes
scan it. At last, Melampus—prophet son
of Amythaon—asked, "Amphiaraus,
do you not notice that within the vast
dominion of the breathing winds of heaven,
none of the birds are flying steadily,
none of them hang and glide in fluid circles
or soar while they sing songs foretelling peace?
There are no ravens—birds of prophecy— 506
no eagles bearing thunderbolts, no owls—
fair-haired Minerva's hooting, hooked-beak birds—
who might bring better auguries. But there
are vultures overhead and hawks that prey;
monsters are flying; birds of evil shrieking
high in the clouds; nocturnal screech owls screaming:
the horned owl chants of injuries and dying.

"Which portents of the gods should we attend? 512
◆ Do these, o god of Thymbra, rule the heavens?
Winged birds fly madly. With their hooked-back talons
they strike each other's eyes. They rouse the winds
with the distressful sounds of beating pinions;
they pluck plumes from their breasts."

And his companion
answered him, "Father, I have often read 516
many and various omens of Apollo.
When I was young and green, the pinewood ship
from Thessaly—the *Argo*—carried me
among the demigods and kings. Their captains
fell silent when I sang of trials on land
and sea, and Jason, when he wondered what
would happen, often did not listen more
attentively to Mopsus than to me,
as I made my predictions. But I never 522
before saw similar forebodings, or
skies more prodigious, strange. And there is worse.
Turn your attention here: swans without number
in this clear region of the deepest air
have shaped themselves in one battalion. Whether
Boreas blows them from cold Strymon's shores
or fertile Nile's tranquillity invites them,
they hold their course. Imagine them as Thebans, 528
for they fly slowly, spiraling in silence,
and peaceful, as if bound by walls or trenches.
But look, a stronger squadron moves through space.
I see a tawny line advance—a troop of
seven bold armor bearers of great Jove.
Think of these eagles as Inachian princes. 533
They open their curved beaks, unsheathe their talons,
and threaten slaughter as they swiftly rush
to strike the snow-white flock of circling swans.

"The wind rains blood, and feathers fill the air, 536
but here is something new. Jove's anger flares;
he sends an evil omen. Something drives
the victors unexpectedly to die.
The one that seeks the highest point—alone—
burns in a sudden flash, and boasts no longer.
Tender wings fail, which would pursue flight paths
of greater birds. Here enemies, entwined
together, fall together. There, retreat
sweeps one who leaves his comrades to their fate.

Another drowns in pouring rain. One gnaws,
while dying, on a living victim. Blood
splatters the hollow clouds."

"Why do you cry
in secret?"

"Reverend Melampus, I
◆ know all too well the last, who falls and dies." 547

The pair of prophets trembled. Terror seized them.
They'd turned their thoughts to what the gods forbid
and pierced the secret councils of winged creatures.
Now they repent and hate the gods who heard them.

When did this worldwide, sick obsession 551
to know the future first infect sad mortals?
You say it is the office of the gods,
but we ourselves inspect our birthdays, seek
to know where we will die, and what the gods'
kind father and firm Clotho have in mind.
◆ *Hence entrails, sermons birds that fly deliver,*
revolving stars, the mapped course of the moon,
horrors in Thessaly. Our father's blood was golden;
our race descended from great oaks and caves.
We had one passion: not to prophesy
but tame the forests, cultivate the soil.
It was a crime for men to know the future.
But we depraved, we pitiable people
too deeply scrutinize the gods. Hence terrors
and rage; hence crimes, deceit, immodest vows.

And so Amphiaraus stripped his fillets; 566
he tore the hated garland from his temples,
let fall his sacred branch, and from the mountain
the priest returned unseen, unsought. The horns of war
reached him from distant Thebes; he felt the roar
but sought seclusion. He would not reveal
the prophecies of heaven to the people,

in private conversation with Adrastus,
or in a gathering of leaders, but
covered himself in darkness. (You, Melampus, 573
felt too much shame and care to come to town.)
Twelve days he held his tongue. Delay prolonged
the questions of the chiefs and commoners.

–◆–◆–◆–

The high charge of the Thunderer by now 575
had shaken farmers' fields, unmanned old towns.
From everywhere the war god gathered soldiers
happy to leave their homes, the wives they loved,
and children weeping on their outer thresholds.

Mars had confounded them. With reverence 580
they took their family armor down from posts
and from the inner chambers of the gods
brought chariots. Whetstones rejuvenated
worn out and rusty javelins. Their swords,
which had been stuck in scabbards, were restored
to savage sharpness. Some men handled smooth,
round helmets, hefted corselets of sutured
bronze plates, or fit their abdomens with panels
of Chalybean steel that creaked from rust.
Furnaces glowed red-hot as they devoured
curved mattocks, sickles, pruning hooks, and plows.
Venerable trees were felled for robust spears; 590
there was no shame in dressing shields with hides
of worn-out oxen. Bursting into Argos,
they cried and clamored, heart and soul, for war
as loud as when Tyrrhenian salt seas roar
and fiery Aetna thunders over caverns
◆ and Sicily's Enceladus shifts sides,
◆ craters pour lava, seas beyond Pelorus
contract, and floodlands hope to reemerge.

◆ Excited Capaneus moved among them 598
because he loved the power of Mars and long
had hated the protracted peace. His heart
was swollen, proud: he was of ancient blood,

a man of full nobility, who yet
had overpassed, by his own hands, the deeds
of his progenitors. He long despised
the gods—and with impunity. He loved
not peace; he was improvident, impulsive,
especially when angry, like a Centaur
inhabiting dark Pholoë, or like
a Cyclops—the fraternity of Aetna.

He stood before your gates, Amphiaraus, 606
among the mob of rabble and its leaders,
and yelled, "What kind of cowardice is this,
o Argives, and you blood-related Greeks?
Do we, so many people armed in iron, 609
hang here before a common person's doorway,
a single citizen's, when we are ready
and willing? I won't wait while some pale virgin
utters her warning riddles for Apollo—
if he exists, if he is not a rumor
or something for the timid to believe—
secluded deep within his crazy cavern,
beneath the hollow peak of Cirrha, moaning!
My god is my own strength, this sword I hold!
Now let that timid priest, that fraud, emerge—
or I will demonstrate the power of birds!"

The rabble howled with joy, and their approval 618
encouraged Capaneus, when at once
Amphiaraus, son of Oecleus, broke
his silence. He had come forth. "It is not
this irreligious man's unbridled bawling
that draws me from the shadows. Let him threaten.
I do not fear his ranting. Mortal arms
cannot assail me—I am fated for
another end—but I fear civil war.

"Pressed by my love for you, urged by Apollo, 625
I will reveal your fortune, your whole future—
but not yours, madman! Phoebus has forbidden
me to admonish you. But miserable people,
where are you going? Both the fates and gods

oppose your expedition. Are you driven
blindly by vengeance? Do the Furies lash you?
Is Argos hateful? home unsweet? the omens
pointless? Why did you send me to intrude
on secret gatherings, to climb the mountain
with trembling steps to Perseus' hidden peaks?

"I would prefer not knowing this war's outcome, 635
the causes of our common destiny,
the time and place of our dark day, my fate.

"I can report the secrets of the world 637
on which I gazed, what birds communicate,
and signs of future things that I endured.
I prayed to you, Thymbraen god—Apollo—
and you were never crueler. You showed me
the secrets of the cosmos I consulted.
The birds have spoken, and I have perceived
the signs of what's to come. I have seen portents
of great destruction, men and gods in terror.
Megaera is delighted. Lachesis
cuts short our lives, and her thread turns to dust."

Then Capaneus once more spoke to him: 647
"You are the only subject of your fury,
your auguries! You will complete your years
empty of honor; you will never hear
the sound of Tuscan trumpets in your ears.
Why do you thwart the vows of better men?
You want to stay home with your lying birds, 652
enjoy your wife and children, I suppose,
while we say nothing and do not avenge
the pierced chest of great Tydeus or the ambush
that broke a treaty's terms. If you would keep
the Greeks from waging hot war, go yourself
as legate to the enemy in Thebes.
Your garland will protect you. Can your words
really elicit, from unmeaning skies,
the hidden why and wherefore of the world?

I pity gods above if they must pay
attention to our human chants and prayers.

"Men of the world created gods from fear: 661
yet you are safe here. Go ahead; act crazy—
but from when first the battle trumpets wail
to when we drink from helmets—from the Dirce,
from hostile Ismenos—I warn you, keep
your distance. Do not try to cross my craving
for trumpet calls and combat. Search no veins,
look at no birds. Do not defer the day
of war but keep your soft wool fillets and
your mad Apollo's ravings. Stay away!
The augur will be me and those prepared
to join me in my own insanity."

Roars of approval thundered; a vast tumult 669
soared to the stars, as when late winter winds
strengthen a stream in spate—ice uncongeals,
and mountains thaw; a river winds through fields,
but hills prevent its outflow; swirling floods
sweep away buildings, plowlands, men, and cattle,
until a dam, just smaller than a hill,
forms a retaining wall along the banks.

Night intervened. It stopped their bickering. 677

–◆–◆–◆–

Argia could, with equanimity, 678
no longer bear her husband's groans—a grief
her heart and soul shared—so she went—without
adornment, hair disheveled, mangled, cheeks
furrowed with tears—to her respected father's
imposing palace, bearing, by her breast,
◆ little Thessander to his doting grandsire. 683

It was late night, the hour before the sunrise—
the Great Bear, left alone in northern skies,

envied the stars descending to the Ocean—
when she passed through the gates, and her great parent
embraced her.

"Father, you know why I weep,
why I, without my mournful husband, seek
your threshold in the night. I should be silent
but come as suppliant because I lie
awake in anguish. I have not been sent.
I swear this by the gods of lawful marriage.

"Ever since Hymen and unlucky Juno 691
first moved the left-hand torch, my husband's
tears and his moans have banished rest. Were I
a fearful tiger, were my heart as hard
as sea cliffs, I would crumble. You alone
have the ability, the sovereign power
to cure him. Father, give us war! See how
humbly your grandson lies, the child of exile.
One day, his birth will be his shame. O father,
remember your first welcome, how the heavens
witnessed your grasping of right hands. They sent
you Polynices, whom Apollo chose.

"I am not raging with the hidden heat 701
of Venus or a sinful marriage. I have cherished
your admonitions; I have feared your rule.
But how can I ignore this sad man's grief?
Can I be such a wild beast? Dearest father,
you do not know, you do not know how much
pure love a husband's wretchedness arouses.

"Now I am miserable. Now I request 706
a harsh and joyless, sad and fearful gift,
but father, I may beg another present
when mournful daylight interrupts our kisses,
when the harsh call of trumpets orders soldiers
to march away and gold cheeks glitter fiercely."

Adrastus kissed her moist face. "Daughter, I 711
never would blame you for complaining. Do

not be afraid. What you request deserves
approval, not denial. But the gods
have weighed my mind with myriad concerns.
Do not abandon hope for what you want,
but there are many fears, the slippery burden
of government. You will not weep in vain;
what you desire will happen—in due time.
Daughter, console your husband. Our delay 718
is just, and not too high a price to pay.
Great preparations make us linger. They
are pathways to the war."

The dawn light broke.
Anxieties had roused him as he spoke.

–♦–♦–♦–

BOOK 4 Thirst

The seven against Thebes: Adrastus, Polynices, Tydeus, Hippomedon, Capaneus, Amphiaraus, and Parthenopaeus. Eriphyle receives Argia's jewels. Atalanta pleads with her son. A woman seized by Bacchic frenzy warns Thebes to prepare. Eteocles consults Tiresias. His daughter Manto. The prophecy of Laius. The Argive army reaches Nemea. Drought. Hypsipyle neglects the baby Opheltes while bringing the Argives to the waters of Langia.

The third year Phoebus loosened wild west winds
and let spring days grow long and unconfined,
the feeble Council, pressured by the Fates,
at last allowed war's miseries their place.

High over Argos, from Larissa's fortress, 5
◆ Bellona first displayed a flame-red torch
then flung a beamlike spear from her right hand
that whistled through clear skies until it reached
the lofty Theban ramparts on the Dirce.

She entered camp and rattled like a squadron 9
among the men who gleamed in gold and iron.
She gave the marching soldiers swords, she clapped
the horses, and she called them to the gates.
Strong men become more strong when she aroused them;
even the timid felt a fleeting courage.

The forecast day had come. Flocks fell, as due, 13
in sacrifice to Mars and Jupiter,
the Thunderer, and augurers, who viewed
the entrails, showed their skill. They did not faint,
but feigned hope for the army. Now the children
mingled with wives, and parents crowded men
and stopped them at high doors. There was no end
of weeping. Shields and helmet crests were damp
with sad farewells. Whole households clung to soldiers-

in-arms and sighed, and some rejoiced to send
their kisses through closed helmets or to bend
crests of grim casques to their embrace.

Those men
who even now were pleased by swords, by death
itself—their anger broke, they wavered, and
they groaned, like those about to take a long 24
voyage at sea: south winds are in the sails,
the anchors weighed. Affectionate women ring
their arms around their sailors' necks; they cling;
their eyes are wet, and kisses cloud them—or
the thick sea fog. At last, when left behind,
they stand upon a rock and watch the sweet
sight of the linen sails departing, grieved
that winds from their own country so increase.

♦ *Hidden Antiquity, you ancient Rumors,* 32
show me the kings I must remember, for
my task is to give length to lives. And you,
queen of the chanting grove, Calliope,
lift up your lyre and play: what men did Mars,
what armies did he move? how many cities
depopulate? When I sip from your streams,
my mind (and no man's more) is never higher.

The king was sad and sick. Cares weighed him down. 38
The years were leaving him. Among the troops
who cheered him on he marched, although reluctant,
content to wear his sword and let his soldiers
carry his armor after. His swift steeds
were tended by a groom beneath the gates;
♦ his favorite horse, Arion, fought the reins.

Larissa sent him men in arms as did
♦ the mountain town Prosymna; Phlius, rich 44
in cattle; Media, renowned for herds;
and Neris, which Charadrus frightens as
it foams through its long valley; then Cleonae,
a town of towers, set on a vast protuberance;
♦ and Thyrea, where Spartan blood will fall.

Those who remember where the king was born, 49
and how he left, now join him: men who tend
Drepanum's rocky fields or olive trees
◆ in Sicyon, and those the quiet stream
lazy Langia washes, or Elisson,
which winds along recurving riverbanks.
This river has an awful privilege; 53
◆ they say its gloomy waters cleanse the Stygian
Eumenides—the Furies—when they raze
Mycenae's evil roofs or homes in Thrace
or Theban dwellings and then bathe their snakes
(which sputter when they drink from Phlegethon)
and wash their faces. Then the river flees.
The venom of the serpents leaves black pools.

Corinth, where Ino solaces herself 59
with plaintive songs, accompanied the king.
Its harbor, Cenchreus, sent men: that is where
◆ the river that inspires poets flows,
formed by the foot of Pegasus, and where
the Isthmos fends off deep and sloping seas.

Three thousand joined Adrastus and rejoiced. 63
Some were adept at whirling woven slings
that circle through the air in unseen rings;
some carried heavy javelins; some chose
oak staves slow flames had hardened. Customs differed.

Equally venerated for his years 68
and his authority the king advanced
◆ like some great bull who wanders through the fields
he has long owned. His neck hangs loose, his power
has faded, yet he leads. The younger bulls
have no desire for combat, not when they
can see horns maimed from fighting and the huge
swellings of scars that run across his trunk.

His son-in-law, the Dircean Polynices, 74
followed, his standards close to King Adrastus.
War favored him; his cohorts tuned their rage
to his demands, and volunteers from Thebes,

his native country, joined him, whether drawn
to help an exile whose distress augments
their loyalty, or they preferred that princes
rotate their power, or they convinced themselves
his grievances were just. Adrastus gave
his son-in-law the rule of Aegion,
Arene, and the wealth of Troezen, which
was ruled by ancestors of Theseus,
because it would have been inglorious
if he led meager ranks or if he felt
the loss of public offices at home.

He wore the very clothes, the man was armed 85
the same way he had been that winter night
when, fated, he became a guest. The hide
of a Teumesian lion draped his spine,
his double-pointed javelins gleamed brightly,
and on the handle of his wounding sword
a sphinx rose by his side—a fearful sight.

Already in his hopes and in his prayers 88
he ruled his realm and dreamed he put his arms
around his mother and his faithful sisters,
but then he saw Argia leaning, frantic,
high in a distant tower where she attracted
her husband's gaze and turned his thoughts from Thebes.

Look here! Among his men was thunderous 93
Tydeus. He marched before his homeland army.
His wounds had healed. The first blasts of the horns
of war brought him delight—like a slick snake
the warm sun coaxes from deep earth, whose youth
renews, whose old scales shed. His menace lies
green in the grass; his mouth produces venom
when some poor peasant wanders much too close.

News of the war brought men from cities in
Aetolia to him: it reached Pylenë, 101
which sits on cliffs, and Pleuron, where the sisters
of Meleager weep, and Calydon,
a hilltown, and Olenos, whose god Jove

challenges that of Ida, and the port
of Chalcis, which receives Ionic seas,
♦ and the grim-visaged river Hercules
polluted when he wrestled. Even now
it hardly dares to lift its mangled face;
down in the depths it weeps, its head submerged
inside green caverns, while its riverbanks
sicken, inhaling dust. Each soldier held
a bronze-ribbed shield before his chest, a set
of fearsome, heavy javelins in hand,
and helmets decked by Mars, their native god.

Select youths ringed the meritorious son 112
of Oeneus, who displayed his wounds like honors
and reveled in the thought of war. His rage
and menace were no less than that displayed
by Polynices, and, indeed, there may
have been some doubt for whom the troops engaged.

Peloponnesian recruits composed 116
a mightier battalion, men who hoed
your stream banks, Lyrcius, and plowed your shores,
o Inachus—you who have precedence
♦ among Achaean rivers. No other torrent
leaves Persean lands with so much violence
when it has drunk the rainy Pleiades
or in the sign of Taurus swells with foam
when Jupiter pours water on his daughter.
And there were those that swift Asterion
circled around, as does the Erasinus,
which washes grain from the Dryopians
in Epirus, and those who tend the fields
of Epidaurus, where the hillsides suit
the grapes of Bacchus, not the grains of Ceres,
♦ whose temple is in Sicily, at Enna.

Hard-to-reach Dyme sent assistance; Pylos, 124
Neleus's city, dense battalions: Pylos
♦ was not yet famous, for though Nestor had
sufficient youth in middle age, he would
not join a doomed campaign. These, then, the troops

whom tall Hippomedon preceded and
filled with a passion for his fortitude.

His head shook his brass helmet, crested by 129
three tiers of snow-white plumage; iron mail
beneath his armor rubbed his sides; a flame-
bright orb was on his torso and displayed,
◆ in living gold, the night of Danaus,
whose fifty guilty daughters' chambers blaze
dark with the wedding torches of the Furies.
This wickedness incites their father's praise—
he witnesses their swords through bloody doorways.

Down from the citadel of Pallas on 136
a Nemean charger came Hippomedon.
◆ War terrified his steed. Its flying shadow
covered the field and stirred long plumes of dust.
◆ Not otherwise Hylaeus speeds—half-man,
half-horse—through forests from his mountain cave,
◆ shaping with both his chests an open path
that frightens Ossa. Fearful cattle, beasts
that cause fear, fall. Even his brothers feel
his terror till he takes a giant leap,
dives in the waters of the Peneus,
and dams the mighty river with his body.

What mortal voice is competent to count 145
the numbers of his weapons, powers, peoples?
Tiryns, the town of Hercules, responded.
She was not barren of brave men or less
productive since when her great son won fame,
but inactivity decayed her fortune;
she had no capital to finance strength.
From empty fields a lonely citizen
might point at towers the sweat of Cyclops built.
Nevertheless, she sent three hundred men
to war—so strong they seemed more numerous.
Their heads and shoulders bore buff lion skins,
the marker of their tribe. They were equipped
with pinewood stakes and inexhaustible
quivers containing sheaves of javelins.

Their spears lacked straps; they could not buy bright swords,
but they sang hymns to Hercules, the god
who cleared the world of monsters and who heard
◆ their song on leafy Oete, far away.

Nemea sent a retinue, as did 159
the sacred vineyards of Cleonae, where
◆ Molorchus lived. His dwelling won renown
for welcoming the god whose arms appear
depicted on its willow doors, while in
its small-scale fields you might see where he set
his club down, and the holm oak where he leaned
his unstrung bow, and where his elbow left
traces of his existence on the earth.

–◆–◆–◆–

Viewing the war a head above the others 165
came Capaneus, who upheld hides torn
from four unmastered oxen and the weight
of heavy layers of stiff bronze on his shield,
◆ which showed a branching, triple-headed Hydra,
recently slaughtered, rigid. Living snakes
shone in relief, engraved in textured silver,
while other features, by a hidden art
of working tawny gold, in death turned dark.
Slow Lerna's steel-blue river rimmed the scene.

His vast expanse of chest and spacious sides 173
were kept protected by a corselet tied
together by uncountable steel joints,
a rugged vest—no woman's work—and on
the top part of his shining helmet stood
a giant. No one else could launch his spear
of smooth-shaved cypress with its point of steel.

◆ The troops assigned to his command were born 178
in ample, lush Amphigenia or
flat Messenë or mountainous Ithome,
Thryon or Aepy, in the highest hills,
Helos or Pteleon or Dorion,

which mourns for Thamyris, the Getic bard.
♦ This Thamyris believed he could surpass
the learned Muses of Aonia,
but he was quickly silenced and condemned
never to sing or play his harp again,
for who can face divinities and scorn them?
He had not heard about Apollo's contest
with Marsyas, which made Celaenas famous
where Phoebus hung the Satyr up to die.

–♦–♦–♦–

By now the fortunetelling prophet's mind 187
was weakening from pressure. He indeed
foresaw disasters, read distressing signs,
but Atropos herself took arms against
his hesitation and she overthrew
♦ the god in him. The ruses of his wife
had not abated, and forbidden gold
already flashed and glittered in his home.

The Fates had warned Amphiaraus that 192
this gold would kill him, and his wicked wife
knew it. Here is the horror then, that she
loved frippery and not her husband's life.
She wore what she had wrangled from Argia
in order to assert her eminence.

Argia saw that if Amphiaraus, 196
the hero blessed with foresight, did not join
the expedition, then morale would suffer
among the men who bore the weight of war,
so she was willing to divest the sacred
bosom her husband Polynices loved.
She did not mourn the loss of ornaments,
but said, "The times are not appropriate 200
for me to wear bright jewels. Why should I dress
my wretched beauty while you march away?
People feel waves of fear—they are the ones
I must beguile. My hair shall be undone
and sweep across their altars. Certainly

it would be reprehensible for me
to wear the dowry of Harmonia,
her wealth in gold, when your face is concealed
inside a threatening helmet and the steel
you wear reverberates. And it may be 206
more fitting and more glorious for me
to outdress other Argive wives when my
husband becomes a king, when he is safe,
and I fill temples with thanksgiving choirs.
Let Eriphyle wear what she desires
and frolic while her prophet husband fights!"

That was the way the fatal jewelry reached 211
the home of Eriphyle, where it sowed
the seeds of powerful impieties
and made the Fury named Tisiphone
laugh loudly and rejoice in destiny.

Amphiaraus drove Taenarian steeds 213
engendered by the Centaur Cyllarus
in secret, so that Castor did not know
the ill-matched intercourse that bred those foals.
He wore Parnassian woolen bands to show
his status as a prophet: olives wigged
his helmet, and white, narrow ribbons twined
and twisted through his purple-colored crest.

His hands were busy with his horses' reins, 220
and trembling iron javelins fenced his chariot.
He threatened, like a comet in the distance;
his bright shield showed the Python Phoebus killed.
◆ Troops joined him from Amyclae, where Apollo
is worshiped, and from Pylos and Malea,
which careful ships avoid, and Caryae,
whose hymns provoke Diana's praise, and Pharis,
and Cytherean Messë, which breeds doves.

A hard band from the stream of swans, Eurotas,
descended in a phalanx from Taygetus.
Mercury (born Arcadian) had trained 228
these men in blood and dust, provoked their stark

aggression, and instilled them with his rage.
He stiffened their resolve and made it sacred
to die with honor. Young men wept if one
should die in battle, but the mother would
accept a funeral wreath. The fate that they
encouraged for their children pleased the parents.
Their javelins had double thongs; their reins
sat in their hands; their backs were unrestrained;
they wore broad, rough wool mantles, and
♦ swan feathers peaked their helmets, nor were they 236
the only ones to serve Amphiaraus:
Elis, which spreads across a hill, had sent
a company, and so had lowland Pisa,
whose people swim your yellow streams, Alpheus,
which flow to Sicily but never take—
however long the journey—sea-wave taint.

Uncountable the chariots that churned 241
the worn-out plowlands, and the horses tamed
for war. The widespread glory of the race
survived the broken axles and the foul
customs of Oenomaus. Foaming bits
rattled the horses' teeth, and white saliva
bedewed the sandy soil their footfalls furrowed.

–♦–♦–♦–

Parthenopaeus, inexperienced 246
and young: you also led Arcadians—
you were so eager to achieve renown.

♦ His mother did not know it yet—or he 249
would not have been allowed to go—for she
(wild Atalanta) with her bow was then,
by chance, establishing the peace in distant
woodlands and chill Lycaeus. Now, her son
was handsomer of face than anyone
who sallied to the hazards of the war,
and he was spirited. Would he had aged
till he was stronger! He ignited flames
in every forest nymph and river goddess

or deity residing in a valley.
They say Diana—even she—forgave 256
her follower when in Maenalian shades
she saw the young man's light steps skim the grass.
She gave him Cretan weapons and a quiver
of Amyclaean arrows for his shoulder.

He ripened with a daring love for war, 260
hot to hear horns and weapons, to befoul
his blond hair with the dust of battle, to
capture a rival's horse and ride it home.
The groves grew tedious; he felt ashamed
his arrows did not yet know human blood.

He shone with flaming purple, fiery gold: 265
Iberian embroidery made folds
along his flowing tunic, and his shield,
unsuited to the wars, displayed his mother's
♦ battles in Calydonia. His bow
♦ rang fiercely on his left. Cydonean arrows
rattled the quiver hanging down his back,
set with pale amber, bright with eastern jasper.

Accustomed to outracing startled stags, 271
his horn-foot horse was now amazed to feel
twin lynx-hide blankets and the extra weight
the young armed hero carried as he rode,
high on his horse—a sight!—with cheeks of rose.

A loyal army was delivered by 275
that ancient people, the Arcadians—
said to be older than the stars and moon,
and born from rigid tree trunks in the woods
when earth first saw the prints of human feet
and felt amazement in the times before
cities or fields or houses or the ways
of married life. Oak trees and laurel trees
bore tender children, and the ash produced
both shade and babies, and the wild ash dropped
young infants it had carried. It is said
that Titan's alternation with the shades

of night perplexed these people, who pursued
the setting sun, afraid of losing light.

Farms on Maenalos lacked inhabitants, and forests 284
on Mount Parthenius were emptied. Rhipe
and Stratië, Enispe with its winds,
sent men to war. Not Tegea or Cyllene—
home to a god and fortunate—stood idle,
nor did Minerva's forest temple at
Alea, nor rapid Clitor, nor the one
named Ladon—who, o Pythian, was almost
father-in-law to you—nor bright Lampia,
on ridges white with snow, nor Pheneos,
believed to send the Styx to darkest Dis.

Azan came too, whose howling mobs could rival 292
those on Mount Ida, and the countryside
of Sicily that pleased the quiver-bearing
Thunderer, bringing laughter to Amores
(divinities of Love); and cattle-rich
Orchomenus was there, and Cynosura,
a town where savage animals abounded.
The fields of Aepy and the peaks of Psophis
were emptied by identical desires,
as were the mountains Hercules made famous
by feats of strength: boar-bearing Erymanthos
and tintinnabulous-in-bronze Stymphalos.

These, then, were the Arcadians: one race, 299
but made distinct by different traditions.
Some bent the lower stems of Paphian myrtle;
some went to war with clubs, like pastoral dwellers;
some drew a bow, and some used stakes for weapons;
some crested horsehair on their helmets; some
wore leather-covered casques, Arcadian fashion,
or fit Lycaon bear-jaws to their skulls.

The neighboring town, Mycenae, did not lend
troops or assistance to the ranks and hearts
sworn to the cause of Mars. This was the time
a feast of human flesh was taking place,

the time the sun moved backward: it was when
two other brothers merged their souls in battle.

Now Atalanta heard reports: her son, 309
as chief, led all Arcadia to war.
Her legs gave out, her weapons fell beside her,
and faster than the flying winds she left
the forest, over rocks, across full rivers—
their banks no obstacles—just as she was,
her blond hair streaming loosely in the wind,
clutching her flowing robes, like some wild tiger
pursuing hunters who have seized her cubs
and ridden off on horseback. Now she stopped,
and leaned her breast against opposing reins—

"O son" (his eyes looked down; his face was pale), 318
"what causes this mad passion? Why must you,
at your age, show unseemly fortitude?
Can you train troops for war, support the weight
of Mars, or join with men who carry swords?
I wish you could! I almost fainted when,
just recently, you pressed your hunting spear
into a deadly boar and fell down backward.
Had I not sped a shaft from my curved weapon,
where would you be? My polished bow and arrows
and this gray horse with black spots you so trust
won't save you in the wars. You are a boy
who seeks to undertake great challenges
but hardly old enough to love a Dryad
or know the older passions of the nymphs
of Erymanthus. Portents tell the truth:
just recently I saw, to my amazement,
the temple of Diana trembling, and
the goddess seemed to scorn me. Votive gifts
fell from the cupola. My bow hand wavered,
I grew unsteady, and I could not aim.

"Your honor will be greater if you wait 335
till you are older. Your pink cheeks will darken.
Your face will lose my features. I will find
you wars, give you the iron swords you crave.

I will withhold my tears and not recall you.
Now bring your armor home! O let him go,
Arcadians! Are you born from oaks and stones?"

She'd have continued, but her boy consoled her, 341
as did the officers. They dimmed her fears.
It was not easy to release her son,
but now the trumpets blew their dreadful signal,
and she unclasped him from her loving arms;
she recommended him to King Adrastus.

–♦–♦–♦–

Now, in another country, in the city 345
founded by Cadmus, citizens of Mars
despaired because their king was mad, and they
were terrified by not unfounded rumors
that said an army had departed Argos.
Because they were embarrassed by their king
and by his quarrel, they were slow to act.
At last they mobilized, but no one felt
driven to draw a sword, nor was it sweet
to put one's back behind a father's shield
or tend the harness of a wing-foot steed—
such joys as warfare brings. There was no fire
or spirit, just reluctance to proceed
and downcast soldiers who complained about
their bad luck to their parents, who concurred.
They grudged the loss of their young wives' best years,
the babies growing sadly in the womb.

Mars, god of arms, inflamed no one. The walls 356
and mighty towers Amphion built had fallen.
Years of neglect lay bare the old, worn sides
of what was once upraised, with sacred faith,
as high as heaven. Now they were repaired,
but inattentively, since no one cared.
Nevertheless, mad keen for war and vengeful,
the cities of Boeotia moved, not to
assist Thebes' evil king, but to aid their neighbor.

That king was like a wolf who storms a sheepfold, 363
who turns his heavy eyes from side to side
as he withdraws. Fouled blood drips down his chest
and gory bits of wool fleck his raw breath.
If when the slaughter is revealed the shepherds
give chase, he runs away, but he is not
unconscious of his fierce accomplishment.

Chaotic Rumor added yet more panic: 369
the Argive cavalry was said to be
scattered along Asopos, wandering.
Some said that Mount Cithaeron had been taken,
home of the Bacchic revels; some, Teumesos.
News came that through the shadows of the night
◆ Plataea burned her watch fires, vigilant;
that home gods strove in Thebes; blood filled the Dirce;
monsters were born; once more the cliff sphinx spoke.
Who did not know, who had not seen these things?
But, in addition, this new prodigy
disturbed uneasy hearts: the queen who led
the woodland choir was seized by sacred frenzy.
She spilled her canister of flowers and ran
down from the Bacchic mountain to the plain,
waving a three-pronged pine torch. Here and there
it cast a somber, scarlet light and her
loud clamoring amazed the startled city:

◆ "All-powerful Nysaean father! you 383
for long have not concerned yourself with our
ancestral people. Even now, you move
unceasingly across the frozen North
and with your iron thyrsus weaken Thrace.
You cover up Lycurgus with your vines.
You race insanely down the swollen Ganges.
You cross the Red Sea's furthest barriers
to eastern lands and—brilliantly triumphant—
◆ let gold flow from the sources of the Hermus.
Meanwhile your progeny among the nations
who consecrate their festivals to you
know war and tears and fear and horrid brothers.

We reap the wages of a king's injustice
and lay aside your ivy-covered thyrsus!

"Transport me, Bacchus, to the land of frost
◆ that lasts forever, past the Caucasus 393
where howls of Amazons in arms reecho:
these I would rather face than tell about
the criminal offenses of our kings
whose family is cursed. You urge me, Bacchus,
but I owe you another frantic oath.
Two equal bulls—of similar renown,
born from one blood—collide. They join their leaning
foreheads and mix their lofty horns together,
vicious in turn and angry, and they die.
You are the worst of these, and must desist:
the fault is yours, Eteocles! Alone
you wreck your homeland to protect your mountain
but everything you do subverts your aim—
another king will rule your forest glade."

She spoke this prophecy. Her face turned cold; 404
as Bacchus dispossessed her, she grew silent.
The king felt sick. This portent left him weak.
Unable to endure his various terrors
he did what those who face uncertainty
do when afraid: he looked for answers from
the skill and shaded wisdom of Tiresias,
the ageless prophet.

And Tiresias said
his method for communing with the gods
was not to slaughter herds of sheep, or watch
birds fly, or seek the truth in quivering entrails.
Rather than quizzing cauldrons, calculating
the stars, or burning frankincense whose smoke
would hover over altars, he raised ghosts
◆ who crossed the threshold of grim Death. By means
of rituals of Lethe he would purge
King Laius, who at that time was submerged
under the waters of the stream Ismenos.

Before he did so, he prepared torn entrails 416
of sheep, incense of sulphur, fresh-grown herbs,
and always while he worked he muttered prayers.

There stands an ancient, deep, capacious forest, 419
sturdy, always in leaf, that sunlight never
penetrates. Winter's shortest days do not
diminish it, nor is it influenced
by warm south winds or cold winds from the north.
Beneath its noiseless canopy, a vague
shiver augments the silence, and a pale
absence of light makes darkness visible.

These shadows know Latona's virgin daughter, 425
who makes her home in groves. These sacred shades
conceal the cedars, pines, and suchlike trees
that hold her effigy within the woods.
Her hounds bay every night, and through the forest
her arrows whiz unseen. She hunts when she
emerges from the threshold of her uncle,
back in her better form, as fair Diana.
When she is weary and the mountain sun
is high and makes her sleepy, she positions
fixed spears around her, then removes her quiver.
She leans her lavish neck on that to rest.

Beside her lie the open fields of Mars, 434
the fertile soil of Cadmus, who was first
to plow it, dared to turn the fatal furrows
before the consanguineous earthmen fought
and spilled decaying blood on lands he dug.
At midday, or the solitude of night,
this ill-starred earth exhales tumultuous winds.
Black earthborn figures rise and fight as phantoms.
The frightened plowman, who has just begun,
now flees and drives his madding oxen home.

The aging prophet found the soil disposed 443
to Stygian rituals; the earth was rich
with living blood. Here he commanded men
to bring him sheep of darkest fleeces, black

cattle, the choicest beasts of all the herds.
Sad Mount Cithaeron and the Dirce groaned,
the valleys rang, then quieted, astonished.

Tiresias entwined their fearsome horns 449
with garlands of dark flowers—he did this
himself—and then, beside the well-known forest,
he first poured, in a hole dug in the earth,
nine lavish offerings of wine and gifts
of springtime milk, Actaean drops of honey,
and blood that pleases ghosts. He poured as much
as arid earth would drink, then called for logs.
The mournful priest asked that three mounds be raised 455
to Hecate, and as many for the Furies
(daughters of evil Acheron). And for
the king of hell—for you, lord of Avernus—
he raised a pile of pine as high above
the ground as it was sunk below. A less
imposing altar he erected next to this
accumulated mass. It was for Ceres,
who dwells beneath the earth. Around these mounds
he scattered cypress branches, signs of mourning.

The cattle held their heads high as the sword 461
and offerings of fresh, whole grains descended,
then fell beneath the blows. Next unwed Manto,
Tiresias' daughter, caught their blood in bowls
and poured the first libations. Now three times,
as she was bidden by her holy father, she
circled each pyre and tossed in still-warm organs
and pulsing entrails, nor did she withhold
fast-burning flames from darkened leaves and branches.
Flames crackled in the sticks; the fires roared
through the sad mounds, and when the heat increased,
when fiery vapors filled his empty eyes
and blew hot on his cheeks, the prophet howled;
he made the bonfires quake: 473

"You, in the seat
of Tartarus—voracious Death's harsh realm;
o you, most savage of the brother gods,

you whom dead shades attend, who portions out
eternal punishments to malefactors
there in the palace of the lower world:
open the silent, void domains of grave
Persephone to one who pounds the gates.
Set free the throngs who populate the night,
and let the ferryman recross the Styx.
Grant a full cargo for his wooden ship;
give passage to those shadows, and permit
more than a single means to reach the light.

"O Hecate, Perses' daughter! O sad Arcas, 482
equipped with staff of office! Lead the pious
Elysians in separate groups, and let
Tisiphone direct to daylight those
in Erebus who died committing crimes,
of whom so many ghosts descend from Cadmus.
Let her lead them with torch of flaming yew;
let her give three swings of her mighty serpent;
and do not let the heads of Cerberus
be obstacles to those deprived of light."

The old man spoke, and waited with his daughter— 488
Manto, Apollo's virgin—both attentive,
fearless, because the god was in their hearts.
Only the king of Thebes, Eteocles,
was overwhelmed by terror and afraid
to hear the prophet's chanting. He was anxious
and wound wool ribbons on his hands and shoulders
and would as soon have left these rites unfinished,
just like a hunter who awaits a lion
driven to thickets by loud clamor in
◆ the forests of Gaetulia: he girds
his soul and waits; he sweats; he grips his weapon;
his face is numb with terror; his knees shake.
What will emerge? How big? He hears the awful
noise of its roaring. Blinded by his panic,
he calculates its distance by the sound.

But nothing happened, so Tiresias 500
cried, "Goddesses—for whom I poured from fatal

beakers on plowed-up earth and moistened flames!
I am unable to endure delay!
You disregard me, though I am a priest.
If a Thessalian woman's raving charms
conjured you, would you come? Would hell
grow pale and shake as often as a witch
from Colchis might apply her Scythian poisons?
I do not care to raise the dead from graves.
I do not carry urns of ancient bones.
Is that why you ignore me? so that I
will not profane celestial gods or those
of Erebus by mingling them, or hunt
pale phantoms with my sword, or pluck diseased
organs from corpses? Goddesses, do not 511
despise, I warn you, my old age or this
dark cloud upon my brow, for even I
am capable of rage. There is a deity
◆ you fear to know, whose name you are afraid
to say, but he is known to me, and I
would conjure Hecate by him, did I not
revere you, o Thymbraean—o Apollo!
He is the ruler of the triple world.
His name may not be known; it is forbidden.
He . . . but I must be silent. My old age,
my years of peace, forbid my saying . . ."

Manto, Apollo's priestess, cut him off: 518
"Father, attend! The bloodless phantoms come!
The chaos of Elysium appears;
the massive canopy of this dark world
bursts open and reveals dark rivers, forests.
Acheron pours black mud, and Phlegethon
curls flames of darkness down its smoking waves.
Styx flows among the phantoms and divides them.
I can discern the king, pale on his throne,
surrounded by Eumenides, who do
his deadly work. And there is Stygian Juno
in grim rooms on her gloomy bridal bed.
Dark Death sits on an eminence and counts 528
the noiseless multitude as more arrive.
The arbiter from Crete turns hard his urn:

◆ this judge is Minos, from Gortynia.
He chooses names and threatens them to find
the truth about their past lives. They confess
the gains that they have gotten from their crimes.
But what concern have you for Erebus,
the god of darkness, and his monsters, his
Scyllas, his Centaurs full of empty rage,
the adamantine chains that bind the Giants,
or hundred-armed Aegaeon's narrow shade?"

Tiresias answered, "O my guide, support 536
◆ of my old age, it's true: there is no need
to tell of these. Who does not know about
the stone that must be rolled back, or the lake
that falsely tempts, or Tityos, who feeds
the vultures, or tormented Ixion, 540
tied to an ever turning wheel? I've seen
the hidden realms myself, back when my blood
was stronger. Hecate guided me, before
the god eclipsed my eyes and put my light
inside me. Better if you call, with prayers,
the souls of Argos and of Thebes. Avert
the others' footsteps. Sprinkle milk four times
and order them to leave this dreary grove.
Now then, inform me how they look and dress.
Who craves the blood you pour? Which race approaches
most proudly? Teach my blindness, daughter. Speak!"

She did as she was told. She sang the songs 549
that make the scattered phantoms come and go,
◆ just like Medea or deceptive Circe
on the Aegean shores (if you ignore
their evils). She described the sacrifice:

◆ "Cadmus is first to lift his sluggish face 553
above the lake of blood, and next to him
the daughter of the Cytherean goddess—
Harmonia—arrives and both have serpents
protruding from their heads, and both snakes drink.

"They are surrounded by the men of Mars, 556
earthborn companions who lived just one day.
Each one holds weapons. Each one grips his sword.
They block each other, clash. They rage like men
who breathe the air, but they avoid the swamp.
Instead, they thirst for one another's blood.

◆ "Next comes a group of daughters and the grandsons 561
◆ they mourn. Here is Autonoë, bereft,
◆ and Ino, panting, looking at a bow
and pressing to her breast her precious infant.
◆ Semele holds her arms before her womb.
◆ Agave moans as she runs after Pentheus, 566
her son, along the banks of wandering Lethe,
her thyrsi broken, for the god has left her.
He flees past Stygian lakes to where his father,
Echion, weeps for him and tends the body
his wife had torn to shreds. I recognize 570
sad Lycus and Aeolides, the son
of Aeolus, named Athamas, whose right
elbow is raised: his shoulder bears the burden
of his son's lifeless corpse. And there is he,
Actaeon, son of Aristaeus, whose
condition and his metamorphosis—
sign of his guilt—have not been altered. Horns
roughen his brow; his hands hold weapons; he
repels the wide-mouthed hounds that tear his limbs.
And here comes Niobe, the envious child
of Tantalus, surrounded by great crowds.
Misfortunes do not dash her. She is proud
of every corpse she mourns, the slain she counts,
and pleased that she has fled from heaven's sway.
Now, even more, her mad tongue has its way."

The virgin priestess chanted while Tiresias 579
listened and white hairs raised his woolen garland.
His gaunt face flushed with blood, and he no longer
leaned on his steadying staff or virgin daughter
but stood erect and said: "Cease singing, Manto;

there is enough external light for me.
The heavy clouds depart, dark shades recede
before my face. A spirit fills my soul.
Daughter, what is its source? The god Apollo?
Or ghosts? Behold, the Argive phantoms lower
their eyes and weep. Grim Abas. Dangerous 589
Proteus. Mild Phoroneus. Pelops—maimed.
And Oenomaus, fouled by bitter dust.
Large tears roll down their faces—therefore, I
predict that Thebes will win the war. But who
are these, compacted in a group? And why
do they regard us so unpeacefully?
Their faces and their breasts are dripping blood.
They raise a silent shout, lift outstretched hands.
Their wounds and weapons show their quality—
the souls of warriors. Eteocles,
am I deceived? Is this the group of fifty?
Do you see Cthonius and Chromis and
Phegeus—and Maeon? He stands out because
he wears our crown of laurel. Do not be 599
angry, o soldiers! Your assignment was
no mortal man's idea, for Atropos,
the Destiny of iron, spun your years.
You met your Fate; we still must face war's horror
and battle Tydeus." So he spoke. The ghosts
pressed for the woolen ribbons in his hair,
but he drove them aside and toward the blood.

Along the sad shore of Cocytos stood 604
Laius, alone. The winged god Mercury
had redelivered him to harsh Avernus
from where, his eyes askew, he watched his grandson,
whose evil face he knew. He had no thirst
for blood or other fluids, like the rest,
but breathed immortal odium. The priest—
Aonian Tiresias—enticed
him forward, "Famous king of Tyrian Thebes!
No peaceful sun has seen Amphion's towers
since your demise. You have sufficiently
avenged your bloody death, and your descendants
have placated your shade. Whom do you flee,

so miserably? He whom you mutter for 614
now lies in endless night, with death close by.
Corrupted blood and dried pus veil his eyes,
which no light enters. Take my word, his fate
is worse than death, but your son's son is guiltless.
Why do you turn from him? Come here and sate
yourself with sacrificial blood. Reveal
the revolutions of the times. Tell who will die
in war: the enemy, or citizens
you pity? I will then arrange that you
may cross forbidden Lethe on the boat
of your desire, and settle you in peace
among the Stygian gods on holy ground."

The promise of reward assuaged King Laius. 624
His cheeks took color. He responded thus:
"We are the same age, priest. Why have you chosen
me from among the many ghosts you raised
to give prognostications of the future?
It would be shameful if my grandsons asked
advice from me. They should adjure the one
so pleased to pierce his father with his sword.
Who crawled back to the womb? who paid his wanton
mother deposit? Oedipus, who tires
the gods and midnight councils of the Furies;
who conjures my dead soul to join his battle.
If I have been selected as a prophet
in times as terrible as these, then let
me say what Lachesis and cruel Megaera
permit me: war comes everywhere, unnumbered
soldiers! Gradivus—fatal god of battle—
goads on the Argive sons of Lerna's swamp.
But they are stopped by wonders of the world,
by weapons of the gods, by glorious deaths,
and those delays decreed by law that keep
invaders from the final funeral fires.
Thebes' victory is certain; do not fear; 641
your vicious brother will not gain your kingdom.
The Furies, your dual wrongs, and your cruel father,
whom your sad swords will make victorious,
will be, to my regret, all that remains."

He slid away when he had spoken, leaving
Tiresias and King Eteocles
in doubt about his ambiguities.

–◆–◆–◆–

Meanwhile, the wandering legions of the sons 646
of Inachus had reached the cooling glades
of Nemea, where Hercules performed
such deeds that thickets still recall his praise.
Already they were busy taking booty,
eager to overthrow and pillage homes.

Who turned their rage? What brought about delay? 649
Why did they stray when they had gone halfway?
Teach us, Apollo! Little now remains.
◆ *Start from the dim beginnings of their fame.*

◆ Liber, the god of wine, who wasted Haemus, 653
was feeble as he rearrayed for war.
Two winter seasons he had taught the martial
Thracians the orgies, mysteries of wine,
to plant on Rhodope Icarian shades,
and make the sides of Othrys green with vines.

And now he drove his chariot, bedecked 656
with leaves and tendrils, to his mother's walls.
◆ Unbridled lynxes followed, left and right,
while tigers licked their harness, soaked in wine.
Behind him came the joyous Bacchanals,
bearing the spoils of cattle, half-dead wolves,
and she-bears torn to pieces. His companions
were not inactive. Here, with steps that staggered,
◆ the members of his sect marched: Fear and Anger,
Ardor, who's never sober, Madness, Valor.

Then Bacchus noticed rising clouds of dust 664
that swirled through Nemea and sunrays flashing
from metal. He saw Thebans unprepared.
The sight unnerved him, he felt faint, he drooped.
He ordered cymbals, pipes, and pounding drums

to cease their playing; in astonishment,
he spoke:

"That mass of soldiers is engaged
to kill me and my followers. Their rage
has simmered over time. The endless anger
of Juno, my stepmother, and fierce Argos
incite this warfare. Was it not enough
that Semele, my mother, burned to dust?
Impious Juno battles idle Thebes—
the relics and the grave of Semele,
her husband's mistress, who was blown apart
while bearing me. Companions, take the field;
meanwhile I will use fraud to weave delay."

His team of Caspian tigers swelled their manes 678
when he gave them the signal to proceed.
He spoke, and just that quickly reached the plain.

It was the moment when the sun had reached 680
its height, borne up by gasping day; when vapors
hang over lazy fields, and groves of trees
admit long shafts of sunlight through their leaves.
He gathered water spirits, and when they
were silent, he addressed them in their midst:

"O goddesses of rivers, rustic Nymphs! 684
I offer you this chance; do me this favor:
obstruct the Argive river at the source.
Constrict the wandering streams and lakes with silt.
Let all the deepest waters drain away
in Nemea, where they attack our walls.
Phoebus will help, if you are resolute.
The sun has reached its height. The Dog Star rages,
and constellations bless this enterprise.
Be of good cheer; hide in the depths of earth.
When this is over, I will call you forth
in overflowing streams, and your reward
will be the ample gifts that deck my altars.
Licentious horn-foot Centaurs will no longer
violate you at night, nor Fauns steal love."

And even as he spoke, a film of mold
withered their cheeks and eyes, and blue-green beads
of moisture radiated from their hair.

Drought dried the plains along the Inachus; 699
streams disappeared; the springs and lakes drained dry.
In empty beds of rivers, mud baked hard.
Sick barrenness was suddenly on the soil.
New-planted grains let drop their slender tips.
Along the riverbanks stood wondering flocks,
and cattle searched for brooks where once they bathed.
So Nile recedes and hides inside deep caves; 705
he swallows down the liquid nourishment
of eastern winters. Waterless valleys steam,
and gasping Egypt waits to hear the roar
of Father Nile's waves in Pharian fields,
when prayers will bring them food, a good year's yield.

The noxious Lerna ran dry. Parched were Lyrceus; 711
the mighty river Inachus; Charadrus,
which rolls down swimming rocks; bold Erasinus,
which never holds its banks; and that well-known
and oceanlike Asterion, which wakes
the shepherds in the highlands, far from roads.
Only Langia nourished secret streams
in hidden shades. She did so as the god
commanded, for Archemorus still lived.
He had not given her his mournful name,
nor made the goddess famous. She preserved
her unfrequented groves, her fountains, waiting
for her great glory, when the Greeks compete
in the triennial contests held to honor
sacred Opheltes, sad Hypsipyle.

–♦–♦–♦–

Hot thirst consumed the soldiers, who'd no strength 723
to bear their burning shields or wear close links
of chain mail on their bodies. Their tight throats
felt fiery, and their fevers made them shake;

their hearts were racing, and their veins congealed;
their blood was spoiled and thickened in their guts.

The earth stunk from the sun and turned to dust;
it gave off clouds of heat; no flecks of foam 729
fell from the steeds, whose tongues drooped, and whose lips
licked dry their chain-link bridles. Flocks obeyed
neither their laws nor leaders: overheated,
they wandered fields. Meanwhile, Adrastus ordered 733
explorers out to find Licymnian lakes
or learn if Amymonë still held water,
but unseen flames had dried up every vein;
there was no hope Olympus would bring rain;
they might as well have wandered through the sands
of Africa or yellow Libya
♦ or Syene, where no clouds offer shade. 745

–♦–♦–♦–

Bacchus himself prepared what happened next.
While wandering a wooded area,
they suddenly beheld Hypsipyle,
whose sorrow made her beautiful. She held
Opheltes to her breast, although the child
was not her own, but the unlucky son
of King Lycurgus, who ruled Nemea.
Her dress was modest and her hair disheveled,
but she was regal, and her face revealed it.
Her sorrows had not overcome her grace.
Adrastus, in astonishment, said this:

"O goddess, you must rule this forest, for 746
your looks and manner say you are no mortal!
You who rejoice beneath these fiery skies
and seek not water, succor those nearby!
Whether Diana or Latonia
chose you for marriage from among the virgins,
or whether love descended from the stars
without humility and made you breed—
for he who rules the gods is not unknown

to visit Argive women in their beds—
behold this suffering army! We have set
our minds on Thebes, which merits punishment!
This bitter drought, though, undermines our spirit,
makes us unfit for war and drains our strength.
Is idleness our fate? this weariness?
Give us a muddy stream, a filthy swamp: 756
anything! Our position makes us shameless.
Nothing is too abysmal. We now pray
to you instead of Jove or Winds and Rain.
Restore our vanished strength. Prepare our hearts
for battle, though we're weak. So may the stars
favor your son in his maturing years!
If Jove lets us return, you will receive
the spoils of war in untold quantities!
I will requite you, goddess, with the grazing
sheep of the Dirce and with numerous slaves!
This grove will hold an altar to your fame!"

He spoke in gasps, as heat cut off his speech. 765
His dry tongue stuttered as he tried to breathe.
Like him, his men were pale, with sunken cheeks;
they panted, and the Lemnian woman answered,
her eyes cast down. "To you I seem a goddess—
indeed, my origin is heavenly—
but what's the use? The grief that pierces me
is more than mortals suffer. I have nothing,
although you see me nursing someone's child.
God knows if my own sons have been embraced
and fed from fruitful breasts. Yet I possessed
a kingdom once. I had a mighty father.

"But why should I recall these things and keep
you weary soldiers from the streams you seek?
Follow along with me. Perhaps Langia
preserves some water in a shallow pool,
for he flows even when the sun's path runs
through burning Cancer, or the Dog Star rages!"

She did not want to slow the Danaans down,
whom she would lead, so she removed the baby

who clung to her and laid him on the turf.
(The Fates—the Parcae—instigated this.)
After she set him there, the baby cried.
To stop the infant's tears, she gathered flowers
and soothed his weeping with her lullabies,
◆ as when the Berecynthian mother ordered 789
excited Curetës—inhabitants of Crete—
to dance around the little Thunderer:
they pounded drums and cymbals in their orgies,
and Ida echoed back the infant's screams.

The baby crawled face forward through the lap
of vernal earth, and as he tottled forward
through waving grass, he trampled tender herbs
and cried for his dear nurse, demanding milk,
but then recovered. He resumed his laughter,
and his young lips attempted to form words.
He grasped at objects lying in his way,
questioned the woodland sounds, inhaled the day
with open mouth, and did not know the dangers
the forest hid. Life felt secure. He strayed.

◆ So did young Mars upon the Thracian snows; 801
so did the wingèd boy along the peak
of Mount Maenalius; and irresponsible
Apollo crawled the same way on the sands
of Delos, and he made the island slant.

–◆–◆–◆–

The Argives traveled through an undergrowth
of aimless paths and devious green shades.
Some raced ahead; some stayed beside their guide;
a smaller group of people only followed.
Hypsipyle moved quickly in their midst
and bore herself in not unhumble fashion.
They neared the river now, and they could hear
the valley echo and the sound of rapids.

Argus exulted first and cried out "Water!"
He bore the standard for the faster troops,

and soon the word had run from mouth to mouth,
a long loud cry of "Water!" like the sound
that rings out from young sailors at their oars.
Their officer commands them to salute
♦ Phoebus, who shows them Leucas (where he's worshiped). 815
Their loud shouts echo from Ambracian shores.

The leaders and their men swam through the flood;
thirst leveled them; there was no sense of order,
no way to separate the mingled ranks.
Horses hauled chariots or dragged along
their armored riders; some were carried off;
some slipped on glistening rocks; none were ashamed
to tread on kings the current swept away
or trample drowning friends who called for aid.

The rapids roared. Far from the river's source,
the channel that was formerly translucent—
a slow, green stream of crystal pools—now swirled
with mud stirred from its depths, with chunks of bank
and clumps of loosened grass and sod. Men drank
the silt and flowing filth, although their thirst
had ended. You would think you saw armed ranks
in righteous battle, raging in the torrent,
or conquerors consume a captured city.

One king, surrounded by the river, cried:
"Queen of green forests, chosen seat of Jove,
o Nemea! You treat us more severely
than you did Hercules when his hands seized
♦ the raging lion's shaggy mane and squeezed 834
the breath from swollen limbs. You have tormented
your worshipers, so therefore be content
as we begin our war. Flow on, horned river,
provider of an everlasting stream.
May your cool waves continue from wherever
they take their origin! No winter stores
white snow for you, nor does the rainbow pour
cool waters stolen from another source,
nor are you favored by the pregnant clouds
that ride the northeast wind. You are your own!

No star can stop your flow, which neither Phoebus'
Ladon nor Xanthus, threatening Spercheos 844
or Centaur-like Lycormas can surpass.
When we return exhausted from the wars—
beneath the cloud of battle or in peace—
I will requite you with a celebration
worthy of Jupiter, a festive meal,
if you will once more open your kind shores
to strangers and recall whom you restored!"

—◆—◆—◆—

BOOK 5 Women of Lemnos

The women of Lemnos fail to worship Venus and the men prefer war. The frenzy of Polyxo. Hypsipyle saves her father Thoas, son of Bacchus. The Argonauts arrive. Jason abandons Hypsipyle. Bacchus saves her. Pirates sell her. She nurses the baby of King Lycurgus. Jupiter's serpent kills the infant Opheltes. Amphiaraus calls for funeral games.

Its thirst relieved, the Argive army left
the ravaged riverbed and shrunken stream;
their horses now ran rapidly through meadows,
and celebrating soldiers filled the fields.

Their spirit was restored, and they renewed 4
their threats and vows, as if they'd drunk the fire
of warfare mixed with blood from flowing springs.
Courageous thoughts of battle filled their minds.

The troops once more pursued the rule of order. 7
Squadrons reorganized, and each man found
his former place and leader and was warned
to recommence the march.

Now the first dust
rose from the earth, and weapons shone through foliage,
just as when winter dims and whirring lines
of cranes, across the sea, abandon bright
◆ Pharus and leave the Paraetonian Nile:
they fly with fleeting sounds, reechoed by
the pathless skies, like shadows on the waves
or over fields, and they endure the rain
and Borean north wind, until they swim
unfrozen rivers and rejoice to spend
their summer on unforested Mount Haemus.

Adrastus, son of Talaus—once more 17
wreathed by a circle of his generals—

by chance stood underneath an ancient oak.
He leaned on Polynices' spear, then spoke:

"Woman, whoever you may be, your glory
is great, and fate has brought us, numberless
soldiers, to owe you debts and honors that
the father of the gods would not despise.
As we speed from your waters, say to us
what is your home and country, from what stars
do you draw life? Who is this father whom
you mentioned? For indeed, you cannot be
far from divinity. Your fortune may
have faded, but your face shows noble blood.
Singed by adversity, it breathes respect."

The Lemnian woman sighed, and for a moment 28
her tears detained her. Then she started speaking:

"The wounds you ask me to reopen, master,
are great—the Furies, Lemnos, weapons brought
within the confines of our beds, our men
undone by shameful swords. Our criminality
comes back to me, our vengeance, our cold hearts!

"O wretched women who endured such madness; 33
o night, o father! I, your friend and guide,
I was the only one, the only woman—
I say this if, by chance, you feel embarrassed—
to bear away her parent, to conceal him.
Why should I weave my problems through 36
a long exordium? War calls you forth,
your great hearts are prepared. It is enough
if you remember this: I am the daughter
of famous Thoas, named Hypsipyle,
and I am now a slave to King Lycurgus."

Her words drew their attention, for she seemed 40
mature, worth honoring, prepared for greatness.
A passion rose in each to learn her fate.
Father Adrastus was the first to speak:

"But come now, while our first troops frame long lines, 43
for Nemea's impenetrable shadows and
overspread foliage prevent broad ranks
from forming: tell of criminality,
your honors and your sorrows, and why you,
ejected from your kingdom, labor here."

–♦–♦–♦–

It pleases those in misery to speak 48
and visit sorrows past, so she began:

"Lemnos lies circled by the blue Aegean.
♦ There, worn by fiery Aetna, Mulciber
exhales and rests, and nearby Athos drapes
the land in giant shadows and casts shades,
shaped like her forests, on the seas. The Thracians
plow the shores opposite—in fatal Thrace,
the source of all our woe. Our country flourished,
as well endowed and populous as famous
Samos, not worse than ringing Delos or
other Aegean islands washed by waves.

"The gods decided to disturb our homes. 57
Our hearts, though, were not guiltless. We had not
lit any sacrificial fires for Venus
nor given her an altar. Anger moves
even the minds of gods, and Punishments
(divinities of vengeance) gain admittance.

"They say she left behind a hundred altars
♦ on ancient Paphos, changed her looks, her hair, 61
took off her nuptial girdle, and dismissed
the doves of Ida. Certainly some women
say that the goddess, bearing other torches
and weapons than the ones that kindle love—
merciless to her faithful husband's people—
flew through our bedrooms with the hellish Furies,
brought cruel fear to the thresholds of our brides,
and filled our homes' dark nooks with twining serpents.

"Next you, Amores, flew away from Lemnos. 70
Hymen was mute, his torches overturned.
Frozen care occupied the lawful couch;
the nights produced no joy; none slept embraced,
but bitter hate was everywhere, and rage,
and discord parted couples in their beds.

"Our men were keen to cross the straits to Thrace, 75
to fight, and decimate that proud, cruel race.
These brutes preferred Edonian winters and
the bluster of north winds, so they ignored
their homes, left children standing on the shore,
and went where they could hear a falling torrent
sound in the silent night that follows war.

"I was relieved of cares, since I was young, 81
a virgin, but our women moped in sorrow.
For consolation they spoke night and day
and wept incessantly or they would stand
and gaze at savage Thrace across the sea.

"The sun was halfway through his work and hung 85
his shining steeds above Olympus' peak,
as if unmoving. Four times thunder pealed
in cloudless skies; four times the smoking caverns
of Vulcan blew emissions from high summits.
There were no winds, yet the Aegean stirred,
and high seas battered shores, when suddenly
an ancient woman named Polyxo felt
an unaccustomed terror, and, in frenzy,
she flew from her abandoned bed. As a
Teumesian Thyiad, ravaged by the god, 92
hears Bacchus calling from the mountain tops
and follows sacred rites and boxwood pipes
of Ida that allure her, so, head high,
her eyes suffused with blood, with rabid cries
that roused the quiet town, she knocked on closed
houses and doorways and convened a council.
Her children went unwillingly and held her,
but other women, no more slow than she,

burst from their homes and reached the citadel
of Pallas on the hilltop. Here we crowded,
congested and disordered, as she drew
a sword and ordered silence and soon urged
our crimes upon us. She dared speak these words:

" 'Driven by gods, by undeserved mistreatment, 104
I authorize our exploit! O you widows
of Lemnos, fix your minds: unsex yourselves!
If you are tired of tending empty homes,
spending the flower of youth in vile neglect,
forever mourning your unfruitful years,
I have a way, I promise, to renew
the work of Venus and respect the gods.
I only ask that you take strength from your
distress and tell me you are strong. Three winters 112
of white have passed, and who has known the bonds
of wedlock or the secret rites of marriage?
Tell me, whose heart is heated by her husband?
Whose labors has Lucina overseen?
Who swells up month by month, makes vows, gives birth?

" 'Even the birds and beasts may copulate: 116
it's instinct, but we linger. Could a Grecian
have given daughters weapons for revenge
to fill their husbands' peaceful sleep with blood
◆ and ease his anguish, while we stand here idly?
If you require relevant examples,
think of the dinner Procne served her husband,
◆ the way that she avenged her bed, her marriage.

" 'I am not safe nor unaffected by 123
the crime I urge you to commit. My house
is full, my task enormous. Here you see
my four sons, each their father's pride and joy.
They may delay me with their hugs and tears,
but I will hold them in my lap and stab them
and throw these brothers in a breathing heap
of blood and wounds. I'll pile their father on them!
What woman here can pledge so many dead?'

"She was continuing, but sails were shining 129
across the sea; it was the Lemnian fleet.
Polyxo, joyous, seized her opportunity
and spoke again: 'How can we fail the gods
when they exhort us? Lo, behold the ships!—
delivered by the God of Punishment
for our revenge. He favors our design!

" 'My dreams are not vain images; I see 134
Venus with naked sword drawn when I sleep!
She seems so clear: "Why do you lose your youth?"
she says. "Your husbands hate you. Rid your beds:
I will arrange new marriages myself,
better arrangements." Then she sets her sword 139
along my couch: believe me, this same sword!
Decide while you have time, o miserable women!
Look who arrives: strong arms stir foaming seas;
your husbands may be bringing Thracian wives.'

"This was a mighty spur, and a great roar 143
rose to the stars. You might have thought a horde
of Amazons were swarming over Scythia,
bearing their moon-shaped shields when Jupiter
indulges them by opening the gates
of foreign wars. There was no murmuring,
no differing, no dissent that causes factions,
such as may seize the commoners. The same
anger was felt by everyone, the same
craving to desolate their homes,
to murder young and old, tear babies from
full breasts, stab every man of any age.

"Inside a verdant grove—a grove that's dark, 152
that shades the ground but also lies beneath
the shadow of the mountain of Minerva
(and so two shadows dim the sun)—the women
pledged faith. The witnesses were you, Enyo
(goddess of war), and you, infernal Ceres.
The deities of Styx anticipated
their call and left reclusive Acheron

as Venus mingled everywhere, concealed:
Venus bore weapons. Venus gave them zeal.

"They did not make a normal sacrifice. 159
The wife of Charops seized her son, and women
girded themselves and stabbed their greedy knives
through every portion of his lovely body.
They swore to sweet revenge in blood still warm,
and the new ghost flew rings around his mother.

"Horror ran through my bones as I observed; 164
my facial color faded; I felt like
a deer surrounded by bloodthirsty wolves
whose tender breast lacks vigor, who
lacks faith in her ability to run,
who waits, who flees, who thinks she has been caught,
who hears, just out of reach, approaching jaws.

"Keels struck the outer beach. The men arrived 170
and struggled to be first to jump ashore.
Unfortunates—these men—whose horrid strength
had not consumed them in the Thracian wars
nor storms in midsea drowned. They filled high shrines
with incense for the gods and offered flocks
as promised, but the altar flames turned dark.
♦ No vigorous god inspired a single entrail.

"Jupiter slowly drew down night from damp 177
Olympus, and with kindly care, I think,
delayed the turning skies, which Fate forbids.
Never were shadows longer after sunset.

"Late stars appeared at last, but only shone 181
♦ on Paros, on the many Cyclades,
♦ and Thasos with its forests. Shadowed Lemnos
lay hidden under heavy skies, dark clouds,
the woven zones of blackness. Lonely Lemnos
remained unseen by mariners who roamed.

"And now the men poured from their homes and entered 186
the darkness of the sacred groves where they

indulged themselves in rich feasts. They drank deep
from massive, golden goblets. They had leisure
to sing strife in Strymona, to recount
labors that made them sweat on frozen Haemus
or Rhodopë. The wicked crew of wives
even reclined among the banquet flowers,
dressed in their finest clothes, as Venus vainly
granted their softened husbands one last evening—
after so long a time, a little peace.
She breathed a dying flame on those sad men.

"The choristers fell silent. It was time 195
to end the feasting, cease licentious games.
The noises of the early night decreased.
Befouled by darkness from his brother Death,
Sleep seized the city that would die. He dripped
with Stygian moisture, and he poured out heavy
fatigue from his resistless horn. He set
the men apart, while wives and younger women
remained awake, preparing for their crimes.
The Fatal Sisters laughed and honed fierce weapons.

"They started their assault. Each female heart 202
was governed by a Fury of Revenge,
just as Hyrcanian lionesses pen
the flocks they chase along the Scythian plains.
Hunger first brings them out from under cover—
that, and the need to nurse their hungry cubs.

"Which deaths, out of the thousand murders done,
should I describe for you? Let me consider! 207
Gorge was brave but rash. She hovered over
Helymus, who was sleeping, crowned with vines,
high on his tapestries, and breathing wine
that bloated him. She slipped her hand inside
his loosened clothing for a place to wound.
As death approached, his miserable sleep
deserted him. Uncertain whom he faced,
confused, his eyes scarce opened, he embraced
his consort, but she did not hesitate
to stab him from behind, as he held on,

nor stop until her knife-blade touched her breast.
His eyes implored her, while his arms remained
around her faithless neck. He murmured 'Gorge,'
trembling. That was the end of it. I won't
describe the other deaths, for they were gruesome,
only the sorrow of my relatives:

"I saw my two half brothers die: Cydon, 220
a blond, and Crenaeus, whose uncut locks
hung loose around his neck: we shared our mother
but not our father. My fiancé was Gyas:
a strong man who inspired fear in women.
I saw fierce Myrmidonë murder him,
and Epopeus, while playing with wreathes on couches,
was barbarously slaughtered by his mother.
Lycaste, who cast down her weapon, wept 226
◆ for Cydimos, her twin, as she beheld
a face like hers, but in a body that
must die. His cheeks glowed. She herself had woven
gold through his hair. But her fierce mother, who
had killed her husband, hovered over her,
made threats, and forced the girl to seize her sword.
Then like a beast that has unlearned its madness 231
under a kindly master—it is slow
to skirmish, to resume old habits—she
fell on her fallen brother. She absorbed
his life-blood in her bosom as it flowed
and pressed her shredded hair where he was gored.

"Alcimede was carrying the head 236
she severed from her parent. It still murmured.
I felt fierce horror and my hair stood up,
because that could have been *my* father, Thoas;
her dreadful right hand could have been my own.
Greatly dismayed, I sought my father's chambers, 240
where, in the meantime, he was wondering
what caused this uproar, why these sounds at night,
why, in a time of quiet, so much noise?
Our house stood in a side part of the city;
his worry nonetheless kept him awake.

I told him a disordered story of
impieties, complaints, and female valor.

"I urged the miserable man to follow me: 245
nothing could stop the madness; women raged,
and he and I would die if we remained.
My words aroused my father from his bed;
dark hid us as we traced the empty town
through alleys, and we saw enormous mounds
of those who died that night, men who lay down
to sleep in sacred groves that awful evening.
One could see cushioned couches pressing faces,
sword-handles sticking up from riven breasts,
the splinters of great spears, clothes torn by knives,
overturned chalices. The food from banquets
floated in blood that spilled from open throats,
mingled with wine, and trickled into goblets.
Here there were adolescents, there old men
whom weapons should not threaten, also small
children who sobbed away their trembling souls,
abandoned, on their fathers' moaning faces.

"Not wilder are the feasts the Lapithae
◆ hold on cold Ossa where the cloud-born gods
grow hot from stoops of wine, then, pale with anger,
rise suddenly and overturn their tables.

◆ "We were in fear, when Bacchus—called Thyoneus— 265
made himself visible to us that night.
He shone with sudden light as he assisted
Thoas, his son, to face this deadly crisis.
I recognized the god, although no garlands
adorned his bloated temples, no white grapes
set off his hair. His eyes dripped angry tears;
his mood was melancholy, and he said:

" 'When you ruled Lemnos, as the Fates decreed, 271
and made her feared abroad, I never ceased
to be solicitous in your just cause,
but those sad Destinies, my son, have sheered

your threads without remorse. I poured out tears
and supplicated Jove, but I could not
avert disaster. He has granted this
despicable endearment to his daughter,
to Venus; therefore you must guide your father— 278
o dutiful young girl, my progeny—
along the city's twin walls to the sea.
You might imagine that those gates are peaceful,
but murderous Venus stands there, girt with steel,
assisting maddened women. Where did she 282
acquire such force and such a warlike heart?
Commit your father to the wide, deep seas.
I will attend your worries.' 284

So he spoke,
then he dissolved in air. But he was kind:
when shadows took our sight, he gave us light.
I followed where he signaled us to go
and hid my father in a ship's curved hold.
Aegeaon, who surrounds the Cyclades,
the winds, and other sea gods had my faith.
We never would have ceased our sad farewell
had Lucifer not set the eastern stars.
At last, but very much afraid, I left
the murmur of the sea. My steps were quick
but fear crept through my breast. I scarcely trusted
Bacchus Lyaeus, who relieved our cares.
There was a sunrise, but I could not rest.
I gazed upon the sea from every cliff.

"Day broke, ashamed. Titan unveiled the skies 296
and shone across from Lemnos. Though he veiled
his horses in an intervening cloud,
the madness of the night was manifest.
First light made everyone afraid. They felt
their infamy at once and shared their guilt.
They buried their impieties, their crimes,
or burned them over fast-devouring fires.
The Furies who possessed the city left,
and Venus, too, departed, anger slaked.

"The women now could know what they had dared; 303
their eyes were wet with tears; they tore their hair.
This island, rich in fields, possessions, men
and arms, this notable locality,
just now made wealthy by its Getic triumph,
had lost—not to eroding seas, foul weather,
or enemy invasion—all its native
men. It lay desolate, alone, bereft;
nobody plowed the fields or sailed the seas;
houses were silent, deep in blood, and smeared
with lucent, thick red gore. Except for ghosts
who breathed along the city walls, we lived
alone, ringed by the lofty towers of Lemnos.

"Inside a central room, I lit a fire, 313
like other women, and I threw my father's
scepter and armor in the mounting flames,
his royal robes and well-known clothes, while I
stood mournfully beside the pyre, my hair
disheveled, with a bloody sword, afraid
my fraud—his empty bier—would be discovered.
Meanwhile, I prayed it would not be an omen
of death, either for me or for my father.

"Deception—my false crime—had won belief 320
and earned me this reward: the throne and kingdom
my father'd held were reassigned to me.
What punishment! Could I deny what women
insisted on? So I accepted: I
frequently prayed the gods to witness my
good faith and guiltless hands. My power was ghastly—
bloodless dominion, Lemnians lamenting
lost husbands, as our sorrows more and more
tormented sleepless senses. Women were
in mourning and grew conscious of their crimes,
and gradually Polyxo was despised.

"Now prayers were granted to the buried ashes; 328
now spirits of the dead accepted shrines.
The same occurs when female cattle tremble
to see the leader of their herd, their husband—

he who defeated other bulls and ruled
◆ their pasture—torn apart by a Massylian
lion: the maimed herd moves along, dishonored,
in silence, grieving for its king, whose loss
even the fields and rivers also mourn.

"Yet now the bronze prow of the son of Pelias, 335
the pinewood ship of Jason, cut the seas.
He came, a stranger, to our unknown waters.
◆ The Minyans, those Argonauts, rowed hard:
twin waves of foam turned white the ship's high bulwarks.
You would have thought Ortygia moved, torn from
her roots, or that a mountainside reached shore.
The oars stopped, and the sea was silent. Then 340
a voice came from the middle of the ship,
sweeter than that of swans before they die,
or Phoebus' harp. The seas themselves drew nigh.
There Orpheus, Oeagrus' son, was singing,
leaning against a mast amid the rowers,
persuading them to end their many labors.
Their path was north, toward Scythia. They were 346
the first to pass the Black Sea's tight approach
◆ between the islands called Symplegades.
This we learned later. At the time we thought
that they were warriors who came from Thrace.
We fled like birds to reach our homes. We ran
in various directions, like stampeding
cattle. Where were our Furies now, our anger?

"We climbed the lofty towers and the walls 350
that ring the port and shore where we could view
the open sea. Here anxious women brought
boulders and sharpened stakes, swords stained with blood,
the melancholy arms of men, and, unashamed,
they put on woven corselets and slipped helmets
over their faces as Athena watched.
She blushed at these audacious women. Mars
laughed on Mount Haemus, opposite—then our 358
rash madness ended, and our minds were freed.
We thought we saw the justice of the gods,
not just a ship, and we believed it sailed

the seas to punish us. Its distance from
the shore was what Gortynian arrows fly,
when Jupiter produced a heavy cloud
and set dark rain above the Greek ship's halyards.
The seas swelled high, and shadows veiled the sun,
and soon the missing sunlight dimmed the waves.
Winds slashed at concave clouds and rent the sea.
Black whirlpools stirred wet sand. The waters hung
suspended by opposing northern blasts;
high arching breakers almost reached the stars.
The vessel was uncertain of its course;
it tottered, and the Triton on its rostrum
drove deep into the sea or aimed at heaven.
The wild mast whipped the ship from side to side;
it heeled the gunwales underneath the swells
and forced men's chests against their useless oars.
The sailors faced fierce seas and southern winds— 376
those demigods, those heroes, lost their strength—
while we hurled weapons with weak arms from walls,
from every rock and hill. What did our hands
not dare? We aimed at Telemon and Peleus.
Hercules was a target of our arrows.
Because they fought the sea and fought a war,
some of them flanked the ship with banks of shields
while others bailed out water from below.
Some battled, but their bodies barely moved;
even a slight exertion drained their strength.

"We doubled our attack. Our iron rain 385
contended with the weather. Fire-hard stakes,
pieces of boulders, arrows, flaming missiles
that streamed like comets hit the ship and shore.
The covered vessel echoed, and the floorboards
within the battered ship's hold groaned, just as
when Jupiter lets northern snowfalls lash
farmlands of crops, and all the field beasts perish
along the plains: birds drop, caught by surprise;
frost ruins harvests; mountains roar; streams rise.

"But then, indeed, a lightning bolt, sent down 394
by Jupiter, tore through the clouds; its flash

revealed the great size of those mariners,
and our hearts stopped; our unaccustomed weapons
dropped from our falling hands, and we felt horror.
The nature of our sex returned to us.

♦ "We saw the sons of Aeacus: Telamon 398
and Peleus. We saw immense Ancaeus
threatening our walls, and Iphitus, who batted
boulders away with his long spear. But most
remarkable among that wondrous host
was Hercules, whose heavy weight inclined
the ship to either side. He seemed prepared
to leap into the sea. And there was Jason,
as yet unknown, who had not hurt me yet.
He moved with speed among the rowers' benches,
the oars and straining backs of comrades, shouting
encouragements and signaling commands
♦ to Meleager, Idas, and Talaus,
♦ and, dripping white sea foam, Tyndareus's son,
and Calais (Boreas' son), who worked aloft
inside his father's freezing clouds to reef
the sails along the mast. He and his sailors
attacked our walls and rowed, but those white waters
never subsided, and their spears bounced back.

♦ "Tiphys himself grew weary as his helm 413
could not control the ship. He struggled with
the stormy sea, grew pale, and many times
he had to counteract his own commands.
He steered the vessel left and right through crests
and turned the prow from rocks where it would wreck.

"Finally, the son of Aeson held the branch 416
of Pallas on the pointed bow, extending
the olive worn by Mopsus as a garland.
He asked for peace despite objections from
his friends; his words were overwhelmed by winds,
but then the weary weather quieted,
the fighting ended, and the sun returned
to heaven's clouds. The fifty moored their vessel
according to their custom, and the shore

trembled as they leaped off their ship's high stern,
eminent, elegant, nobly born—and now 424
that fear and rage did not disfigure them,
their faces shone, and their demeanor spoke.

"They say the gods emerge through secret doors
to visit Aethiopia's Red Sea shores,
the houses where they feast at minor banquets,
and all the rivers and the mountains ease
their passage and the lap of earth rejoices;
there Atlas, who sustains the heavens, rests.

"We saw proud Theseus, who had recently
freed Marathon. We saw the North Wind's children, 431
brothers from Thrace, whose temples sang with feathers
like red wings, and we saw Admetus, one
whom Phoebus granted precedence, and then
Orpheus, mild, unlike the other Thracians.
We saw the son of Calydon, then Peleus,
the son-in-law of Nereus. The twin
Oebalidae deceived our sight with their
confusing ambiguity: both Castor
and Pollux wore a purple cloak and carried
javelins, and they each exposed their shoulders;
their cheeks were shaved; their hair shone like twin stars.
Young Hylas tried to match the mighty stride
of Hercules, whose bulk made him move slowly.
He managed with some difficulty, bearing
Lernaean weapons, proud he could perspire
under the burden of a massive quiver.

"Venus, as a result, returned, and Cupid 445
with silent flames aroused love in
the hard hearts of the women left on Lemnos.
Juno allowed our minds to dwell on thoughts
of noble arms and manly dress, the signs
of breeding and distinction. We competed
to open up our doorways to these strangers.
We lit our altars and forgot the crimes
that for so long preoccupied our minds.
We feasted and slept well through quiet nights.

"We women told what happened, and the gods 452
protected us, I think. O gentlemen,
perhaps my destiny would interest you!
My error was excusable. I swear
upon the ashes and the Furies of my family,
I did not light a stranger's marriage torch
because of my desire or ill intent.
The gods know it was Jason's charming manner
that bound another virgin in his chains.
He broke the law in Phasis, spilling blood.
◆ In Colchis, he discovered other love.

"Soon frost had melted, and the stars were warmed 459
by longer days. The rapid year revolved.
Women made vows in childbirth, and a new,
unlooked-for generation cried in Lemnos.

"Brought to the marriage bed by force, and made 463
a mother by a brutal foreigner,
I bore twin sons, and I named one for his
grandfather. What their fortune is, or if
the Fates have let them live, who knows? Four times
the span of sixty months has passed since I
left them in Lemnos in Lycaste's care.

—◆—◆—◆—

"A milder, southern breeze allured the sails. 468
The spirit of the sea grew calm. The ship
disparaged quiet haven and delay;
she strained against the rock that held her chain.
The Argonauts were set to leave, and that vile
Jason assembled his adventurers.
I wish that waves had borne him past our shores,
for Jason never loved his children or
respected promises. His fame in far-
off nations is well known: he won the fleece,
the one that Phrixus carried overseas.

"On the appointed day, the sun set west; 476
Tiphys, the helmsman, sensed the coming breeze;

Phoebus descended to his scarlet bed.
Women lamented. It was night again.

"The order for departure came from Jason, 479
on his high deck, when day had hardly broken.
That leader was the first to lash the sea.

"From cliffs and from the highest mountain summits 481
we watched them cleave the foaming main's expanse
till light deceived our eyes and heaven seemed
to merge into the margin of the surface;
it blended in the distance with the ocean.

"There was a rumor running in the port 486
that said my father Thoas crossed the seas
◆ to Chios, to his brother, where he ruled;
that I had spared my parent; that the bier
I burned was empty. Driven crazy by
their sense of guilt, the common women called
for punishment and shamelessly complained.
The rabble's secret whisperings increased:
'Why must we mourn our dead while she alone 491
kept faith and saved her family? Were not
these things commanded by the gods and fate?
Why should that wicked woman rule our city?'

"Terrified by their murmurings—my royalty 493
useless against impending retribution—
I left the bloody walls and, unaccompanied,
wandered along the pathless shores in secret—
the route that I had followed with my father.
No Bacchus met me this time. I was seized—
I did not scream—by pirates on the beach,
who brought me to your shores to be a slave."

–◆–◆–◆–

These words, addressed to those Lernaean leaders, 499
allowed the Lemnian exile to assuage
her grief, but she forgot her absent baby.
The fault lay in the stars! Weary from playing,

he lay his heavy eyes and languid face
along the ground and fell asleep, while grasping,
within his little hand, a clump of grass.

♦ Meanwhile, a dragon born of earth, the sacred 506
curse of Achaean groves, appeared. He moved
with tract indented on the ground. He drew
his bulk first forward, then behind his torso.
Blue flames burned in his eyes, his jaws foamed green
with venom, three tongues flickered from curved teeth
arranged in triple rows, and from his brow
of burnished gold a gruesome crest protruded.

Along the Inachus the farmers say 511
he's sacred to the Thunderer, whom they
worship at woodland shrines in their small way,
and he protects them. Now the serpent slid
and looped around the temples of the gods;
his loose folds ravaged forests, crushing oaks,
huge ash trees, and his serpentine, coiled length
lay over rivers, bank to bank, which once
bubbled beneath his scales as he cut trenches.
But now, as Bacchus had commanded, all
the land was panting and the nymphs of streams
lay hidden in the dust. The serpent twisted
his convoluted curves on crumbling ground
and burned up with the heat of drying venom.

He wound and wandered where old swamps had been, 522
on burning lakes and buried springs, through valleys
empty of rivers. Now he raised his head,
uncertain, and he licked the liquid air.
The serpent scraped through groaning fields; he slid
along his belly on the ground in search
of fresh grass, and whichever way he turned
his scalding breath, fields died and pastures withered.

♦ His size recalled the dragon that divides 529
the Great Bear from the northern pole of heaven
and reaches to the other world's south winds,

or him whose coils contained the sacred horns
of Mount Parnassus, until you, Apollo,
pierced him a hundred times with wooden arrows.

Why has God given you, o little one, 534
by accident, the weight of such misfortune?
Were you, who had just reached the gates of life,
doomed by your enemy? Is this why you
for centuries were sacred to the Grecians
and why you earned so great a funeral?

The serpent did not know, but its long tail 538
struck you and killed you, child! At once
sleep left your limbs; you opened up your eyes,
only to die, but first your frightened cries
were carried through the air, and when they ceased,
your voice fell silent, as occurs in dreams.

Hypsipyle was listening; she breathed 544
softly, too sick to run; her knees grew weak.
Convinced that something awful, some ill omen,
had happened, she looked everywhere; she crossed
the fields repeating words the infant knew
but found no sign of him. The child was gone.

Meanwhile, her sluggish enemy, the dragon, 549
stretched over several acres in a circle
of venom, with his neck back on his belly,
unmoving, unafraid, despite the screams
of awful fear resounding through the forest.

The Argives' ears, however, heard her wails 554
of misery, and the Arcadian,
Parthenopaeus, at his leader's urging,
took off at once, then brought back his report.

And now the dragon turned his scaly neck 556
toward flashing weapons and the sounds of men.
With great strength, huge Hippomedon uplifted
a boundary marker stone and hurtled it

through empty air, just as a catapult
casts balanced boulders at a city's doors
in wartime. But the hero's strength was useless.
The dragon drew its head back. It avoided
the blow, which tore a pathway through the forest
of tangled branches till it struck the earth.

"Even if giants join you and assault me,
you won't avoid *my* blows," cried Capaneus, 565
who held his ash spear out and faced the serpent,
"wherever you inhabit fearful groves
or entertain the gods—oh, yes, those gods!"

His quivering weapon took advantage of 570
the monster's open jaws; it flew inside
and slit the sinews of its triple tongues;
it exited his brilliant head and crest,
draining black blood and brains, and pierced the earth.
The pain had scarcely reached its total length,
when it threw rapid coils around the spear,
extracted it, and took it to its cave,
the temple of the god, where all was dark.
There its great bulk collapsed; the creature sighed,
lay down before its master's shrine, and died.

Lerna's swamps (kindred spirits) mourned the serpent, 579
as did the Nemean fields where it had crawled
and Nymphs whose vernal flowers covered it.
O woodland Fauns, you groaned and dashed your pipes!

Jupiter—even he, in his high heaven— 584
gathered the clouds of winter, called for weapons,
but then dismissed his anger. Capaneus
must be preserved for greater punishment.
One lightning bolt, however, cut the air
and blew aside his towering helmet crest.

Already the unhappy Lemnian 588
had wandered over many fields in which
the serpent once had dwelled; then she beheld,
not far away, a grass knoll stained with blood.

Carried away by grief, her face grown pale, 591
she hurried there, and when she recognized
the tragedy, she tumbled, thunderstruck,
on the offending earth, incapable
of weeping or of speaking, only seeking
life in the baby's limbs, still warm. She leaned
over him, giving kiss on kiss, although his skin
was rent, and she could not distinguish his
face or his chest. She viewed his tender bones—
his fresh blood dripped in beads along his tendons—
as when a bird returns to her holm oak 599
within whose shady leaves a tedious snake
has ravaged her young brood and torn her nest;
she marvels at the quiet of her home;
she hovers, in confusion; then, dismayed
and horrified, she drops the food her beak
has carried; she sees blood around her tree
and floating feathers drape her captured nest.

When she upheld his torn limbs to her breast 605
and veiled him with her tresses, she expressed
her grief and let her groans form words. At last:

◆ "Archemorus, sweet image of my sons!
You were a solace for my loneliness,
my country, all I'd lost. You were my one
reward for servitude. What guilty gods
have murdered you, my joy, whom I had left
playing and crawling, worrying the grass?
Where are your star-bright eyes? those words you half 613
pronounced? your laughter and your murmurings
only I understood? How many times
did I discourse of Lemnos and the *Argo*
and sing you lulling songs so you would sleep?
You were my consolation, little one!
I nursed you at my breast. Now you are gone;
my milk comes down in vain; it trickles on
your injuries like melancholy rain!

"I recognize the workings of the gods. 620
My dreams have been portentous, fearful nightmares.

There always is some cause when Venus comes
and shows herself in shadows to amaze me.

"Which gods should I reprove? Why should not I 624
confess, who am to die, that it was I
who left you unattended to your fate?
What madness overcame my mind? Can great
preoccupations cause such disregard?
I—who retold my country's history
and my ambitious origins and fame—
o Lemnos, I excuse you for your crimes!

"Gentlemen, if you all appreciate 628
my worthiness and hardships, if my words
have stirred your gratitude, place me before
the deadly snake or kill me with your swords,
but do not make me face the family
whose slave I am or see Eurydice
in her bereavement—though she cannot grieve
more than I do. Am I to bear the weight
of this dead baby to its mother's lap?
May earth first bury me beneath deep shades!"

Blood and dirt grimed her face while she was speaking, 635
then silently she turned and walked behind
those princes as they mourned—those men she blamed
for what the journey to the river cost her.

—♦—♦—♦—

News reached the household of devout Lycurgus 638
and left him and his family in tears.
He was returning from the sacred heights
♦ of Perseus's mountain, where the Thunderer
had angrily refused his sacrifice.
He wondered why the entrails were averse.

He had remained aloof, while Argives armed, 643
to tend his shrines and temples—not a coward,
but mindful of responses of the gods
and ancient warnings given by a voice

that from beneath his altar spoke: "Lycurgus,
the first death in the Dircean war is yours!"
He heeded, but it tortured him to see
the dust of Mars so near, and he felt envy
for those whom trumpets forewarned death in battle.

See how the gods maintain their promises! 650
She who'd escorted Thoas now conveyed
the lacerated remnants of a baby
before his mother and her women and
long lines of mourners. How his pious heart
impelled Lycurgus! He was overwhelmed
but held paternal tears back and advanced
despite his frenzied anger and his pain
with quick steps over intervening fields.

He cried out, "Where is she for whom my blood
matters so little, who rejoices in
my harm? Is she still living? Seize her then,
and bring her quickly, friends! I'll put an end
to all her tales of Lemnos and her father,
her lies and pride in sacred origins!"

He raged, his sword was out, and he stepped forward, 660
about to murder her, when Tydeus
stopped him and rammed his shield against his chest:
the Oenian hero quickly intervened,
gnashing his teeth, and saying, "Stop this madness,
whoever you may be. Don't play the fool!"

Now Capaneus backed him up, and brutal 664
Hippomedon held out his sword, as did
Parthenopaeus, and the flashing glints
weakened Lycurgus's will, and that of his
supporters, who were only farmers, till
mild-mannered King Adrastus intervened.

Amphiaraus, who respected him 669
because they both were augurers, exclaimed:
"Desist, I pray you! Put away your swords!
We are one people. Do not yield to anger.

Tydeus, you first!" But Tydeus could not ever
control himself. "She saved a kingdom and
her father Thoas. Glorious Bacchus was
the founder of her race. She was our guide,
the savior of the Argive troops. And do
you think that to avenge so small a death,
all these ungrateful troops will let you stain
a gravesite with her blood? You are a coward!
Armies move everywhere, but you alone
have peace in time of war. That should suffice!
No doubt when we return victorious,
we'll find you blaming fate at your son's tomb!"

He spoke. Lycurgus answered, but his speech 680
was moderate, his rage restrained: "Indeed,
I did not realize your goal was Thebes.
I took you for a hostile force. Proceed
with your destruction, if your pleasure is
the blood of kindred. Stain your civil swords.
What is not lawful? Exile piety,
for it has long been useless. Burn Jove's temples.
I thought I was my low slave's lord and master,
but that sticks in your throat and makes you grieve.
The king of gods sees your audacity.
His anger may be slow, but it will be."

He spoke, then looked back at his city, where 689
another contest echoed from the roofs.
It seemed like war. Fresh Rumor had outstripped
the flying wings of horsemen, and her pinions
transported trouble of two kinds. Some said
Hypsipyle was carried to her fate;
some said she was about to die—as she
deserved. Some gave the rumors credence, and
their anger was immediate. Their javelins
and torches struck the palace of the king.
The people called for revolution, to
topple Lycurgus and his shrines to Jove.
The buildings echoed with the chants of women.
Grief for the boy gave way to fear of war.

A chariot, drawn by wing-footed steeds, 699
carried Adrastus high above the crowds
of raging warriors. He brought the daughter
of Thoas to their midst and cried, "Desist,
desist! No outrage has been done. Lycurgus
does not deserve death. Here you may observe
the one who found the river that preserved us!"

At times diverging tempests—Boreas, 704
Eurus, and Auster—darken seas with rain,
day vanishes, and winter weather reigns.
The high king of the ocean guides his steeds,
◆ and by his foaming reins the two-formed Triton
signals the waves he swims to moderate:
◆ Thetis lies flat; the coasts and hillsides rise.

Which of the gods to whom she prayed consoled 710
her losses and requited tears? You, Bacchus,
the founder of her people, made her fate
miraculous, by carrying her twins
from Lemnean shores to Nemea. They'd traveled
to find their mother, and Lycurgus had
given them hospitality before
he heard a messenger inform him that
his son, dismembered horribly, had died.

The minds of men are blind to destiny. 714
The sons of Jason offered their support,
favored the king, but when they heard the sound
of "Lemnos," the word "Thoas," they rushed past
the weapons and the soldiers to embrace
their mother in their eager arms. They wept
and hugged her, alternating, each in turn.

Like some rock cliff, she could not move her face, 723
dared not believe the gods to whom she prayed.
Her mourning ended when she recognized
their faces, Jason's shoulders, and some signs
of Argos on the swords that Jason owned.
She fell down, overcome by her good fortune,
and tears were overflowing from her eyes.

Heaven gave demonstrations of the god, 729
and joyous revels echoed through the air,
the sound of cymbals, and the beat of drums.

When silence settled on the angry mob, 731
Amphiaraus, pious son of Oecleus,
addressed attendant ears: "Hear what Apollo
commands you and makes clear that you must do,
o king of Nemea, and chosen Argive
leaders! This tragedy has not been un-
appointed from of old. Straight runs the line
drawn by the Parcae, who control our fate.
The drought, the interdicted streams, the snake
that kills, the little boy, whom it is now
our destiny to name Archemorus:
all these descended from the gods' high minds.
Postpone your purpose. Lay aside your weapons.
This infant must have honors that endure.
Truth is, he merits them. Let Virtue's hands
pour out libations, blessings to the gods.

"Continue interweaving more delays, 742
o Phoebus. Keep us out of fortune's frays,
and let the thought of Thebes just fade away.

"But you, o happy couple, whose good fortune 746
surpasses that of other noble parents,
your name will be remembered through the centuries.
While there is swamp at Lerna and a current 748
for father Inachus, while Nemea's
shadows fall trembling on the ground, do not
profane these sacred rites with weeping or
be plaintive to the gods, for he himself,
your own son, is a god. He'd not have wanted
old age to be his destiny, like Nestor,
or live long years, as Priam will." He ended.

Dark veiled the infant's shade. The night descended.

–♦–♦–♦–

BOOK 6 Funeral Games

The Argives found the Nemean games in honor of the infant Archemorus. The mourning of King Lycurgus and his wife Eurydice. Two funeral pyres. The parade of figures from the history of Argos. The chariot race won by Amphiaraus, the prophet. Parthenopaeus, the Arcadian, wins the foot race. Hippomedon wins the discus. Capaneus boxes. Tydeus is the champion wrestler, despite his smallness. The omen of Adrastus's arrow: he alone will return.

Far-wandering Rumor flew through Grecian cities.
The men of Argos, sons of Inachus,
would solemnize, with games, the infant's death.
Their purpose—to prepare for war, perspire
beforehand, lend their fortitude some fire.
◆ Such contests were the custom of the Greeks. 5

The pious Hercules was first to fight
in Pisan fields for glory; there he wiped
◆ wild olive leaves across his dusty forehead.

The next games were in honor of Apollo, 8
whose bow and arrows, when he was a boy,
freed Phocis from the tangles of a serpent.

Dark, superstitious rites began in Corinth, 10
soon after Delphi and Olympia,
to serve Palaemon, where Leucothea
would sojourn in the time of festival
on friendly shores and moan. Her lamentations
would shake both sides of Isthmos, and sad Thebes,
Echion's city, would reecho these.

–◆–◆–◆–

And now the leading men, whose breeding gives 15
Argos a link to heaven, men whose names

grieve mothers in Aonia and Thebes,
joined in their naked prowess to compete.
So bireme ships that dare the unknown seas,
Tyrrhenian rainstorms, or the smooth Aegean,
first practice on a tranquil lake and learn
to row together, steer, and handle danger.
Only with this experience do they
attempt upswelling waves and distances
where shores fade and no longer hold their gaze.

The horn of Sleep was empty. He and Night 25
left heaven as the chariot of bright
Aurora brought day labor, and pale light
the wakeful horses of the goddess cast
pursued them. Lamentation in the streets,
low sounds of groaning in the mournful palace
sounded through pathless forests far away
and there reechoed. He, the father, sat
divested of the honor of his fillets,
covered with ashen grime. His face was filthy,
his beard unkempt. More bitter was his wife:
her lamentations stirred her female servants 33
to act as if they too were childless parents.
She longed to lie on top of her torn baby;
she would have done so, but they led her off.
Even the king condemned her excess grief.

Soon the Inachian leadership arrived 37
and they behaved with solemn dignity,
but when they reached the inner atria
it was as if the infant died again,
as if the fatal serpent had slipped in
to scourge him with another deadly blow.
The cries redoubled, although breasts were weary.
One followed from the next until the sounds
combined and made the doors reverberate.
The Greeks sensed this ill-will and showed
their own tears in atonement for their crime.

As often as the stricken house was silent, 45
during the intermissions in the tumult,

Adrastus offered words of consolation
to King Lycurgus, uselessly observing
how hard Fate makes men's lives, how short
the thread of life lasts, saying gods would grant
permanent pledges to him, other children,
but even as he spoke, laments renewed,
and he was listened to no more than are
Ionian sailors' vows when fierce seas seethe
or slender clouds no wandering lightnings heed.

It was with sadness that the infant's bier—
the bed on which he would be burned—was wrapped
◆ with branches and young cypress. Country fruits 54
lay deep and green upon that site, beneath
a more painstaking layer of woven grass,
a colored mound of flowers that will fade.
A third layer was arranged of eastern spices, 59
the riches of Arabia, white glebes
of incense, and Egyptian cinnamon.
Gold crinkled in the canopy they raised, 62
soft cloth of Tyrian purple, which displayed,
among acanthus leaves and polished jewels,
◆ an infant Linus and the hounds of death—
ill omens that his mother always hated.
Despite its craft, she would avert her gaze.

The pyre was circled by ancestral arms 67
and relics—monuments of glory dimmed
by suffering and family defeats—
as if the weight of great, enormous limbs
were borne within the coffin, not an infant.

The mourners celebrated him despite
his nonaccomplishments and barren fame
and with their pomp enhanced the infant's shade.
And thus with joyful sorrowing, with tears 72
of exaltation, they bore gifts for burning
more precious than his years. His prayers too hasty,
his father had already dedicated
a quiver and a small-scale spear to him
and arrows that knew no impieties

and stabled horses of the best-known breeds:
he'd kept these in his name with belts of bells
and armor that would wait till he grew strong.
His mother'd had great expectations also: 79
what clothes had she not ordered, in her zeal,
cut out of purple cloth, inwoven with
royal insignia? She'd even chosen
a little scepter. Now her cruel husband
ordered it all conveyed to those dark flames,
as if this desecration could erase
the misery that made his mind feel crazed.

–◆–◆–◆–

Elsewhere the Argive army, at the urging 84
of its wise augur, built an airy pyre
high as a mountain, made of fallen forests
and trunks of trees, to burn away their guilt—
they'd killed a sacred snake!—and to appease
◆ the deities for their ill-fated war.

They lay the groves of shady Nemea 88
to earth, and with their efforts, they exposed
its valleys to the sun; they now cut down
a virgin forest, ancient growth no ax
had ever touched, whose shades were thicker than
in any vale between the Argolis
and Mount Lycaeos, where trees reach the stars.

◆ Sacred it stood, divine with age. They say 93
not only ancestors of men, but nymphs
and flocks of fauns dwelled there in olden days.
The metamorphosed ones remained, but ruin
and misery now overcame the forest;
the wild beasts fled; fear drove birds from warm nests;
great beeches fell, as did old oaks and cypresses
that winter does not harm. Pitch pines were hewn
to feed the funeral flame; and mountain ash
and trunks of holm oak, yews with poison sap,

and those ash trees that drink cursed blood in wars
as well as oaks impervious to rot.

They cleaved the daring firs, the pines whose wounds 104
are scented, vine-propped elms, and alder trees
that lower to the earth their unshorn branches.
♦ Earth groaned, and more trees fell than on Ismara
when Boreas escapes his broken cave;
the trees fell faster than nocturnal flames
incited by the roll of southern winds.

♦ Hoar Pales, deity of shepherds, left 111
the pleasant leisure of the groves. So did
♦ Silvanus, king of shadows, and the flocks
of demigods, and as they went, the forest
despaired and moaned, for trees could not release
the nymphs from their embrace. It was as when
a leader gives the signal to his troops
to sack a conquered town. The victors scarcely
hear it before the city disappears.
Without restraint they enter, raze, take flight:
they bear off loot with more noise than they fight.

Their work produced two pyres of equal size, 118
one for sad ghosts, one heaven's deities.
Then the low murmur of a spiral flute—
the Phrygian custom when an infant dies—
signaled the start of mourning. It is said
King Pelops instituted this sad chant
and funeral ritual, the same used when
Niobe brought twelve urns to Sipylus,
♦ where she mourned when two quivers had undone her.

Grecian commanders carried offerings 126
on platters, sacrifices for the flames.
Their titles and their honorable names
served as a testament, and then the bier,
after a lengthy interval, was borne
upon the shoulders of young men the king

himself selected from his multitudes.
The clamor was ferocious. Lernaean
princes enclosed Lycurgus. Gentle women
walked with his queen; nor was Hypsipyle
without her followers; the Argive women
protected her and showed consideration;
her sons held her bruised arms, and they endured
the lamentations of their newfound mother.

At that point, having left her fatal palace, 135
Eurydice, breast bare, began to speak,
a prelude to more moans and longer wailings:

"I never, son, in my most foolish dreams
imagined anything this horrible:
to follow you, surrounded by a train
of Argive matrons! How could I have known
at this time in my life that I would need
to worry you'd be harmed by war in Thebes?
To which god is it sweet to make us bleed
in battle? Who has sworn to harm our army?

"The house of Cadmus has not yet known grief 144
for any Tyrian infant born in Thebes!
The first to suffer tears and bitter death—
before the horns have played, before a sword
is drawn—is me, for I am she who trusted
a nurse to take my baby to her breast!

"Why not? The woman told us how her tricks 149
had saved her father from an evil mob,
and we believed that she alone abjured
the ritual of death—that she, alone,
was guiltless of the madness that seized Lemnos.

"Can you believe that one so brave, so pious, 152
could be so reckless as to leave behind
in unattended fields a lord and king—
as well as someone else's child? She was
so negligent! She left him on a path

of peril in the forest, where he might
be killed not only by an awful serpent—
whose mass more than sufficed to cause his death—
but by strong breezes, falling limbs when north
winds blow, or baseless fears. I am bereft,
but I blame nobody except the nurse
who cast on me this long, unhealing curse!

"My son, you liked her best, knew only her. 161
I never shared the joys of motherhood.
Hers was the voice you heard; mine was unknown.
That impious woman knew your laughter, cries,
and tears; she heard the sound of your first words;
she was your mother while you were alive.
Now I am she—and miserable that I
can't punish her as she deserves! Great men,
why do you bear these offerings, these empty
gifts to the fire? His ghost demands no less
than her—his nurse. I ask, I plead! you leaders,
by this first death of war, the son I bore,
sacrifice her to me (the murdered mother)
and to his ashes. Let Ogygian matrons
mourn at their funerals as I have mourned!"

She tore her hair, and she renewed her prayer: 173
"Bestow her, but don't call me cruel or say
I seek her blood. I will go down to death—
let us be cast within a single fire—as long
as I can satisfy my eyes that she
feels punishment!" Her voice resounded; she
made gestures at Hypsipyle, who grieved
elsewhere, far off (for she too tore her hair
and beat her breast). Indignant that she shared
her pain, Eurydice continued, "Grant 180
me this, at least, great men! Behold this woman,
who flung away the treasure of my marriage:
banish her from these rites, and keep her distant,
far from our sight! Why should that woman's presence
pollute our mourning and offend a parent?"

She spoke. At once her lamentations ceased, 185
and she was like the mother of a calf
that still sucked milk from which it drew its strength,
however little. When her calf is captured
by some wild beast or shepherd for his altar,
the lonely mother wanders over valleys
and mourns beside the rivers; now she asks
the herds for news; she questions empty pastures
and lingers in the fields of desolation,
which she is last to leave; she can't endure
her stable and refuses food before her.

Father Lycurgus, though, was strong enough 193
to cast his finest scepter in the flames
along with badges of the Thunderer.
His long hair, which hung back and down his chest,
he cut off with a knife and let the locks
drop on the tender limbs of his dead son,
and doing so he mingled words with tears:
"Perfidious Jupiter, I dedicated
my hair to you for other reasons, when
I vowed to make a present to your temple—
if you consented—of my son's first beard.
I prayed in vain; the priest did not respond.
My son's ghost merits these tufts more than you!"

The first torch lit the faggots. Flames exploded. 202
Stiff task to hold the frenzied parents back!
Danaans under orders raised their weapons
to bar the dreadful sight and maintain distance.
There never was a fire as opulent;
the flames grew rich: jewels popped, massed silver melted;
embroidered needlework exuded gold;
over piled logs Assyrian nectars dripped;
hot honey hissed pale saffron; foaming bowls
of wine were overturned, and vessels poured
dark blood and fresh-drawn milk the lost boy welcomed.
Greek kings, their arms reversed, led seven squadrons—
a hundred horsemen rode in each—according

to custom, in a leftward ring, beside
tall flames, and they kicked dust upon the pyre.

Three times they made their circle, then they struck 217
their weapons on their weaponry four times,
causing a horrid crash of armor while
four times the women's forearms beat soft breasts.

The other altar burned half-living flocks 220
and breathing animals. Amphiaraus,
the prophet, ordered lamentations cease,
because he recognized the signs, the true
omens of future funerals. The riders
wheeled to the right and shook their spears. Each one
removed a token from his armament
to throw into the fire—the shadowing
crest of a lofty helmet, reins, a bridle.

♦ [Surrounding fields emit concordant groans. 227
Sharp trumpets strike the ear. Their clamor
frightens the forests. Horns uproot the standards
of battle. Rage is not yet hot, or swords
reddened by blood. The first face of the war
is that of honor. Mars sits on high clouds,
uncertain of which side he will support.]

And then it ended. Mulciber, the god 234
of fire, exhausted, turned to pliant cinders.
The flames were beaten out; the pyre was drenched
with water. Men worked wearily till sunset
and scarcely finished as the shadows lengthened.

♦ Nine times had Lucifer already chased 238
damp stars from heaven. He had heralded
moonlight and changed his horses and had not
deceived the conscious stars, who understood
that he who rose and set were one, the same.

It was a miracle how fast they worked.
They made a monument of stone—a great

temple to hold the ashes—and incised
the history of what had happened. Here
Hypsipyle shows weary Greeks a river;
there is the infant they will weep for, crawling,
then sleeping, as the scaly serpent digs
through earth around a hillside. You'd expect
to hear its bloody mouth hiss as it winds
itself around a marble spear and dies.

–♦–♦–♦–

Now Rumor called the multitudes away 249
from field and city, people keen to view
♦ the unarmed contests, those whom youth or age
kept home, who did not know the horror of war.
They came—more than would gather for
the Isthmian or the Olympian games.

There was a vale surrounded by a ridge 255
of rugged forests and encircling mountains
that formed a crown, a soft embrace, a seat.
A berm marked out by pairs of boundary stones
embraced a long and level field. It sloped
up gently, winding, with no sudden drops,
and shaped a summit, soft with living turf.

Dawn, and the sun's red rays traversed the field. 261
Cohorts of soldiers sat there, pressed together,
and as they saw their numbers and each other's
faces and uniforms, they felt some pleasure;
their confidence renewed, and they felt better.

One hundred black bulls, strongest of the herd, 265
slowly paraded, then an equal number
of cows of that same color with their calves
whose brows were not yet crescented by horns.

♦ A series of amazing effigies 269
was borne along, the likenesses
of high-souled ancient ancestors.
The first was Hercules, whose strong embrace

crushes a gasping lion, breaks his bones.
The Argives found it frightening to view
that figure, not a real man, only bronze—
and they were his descendants! Next in order
was father Inachus, reclining on
his left side by a mound of brookside reeds.
They showed him pouring water from his urn.
Io was next, already on all fours, and she
◆ saw starry Argus, ever vigilant,
behind her, and her father grieved. But then
in Pharian fields in Egypt, Jupiter
lifted her kindly, and Aurora kissed her.

Now father Tantalus was drawn along, 280
not he who hovers near deceiving waves
or snatches at the air when trees recede,
but the great Thunderer's guest, a pious man.

Elsewhere triumphant Pelops drove the reins 283
and car of Neptune, while the charioteer
◆ Myrtilos grappled for his swimming wheels
but fell behind the faster vehicle.
◆ Then came the grave Acrisius, and the harsh
face of Coroebus. They showed Danaë,
◆ and rain poured on her lap. Amymone
appeared in sadness by the stream she'd found.
Alcmena held the infant Hercules,
her pride and joy, and three moons veiled her hair.
◆ The sons of Belus shook discordant hands,
a truce of enmity. Aegyptus stood
nearby with milder aspect, but the face
of Danaus revealed his treachery:
he planned a future evening of destruction!
Unnumbered pageants satisfied the soldiers,
but then their prowess called the best to contests.

—◆—◆—◆—

The sweat of horses first. Recite, Apollo, 296
the names of famous riders and their steeds.

There never was a gathering of more 297
noble, wing-footed horses. These resembled
a flock of birds aligned in V-formation,
or Aeolus, whose mad winds clash on shore.

Leading the others, clearly visible 301
because his red mane flamed, Arion pranced.
His lord, they say, was Neptune and the first
to hurt his tender mouth with his sharp curb:
he tamed that horse along a sandy shore
without a whip, for his desire to race
could not be satisfied—he was inconstant,
like winter waves, and joined with swimming steeds
he often drew his blue-haired master safely
through the Ionic and the Libyan seas
while storm clouds marveled to be left behind
and north and south winds struggled to pursue.
With equal speed he carried Hercules, 311
son of Amphitryon, when he engaged
◆ in King Eurystheus's toils and traced deep furrows
through meadowlands. Even to him he was
disorderly and difficult to hold,
but soon—a gift of heaven—he accepted
the rule of King Adrastus. He grew tame
with age till on this day the king permitted
his son-in-law to ride him—yet he gave
warning to Polynices not to raise
a stern hand should the horse bolt, but use skill,
the arts of riding. "Do not let him free
and off the bit!" he warned. "Urge other steeds
with whips and threats! This horse has all the speed
you'll need!" In just that way, Apollo gave
◆ his happy son his fiery reins and car
but wept while he instructed him which stars
were treacherous, which zones could not be crossed,
and what was temperate between the poles.
His son was pious, duly cautious, but
young, and the harsh Fates would not let him learn.

The next contestant for the palm wore white, 326
harnessed white horses, and wore bands of wool

whose color matched his casque and crested plume:
Amphiaraus, guiding Spartan horses.
◆ These were your offspring, Cyllarus, begotten
by stealth when Castor, by the shores of distant
◆ Scythia, traded Amyclean reins
for oars along the Black Sea where he sailed.

Admetus, blessed with steeds of Thessaly, 332
could hardly curb his barren mares, offspring
of Centaurs, it was said. They scorned their sex
and used their female heat to fashion strength.
They were like night and day, dark-grained and white,
so bright they could be easily believed
to stem from that same herd that would not eat
as long as they, enchanted and amazed,
could hear Apollo play Castalian reeds.

The next were sons of Jason, whom their mother 340
Hypsipyle had recently discovered.
The name of Thoas was one's mother's father;
Euneos was a word derived from *Argo*.
Their faces, horses, chariots, and clothes
and equal and harmonious vows to win—
or come in second only to a brother—
made the twins similar in all they did.

Here were Hippodamus and Chromis—one 346
descended from great Hercules, the other
from Oenomaus. Who could tell which one
handled his reins more fiercely? Getic steeds,
bred by Diomedes, for one; the other
had horses from his Pisan father. Stains
of blood marred both war carts—and foul remains.

One of the goalposts was a strong, bare oak, 351
whose branches had been stripped; opposed, a stone
protuberance, the kind that limits fields.
It was the length four javelins could reach
or three times longer than an arrow's flight.

—◆—◆—◆—

Meanwhile the singing of Apollo charmed
the Muses, in their glorious assembly.
He touched his strings, and gazed down from Parnassus,
then sang the first beginnings of the gods,
for often he had sung of Jupiter,
or Phlegra, or his own fight with the serpent,
or told, with piety, his brothers' deeds.

He opened with what spirit moves the stars,
the bolts of lightning, what soul animates
the rivers, feeds the winds, provides the source
of life for oceans. He revealed the sun's
pathways that hurry nightfall or delay it
and how the universe holds middle earth
deep down and bounded by an unseen world.

He finished, and although the Sisters wished
to hear more, he dismissed them and removed
the laurel from his instrument, unwove
the chaplet from his bright head, and released
his waist's embroidered girdle. Then he saw,
in Nemea, the land of Hercules,
commotion—not far off—a great assembly
of four-horse chariots prepared for racing.

By chance Amphiaraus and Admetus
stood in a nearby field. Apollo knew them
and asked himself, "What god put these two kings,
my loyal followers, in competition?
Both men are pious. Both are dear to me.
I do not know which one should be preferred!
When I served in the fields of Pelias,
as Jove ordained, and midnight Fates desired,
one offered incense—though I was a servant—
and never made me feel inferior.
The other is companion of the tripod,
a faithful student, skilled in augury.
The merits of the one should be preferred,
but then, the other's thread of life is short.
Admetus will receive old age, die late,

but you, Amphiaraus, have no space
for joy between the dark abyss and Thebes.
◆ You know this; you have heard the sad birds sing!"

He spoke, and his hard face, unused to tears, 384
was moist. Then suddenly he bounded through
the brilliant air to Nemea, more swift
than his own arrows or his father's lightning.
He landed as the skies retained his traces;
the winds revealed his brilliant path of flight.

–◆–◆–◆–

Prothous tumbled markers in a bronze 389
helmet to choose positions for the start.
Horses and drivers were their countries' finest,
descendants of the gods. Their hearts unsettled,
with nervous confidence and hope, they waited.
Enclosed, they strained to be released as chills
ran through their limbs—not only fear but thrills.

The horses shared the passion of their masters. 396
Flames filled their eyes. Bits rattled in their mouths.
Blood and saliva scalded bridle rings.
They pressed the posts and scarce-resisting gates
and exhaled rage like smoke. Distraught, they waited,
and lost a thousand steps before they started;
their heavy hooves upchurned the absent fields!
Trusted attendants smoothed their knotted manes,
settled their spirits, whispered, planned their race.

Tyrrhenian trumpets played; the steeds leaped forward. 404
What sails at sea, what weaponry in battle,
what clouds so swiftly race across the sky?
There is less force in winter streams and fire;
stars fall more slowly, so do drops of rain
and rivers from high summits to the plains.

The Grecians watched them start but soon lost sight 410
of separate horses in the blinding dust.

A single cloud obscured them, one so dark
they scarcely saw or heard each other's cries.
Then the pack thinned. The chariots formed lines.

The second circuit smoothed out former furrows. 415
The eager drivers leaned and touched their yokes,
flexed with their knees, and doubled tight-held reins.
Neck muscles bulged. Winds combed the flying manes;
◆ wheels squealed; hooves pounded; parched earth drank white rain.
Hands never paused; whips whistled through the air.
Cold hail does not fall faster in north winds
nor water tumble from the horns of winter.

Astute Arion could detect the guilt 424
of Polynices, son of Oedipus,
the dreadful foreigner who held his reins.
He felt his future, and he was afraid,
unruly from the start, as his oppression
angered him more than usual. The Greeks
thought him provoked by praise, but he was fleeing
his driver, running mad, his unrestraint
threatening his charioteer, while through the field
he searched for King Adrastus, his right master.

Amphiaraus came before the others, 431
but he was far behind in second place.
Admetus, the Thessalian, raced with him.
Then came the twins; now Euneos was first,
now Thoas. One advanced; one fell behind.
◆ Though each desired to win, they never clashed.
Desperate Chromis and Hippodamus
followed, slowed by their horses' weight, not lack
of talent, and Hippodamas, out front,
could feel the heat of panting mouths behind him.

The auger of Apollo hoped to take 440
the shorter, inside path around the goal
by drawing in his reins so he could pass,
and the Thessalian hero, too, perceived

an opportunity because Arion
ran unrestrained in circles to the right.

Amphiaraus was first, Admetus now 445
no longer third, but they were passed, their joy
short-lived, as Neptune's horse rejoined the circuit
from which he'd strayed. The crowd rose to its feet;
the heavens shook and tumult struck the stars.

No longer could the Theban Polynices 450
manage his reins or dare to use his whip,
like an exhausted helmsman who no longer
looks to the stars but only hopes for luck
while sea waves sweep his ship against black rocks.

Again they circled right in full career 454
and strove to hold their course around the field.
Axles collided; treacherous spokes struck wheels;
a thousand horsehooves pounded on the plain.
The riders feared, and also threatened, murder.
Their craving for renown was unrelenting.
Their violence was equally intense
as when they went to war with horrid weapons.

They needed more than whips; they shouted names: 460
Admetus called on Iris, Pholoë,
and Thoë, his best trace horse. The Danaan
augurer urged on Cygnus, that white steed,
and Ascheton. The son of Hercules—
that's Chromis—called on Strymon. Euneos
shouted for fiery Aetion. Thoas named
dappled Podarces, and Hippodamus
pressured slow Cydon. In his chariot,
only Echion's son maintained sad silence,
afraid his voice would tremble as he swerved.

The horses were just starting their true task 469
as they began the fourth, most dusty lap.
Limbs weary, hot with sweat, their thirsty throats

flaming, they found their forward progress flagged;
thick clouds of vapor marked their respirations,
and constant panting flattened out their flanks.

Now wavering Fortune, which had only watched, 474
first dared to intervene. As Thoas strove
madly to pass Admetus, his car crashed,
nor could his brother help, although he tried.
He failed because Mars-like Hippodamus
obstructed him, and his car intervened.

Then Chromis, using all his father's strength— 479
the might of Hercules—locked axles with
Hippodamus to take inside position
going around the goal. Their horses fought
to free themselves. They tensed their necks and bridles
to no effect, as when the tides detain
Sicilian vessels while the north wind rages
and swollen sails stand motionless at sea.

Then Chromis flipped the other's chariot 485
and raced ahead, but when the Thracian steeds
saw that Hippodamus had fallen, hunger
came over them. They would have madly ripped
their charioteer to pieces where he lay
had Chromis not retrieved them by their bridles.
He quit, defeated, but he earned high praise.

The race drew close; the winner was uncertain. 491
It was Apollo's wish, Amphiaraus,
that you should have the victory he'd promised.
He thought the time was right to favor you
and there within the dusty circuit's confines
he called from hell, or cunningly constructed,
the figure of a monstrous, crested serpent.
Its face was horrible to see. A thousand terrors
clung to this wicked thing he brought to light.

Neither dark Lethe's fearful guardian, 498
the horses of the sun, the team of Mars,
or Furies could have seen it undismayed.

Arion's golden mane stood stiff as he 501
stopped at the sight. He lifted up his shoulders
and raised his yoke companion and the other
horses who shared his labor by his side.
This forced the exile from Aonia to fall
and tear away the reins that crossed his back,
and, disattached, his chariot escaped 506
as he lay in the dust. The other cars—
from Taenaros and Thessaly and Lemnos—
avoided him by swerving just off course.

He managed to uplift his clouded head
after assistance reached him and to pry
his weak limbs from the ground before returning,
unlooked for, to Adrastus, his wife's father.

Theban, the place was fit for you to die, 513
if harsh Tisiphone had not denied it.
Think how much warfare could have been avoided!
You would have been lamented by your brother,
for all to see, as well as Argos, Thebes,
and Nemea. Like suppliants Larissa
and Lerna would have offered you their hair.
The funeral Archemorus was given
would not have equaled what yours would have been.

Truly Amphiaraus, son of Oecleus, 518
tried to defeat the empty car as well,
though victory was certain as he followed
Arion, driverless, who raced ahead.
Phoebus lent strength, refreshing him. He drove
fast as an eastern wind, as if the gate
has just been dropped, the race has just begun.
With lash and reins he whipped the backs and manes
of fleet Ascheton and his snow-white Cygnus.

Now that the prophet raced in front alone 525
his hot wheels tore the track and scattered sand.
Earth groaned—a warning, a fierce premonition—
and Cygnus might have come in first and beaten
Arion, but the Father of the Sea

denied him that, yet gave a fair exchange:
the horse gained fame, the prophet won the race.

A pair of twins delivered him his prize, 531
a Herculean cup. This the Tirynthian
would lift one-handed when he raised his throat
and let pour foaming wine to celebrate
his conquest of some monster or a war.
Engraved artistically in gold, it showed
fierce Centaurs slaughtering the Lapithae
as torches, stones, and drinking bowls went flying:
Hercules held Hylaeus by his beard
and clubbed him while the rioters were dying.

As your reward, Admetus, you were given 540
a cloak with purple border, deeply dyed,
that showed Leander braving Phrixean seas,
his figure carved in blue beneath the waves.
You would have thought the dry cloth held wet hair.
There he swam on his side, exchanging strokes,
while opposite, in Sestos, waits a light—
filled with anxiety—that slowly dies.

These gifts Adrastus ordered for the victors 548
and to his son-in-law he gave a slave girl.

–♦–♦–♦–

Adrastus now requested those with speed
to run a footrace for an ample prize.
This sport suits agile men, not strong or hale. 550
Proper for peacetime and the sacred games,
it may yet serve in war when right arms fail.

Idas stepped forward first, who recently 553
shaded his brow with an Olympian garland,
and young Pisaeans and the Elean
squadrons rejoiced. Alcon of Sicyon
came next, and Phaedimus, who twice was crowned
and heard the crowds cry on the sands of Isthmos,

and Dymas, slowed by age, who once outraced
wing-footed horses. Soon a silence greeted
those whom the crowd found unfamiliar when
they entered here and there, yet murmurs moved
around the packed arena when the crowd
hailed Parthenopaeus, the Arcadian.

His mother was renowned for speed. Who knows 563
not Atalanta, her great fame, her feet
pursued by suitors? Her celebrity
weighed on her son, but he, they say, was known
for chasing helpless deer through open fields
on Mount Lycaeus. He could fling a weapon
and run to catch it. He had been expected!
Now he leaped forward through the crowd, released
a clasp of twisted gold, and dropped his cloak.
His torso glowed; his beauty was apparent: 571
the massive shoulders, hairless chest, smooth cheeks,
the body no less handsome than his face,
but he disdained admirers and despised
their compliments. With skill he took the balm
of Pallas—olive oil—and rubbed his skin,
while Idas, Dymas, and the others glistened,
just as when tranquil seas reflect the stars
and images of constellations shimmer.
The brightest lamp of these clear lights
is Hesperus, whose rays extend as wide
through the blue waves as he mounts heaven's heights.

Idas was not much older, not much slower, 583
and almost matched his beauty. His cheeks showed
a sheen induced by ointments in the gym,
and tender peach-fuzz peeped through waves of hair.

Now they confirmed their quickness, honed their steps, 587
and stimulated limbs by various means;
they feigned excitement to resist fatigue;
they crouched and bent their knees; they slapped their chests,
poured on slick ointments, and their fiery feet
suddenly started, then as suddenly ceased.

When the bar dropped and left the gateway clear, 593
they quickly drew together and the field
shone with their naked bodies till it seemed
the chariots had raced at slower speed.
♦ They flew like arrows of Cydonian plebes
or fleeing Parthians. Not otherwise
♦ across Hyrcanian wastelands race swift deer
who congregate, astonished, blind with fear,
and clash their tangled antlers when they hear,
or think they hear, far off, the hungry roar
of lions. 602

Faster than rapid winds
raced Parthenopaeus, pursued by Idas,
whose rugged body shadowed his bare shoulders,
who panted at his back, while after them,
Dymas and Phaedimus contended, followed
at an uncertain distance by fast Alcon.

Parthenopaeus, the Arcadian, 607
had dedicated, since he was an infant,
♦ his blond hair to Diana (Trivia).
It streamed behind him. He had never cut it.
Boldly, but vainly, he had promised her
to immolate it on his country's altars
when he returned from these Ogygian wars.
Spread out upon his shoulders and unbound,
it slowed him as it followed in the breeze
and it obstructed evil Idas too,
but also gave the man a way to cheat.

As they approached the line, and victory 615
awaited Parthenopaeus, Idas seized
his hair. He took his place. He won the race.

Arcadian soldiers cried for war, prepared 618
with weapons to defend their king if what
he won and he deserved was not returned.
They were about to enter the arena,
but others there admired the craft of Idas.

Parthenopaeus rubbed his face with dirt. 621
His tears streamed down and added to his beauty.
He mourned and clawed his undeserving cheeks
and chest with savage nails and rent the hair
that caused his loss. Noise rose on every side,
the dissonance increased, as old Adrastus
paused, for his decision was uncertain.

At last he said, "Young men, cease quarreling! 627
Your prowess must be tested once again,
but do not run along a single lane.
Idas will take this side, and you take that;
all cheating must be banished from the race!"
They listened and agreed to his decree.

♦ Then the Tegaean youth prayed silently, 632
"O mighty goddess of the forest groves—
for it is you to whom I vowed this hair,
an oath that has resulted in disgrace—
if ever mother or myself has earned
some honor by our hunting, do not let
me go to Thebes with such an omen, or
subject Arcadia to this dishonor!"

The answer to his prayer was manifest: 638
the meadow scarcely felt his flying feet;
he barely moved the wind or skimmed the dust
and sped across the line as watchers roared,
then went back to Adrastus, whose reward
absolved his sighs and gasps as he received
a horse, while odious Idas got a shield.
The other runners treasured Lycian quivers.

–♦–♦–♦–

Adrastus then invited athletes skilled 646
at discus to step forward and compete.
Pterelas came at his command and brought
the slippery burden of the bronzen weights.
They bent his body; he tossed down that mass.
Greeks stared in silence, pondering the task.

Soon the crowd moved: two from Achaea, 651
three Ephyreians, one from Pisa, seven
Arcanians, and others would have joined,
had not Hippomedon appeared, that giant!
Urged by the audience he rose and balanced
between his hip and hand another discus.

"Instead, try this one, you young men, whose prowess 656
will soon stone walls and throw down Tyrian towers!
Whose right hand cannot hurl that other weight?"
He tossed the first aside with little strain.

Just Phlegyas and green Menestheus stayed
in competition, who, compelled by shame,
sought to maintain their families' good names.
The other young men willingly conceded,
forced to renounce the discus they esteemed,
for they were so astonished by that giant 660
that they knew they would lose, and so withdrew,
just as in Thracian plains the shield of Mars
rings when the god's spear strikes it and emits
an evil light that reaches Mount Pangaea
and shines so bright it terrifies the sun.

The Pisan, Phlegyas, began to work, 668
and drew all eyes upon himself. The force
his body had was visible, but first
he dusted up his disk and hands with dirt.
He quickly shook the excess off and turned
the object in his fingers to discern
which side felt best, which fit his middle arm.

He knew the art; this game had been his love, 673
not only in his country's festivals,
but when he would connect the banks of Alpheos,
however wide apart, and never sink
his discus when his throw traversed that stream.

Trusting his prowess, with his right hand he 678
now measured not the nearby mountainside
but heaven as he drove his flexed knees down,

twisting with all his force. He hid the disk
up in the clouds. It sought the height with speeds
that grew like something falling, then returned,
after a pause, more slowly to the earth
and buried in the field. Thus falls the moon,
the sun's dark sister, when it is removed
from the astonished stars, as distant people
rattle bronze instruments to stay her course
(senselessly scared) while the Thessalian witch
laughs at the panting steeds that bide her charms.
Danaans cheered, but not Hippomedon,
as Phlegyas tried a flatter, longer throw.

Suddenly Fortune intervened, for she 691
delights in disappointing undue hope.
What claims has anyone against the gods?
As Phlegyas prepared substantial space, 693
he bent his neck, his side was turning back,
but the weight tumbled at his feet; his hand
fell forward, empty, and the throw was useless.

Everyone groaned, although to some the sight 697
was pleasing. Then Menestheus, diffident,
made his attempt with care and skill and prayed
continually to you, o son of Maia!
He dusted his slick disk so it won't slip.
It flew from his huge hand with better luck
and covered no small portion of the circuit.
A cry went up. An arrow marked the spot.

Hippomedon, the third in this stiff contest, 704
moved with slow steps, and bore in mind the fate
of Phlegyas, the fortune of Menestheus.
He raised his burden with familiar ease
from warfare and sustained it, drawing strength
into his rigid side and brawny arm.
He coiled and hurled the weight. His body followed.

With a tremendous bound the discus flew 710
through empty air, and even at a distance
recalled his hand and held its path. It passed

beyond Menestheus' mark and landed far
distant—an envious throw—not even close!
It shook the theater's dark heights, its green banks,
as if the whole mass fell in widespread ruin,
as if blind Polyphemus threw a stone
from smoke-filled Aetna at Ulysses' ship,
guided by enemy sounds, and nearly hit it,
or like the sons of Aloeus when they
made Ossa tread Olympus and then piled
Pelion on top to conquer trembling heaven.

Talaus' son, Adrastus, ordered that 722
a tiger skin be given to the victor.
A yellow border hemmed its brilliant surface;
gold smoothed the edges of its long, sharp claws.

♦ Uncertain arrows and a Cnosian bow 725
were given to Menetheus. "But to you,"
he said to Phlegyas, "because of your ill luck,
we give this sword, the glory of our own
Pelasgus. We are sure Hippomedon
will not feel envy! Now we look for bravery:
strap on the deadly gauntlets, pugilists!
Fight hand to hand, for no sport is more warlike."

–♦–♦–♦–

The Argive Capaneus was enormous, 731
tremendous to behold, a fearful sight,
and while he bound raw leather, black with lead,
about his arms, hard as his gloves, he said,
"Select from all these thousands of young men
someone Aonian as my opponent,
someone I can legitimately kill,
so civil blood won't stain my reputation!"

All were astonished, silent in their terror, 738
when suddenly, unsought, Alcidamas
stepped forward from the nude Laconians.

The Doric leaders wondered, but his friends
knew he relied on Pollux, his instructor.
He'd grown up in the god's gymnasium.

Pollux, the deity, had taught him how 743
to hold his hands, and he had trained his arms.
Both of them loved the sport and often sparred.
Pollux would proudly seize Alcidamas
when he discerned in him his own ill-temper
and hug his naked strength against his chest.

As if in pity, Capaneus taunted 747
and called for someone else. He scorned this challenge,
but when he saw Alcidamas determined,
he felt provoked and swelled his long neck's tendons.

Both stood up tall, feet firm, heads back, and raised 750
their lightning hands, their arms in mirror stances
to guard against attack. This one was large,
big-boned and savage, long of limb, as if
the gruesome vultures had let Tityos
ascend from Stygian fields. The other was
a boy till recently, but he was strong,
more than his years. His young enthusiasm
promised a famous future. Nobody
wanted to see him beaten up and bloody;
they feared the outcome, and they prayed for him.

The boxers eyed each other, seeking advantage. 760
They did not throw wild punches; they restrained
their eagerness; they showed some fear and caution.
They leaned their arms against quick jabs and tested
their leather gloves by rubbing them together.

Alcidamas, more skilled, postponed attack; 765
worried about the future, he delayed;
he saved his strength. However, Capaneus
was prodigal, unmindful of his safety;
he hurried in with everything; both hands

flailed uncontrollably; he ground his teeth—
to no effect; he only harmed himself.

Alcidamas was prudent, dexterous, 769
skilled in his homeland's art (Laconia: Sparta).
He blocked some blows; he dodged some; some he ducked.
He sped away from danger, bobbed his head,
lifted his hands to parry jabs, stepped forward,
yet he held back his head. His strength was in
his skill; he had so much experience
in his right hand, that often, though his foe
was strong beyond all reason, he made bold
to step in, block him out, and strike high blows.

Just as a wave precipitates its mass 777
on threatening rocks and breaks and then retreats,
so he attacked that madman. He raised up
his hand and kept it forward, menacing
his face and ribs; then as his rigid arm
held the attention of his wary foe,
he threw a skillful, unexpected punch
that hit him on the brow and left a mark.
A flowing stream of warm gore streaked his temples,
and Capaneus, unaware of it,
was wondering why those watching suddenly gasped
until by chance he drew his flagging hand
across his face and saw the blood-stained leather.

No lion or speared tiger ever raged 787
as he did as he pushed Alcidamas
backward until the youth lay on the ground.
His teeth made awful noises as he spun
and multiplied his blows, although the air
absorbed his efforts, while the Spartan caught
some on his gloves with sharp moves and avoided
a thousand deaths directed at his temples.
He showed quick footwork. He recalled his skills
even in flight and parried many punches.

And now they both were weary from their efforts 796
and breathed in pain; now Capaneus pressed

more slowly, and Alcidamas retreated
less skillfully. Knees buckled. They craved rest.

They were like wandering sailors whom long seas 799
have wearied, who relax their arms a minute
after they hear a signal from the stern,
before a voice recalls them to their oars.

And so Alcidamas again eluded 802
the furious onslaught; he dropped back and ducked,
hunching his shoulders, while the other fell
over his head, and as he tried to rise,
the gallant young man landed one more blow
and Capaneus paled at this surprise.

The shouts of the Inachidae were louder 806
than noises from the seacoasts or the forests,
but when Adrastus noticed Capaneus
rising and tightening his fist, preparing
what could not be endured, he cried, "I pray,
o comrades, hurry! Go and stop his rage!
He is convulsed! Bring him the palm and prizes!
The Argive will not spare Alcidamus
until he breaks his head and spills his brains!
Seize the Laconian, or he will die!"

Tydeus leaped forth at once; Hippomedon 813
did not ignore the order, but they both
could hardly hold resisting Capaneus.
They gripped his hands and spoke to quiet him.
"You are the winner here, so stop! It is
a noble thing to spare this young man's life!
He's one of us, our comrade in the wars!"

But nothing calmed that warrior, who shoved 817
their proffered palm and cuirass back and shouted,
"Let me alone! Let me destroy those cheeks
with which that sissy curries minions! I'll
turn them to bloody pulp, and I will make
a gift for his instructor back in Sparta,
where I'll send his maimed body to its grave!"

Friends led him off. Meanwhile the pupil of 823
famous Taygetus was congratulated
by the Laconians. They mocked the words
of Capaneus as he called for more.

–◆–◆–◆–

Self-conscious of his prowess, having heard 826
other men lauded, Tydeus ventured forward.
He could throw disks with skill, compete in racing,
or hold his own in boxing but preferred
before all other sports the oil of wrestling.

He spent his leisure from the war this way. 830
It was his custom to relax his weapons
and, on the banks of Achelous, compete
against the strongest in a pleasant school
where Mercury instructed in the art.
So, when ambition for achievement called
the young men to that contest, the Aetolian
doffed his great cloak, the skin of native boar.

Agylleus, a tall braggart, rose against him; 836
◆ his limbs were long, his homeland was Cleonae,
and he, not less than Hercules in size,
possessed enormous shoulders, and he towered
high over other men, beyond all measure,
but he lacked tone; he did not have the strength
of Hercules; his limbs were loose and flabby;
blood bloated them and therefore Tydeus had
enormous confidence that he would beat him.
He was a little man, but strongly built, 843
with bundled muscles that belied his size.
Nature had never put such spirit in—
or dared to give such strength to—someone small.

After their skin enjoyed a bout of oiling, 847
each sought the center ring and scooped up dust
and dried his limbs in turn, then raised his shoulders
and, hunching forward, bent his outstretched arms.

Tydeus had skill enough to draw Agylleus 851
down to his height by stooping till his knees
were almost in the sand, but his opponent
was like a cypress tree, queen of some mountain,
that when the wind blows lowers down its head—
its roots can hardly hold—to graze the earth,
until at last it springs back through the air.
Not otherwise does tall Agylleus bend
his mighty limbs above his smaller foe
and as he does so, groans. Both alternated
quick hand assaults at brows, necks, shoulders, sides,
chests, and retreating legs; sometimes they leaned
their arms against each other for support;
sometimes they locked their hands then struggled free.

Two bulls, the leaders of two herds, do not 864
make fiercer war when one white heifer waits,
expectant, in the field where they confront
and crash their chests together goaded by
love—that same love that numbs and heals their wounds.
Thus do two boars clash lightning tusks, or two
rude bears compete and tear each other's fur.

Tydeus had strength that never failed; his limbs 870
did not grow faint from sun or dust; his skin
was firm and well conditioned from hard work,
his muscles hard, but his foe was unsound,
his breathing labored, he was weak, he panted,
and sticky sand rolled off in streams of sweat
as furtively he grasped the ground to rise.

Tydeus took action, crowded him, then faked 876
and—threatening his neck—he grabbed both legs
but could not stretch his short arms where he wanted.
Agylleus tumbled down and buried him
under his massive bulk, not otherwise
than when a miner in the hills of Spain
goes underground far down from light and life.
He will lie broken in a mass of rubble
should tunnels tremble, arching vaults collapse;
his angry soul will never reach the stars.

Tydeus was stronger, with more heart and courage, 886
and soon slipped from that evil grasp and weight,
and when he faltered, whirled behind his back.
He quickly gripped his side and held his groin,
and when Agylleus tried to seize his flank
and struggled to escape, he strained his thighs
and bent his knees and lifted him. The sight
was terrible, his strength miraculous.
◆ Thus, it is said, the earthborn Libyan 894
was lifted in the air by Hercules,
who would not let his feet touch mother earth
after he learned the secret of his strength.

The air resounded. Spectators applauded, 897
happy to watch him hold that man aloft
until, to their surprise, he suddenly flung
Agylleus on his side and threw himself
on top and seized his hips between his legs. 901
The beaten man—his belly on the ground,
prone on his chest, his neck in Tydeus's hand—
faded and only fought to save his pride.
At last he rose unhappily to leave;
the earth was stained by marks of his defeat.

Tydeus received the palm with his right hand 905
and took the shining armor with his left.
"What if the Dircean plain had not received
a portion of my blood, as you have seen,
when my wounds made a treaty with the Thebans?"
He showed his scars and gave his prized rewards
to his companions, and he sent the cuirass
after Agylleus, who had left the field.

–◆–◆–◆–

The next were those who fought with naked steel: 911
Agreus from Epidaurus and the Theban,
not yet condemned by fate. They took the field
with others, armed and ready, but Adrastus,
the son of Iasus, called a halt. "Enough
of death remains, young men! Preserve your spirit!

Hold back your longing for opponents' blood!
And you, for whom we desolate fair cities
and our ancestral countryside, do not
allow so much to chance before the battle,
nor, God forbid, fulfill your brother's prayers!"

He spoke, and he awarded both men helmets 920
of gold; then, lest his son-in-law lack honor,
he ordered that his brow be garlanded
and that the Theban be proclaimed the victor—
an omen that the deadly Fates ignored.

–◆–◆–◆–

The leadership now urged the king to add 924
some exploit of his own to grace the games
and offer final honor to the tomb.
And so that every prince would have a prize,
◆ he should shoot arrows from his Lyctian quiver
or throw his slender spear shaft through the clouds.

He joyfully agreed and, crowded by 929
his most important men, descended from
the green berm to the field, while his arms bearer
brought him his lightest arrows and his bow.
He pointed to an ash tree in the distance
across the circuit's length. He aimed at this.

Who can deny the secret source of omens?
We know our destiny but disregard
the warnings and refer to them as chance.
Man is too lazy to attend his fate.
Thus Fortune gains her power to do us harm.

The fatal arrow quickly crossed the field,
rebounded from the tree, and—horrible
to see—flew back on that same path, then fell
beside the mouth of King Adrastus' quiver.

The leaders offered many explanations,
but all were wrong. Some laid the blame

on clouds, some sky-high winds, while others said
the arrow struck the tree and bounced away.

The secret of our death is deep and hidden,
but also visible. The arrow promised
its master's sad return from war—alone!

–♦–♦–♦–

BOOK 7 Earth Opens

Jupiter sends Mercury to the house of Mars. Adrastus addresses the shade of Archemorus. Panic in Thebes. Bacchus appeals to Jupiter. Eteocles prepares Thebes for war. Catalog of Theban allies and champions (Creon and his sons Haemon and Menoeceus, Dryas, Eurymedon, and Hypseus). Hippomedon leads the Argives, despite ill omens, across the Asopos River. Tisiphone stirs both sides. Jocasta appeals to Polynices. The Fury Tisiphone rouses two tigers of Bacchus, whose deaths ignite the first battle. Earth opens for Amphiaraus.

Not with an even heart did Jupiter
watch the Pelasgians delay their task
of waging war against the Tyrians.
He shook his head, and that hard motion made 3
high stars fall from the sky and Atlas howl
as his distended neck absorbed his burden.
He then spoke to swift Mercury, his son:

"My boy, leap quickly. Ride the northern winds 6
◆ to Thrace, where the Parrhasian dipper feeds
my winter clouds, and my own winter rains
those fires that never touch the ocean streams.
There houses lie beneath the pole star's snow.
There Mars dwells, either leaning on his spear
to breathe, though he hates peace, or—I believe—
he takes his fill of arms and winding trumpets
and wallows in the blood of clans he favors.

"Hurry this warning: say his father angers; 13
spare nothing! After all, I long ago
commanded him to spark the Argive army
drawn from the areas below the Isthmos
of Corinth or surrounded by Malea,
which raves and echoes. These young men of war
had hardly left the city's walls and gates

when they held games, like conquerors, as they
paid homage to the tomb their crimes created.

"Is this the rage of Mars? To hear a discus 20
bounce and Oebalian boxing gloves collide?
Mars boasts about his madness, his insane
desire for warfare; therefore, let him show
impiety and render unto ashes
innocent cities, carry fire and sword,
smash to the ground those people who implore
the Thunderer: exhaust the wretched world!

"Now I am angry, but he moderates 26
contention: he abates! But he must start
a battle sooner than I speak these words
and drive the Argives to the walls of Thebes
or I will change things: there will be no cruelty!
Let his divinity be mild and good
and let him turn his unrestraint to leisure;
let him return my steeds and sword and lose
his power over blood! I will survey
the earth and tell the world it must make peace!
Athena will suffice for war in Thebes."

He spoke these words, and the Cyllenian 34
descended into Thrace. Continuous
tempests exhaled from heaven's northern gates;
long lines of clouds stretched out; the heavens blew,
and northeast storm winds struck him as he flew.
Hail rattled on his golden cloak. His own
Arcadian helmet offered small protection.

Here he saw lifeless trees and shrines to Mars 40
and shuddered at the sight. A thousand Furies
surrounded War's fierce domicile, which lies
under and opposite Haemus. It has walls
of fitted iron, narrow iron gates
so tight they scrape, and columns bound with iron
that prop the roof. The radiance of Phoebus
weakens on contact with this seat of Mars;

it makes the light afraid, and its hard gleam
saddens the stars. The posted guards befit it: 47
mad-moving Haste, who leaps through outer gates,
blind Wickedness, pale Fear, and blood-red Rage.
Deception carries hidden knives, and Discord
a two-edged sword. Innumerable Threats
howl through the inner court where in the middle
Valor stands sadly and exultant Madness
and armored Death (gore blots his face) mount thrones.

The plundered flames of burning towns and blood 55
of war lie on his altars, and the spoils
that he has pillaged from surrounding lands.
The temple's high facades are lined with captives,
fragments of gates designed in iron, ships
for warfare, empty chariots, heads crushed
by war-cart wheels, and even what seem groans:
all kinds of violence, and every wound.
The god is everywhere and never languid. 60
Mulciber etched him with his godlike art
before the sun's rays caught him in adultery,
the bond of marriage broken, chained in bed.

The winged Maenalian had just begun 64
to seek the temple's ruler when, behold,
◆ earth shook and torrents roared in hornèd Hebrus
as horses bred for war disturbed the valley;
foam flecked the trembling fields—a sign!—and gates
bound with eternal adamant released.
Mars was returning in his chariot,
leading his spoils, his ranks of weeping captives. 69
Hyrcanian blood made him illustrious
and feared; the scattered drops deformed wide fields.
He traveled through the high snows and the trees
while dark Bellona, grim-faced charioteer,
guided his team and brandished her long spear.
Mercury stiffened and he lowered his eyes.
Even his father would have shown respect
(if he had been there) and toned down his threats
or changed his message. Mars was first to speak:

"What orders from our father have you borne 77
through the great ether, brother? It's not like you
to travel north alone to my cold climate.
Maenalus with its dews and warm Lycaeus
provide the milder airs that you prefer!"

When Mercury delivered Jove's decree 81
Mars did not wait for long but urged his yoked,
perspiring, panting steeds, indignant at
the Argives that they had not left for battle.

The mighty Father watched. His anger lightened. 84
Slowly, with gravity, he lowered his head.
Just so east winds decline and leave the seas
they stir to fury; skies grow peaceful; storms
diminish and depart. Swells settle down
till sailors who have not had time to breathe
can resecure the riggings of their ships.

–♦–♦–♦–

The war games, rites, and funeral 90
had finished, but the crowds had not departed
when King Adrastus poured wine on the ground,
while everyone was silent, to placate
the ashes of Archemorus:

"Small one,
allow us to observe your holiday
every three years, for years to come. Do not
let wounded Pelops choose Arcadian altars
nor let his ivory joint strike Elean temples.
Guard the Castalian altars from the serpent.
Keep Melicertes' shade from Corinth's pines.
O child, we hold you back from sad Avernus 98
and join your sad solemnities to stars
that never die. We hurry off to war.
But if you let our army overturn
the houses of Boeotia, you will earn
much greater altars; your divinity

will be maintained by all Inachian cities,
and men will swear by you, a god, in Thebes!"

He spoke for all, and each man's vows were these.

–♦–♦–♦–

By this time Mars had pressed his outstretched steeds 104
along the shores of Corinth, where the city's
citadel lifts its head high through the air
and casts its shade in turn on either sea.

One of his dreadful followers, named Panic,
announced his chariot, at his command. 108
There's nothing Panic cannot make us think.
His horrible approach drives cities crazy.
No one is better at instilling fear,
more fit for draining courage from men's souls.
This monster's hands and voices have no number;
he can assume whatever face he wants.
He makes the common people think they see
stars tumble from the sky, twin suns appear,
earth totter, and the old-growth forests walk.
Panic conceived this excellent device:
across the Nemean plains he swirled false dust.

The leadership observed and wondered at 119
the dark cloud overhead; then Panic added
false clamors to the noise and imitated
the pulsing sound of mounted men and arms;
he filled the wandering winds with fearful cries.

Their spirits soared, but common people murmured
because they were in doubt. "What makes this sound?
Or do our ears deceive us? Why does this
cloud of dust hang in heaven? Could it be
Ismenian soldiers? Yes, it could. They're coming!
But is there such audacity in Thebes?
Did they make haste while we interred the child?"

These were the things that Panic made men think. 127
Having astonished them, he then assumed
various faces in the different ranks:
now he was one among a thousand Pisans,
a Pylian, then a Laconian;
he swore the enemy was near, and he
disrupted soldiers with his empty fears—
nothing seems false to people when they panic—
but then he fell upon the madding crowd
in his true guise, and he was whirled by winds
up to the summits of the sacred vale.
Three times he shook his spear and flailed his steeds
and three times bumped his chest against his shield.

Madness drove men to brace, to take their own 135
or unaccustomed arms of other soldiers.
They harnessed stranger's horses, transferred helmets.
A raw desire for death and slaughter seized
each heart; there were no obstacles to ardor.
Their hurrying redeemed delay; the shores
echoed as winds arose and ships left port;
sails fluttered everywhere, and loose ropes dangled;
anchors were weighed; oars swam; across deep seas
friends who remained and fair fields disappeared.

The rapid progress of Inachian cohorts 145
was viewed by Bacchus, who made moan and turned
toward Thebes, his second home. There Jove had burned
his mother, he recalled. His handsome face
and heart were sad; his hand released his thyrsis;
his garlands and his curls fell out of place;
his horn of plenty dropped unblemished grapes.

And so in tears, unsightly, cloak askew, 151
when Jupiter by chance was all alone
in heaven, he, in this unwonted guise
(the reason was not hidden from his father)
addressed him as a suppliant:

"Will you,
progenitor of gods, destroy your Thebes?

Is your wife still so angry? Have you no
feeling for your loved land, the household gods
whom you deceived, the ashes of my mother?
Is it not so, as we believe, that you
once threw unwanted lightning from the clouds?
Again you set dark flames upon the land,
but you are not adjured by Styx; no guileful
mistress beseeches you. What are your limits?
Lightning when you are angry, and the same
when satisfied? Are you our father who
visited with changed features Danaë,
Callisto's groves, and Leda's town Amyclae?
Am I the most neglected of your sons?
Yet surely I'm the precious weight you bore
because you condescended to restore
my mother's months and open womb. You carried
me to the gates of life.

"Another thing:
my people almost never go campaigning;
they never sit in camps; they only know
my wars: they weave their hair with leaves; they dance
inspired by flutes in circles. How should they
endure Mars' trumpets, they who fear the wands
of newly married girls and scuffling matrons?
Look at how passionate Mars is! What if
he led your worshipers in Crete to battle
and ordered them to fight with fragile armor?

"And why do you choose Argos, which you hate?
Is there no other enemy? O father,
worse than our perils is that you decree
our ruin to enrich your wife's Mycenae.
I yield, but those my mother bore for burial,
the sacred altars of these conquered people,
where would you have me take them? In-
to Thrace, and to the forests of Lycurgus?

"I conquered India. Should I flee there
and be a prisoner? Or will you harbor
a fugitive? My brother fastened down
Delos, Latona's rock, and so procured

a place at sea. It's not that I feel envy,
◆ but Pallas saved the citadel she loved
from threatening waves; myself I saw
◆ Epaphus giving laws to eastern lands.
No trumpets threaten lonely Cyllene
or Cretan Ida. So why do our altars
offend? It seems that I am powerless
to please you, but I know you spent fair nights
in Thebes conceiving Hercules; you knew
the pleasant passions of Antiope.
Please spare Agenor's sons, the Tyrians,
◆ whose bull fared better than my flaming mother."

His jealousy brought smiles to Jupiter, 193
who lifted him—knees flexed, his hands outstretched—
gave him a kiss and answered him like this:

"It is not—as you think—my wife's advice
or fearsome importunity, my son,
that binds me, but the steadfast wheels of fate.
Old and new grievances have caused this war.
What god has quieted his anger more
or made as frugal use of human blood?
For ages heaven and my timeless house
have seen how often I have set aside
my twisted thunderbolts, how seldom I
have ordered conflagrations on the earth.
Only against my will—since they had suffered 203
great wrongs that called for vengeance—did I give
◆ the ancient Calydonians to Diana
and let Mars kill the Lapithae. Those losses
exceeded bounds, and it was noisome to
create new souls, bring bodies back to life.
I hesitate to slaughter Thebans—sons
◆ of Labdacus—or Argives, Pelops' seed.
You yourself know how prompt the Thebans are
to blame the gods. I leave the Argive's crimes
aside. You also . . . but I will not speak.
My former animosity has faded.
The shredded corpse of Pentheus weighs your altars, 211
even though he was innocent. His father's

blood did not splatter him, nor had the man
defiled his mother's couch, nor bred bad brothers.
Where were your tears and skillful pleading then?

"I do not judge the sons of Oedipus 215
by my own grievances; the earth and heavens
demand this, as do Piety and wounded
Faith and the ways of the Eumenides.
Cease to be worried for your city. I
have not decreed the end of the Aonians.
There will be other dangers, other victors.
Juno, our royal queen, will not be pleased."

At these words Bacchus raised his face and donned 222
his cloak, as when a rose bush, burned by sun
and the cruel south wind, droops but then is lifted
skyward by brilliant days and western winds:
its beauty is restored, its blossoms glow,
and shapely offshoots ornament its glory.

–♦–♦–♦–

That Grecian leaders guide long lines of troops
and that their march approached Aonian fields
by now a messenger had ascertained 227
and told Eteocles, whose ears were stunned.
Wherever they advance, the people tremble
and feel compassionate for Thebes, he said,
and he described their clans, their names, and weapons.

Eteocles insisted on attending; 232
he hid his worries, yet he loathed the teller;
then with his own address he roused his men
as he informed them of his plan for action.

–♦–♦–♦–

Mars had inspired Aonia, Euboea, 234
and fields near Thebes at Phocis; Jove was happy.
A password tablet flew from rank to rank
as armies hurried to appear in arms 237

and camped beside the city on the plain.
Fated for war, this open field awaited
the coming of the enemy, the madness.

Mothers in trembling clusters climbed the walls 240
to show resplendent armor to their children;
they pointed out the casques of handsome fathers.

Nearby, her soft cheeks veiled in black, upon 243
an isolated tower, out of view,
Antigone was standing by a man
who formerly served Laius; she revered him.

The royal maid spoke first: 247

"Will these troops be
enough to counter the Pelasgians, father?
We're told that all the Peloponnesians
are coming. Please identify the foreign
armies and generals, for I can see
the sign of our Menoeceus, the platoons
that Creon leads, tall Haemon's sphinx of bronze."

So young Antigone. To whom old Phorbas:

◆ "There—look!—how Dryas leads a thousand archers, 255
inhabitants of cold Tanagra's hillside.
Here great Orion's grandson, not disequal
◆ in prowess, shows a rough, gold bolt of lightning
◆ and trident on his armor. May unmarried
Diana's ancient anger be dismissed
and the paternal prophecy kept distant!

"Ocalea and Medeon have come 259
to join our camp and serve our king as have
thick-wooded Nisa, and then Thisbe, where
the cooing of Dione's doves reechoes.

"Next is Eurymedon, who imitates 262
the country weapons of his father Faunus:
hung with pine needles like a horse's mane,

the terror of the forest, he will be
a savage in this bloody war, I think.

"Erythrae, rich in flocks, attends our cause, 265
dwellers in Scolon and dense Eteonon,
where slopes are steep; and Hyle, where the beach
is narrow, and the proud inhabitants
of Schoenon, Atalanta's town: they farm
the fields made famous by the goddess's footsteps;
they wield long, Macedonian spears and carry
shields that can barely tolerate hard blows.

♦ "Listen! the noise of Neptune's progeny 271
who rush down from Onchestus, they whose ranks
the pines of Mycalessos feed, Minerva's
♦ stream Melas, and Gargaphie, Hecate's valley,
whose crops are bountiful and grass is deep,
whose young grains Haliartos sees with envy:
their weapons, logs; their helmets, lion skulls; 276
their shields, the bark of trees. They lack a king;
therefore, Amphion has assumed command.
You can behold him, maiden. His ancestral
bull decks his helmet, and he wears a lyre.
O go thy way, brave youth! He will oppose
his naked breast to swords for our dear city.

"O Heliconian peoples, you too come 282
♦ to join yourselves with us; and you, Permesse,
♦ and pleasant Olmius, home of singing swans,
you arm inhabitants unused to war.
You hear the acclamations of your people
praising their city as, when winter fades,
♦ swans sing again on shining Strymon's stream.
May honor never die, and may the Muses
sing of your wars forever. O, be joyous!"

He spoke, and then the maiden interrupted 290
briefly: "Those brothers: what's their origin?
Their arms are similar, their helmet peaks
protrude an equal distance in the air.
Would that my brothers showed such harmony!"

The old man smiled and said, "Antigone, 294
you're not the first whose eyes make that mistake.
Many have called them brothers. Ages lie.
That is a father and his son, but years
confuse appearances. The nymph Dercetis,
a shameless bride, hot with desire, too soon
corrupted Lapithaon, who had no
experience of marriage—a mere boy.
Handsome Alatreus, not long afterward,
was born, and in the flower of youth, he followed
his father, took his features, blurred their years.
Now the false name of brothers makes them bold;
more so the father, who's both young and old.

"He leads three hundred horse to war; his son 305
an equal number who once cultivated
◆ meager Glisantan soil, where grapes are grown,
and rich Coronia, where they talk of grains.

"But see the spreading shadow Hypseus casts 309
over his lofty horses: on his left
a shield of seven bulls' hides; on his chest,
a triple layer of iron—on his chest,
but not his back, for he is fearless. His
spear is the glory of an ancient forest.
When thrown, it always finds a passage through
armor or bodies, always heeds his prayers.
◆ They say he owes his breeding to Asopos,
and he is worthy of such a father, who
flows swiftly under broken bridges, swells
in vengeance for his virgin daughter, pounds
his waves and scorns the Thunderer, her lover,
for it is said Aegina was borne from 319
her father's stream and hid in Jove's embrace.
The river raged, prepared to fight the stars—
even the gods were not yet granted this.
He overflowed with anger—very daring—
and looked and prayed for help, but he found none,
till overcome by thunder and the fiery
trident, he ceased; but even now the proud
whirlpool, confined within its banks, exhales

signs of his mighty torment—fire and ashes—
and breathes its Aetnaen vapors through the sky,
just as, if Jove is happy with Aegina,
we shall see Hypseus on the Cadmean plain.
He leads Alalcomenaeans—men of 330
Minerva—and Itonaeans, and those
Midea sends, and Arne of the vines,
and those who sow at Aulis, Graea, and
verdant Plataeae; those who cultivate
◆ and master Peteon, and hold Euripus—
the part within our boundaries—which flows
backward and wanders; and, Anthedon, you
◆ from whose grass coastline Glaucus jumped
into the sea that beckoned, ocean-blue
in hair and face already, soon to be
a fish below the waist. These men are trained
to cleave the air with lead balls, twisted slings.
Their javelins surpass Cydonean arrows.

"You would have sent your son too, Cephisus— 340
no one was handsomer than your Narcissus—
but that fierce boy turns pale in Thespian fields,
a flower, father, bathed by your grieved waters.

"Who can describe to you, Antigone, 343
the troops of Phoebus and of ancient Phocis?
Of Panope, and Daulis, Cyparissos;
your vales, Lebadia? Hyampolis,
nestled beneath a steep cliff? those who plow
two sides of Mount Parnassus with their bulls
or Cirrha, Anemoria, Corycian
groves, or Lylaea, from which springs the cold
◆ stream Cephisus, the place the Python, panting
and thirsty, blocked the river from the sea?

"Look at the laurel woven through those crests, 351
that armor, which shows Tityos or Delos,
◆ those quivers that supplied the god's mass killings.
They follow Iphitus, a valiant man,
whose father, son of Hippasus, Naubolus,
recently died. He sheltered you, good Laius!

but I still held your reins and drove your chariot
while you were being trampled by your horses,
neck torn and bloody. Would that blood were mine!"

He spoke. His cheeks were wet, his face full pale, 359
and sudden sobs cut off his path of speech.
The woman, who was dear to him, revived
the old man's languid spirit. He continued:

"Antigone, you are my greatest joy; 363
unmatched in your solicitude toward me.
My own death is delayed; perhaps I act
badly, postponing it, until I have
brought you, intact and suitable, to marriage.
That done, the Fates may take my weary life.

"But look, how many generals have passed 368
while I have been recovering my strength:
I have not mentioned Clonis, or the sons
of Abas, who wear long hair down their backs;
nor you, Carystos, built on rocks; low-lying
Aegae and high Caphereus. My eyes
grow dull and do not serve me. All is still.
Your brother orders silence from the soldiers."

The old man on the tower had hardly finished, 374
when, from a mound, the king began:

"High-minded
leaders, whom I myself, your general,
would not refuse to follow to defend
my city Thebes! I do not come prepared
to rouse you: you have freely taken arms.
Unforced you've sworn to serve my blameless rage.
Nor do my skills suffice to give you praise
or proper thanks. That task is for the gods,
for armies when their enemies are beaten.

"You've come from friendly lands to save this city
that native enemies assault—not some

warlike destroyer from a foreign shore
or far-off population. He who rules
the camps that face us has a father here,
a mother, sisters joined to him by blood—
he had a brother! Everywhere he looks,
the monster plots, with his impieties, his family's
annihilation, but I am not left
alone: the people of Aonia have come
without coercion. It is proper that
he know that they insist I keep this kingdom."

He spoke, then issued orders: who should wage 390
the war, maintain the walls, which squadron would
be first in battle, which should hold the middle.

When earth is fresh and doorways let in daylight, 393
a shepherd opens up his wicker gates:
he lets the leaders out first, then the crowd
of flocking ewes, and then he lifts, himself,
the pregnant ones whose udders sweep the ground;
♦ he carries suckling youngsters to their mothers.

—♦—♦—♦—

Meanwhile Danaans, night and day in arms, 398
carried away by rage, marched night and day.
They scorned rest, barely slept or took time out
for meals. Against the enemy they rushed
as if the enemy were in pursuit, nor did
portents that point to certain death detain them,
or songs of marvelous occurrences.

And there were many: birds and animals 404
gave cautions; stars, and rivers that ran backward.
Jupiter thundered warnings; lightning flashes
menaced; shrines issued terrifying voices.
The doors of temples shuttered on their own.
Now it rained blood, now rocks. Old men encountered
ghosts flitting by. Apollo's oracle

Cirrha was silent, and Eleusis wailed
all night in unaccustomed months. The brothers
Castor and Pollux battled—a disgrace,
◆ a portent—in the open shrines of Sparta.

◆ The Arcadians said Lycaon's frenzied ghost 414
barked through the quiet night, while Pisans claimed
their own Oenomaus drove the savage plain.
The wandering Acarnan—Tydeus—
deformed the Achelous, which had lost
a horn to Hercules; the effigy
of Perseus wept, to which Mycenae prays;
the ivory of Juno was embarrassed;
farmers said mighty Inachus made moans;
inhabitants between the seas told how
Theban Palaemon wailed along the deep.

◆ The Peloponnesian phalanx heard these things, 422
but their desire for battle banished fear
and they ignored the counsels of the gods.

—◆—◆—◆—

The army had already reached, Asopos,
your banks among the rivers of Boeotia
but did not dare to cross your hostile stream.

By chance the river flooded trembling fields, 426
swelled by a rainbow or by mountain clouds;
perhaps the river father purposely
created obstacles to block the army.

Then wild Hippomedon drove down the bank; 430
it crumbled; it confused his horse, but he
held high his reins and weapons in the stream
and called out to the soldiers he preceded:

"Forward, you men, and I will take the vanguard
and lead you to the walls I've vowed to shatter—
the Theban ramparts!"

Everyone raced forward,
into the river, humbled to have followed,
as when before an unknown stream a herd,
pushed by its pastor, sadly hesitates,
fearing the distance to the further shore:
the lead bull enters, and he swims across;
he makes the water seem more tame, the jump
less difficult, the other bank look closer.

Not far away they found a suitable 441
field on a hill to place their camp in safety.
From there they could behold Sidonian towers,
even the city. Under this pleasing and
secure location on the heights was spread
an open field. No mountain overlooked it,
nor did it take much work to fortify—
a miracle how Nature favored it.

High rocks formed walls; the plain sloped into trenches. 448
By chance four mounds shaped ramparts. They themselves
did what remained, until the sunshine crept
from hills; the men were weary, so they slept.

–♦–♦–♦–

What words suffice to show the plight of Thebes? 452
Dark night is terrifying to a town
facing the worst of war, and day brings fear.

Men raced along the barricades in terror; 455
no walls seemed safe; Amphion's ramparts, worthless.
Rumor increased the ranks of enemies,
fear added more. They saw Inachian tents
and foreign campfires opposite, in their
own hills, and begged the gods and prayed or chose
weapons for battle, urged their warlike horses,
wept and embraced their dear ones in despair.
Some ordered funeral pyres against the morrow.

And if some slender sleep should shut their eyes, 463
they dreamed of war, of the advantages

delay brings, of the weariness of life.
Confused, in shock, they feared, and prayed for, light.

Tisiphone ran wild on either side. 466
She flailed her double snake and stirred the brothers
whom Oedipus despised. He left his shadows
and wished that he could see them hate each other.

–♦–♦–♦–

Now the cold moon and fading stars were dimmed 470
by the first light of day. The Ocean swelled
with newborn flames the Titan sun revealed
as he calmed panting horses; now Jocasta,
like the most ancient of Eumenides,
majestic in her suffering, emerged
through the town's gates. Her eyes were wild, her cheeks
pallid, her gray hair dirty, her arms bruised.
♦ She bore an olive branch with black wool twists.
Her daughters, now the better sex, supported
the aging limbs she forced to move along
faster than she was capable of walking.
She bared her breasts before the enemy
and struck the facing barricade. Her voice
appalled them as she begged to be admitted:

"I am the mother of impieties 483
and war; I tell you to unlock these doors:
my womb has earned the right to curse this camp!"

The trembling soldiers feared the sight of her, 485
but more, her words. A messenger returned
from King Adrastus and, as ordered, they
unbolted and gave passage through their swords.

As soon as she beheld the Achaean leaders, 488
maddened by grief, she raised a fearful clamor:

"Beneath what helmet will I find my son,
the enemy I bore, you chiefs of Argos?"

The Cadmean hero wept with tears of joy 492
and held the frantic woman in his arms.
He soothed her and kept saying "Mother! Mother!"
He hugged her and conversed with his two sisters.
The woman's tears were angry, and she sighed: 495

"Why do you feign soft tears and reverence
for me, your hated mother? Iron presses
against the neck your arms clasp. Are you not
a wandering exile and a wretched guest?
Who is not sorry for you? Long battalions
wait your commands; swift swords shine by your side.
Are you the man I wept for night and day? 503
We mothers are so miserable! If you respect
the words and admonitions of your family,
I order you, I beg you as a parent—
now while the camps are still, and wavering
Piety scorns this war—to join me. Look:
your household gods, the buildings that will burn,
even your brother! Why avert you eyes?
Speak to Eteocles; I'll mediate.
Either he'll yield, or you can recommence 510
your struggle, better justified. Do you
fear some deceit, a mother's trick? Your house
retains its sense of right: you would be safe
even if Oedipus had come, not me.
I married and, alas, conceived in sin,
but yet I love you; I excuse your rage.
Still, if you must persist in being cruel, 516
I will surrender. Bind your sisters' hands.
Carry away your father and his burdens.

"But sons of Inachus, you men of honor, 519
you who have left your children and your parents
and those like me who weep at home: I pray,
believe a mother's feelings. If my son—
I hope it's true—became so dear to you
so quickly, what must I—and my womb—feel?
If I asked Thracian or Hyrcanian kings
or any crueler race to halt this strife, they'd do it.
If you must fight, I'll hold him till I die."

Her words struck those proud squadrons; you 527
could see the helmets of the soldiers nodding,
their armor sprinkled by their pious tears.

Irresolute Pelasgian hearts were bending. 529
They were like lions that have scattered men
and met their weapons with impulsive chests;
their rage grows less as they enjoy their captives
and satisfy their appetites in safety.

While they were watching, Polynices turned 534
to kiss his mother first, then young Ismene,
and then Antigone, whose tears adjured him.
Commotion gripped his soul, and he forgot
his kingdom's cause: he wished to go, and mild
Adrastus was no obstacle, but Tydeus,
mindful of righteous anger, interrupted:

"It would be better, o companions, to send me 539
to see the king; I have experienced
the goodwill of Eteocles and bear
his brand of peace and good faith on my chest.
Where was this mother mediator then—
that night I was hospitably detained?
Is this the trade for which your trained your son?
Why don't you lead him to the reeking field,
rich with the blood of Thebans and my own?

"*You* are too soft! Will you forget your friends? 546
Will you be led by her? When hostile hands
unsheathe their swords around you, will she weep
and end the conflict? Will Eteocles—
you fool—dismiss you to the Argive camp
when you are trapped in Thebes and prey to hate?
This lance will first sprout leaves and lose its point
and both our native rivers flow reversed.

"You seek peace and a gentle colloquy 553
among fierce weapons. Well, this camp is open;
nothing to fear out here. Am I suspected?
I will depart and leave behind my wounds.

Let him approach. His mother and his sisters 557
can mediate, but why not just defeat him
and make him leave as he agreed to do?
Why should you alternate?"

His rhetoric
once again swayed the army, just as when
the south wind in a tempest steals the sea
away from Boreas. Mad weapons pleased
once more; the fierce Erinys found occasion
to sow the causes of the first encounter.

–◆–◆–◆–

Two tigers wandered by the river Dirce, 564
a harmless team that Liber recently
freed in Aonian fields on his return
◆ from victory on Erythraean shores—
Bacchus, the devastator of the East.
They had forgotten blood; they wore the scent
of aromatic herbs from India.
The god's retainers and an elder priest
adorned these tigers, following their custom,
with various fruits and flowers and mature
clusters of grapes: they wove their stripes with purple.

Who would believe it? Nearby heifers lowed, 572
the hills and herds embraced them, and they threatened
no one; they fed from human hands when hungry
and turned rough faces up for wine that flowed.
Untouched they roamed; each house and temple glowed
with sacred flames, and they reached town in peace:
their followers believed Lyaeus entered.

Tisiphone restored their wildness 579
by whipping them with vipers three times each.
The meadows did not recognize their speed:
as when two lightning bolts in different zones
of heaven burst and trail their long hair down,
these tigers raced across the fields and seized
your charioteer, Amphiaraus! They leaped

together. Was it not an evil omen
that on this one occasion, and by chance,
the driver fell beside a hellish lake?
Next they seized Idas, a Taenarian, 588
and Acamanteus the Aetolian
whose steeds raced through the fields until Aconteus—
a strong Arcadian hunter, chased
those tigers and flung darts. The wild beasts sought
the walls they trusted, but he thrust his spear
three times, withdrew, and then a fourth time pierced
their backs and necks. Stuck full of shafts, they trailed
blood to the city gates, half-dead, and leaned
their wounded bodies on the walls they loved.
Their groaning seemed like human lamentations.

You would have thought the city had been seized, 599
that wicked flames burned Thebes, such clamor rose
when the gates opened. Tyrians would rather
have lost the marriage bed of Semele,
Hercules' cradle, or Harmonia's bower.

Phegeus, a follower of Bacchus, drew 603
a weapon and approached unarmed Aconteus
as he was boasting of his double killing.
Other Tegean soldiers came too late
to save their comrade; his dead body covered
the tigers: mournful Bacchus was avenged.

The sudden tumult in the camp disrupted 608
the Grecian council. Now Jocasta fled
past enemies in arms, no longer daring
to sue for peace, as those who'd been so welcoming
resented her two daughters and her presence.

Next Tydeus seized his opportunity:
"This is the peace you hoped for and the faith! 612
Could he have not delayed his crimes and waited
until his mother finished and returned?"
That said, he called to friends and drew his sword. 614

Rage heated either side, and all was chaos.
Men shouted out for war as leaders merged

with commoners; their orders were ignored.
Horsemen and rapid chariots and ranks
of infantry were intermixed, unsorted,
a pressing mob, and no one took the time
to show himself or know the enemy.
The Argives and the Thebans troops engaged 621
in rapid-moving groups that raced before
ensuing horns and standards seeking war.

So great a battle from so little blood— 624
as when a tempest gathers strength among
the clouds, it softly blows through leaves and treetops,
then soon takes forests and engulfs dark mountains.

—♦—♦—♦—

Pierian sisters, we consult you now 628
not on some distant matter, but the strife
you witnessed in your own Aonia.
The lyres of Helicon, so close to war,
echo the tumult of Tyrrhenian horns.

The steed of Pterelas of Sidon was 632
untrustable in war and ran away,
crossing the field of foes. Its rider yanked
his racing horse's reins till he was weary.
The spear of Tydeus hit him in the shoulder 634
then hollowed his left hip and, as he fell—
no longer holding either reins or weapons—
it pinned him to the horse, which, joined to its
dead master, galloped—like a dying Centaur,
one that, still clinging to its double life,
falls back and lies recumbent on itself.

War started. Furious Hippomedon 640
slew Sybaris; Menoeceus killed the Pylian
Periphas; Parthenopaeus slaughtered Itys:
a bloody sword felled Sybaris, a spear
dropped savage Periphas, an arrow Itys,
who never saw it; then bold Haemon cut
the throat of Argive Caeneos, whose open

eyes looked across the slit to find his trunk—
his vital spirit tried to find his head—
while Abas stripped the armor from his body
until, stopped by an Argive spear, he dropped
his own shield and the other's as he died.

Eunaeus, who convinced you to abandon 649
the cult of Bacchus? Priests are not allowed
to go outside his sacred grove. Why change
the madness Bromius inspires? Whom can
you terrify? The cover of your shield
is vulnerable and crowned with wreathes of pale
Nysaean ivy; your javelin is vine wood,
wound with white flounces; hair obscures your shoulders;
soft down is on your cheeks, and your unwarlike
corselet is woven through with Tyrian purple.
Bracelets bedeck your arms; your shoes are pinked;
you wear a linen tunic and your cloak—
Taenarian—is pinned by tawny jasper
set in a smooth, gold clasp; your slick-cased bow
is slung beside a gold-laced, lynx-hide quiver.

Eunaeus felt the fury of the god. 662
He hurried toward opposing ranks and shouted:
"Restrain your soldiers! Phoebus's righteous omens
and the Cirrhaean heifer chose these walls.
Stones rolled here of their own accord, so spare them.
Our race is sacred; Jove is our son-in-law.
Our father-in-law is Mars. I do not lie:
Thebes was the home of Bacchus and Alcides!"

Angered by their vain words came Capaneus 668
to meet him with a long spear bound with bronze.
He's like a lion in a cave who wakes
to first wrath in the morning; when he sees
a deer or hornless bull, he roars for joy;
intent upon his prey, he scorns the wounds
of hunters and their spears. So Capaneus
exalted that the conflict was unequal;
he set his heavy cypress spear to throw,
but first he said, "If you must die, why frighten 677

men with your feminine laments? Would that
Bacchus were here, for whom you act so madly!
Go howl at Tyrian women!" And with that
he threw his spear, which no force could impede.
It made Eunaeus' shield ring, pierced his back;
his weapons fell; long sobs choked his gold throat; 682
blood overflowed his breast. You dared, you died—
another favorite of Aonian Bacchus!
◆ The languid town of Ismara lamented
◆ and broke the thyrsi, as did Tmolos, Naxos
(the Thesean island), fertile Nysa, and
the Ganges, sworn (from fear) to Theban orgies.

The Argive army saw Eteocles 688
unhesitant, but Polynices bristled
because he put Thebes's citizens at risk.

Amphiaraus stirred up clouds of dust. 690
Although his horses feared the meadows, and
the plains he churned disdained him, Phoebus lent
some empty glory to his follower
and mourned his coming downfall. He bestowed
a starlike splendor on his shield and helmet,
nor were you late, Gradivus, to command
that by no hand or mortal weapon would
the prophet fall in war; instead his corpse
would enter Dis inviolate and blessed.

The augur Amphiaraus drew
strength from the certainty of death, and fought;
his force increased; his limbs were magnified;
heaven seemed propitious; and he could have read
the stars as well as ever, given time.
His hand was strong, his burning soul exultant; 700
he flamed with unrequited love for Mars,
and Death, who follows Valor, kept his distance.
Is this the one who rescued men from chance 705
and took away the power of the Fates?
How different, all at once, he was from when
he read the tripod and the sacred laurel
and knew what Phoebus' birds in each cloud meant.

Like a plague year or evil influence 709
of some opposing star, he slew innumerable
victims to honor his impending ghost.
His javelins killed Phlegyas, proud Phyleus.
The scythed wheels of his chariot mowed down
Clonis and Chremetaon—one had stood
in front of him; one had his hamstrings cut.
His spear struck Chromis and Iphinous
and Sages and a man with long hair: Gyas.
He struck, unknowingly, Apollo's priest
Lycorus—he had hurled his strong ash spear
before he saw the fillets in his hair.
He stoned Alcathoüs, a poor old man
♦ who lived by Lake Carystos with his wife.
His children loved its shores; he fished its waters.
Dry land deceived him. As he died, he praised
dangers he knew: north winds and storms at sea.

Asopian Hypseus had been watching this 723
slaughter of stragglers for so long that he
burned to reverse its course, yet he had not
been ineffective from his chariot
against Tirynthian forces. Then he saw
the seer. His soul and weapons longed to slay
that man, and he lost interest in his prey.

A dense wedge of the Argives blocked his way. 727
He took a weapon from his father's river,
but first said: "Asopos! O rich dispenser
of waters in Aonia, once famous
for the remains of giants. Grant my hand
strength for this task. It is your son who asks.
My spear grew on your shores. I'll fight Apollo
as you once fought the father of the gods.
I'll sink that prophet's armor in your stream;
his sacred bands will mourn to lose their seer."

His father heard, but Phoebus barred his prayer 736
and turned the blow against his driver, Herses,
who fell. The god himself assumed the reins
and took the form of Haliacmon of Lerna.

No soldiers tried to block their hot pursuit. 740
Everyone fled in terror, and a coward's
death came to those who quailed but showed no wounds.

Whether the added weight increased or slowed 744
the chariot's speed could hardly be discerned,
as when a winter windstorm, or the dry
decay of aging, loosens up the side
of some cloud-covered hill and makes a slide
of men and ancient oaks through bounded fields;
there terror reigns until the avalanche
weakens because it carves another valley
or intercepts a river in midstream.

Not otherwise the chariot, which bore 750
the burden of a man and mighty god,
swerved here and there through blood. Apollo
handled both reins and weapons from his seat,
steadied his aim, deflected flying missiles,
and took the fortune from incoming spears.
They overthrew Menaleus, who walked,
and Antiphus, whose large horse was no help;
Aetion, born of a nymph of Helicon; 755
disgraced Polites, who had killed his brother;
and Lampus, who had tried to stain the bed
of Manto, Phoebus' prophetess: the god
himself attacked him with his sacred arrows.

Dead bodies made the horses shy and snort 760
and scrape away the earth, and chariot tracks
carved furrows over limbs and filled with blood.
The heartless axle ground unconscious men,
and others, half-dead, wounded, saw it coming
but had no strength to move. The reins were slick
with gore; the chariot was soaked; blood clogged
the wheels; they had no solid place to stand,
and mangled entrails slowed the horses' hooves.

Amphiaraus raged. He tore protruding 768
weapons from heaps of bones and spears from bodies.
His chariot was pursued by shrieking ghosts.

At last Apollo let his servant see 771
his godhead, and he told him, "Use your life
to earn eternal fame. Death does not stop,
although he sees my presence: we are beaten.
You know the unkind Fates spin no more strands.
Enter Elysium, where you have been 775
sought after and long promised. You need not
suffer the rule of Creon or lie naked
when his decree forbids your burial."

Amphiaraus answered while he paused 778
a moment in the war: "Cyrrhaean father,
for some time I have sensed you sitting on
the axle of my trembling chariot
and known that I will perish. For how long
do you delay the doom pressed down on me?
I hear the flow of rapid Styx, the dark 782
rivers of Dis, the triple howls of its
evil custodian. Take back the wreathe
with which you honored me; receive my laurels,
which Erebus does not permit. My last
request, if a departing seer may ask,
is this: I leave my lying household—my
impious wife—for you to punish, and
my son, whose madness ought to be excused."

Apollo hid his tears as he descended 789
and sadly left the chariot. The horses
groaned, as when northwest winds raise storms that blind
and ships know they will perish if at night
♦ Castor and Pollux let their sister shine.

Now the earth fissured and began to split; 794
it shuddered and the surface gaped and spit
burdensome dust clouds; subterranean murmurs
echoed along the fields. The cowering soldiers
thought it was war, the noise of distant battle,
but then another tremor knocked them over
and stunned their steeds. Ismenos' banks gave way;
the stream flowed backward; walls and green hills swayed.
Anger decreased; men planted flexing spears

into the earth, then wandered as they leaned
on quivering shafts. They met and were repulsed
by one another's pallor, just as when
Bellona scorns the sea and lets ships battle:
even small tempests make men sheathe their swords,
as they expect the worst—shared fears bring peace—
as happened on this field of wavering war.

Did earth conceive from flames, go into labor, 809
to then deliver mad winds, pent-up fury?
Did hidden springs consume worn, crumbling soil?
Did the machine of spinning heaven lean
its weight? Did Neptune's trident move the seas
and burden distant shores with too much water?
Was all this noise a tribute to the prophet?
Perhaps the world gave warning to the brothers.

Behold, earth's face revealed a deep, sheer chasm; 816
stars feared the shadows, and the shadows stars.
The huge abyss engulfed Amphiaraus;
it swallowed up his horses as they crossed.
He did not drop his weapons or his reins,
but just so, steered his chariot to hell:
a last glimpse of the heavens, then he fell.

Earth groaned, then reunited, and there followed 821
a softer, distant tremoring as fields
conjoined to keep Avernus from the sun.

–♦–♦–♦–

BOOK 8 Savage Hunger

Amphiaraus in hell. Pluto's complaint. Mourning among the Argives. Celebration in Thebes. Oedipus emerges. Thiodamas, the new seer, conducts an empty funeral for Amphiaraus. The seven gates of Thebes. Hypseus kills Menalcas. Other deaths. Tydeus excels, driving back Haemon. The death of Atys, betrothed to Ismene. Eteocles falls back. Tydeus gnaws the head of Melanippus.

Each ghost along the shores of Styx knew fear
when, suddenly, Amphiaraus, the seer,
flew over shadows through the house of death
and entered secret shrines beyond the tombs:
his body, steeds, and weapons seemed prodigious,
for he had come unseasoned by dark flames—
not burnt remains from some sad urn but hot
with sweating war, blood dripping from his shield,
and dirty with the dust of trampled fields.

The Fury had not purified him yet 9
with sprigs of yew, nor had Proserpina
marked his admittance to the crowds of dead
on her dark doorpost. His arrival took
the fatal distaff by surprise, but when
the Parcae saw the augur, in their fright
they cut at once the threads that spun his life.

◆ Those in the safety of Elysium 15
as well as those in distant, lower worlds—
blind regions weighed by strange shades, different darkness—
warily sought the cause of this commotion.
Then burning swamps and dull lakes echoed groans,
and he who carries ghosts across the waves—
◆ the pallid furrower of waters—moaned
that Tartarus allowed a deep, new fissure
and let ghosts enter by a different river.

It chanced the lord of Erebus was then 21
throned in the castle of his dismal realm,
where he required his subjects to confess
the crimes they had committed when alive.
He pities nothing human, blames each shade.
Furies surround him, varied ranks of Death.
Harsh Punishments clank outstretched chains. The Fates
◆ turn thumbs round to condemn the souls they gather—
so arduous their task!—but moderate
Minos, beside him, urges better justice,
restrains the bloody king. There, standing by,
swollen with tears and flames, are Phlegethon,
Cocytos, and the river Styx, who knows
the gods' false oaths. But then the stars appeared,
and all the upper world fell out of joint
and Pluto felt an unaccustomed fear.
The joyous light offended him. He spoke:

"What ruin in the sky inflicts upon 33
Avernus this detestable, bright ether?
Who rends the shadows, gives the silent ones
cause to remember life? What brings this threat?
Which brother fights me? I defy him. Let
divisions that distinguish all things perish!
Who would be better pleased with that? I've served
the world of harmful things since I was tossed
down from high heaven after having lost
◆ our third encounter. Nor do I possess it,
for it is open to the influence
of baleful stars. Should he who rules Olympus
◆ examine my affairs?—the rattling chains
of giants, his father whom I punish,
those Titans who would tempt the heights of heaven?

"Why does that vicious god prohibit me 44
from bearing my sad leisure, my harsh quiet?
Why won't he let me loathe the light I lost?
I'll open every region, if he wishes:
my Stygian firmament will shade the sun.
I will not send Arcadian Mercury

back to the skies: why should he alternate
◆ between two realms? And I will bar both sons
◆ of Tyndareus. Why torture Ixion
on the consuming wheel? Why do my waves
not wait for Tantalus? Must I see Chaos
desanctified by living visitors?
◆ Bold Pirithoüs rashly tempted me,
and Theseus, his daring friend's sworn brother,
and Hercules, for whom iron gates were silent
when he removed their guardian, Cerberus!

◆ "Even the Thracian bard's laments shamed hell: 57
I saw myself whom he seduced with song.
He drew foul tears from the Eumenides
and made the Sisters spin new threads of life.
My plight was similar, but bound by strict,
tough laws I scarcely dared a single trip
◆ to steal my wife from fields in Sicily.
They said it was unlawful, and at once
an unjust proclamation came from Jove:
six months spent with her mother, six with me.

"But why should I go on? Tisiphone, 65
proceed! Avenge this seat of Tartarus!
If ever you have shown harsh, monstrous forms,
bring forth a prodigy—unusual,
enormous, terrible, as yet unseen
by heaven. Stun me! Be the Sisters' envy!
Then make the brothers alternate their strokes
in savage battle. Let this be the first
moment prophetic of my wrath. Next let
a dreadful man behave like some wild beast
and chew the head of his opponent. Let
another keep the dead from funeral flames
so that their naked corpses foul the air!
Let the fierce Thunderer enjoy such scenes,
but lest their strife offend my realm alone,
search for a man who will assault the gods,
someone whose smoking shield will parry fires
of lightning and repel the wrath of Jove.

I won't have anyone fear black hell less
than piling Pelion on the leaves of Ossa!"

His dismal kingdom was already trembling 80
when he stopped speaking, and the violence
that racked his and the pressing world above
was no less than when Jove's gaze bends the heavens
and makes the poles that bear the stars incline.

"But what should be your fate for falling through 84
the void to these forbidden zones?" he said,
threatening the one who, now on foot, drew near,
his armor disappearing, hard to see,
though even as his visage grew obscure,
he yet showed badges of an augur's honor.
Vanishing ribbon twists adorned his brow,
and he retained a withered olive branch.

"If I may be permitted, if the right 90
of speech is not withheld from holy ghosts,
o Terminator of all human lives,
(but also, since I formerly descried
the cause and origins of things, o my
Creator!) ease your threats and quarreling heart;
do not spend wrath on one who fears your laws!

"I am not Hercules, who sought his prey; 95
I do not set my heart on such affairs,
and by these marks I wear, you may believe
I do not seek illicit love in Lethe.
There's no need for Proserpina to fear
my chariot or Cerberus to flee
and seek his cave. I am the prophet who
is best acquainted with Apollo's altars,
and I swear by the emptiness of Chaos
(for what good, here, to swear an oath by Phoebus?)
no crime has made me suffer my new fate;
no lack of merit lost me nurturing daylight.
The urn of the Dictaean judge knows this;
Minos is able to assess the truth.

Betrayed by my wife's plots and love of gold
I joined the Argive army—my right hand
sent you these recent ghosts, this swarm of shades—
but I was not deceived; I knew my fate.
A sudden whirlwind out of your black night
singled me out from thousands in the fight
and even now my spirit feels appalled.
What was my state of mind as I was falling
endlessly through the hollowness of earth,
revolving through concealing airs? Ay, me!
Nothing that's mine remains for friends or country!
Uncaptured by the Thebans, I won't see
the roofs of Lerna, nor my ashes be
transported to my father, dazed by grief.
I was compelled to come, a wretched person,
unwept by family, without a flame
or mound for burial, my only mourner.
Those steeds avail me nothing; uncomplaining,
I will become a shade, forget my tripods,
since what use do you have for augury,
you who command the Fates who spin our lives?
Let your heart yield; be better than the gods!
Reserve your deadly punishments, my lord:
my wife, that wicked women, may arrive,
and she deserves your outrage more than I!"

Pluto received his prayers but scorned compassion, 123
just as a lion, when Massylian steel
glitters before him, summons rage and power,
but if his enemy should fall, contents himself
to let his victim live, and passes by.

–♦–♦–♦–

Meanwhile the army in the open air 127
looked for the chariot adorned with fillets
and fertile laurel leaves, which even now
put fear in famous warriors. No one
defeated it, and no one drove it off.
The troops, suspicious of the earth, retreated
and traced their steps around the impious field.

In honor of the tombs of hell, they shunned
that place of hungry ruin. It lay still.

The news reached King Adrastus (who was elsewhere, 134
encouraging his troops), delivered by
Palaemon, who was trembling as he galloped,
scarce able to believe what he had witnessed.
By chance he had been near the man who fell,
and when earth opened, that poor soul turned pale.

"Avert your steps, my lord, and flee," he yelled, 138
"back to our Doric lands and native towers—
that is, if they remain! Here is no work
for blood or weapons! Why should we unsheathe
our useless swords against the town of Thebes?
Our chariots, our arms, our fighting men
are swallowed by the earth's impiety;
even this field we stand on seems to flee! 142
I myself saw the road to deepest night
when the firm surface fissured and the son
of Oeclus fell, alas, than whom no one
was better loved by fortunetelling stars!

"I speak of marvels! Even now, my lord, 147
I left the fields and furrows and the horses,
horses that smoked and dripped and foamed. What's more,
this curse is not communal: Thebans stay:
Thebes' children are acknowledged by the earth."

Slow to believe, Adrastus was amazed, 150
but Mopsus brought the same news; so did Actor,
trembling. And Rumor now made bold to bring
new horrors, saying more than one had died.

The army, of its own accord, retreated,
undisciplined, before the trumpets sounded,
but found the road was weary; soldiers' knees
resisted hurry, and their horses balked
defiantly—you'd think they showed some sense!
No exhortation could extend their pace
or make them lift their eyes or raise their faces.

The Tyrian incursion gathered strength,
but now dark Evening drove his lunar steeds—
a short truce, troubled rest, the fear night breeds.

Imagine the morale, once there was time 161
for unrestrained lamenting. Men unlaced
their helmets as their tears fell. They were tired,
and nothing cheered them up. They threw aside
their dripping shields untouched, forgot to wipe
their weapons, praise their steeds, or reunite
the plumes on feathered crests or comb them high.
Large gashes went unwashed, and gaping wounds
were barely stitched together. Such distress
was great throughout the camp, and even fear
of battle could not bring the men to eat
or fortify themselves for war. All sang
your praise, Amphiaraus, and with tears
recalled your heart, that fertile source of truth.
One thought ran through the tents: the gods were gone,
and nothing of divinity remained.

"Alas, where are the laurel-bearing car, 174
all-hallowed armaments, and helmet crest
entwined with sacred bands? Is this the faith
owed by Castalia's tripod, lake, and cave?
Apollo's way of saying thanks? Who will explain
the falling stars, what leftward lightning means,
or why slain entrails should reveal the gods?—
select our roads, decide the time to rest,
predict what savage wars may have success
or when the hour of peace should be preferred?
Who now will read the future or discern
what destiny the birds prognosticate?
You knew the outcome of this war—your fate
and ours (so mighty were your sacred powers)—
and yet you came; you joined your countrymen
in our sad combat! Even when earth called,
in your own fatal hour, you engaged
the Tyrian army and consumed yourself
against opposing standards. Even when
dying, you terrified the foe, and we beheld

your deadly spear in motion as you fell.
Now what is happening? Can you return 189
from Stygian regions, burst to upper earth?
Do you sit, fortunate, beside your friends
the Fatal Sisters, whom (in turn) you teach
and learn from what's to come? And does Avernus'
lord let you enter sacred groves to serve
Elysium's birds? Wherever you may be,
the mourning of Apollo will not cease.
In silence Delphi will forever grieve
this strange and everlasting injury.
Upon this anniversary, the shrines
◆ of Tenedos and Chryse will be closed—
Delos (the island moored for hosting birth)
◆ and secret recesses of unshorn Branchus!
No suppliant on this day will approach
◆ the gates of Clarius, the threshold of
Didymeus, or Lycia's oracle.
Silence will fall on Thymbra in the Troad,
the oracle in Ammon, and the oak
of Jupiter that murmurs in Molossis.
Apollo's rivers will run dry, his laurels
wither; the skies will utter nothing—no
wise prophecies; no wings will fan the clouds.
The day will come when shrines that say what's true
will use your priests; and men will worship you!"

Such were the testimonials the prince 208
of prophecies received, as if they laid
his body in the soft earth and brought gifts
and funeral flames and sad rites to his pyre.
Their hearts were broken, ill-prepared for war.
It was as when the Argonauts were stalled 212
◆ by Tiphys' sudden death when seas refused
to bear the fleet or listen to the oars;
even the winds diminished in their power.
But gradually their talk reduced their grief,
their hearts grew lighter, and sleep softly crept,
as night dimmed sorrows, over those who wept.

—◆—◆—◆—

But elsewhere night was different: in Thebes 218
they made the heavens dance with various games.
Outside the watchmen dozed along the walls;
inside, musicians played Idaean drums,
twin cymbals sounded, and the woodwinds hummed.
They sang in town the sacred hymns of praise 223
to bless their gods, their local deities.
They poured wine, they wore garlands, and they mocked
Amphiaraus, whom they said knew nothing,
and *that* was why he'd died. Then they competed
to sing the praises of their own Tiresias.
Soon they were telling ancient histories;
they sang about the origins of Thebes.

Some told of Sidon and the sea and of 229
Europa's hands that grasped the horns of Jove—
bull Jove, who plowed the furrows of the sea god
Nereus. Some sang of Cadmus, and the weary
heifer, and men of blood born from Mars' field.
Others recalled the lutenist of Tyre,
Amphion, how he brought sharp rocks to life
and how they crawled toward Thebes. Then others praised
the pregnancy of Semele, the Cytherean
nuptial rites and how Harmonia was led
home past the torches that her brothers held.
Each table had its stories, just as if
Bacchus had only recently despoiled
◆ India's Hydaspes River and its jewels
and kingdoms in the East and showed his people
flags of obscure, defeated Indians.

That was, they say, when Oedipus emerged 240
unlooked for from dark places where he'd hidden.
His face was bright, and his own hand had brushed
his white hair free from black grime and removed
the clinging strands that fouled his countenance.
He joined in conversation with his friends,
no longer scorned their sympathy, drew out
a portion from the feast, and wiped away
the dried blood that had fallen from his eyes.
He listened to, and answered, everyone,

where formerly he only would complain
of hell, the Furies, and Antigone,
who guided him. The cause of this was hidden.
It was not Thebes' good fortune in the war
that pleased the man, but war itself. He wished
his son to seek for praise, but not to win.
He longed for that initial clash of swords,
sowing his seeds of hate with silent words,
and so the feast delighted him, and he
showed unaccustomed joy, as Phineus did,
when after his long fast had tortured him,
he learned the birds no longer plagued his house
but was not yet convinced the news was true
until he took a couch beside his table
and raised a bowl untouched by savage wings.

–♦–♦–♦–

The other Grecian cohorts were exhausted 259
by war and worry when Adrastus stood
high on a mound beside his camp and heard
that joyful celebration. His heart broke,
age weakened him, but nonetheless he kept
his vigil and observed the enemy—
the sad task of a man who would be king.
It hurt to hear drunk voices full of pride,
loud horns, harsh drums, and other sounds from Thebes,
and to see tottering torches, short-lived fires.
He stood, eyes open, by himself, like some
pilot who stands on deck, while on the flood
his ship sails silently, submerged in sleep,
men trusting in the safety of the sea
and guided by the god carved on their keel.

The time was dawn, when Phoebus's fiery sister, 271
hearing a yoke of horses and the roar
of Ocean's hollow caverns, gathers her
stray beams as light accumulates above;
she drives away the stars with her light lash.
The king called his sad council, and he asked
the mourners who should next assume the tripod,

receive the vacant dignity of wearing
laurels and woolen fillets. They agreed,
without delay: Melampus' famous son,
Thiodamas, renowned for sanctity,
must be the one, for he'd already learned
the secrets of the gods and had observed
the flights of birds with him who gladly shared
his art and said they both could be compared.

He was dumbfounded by their great acclaim 283
and humbled by this unexpected glory.
Duly submissive, reverent, he took
the proffered crown of leaves, but he disclaimed
all worthiness and tried to be constrained,
just as a Persian prince, if young, accepts
his father's throne and people, weighing joys,
uncertainties, and fears. His safety would
be greater had his father lived. Can he
trust the nobility? Or will citizens
rebel against his rule? Whom should he send
to guard Euphrates, whom the Caspian gates?
Then he must take his father's bow and mount
his awe-inspiring horse, attempt to wrap
his hand around the scepter, fill the crown.

When he had fitted twisted, woolen bands 294
around his head, he prayed to heaven's gods
then went through camp rejoicing, made glad sounds,
and in his first official act as priest
prepared to placate Mother Earth, fulfilling
the wishes of Danaans who lamented.
Straightway he ordered double altars built,
covered with aging sod and living branches.
He piled innumerable flowers for the Goddess,
gifts she had given, and he added fruits
and anything the busy year produced.
He sprinkled altars with unspoiled milk,
and then began: 303

"Eternal Maker! You
created gods and men; you made the streams;

you grew groves for the gods and sowed the seeds
of life—Promethean man, the stones of Pyrrha!
You give variety to men; you feed
the hungry, and you let men rule the seas.
You give us power to tame the gentle flocks,
wild beasts, and birds. The swift machine of heaven
circles around you through an empty vacuum.
You are the source of strength that never falters
and you make firm the pole that never sets.
You are the center of the universe!
Two chariots surround you; the three brothers
of heaven, earth, and ocean share your lands.
You are the *alma mater* to great cities,
to many clans and races. You suffice
to hold the sky above and hell below!

"You hold up Atlas, he who bears the stars,
who strains to hold the weight of heaven's home—
and do you then refuse to bear *our* weight?
O goddess Nature, are you so oppressed?
What crime do we unknowingly atone?
I pray you tell us! Is it that we come
as strangers from the banks of Inachus?
The soil is every person's right by birth,
nor does it suit you, worthy goddess, to
distinguish by such insignificance
those who are—here and everywhere—your own.
Be neutral; let our weapons move about.
I pray you, let it be the course of war
that fighting souls who die may enter heaven.
Don't take our bodies to the living grave
before their time, for we, like everyone,
will follow down the necessary road.
Keep the field smooth for us Pelasgians,
and do not speed, we pray, the rapid Fates.

"Amphiaraus, some god favored you!
No human hand or Theban sword destroyed you.
The goddess Nature opened up her lap
as if you merited an opening
in Cirrha's shrine, near Delphi's oracle.

She took you; she embraced you; so, I pray,
rejoice and educate me in your ways,
teach me what you have ready for your people,
and I will bear your sacred prophecy,
be your interpreter in Phoebus' absence,
and call on your divinity, your name.
The place where you have fallen is, to me,
a better place to situate a shrine
than anywhere on Delos or near Cirrha!"

When he had spoken this, he gave the earth 338
black sheep and dark, live cattle and poured piles
of undulating sands upon the rest—
an image of the prophet's living death.

–♦–♦–♦–

Such things among the Greeks. Then horns of war 342
blared opposite, and bronze sounds roused fierce swords.
Bitter Tisiphone blew sonorous:
upon a peak in Teumesus, she mixed
the hissing of her hair with that shrill brass,
and stunned Cithaeron's dankness and the towers
that followed other music, other sounds.

And now Bellona pounded trembling doors 348
and barricaded entrances, and Thebes
turned many hinges. Now the cavalry
scattered footsoldiers, and the chariots
impeded their advance, as if Danaans
were pressing from the rear, and every soul
♦ was squeezed and stuck in each of seven gates.

The lottery sent Creon through *Ogygia,* 353
Neistae Eteocles, and Haemon through
high *Homoloidae; Proetiae*
sent Hypseus; *Electrae* lofty Dryas.
Eurymedon's battalion shook *Hypsistae,*
and great Menoeceus exits through *Dircaea.*
All moved, just as the Nile divides its waters
and flows through open fields in seven streams,

carrying to the main the cold and nourishing
frost from the far horizon he imbibes
in secret with his great mouth: Nereids
hide in his depths, afraid to face fresh seas.

The sad Inachian youth took tardy steps, 363
especially the Eleans, the Spartans,
and Pylians, who felt defrauded by
the sudden choosing of Thiodamas,
the augur they, reluctantly, must follow.
But yours are not the only troops complaining,
o prince of tripods. All the army knew
someone was missing, for Thiodamas
rose less than lofty in the seventh rank,
as when a cloud that envies brilliant skies
obscures the constellation Ursa Major.
It dims its glory by one missing flame
and obfuscates the axle that should guide
uncertain mariners, who count the stars.

—◆—◆—◆—

But now the war is beckoning. Calliope, 373
renew my strength. Apollo, touch my lyre.
Those who demand a day of destiny
confront their fatal hour. Death has emerged
from Stygian shadows to the open air;
Death floats in flight above the fields of war;
Death beckons men with black and gaping maw.
He pricks to die those of distinguished life;
he marks the brave, not commoners, with blood.
The Sisters cut the threads of piteous lives.
The Furies steal the weavings of the Fates.

Mars stood midfield, his sword still dry, and turned 383
his shield against each side and shook his spear;
he blotted thoughts of children, houses, wives;
he overcame men's longing for their homes
and, harder to erase, their love of light.
What is the wonder if these men grew hot?
Rage tightened angry hands on spears and pommels;

hard-breathing spirits swelled in straining corselets;
stiff crests of horsehair trembled on their helmets;
their horses flamed against the enemy
and wet the crumbling dust with flecks of foam.
Steeds wore their masters' anger just as if
they intermixed their bodies with their riders;
they tugged against their bits and neighed for battle;
they bucked and flung their armored riders backward.

They charged. The forward ranks approached through dust. 395
Both sides moved equal distances and saw
the field between them gradually decrease.
Now shields and targets fended shields and targets,
swords threatened swords; feet, feet; and lances, lances.
Battle lines leaned together; each breathed smoke;
tall war crests dangled over foreign helmets.

The siege was still a handsome spectacle: 402
there was a driver for each chariot,
helmets stood high, men wore full armament,
weapons held firm; shields, painted quivers, belts
still shone with gold that blood had not defiled,
but when unsparing rage and force began 406
to dominate, the pounding was more fierce
than when the northern wind in Capricorn
lashes the vales of Rhodope with hail
or darkling Boreas pounds Libya's
Syrtes with freezing rain from Italy,
and Jupiter rolls thunder through the heavens.

Arrows obscured the day, an iron mist 412
so dense that no more missiles could have fit.
Some perished in the serve, some in the volley.
Shafts met in flight and lost their impetus.
Long ash spears flew. Swift slings slung screaming stones.
Sharp pellets and dread arrows that killed twice
forked down like lightning. Each projectile hit
someone, because there was no space to spare.
Men perished and they killed they knew not how:
they often did by chance their deeds of prowess.

Armies receded then in turn advanced,
took land and lost it, just as threatening Jove
loosens the reins that hold back wind and water
and lashes earth with alternating storms:
opposing lines of battle fill the sky;
◆ first Auster's winds prevail, then cold Aquilo's,
till too much rain, or clear skies, stop the storm.

In the beginning of the fighting, Hypseus 428
drove back the Spartans after that proud race
broke the Euboean lines with forceful shields:
he killed Menalcas, who had led that wing.
A true Laconian, raised near mountain streams
and proud of his progenitors, he seized
the spear stuck in his breast and pulled it out
through flesh and bones before it pierced his back,
a sign of shame, and as his hand grew faint,
he flung the bloody object at his foe
and then imagined in his dying eyes
◆ his favorite ridges of Taÿgetus,
his battles, and his mother's admirable floggings.

Dircean Amyntas aimed an arrow at 438
Phaedimus, son of Iäsus. Alas,
how swift is Fate! for Phaedimon hit ground
even before Amyntas' bow was silent.

Agreus, the Calydonian, removed 441
Phegeus' now useless right arm from his shoulder:
it gripped his sword and grappled in the dirt.
Acoetas stabbed that arm through scattered weapons:
it terrified him, even unattached.

Dark Acamas struck Iphis, fearsome Hypseus 445
Argus, and Pheres carved through Abas—these
lay moaning from their different wounds: the rider
Iphis, footsoldier Argus, driver Abas.

The savage ignorance of war! Inachian twins 448
had slain twins borne from blood of Cadmus, hidden

by helmets till they stripped them off as spoils
and saw their impious deed and in dismay
looked at each other and bemoaned their error.

Ion (who prayed at Pisa) toppled Daphneus 453
(who favored Cirrha), and their horses stumbled.
Jupiter praised the first from high in heaven;
Apollo pitied, but too late, the other.

There were two men whom Fortune rendered famous:
they were opposed in blood, of different race.
The Theban Haemon sundered and he slew;
Danaan Tydeus chased the Theban crew.
Pallas helped one, and Hercules the other,
just as two winter torrents from two mountains
burst forth upon a plain in twofold ruin:
you would believe that they compete as they
overwhelm fields and trees and sweep away
bridges; it seems they want to see who's deeper,
and when one vale receives and mixes them
they keep their independence and refuse
to travel to the sea while intermingled.

♦ Onchestian Idas waved a flaming torch 466
that parted and confused the ranks of Greeks:
he carried forth his fire, but Tydeus' spear
caught him up close and pierced his riven helmet.
He fell back, and his torch enflamed his temples.
Tydeus pursued him:

"Theban, you can't say
that Argives are uncivilized! A pyre
is granted you—so burn in your own fire!"

Then like a tiger savoring first blood
who now desires to murder all the flock,
Tydeus dismembered Aon with a rock,
Pholus by sword, and Chromis, too, by sword.

He speared a pair of Helicaonians
♦ whom Maera, priestess of Aegean Venus,

had borne despite the goddess's command:
she tends her shrine as Tydeus kills her sons.

No less did Herculean blood impel 480
Haemon to sate his sword on countless people.
◆ First he laid low proud Calydonians,
next, fearsome squadrons of Pylenians
and then the children of embittered Pleuron.

At last, his spear exhausted, he confronted
Olenian Butës and attacked that man
who blocked his army and refused to move.
Butës was but a boy and had a boy's
smooth cheeks and uncut hair; he did not see
the Theban's double-sided battle ax
aim at his helmet, separate his temples,
or drop his severed locks on either shoulder.
Unwarned, he left the gates of life, still fearless.

Then Haemon killed Hypanis and Polites, 491
both with blond hair. One saved his beard for Phoebus,
the other kept his locks unshorn for Bacchus,
two savage gods. Then to these victims Haemon
added Hyperenor, and then Damasus,
who turned to flee, but Haemon threw a spear
that pierced his armor and his chest before
its sharp point tore his target from his grasp.
Ismenian Haemon would have still been killing
Inachian enemies (for Hercules
pointed his weapons and supplied his strength),
but Pallas sent fierce Tydeus to confront him.

Now they met face to face, as adversaries, 500
but first Tyrinthian Hercules remarked:
"What fortune, faithful sister, makes us meet
here in the dust of battle? Is it Juno,
the queen, who causes this impiety?
Sooner may she see me face lightning bolts—
a sacrilegious thought!—or fight great Zeus,
my father, than confront you. This man's birth . . .
but I refuse to recognize the Theban,

because I see you favor his opponent.
I would not do so, should the spear of Tydeus
◆ chase my son Hyllus or Amphitryon 509
(should he escape the underworld of Styx).
I can remember, and I always will,
how often, goddess, your right hand and aegis
assisted me, while I, a toiling slave,
wandered the world. I know you would have come—
if Acheron had not excluded gods—
to Tartarus with me. To you I owe
my home in heaven: what can equal that?
If you have set your mind on Thebes, it's yours.
I pray you pardon me; I yield you all."

He spoke and turned, and Pallas was appeased.
Her face regained the ardor it had lost;
◆ the snakes that bristled on her breast relaxed.

Haemon, the Cadmian, could sense the god 519
had left him, that he threw his spear less hard.
He could not recognize his own weak blows,
as more and more his strength and spirit failed;
he felt no shame in yielding when assailed
by Tydeus—he, the Acheloan hero!
Hefting a spear that no one else could lift,
he aimed between the margin of the shield
and Haemon's helmet—at the jugular,
that gleaming, vital spot. Nor was his hand 526
uncertain, for his spear flew, bringing death,
but Pallas interfered and drove the lance
at Haemon's shield, a favor for Apollo.

Haemon no longer had the confidence 529
to hold his ground or charge or dare to look
at Tydeus' savage face. His spirit weakened,
◆ as happens in Lucania when a spear
scotches the bristling forehead of a boar—
the aim not true. Not wounded to the brain,
he vents his rage by slashing side to side
but will not face again the spear he tried.

Look, here is Prothoüs, the leader of 536
an enemy battalion, happily
flinging his darts. How he made Tydeus angry!
Enraged he struck two bodies with one blow;
both horse and rider fell: as Prothoüs
groped for his dangling reins, his horse's hooves
trampled his helmet on his face and kicked
his shield against his chest; the horse then flicked
its bridle off and, wounded, losing blood,
reclined and lay its neck against its master.
♦ So on Mount Gaurus vine and elm fall down: 545
some farmer's double loss, but greater for
the elm, which dies while losing its support.
Nor does it mourn its fallen limbs as much
as friendly grapes it had no wish to crush.

Corymbus, from Mount Helicon, who'd been 548
a comrade of the muses, now took arms
against Danaans. His demise had been
predicted by the placement of the stars,
♦ because Urania long before beheld
his Stygian destiny, but nonetheless
he sought out enemies and wars, perhaps
so men would sing of him. He now lay dead,
worthy of chants and lengthy praises, though
the sister muses mourned his loss in silence.

Young Atys joined in the defense of Thebes— 554
he who had been engaged to chaste Ismene,
Agenor's progeny, since he was young.
Although he came from Cirrha, he had not
disdained his in-laws for their wicked deeds.
The spotless squalor of his future bride
and undeserved decline commended her,
for he was virtuous, nor had the girl
renounced him in her heart. They would,
if Fortune should allow it, please each other,
but war has interrupted plans for marriage.

Angered by this invasion, Atys would
sometimes outrace his lines and charge Lernaeans

on foot, with just his sword, or ride, reins high,
as in some spectacle. His mother had
enfolded his smooth chest and growing shoulders
in triple pleats of purple cloth and tipped
with gold his breastplate, arrows, belt, and bracelets—
even his helmet was engraved with gold—
an outfit to impress his future wife.
He trusted it, and he defied the Greeks.
He threw his spears and chased retreating troops. 570
He took the armor of the men he slew,
returning back to safety like a lion
in Caspian forests of Hyrcania,
still innocent of massacres and sleek,
not yet a terror, huge and tawny maned,
who slaughters sluggish cattle close to home
while their custodian is gone and slakes
his hunger by consuming tender lambs.

The arms of Tydeus were unknown to Atys: 577
he did not know enough to be afraid
and judged him by his smallness—so he dared
to throw his fragile weapons at this soldier
who threatened and pursued so many others.

Tydeus laughed horribly when he first felt 580
those useless blows and said, "For sometime now
I have been noticing your great desire
to die a hero's death, you shameless fool!"

He spoke, and scorned to use his spear or sword 583
but with his fingers flicked a feeble dart
that nonetheless drove deep in Atys' groin
as if it had been hurled with all his might.
Sure he would die, he passed him by, too proud
to stoop and strip away his armaments.
"We would not hang these trophies up for Mars
or you, o warlike Pallas! They are worthless,
to be rejected as not even fit
to give Deipyle should she enlist
for war and join me here outside her chamber!"

These were his words, and now he turned his mind
to winning greater trophies in the war,
as some strong lion, who can choose his victims,
passes defenseless heifers and young calves,
raging, intent to bathe in blood, who will
not stop except to break a great bull's spine.

But Atys did not fail, when he had fallen, 597
to call Menoeceus with a fainting voice.
Menoeceus turned his chariot and steeds
and quickly drove to where the Tyrians
allowed Tegeans to surround their man.

"For shame, young men of Cadmus! It's a lie 600
that says your fathers grew up from the ground!
Are you degenerate that you permit this?
Is it ignoble that a stranger died
fighting for us? He was unfortunate,
this foreigner, and had not yet impressed
his promised bride! Are we such faithless men?"

Thoughts of the wives and children they esteemed
stiffened the will of those embarrassed soldiers.
Meanwhile, Ismene and Antigone 607
sat in the inner recess of their rooms,
far different from their brothers, innocent
offspring of wretched Oedipus. They made
various lamentations as they talked,
not about current evils, but the distant
origins of their fate. This girl bemoaned
their mother's marriage; that, their father's eyes;
this one the brother who maintained his rule;
that one the brother who had wandered off.
But both complained about the war: their prayers
were hesitant and sad, and they were swayed
two ways—by fear of who would win the contest
and who would be defeated, yet they favored,
without admitting it, the exiled one.
So King Pandion's daughters, Philomela
◆ and Procne—nightingale and swallow—seek 616

trustworthy hospitality, the homes
they leave when winter weather drives them out.
Their voices seem like words. They think they speak.
They perch above their old nests and recall
their fortunes—feeble murmurings, unclear.

After the women wept and then were silent, 621
Ismene said, "What is this fantasy
we mortals have? Why is our trust deceived?
Do cares attend us as we sleep? Does sleep
bring clarity of vision to our souls?
I could not bear to think of marrying,
not even when we were at peace, but lo!
to my embarrassment, last night I dreamed
I saw my husband! Sister, how can sleep
show me an image that I had forgotten
and barely recognize? Once, in these rooms,
I glimpsed him when our covenants were drawn.
Suddenly, sister, I saw only blurs,
flames separated us, and then his mother
followed me, shouting for her Atys back!
Is this an image of impending doom?
I feel secure as long as Thebes is strong,
the Doric troops retreat, and we're allowed
to reconcile the pride of our two brothers."

Such was their conversation, when stark terror 636
shattered the quiet house, as Atys, who'd
been rescued with great effort, was received.
He had lost blood. He barely clung to life.
He held his hand positioned on his wound.
His neck hung limply from his shield, his hair
fell from his forehead, and Jocasta, who
saw him first, trembling, called his dear Ismene.
The future son-in-law's declining voice
called only for Ismene; cold lips spoke
her name alone. The household servants wept.

His lady held her hands before her eyes,
immobilized by fear; she felt ashamed,
yet entered where he lay. Jocasta granted

the dying man's last wish and let him see—
let him be present with—his dear Ismene.
Four times as death came over him he lifted 647
his eyes and failing vision at her name;
he turned from heaven's light to look at her
and gazed unmoving at the one he loved.
And then, because his mother was not near
and death had shown a mercy to his father,
his bride-to-be received the sad reward
of lowering his eyelids; left alone,
her eyes filled up with tears; the poor girl moaned.

–♦–♦–♦–

While this was happening in Thebes, Bellona 655
renewed the war with fresh flames, other serpents.
Men longed for battle, and their sword blades shone
as if first blows were only now delivered.
Preeminent was Tydeus, even though
Parthenopaeus shot unerring arrows,
Hippomedon's mad horses kicked the dying,
and Capaneus surveyed the array
of distant Thebans as he aimed his spear.

The day belonged to Tydeus; it was he 663
they feared and fled. He cried, "Why flee?
Remain here and avenge your murdered friends
and make atonement for a dreadful night!
I am the man who conquered fifty souls
but feel the need to kill as many more.
Send me more men; no, send as many squadrons!
Are there no fathers or no brothers as
devoted as the fallen you've forgotten?
Where is your grief, your shame that I returned
a victor to Inachian Mycenae!
Are these all Thebes has left? this the king's strength?
Where can I find the great Eteocles?"

Just then he saw the king commanding troops 672
along the left wing, saw his high casque flash.
♦ Tydeus raced not less slowly than the bird

that carries lightning brings a white swan terror,
enveloping and circling him with shadow.

But first: "O just king of Aonia!
We meet in open combat! We draw swords!
Perhaps you'd rather wait for night's dark shadows?"

The king said nothing, but he aimed a shaft 680
of hissing horn in answer at his foe,
but when it reached its mark, the watchful hero
knocked it aside and eagerly unleashed
all of his own great strength to fling his spear.
The deadly weapon, which could end the duel,
flew through the air and drew the eyes of gods
some of whom favored Thebans, some the Greeks,
but the cruel Fury interfered and saved
Eteocles for his disgraceful brother.
The erring point hit Phlegyas, a warrior.

Then a great skirmishing of men began 688
as Tydeus, the Aetolian, drew his sword
and rushed the Theban troops, who covered for
their king as he retreated. Just this way
a band of shepherds makes a wolf abandon
a bullock he has seized and he responds
fiercely, but not at them. He wants his booty—
the prey that, having seized, he now pursues.

No less unmoved was Tydeus by the lines 695
that formed against him as he made his way.
He struck Deilochus and pierced his chest,
the face of Thoas, and the flank of Clonius.
Savage Hippotadas? He stabbed his groin.
Tydeus tossed heads in helmets through the air;
disjointed arms and legs rained over bodies.

By now he had enclosed himself with piles 700
of corpses and the spoils of fallen men.
He was surrounded by the battle line
and every weapon aimed at only him.
Some arrows struck his sinews, some just missed,

some Pallas cast aside, but many stood
stiff like an iron forest on his shield.
The boar skin that he wore, his country's pride,
slipped off his back and shoulders, and his crest
had lost its glory, a tall figurine
of Mars that now no longer topped his helmet.
It fell—no happy omen for the man!

Only bare bronze remained to cover him 709
from thudding rocks that flew around his head.
Blood filled his helmet, and his wounded chest
streamed darkly with a mix of gore and sweat.
He could see comrades urge him, see the shield
behind which faithful Pallas hid her fears:
she left to sway great Jupiter with tears.

Just then an ashen spear cut through the winds, 716
driven by fortune and enormous anger.
At first nobody knew who hurled that shaft;
he did not show himself but tried to hide,
yet celebrating troops discovered him.
It was Astacus' son, named Melanippus,
who shook in fear as Tydeus doubled over,
released his oval shield, and gripped his side.

Aonian cheers mixed with Pelasgian groans. 722
Bands circled to protect the spiteful hero.
He hated Melanippus, whom he glimpsed
far off, beyond his enemies, and gathered
all his remaining strength to throw a spear
that nearby Hopleus offered. The attempt
made his blood spurt, and his unhappy men 728
carried away the one who was so keen
to fight that he denied that he was dying.
He asked for a fresh spear, but he was taken
beside the field and propped against two shields
by weeping soldiers who said he would soon
be back in battle, for the war continued.

But he could sense the heavens dim; extreme 733
coldness came over him; his great strength waned.

He leaned along the ground and cried, "Do what
I ask, Inachidae. Don't take my bones
to Argos or Aetolia. I don't care
for final rites. I hate these useless limbs,
this fragile body that deserts my soul!

"Would there were someone to retrieve your head— 739
your head, o Melannipus! I am certain
you lie dead in the field and that my final
action succeeded. Go, Hippomedon,
if you have any blood of Atreus!
And Parthenopaeus, go—already
famous in your first war! And Capaneus,
now greatest warrior among the Argives!"

Each hurried. Capaneus, first in motion, 745
first to find Melanippus, bent and lifted
him breathing from the dust and carried him
on his left shoulder as his open wound
poured streams of blood and gore along his back—
like Hercules, when from Arcadia's cave
he brought the captive boar to clamoring Argos.

Tydeus sat up and turned his gaze and, mad 751
with joy and anger, saw his gasping face
and glancing eyeballs—and he saw himself.
He had the head cut off and set before him.
His left hand gripped the gruesome, hated object,
and he enjoyed its warmth, while its wild eyes
flickered with wonder. When would they be closed?
Tydeus was happy, but unfortunate.
Vengeful Tisiphone demanded more.

–•–•–•–

• By now Tritonian Pallas had assuaged 758
her pliant father and was carrying
immortal fame to Tydeus, when she saw
that blood and broken brains perfused his jaws,
that slime and filthy stains befouled his face.
His comrades could not stop him. The fierce Gorgon

stood there with outstretched hair, and her horned serpents
stiffened and cast their shadows on Athena.

The goddess turned her face away and fled, 764
nor did she enter heaven till her eyes
had undergone purgation—mystic fires,
ablutions in the guiltless stream Ilissos.

—♦—♦—♦—

BOOK 9 Tide and Time

Disgust with Tydeus. Reactions of Eteocles and Polynices. Hippomedon protects the body of Tydeus until Tisiphone interferes. Hypseus, the Theban champion. The death of Crenaeus, son of the river nymph, infuriates Ismenos, who floods and drowns Hippomedon. Capaneus kills Hypseus. Atalanta's nightmares portend the death of her son. Dryas kills Parthenopaeus. Final message to his mother.

What Tydeus did disgusted every Tyrian
who heard about his angry, bloody deed.
Even Inachians lamented little
that he had fallen. They themselves complained
that he transgressed divine restraints on hate.

Gradivus, most implacable of gods, 4
you too would not approach him. People say
your mad mind is intent on taking life,
but his brutality was so offensive
you turned your frightened horses from the sight.

The desecrated corpse of Melanippus 8
sufficed to stir young Thebans to revenge,
as much as if their fathers' urns were mauled
by monsters and their buried bones disturbed.

The king himself, Eteocles, provoked them: 12
"Who shows Pelasgians mercy anymore?
Tydeus makes curved fangs instruments of rage;
he gnaws our limbs! Did we not slake his sword?
Does he believe he's some Hyrcanian tiger
or savage Libyan lion who attacks us?
He lies in death's sweet solace, yet his jaws
still grip the severed head of his opponent;
he revels in impiety and gore!
We battle Greeks with torches, hardened blades,

and open hate; our anger uses weapons!
Let them enjoy the fame their madness brings,
that you may witness it, great Jupiter.
They wonder why earth opened, why the field
of war retreated. Would their land support
such troops like these?" He spoke, and urged his men.

They charged and shouted loudly; each of them
was mad to gain the corpse and spoils of Tydeus.
Just so do flocks of birds obscure the sky
when lured from far away by evil breezes,
foul air blown from the dead who lie unburied.
Their voices ravenlike, they rush on wings
that beat the winds, and lesser birds give way.

Across Aonia's plain the murmuring 32
of rapid Rumor flew among the soldiers—
bad news moves fast—until that mournful sound
had reached the trembling ears of Polynices.

Slow to believe, he stiffened, held his tears.
He was persuaded, and dissuaded, by
the strength of Tydeus, that he might have died.
A trusted messenger confirmed his death,
and then night overwhelmed his mind and eyes,
his blood chilled, limbs grew slack, his weapons dropped,
he wept inside his helmet, and his shield
fell and rebounded off the warrior's greaves.
He walked on wobbling knees and dragged his spear
in mourning, as if bearing many wounds,
deep ones, on every limb. His friends drew back
and looked at him with sorrow, even as
he shed the armor he could hardly carry
and tumbled prostrate on the lifeless body
of his great friend. He mingled words with tears:

"Is this the thanks I offer you, o son 49
of Oeneus, for your meritorious service
that left you dead in Cadmus's hated fields
while I was safe? Now I will always be

a miserable exile and a fugitive.
My other, better brother has been taken!
I will no longer seek my former fortune,
the perjured diadem of that foul kingdom.
My happiness has cost too much. What can
a scepter you have not presented mean?

"Depart, men! Let me face my wicked brother! 57
Why risk another war where soldiers perish?
I pray you, go! What more is there to offer?
I wasted Tydeus! How can I atone,
even by dying? O Adrastus! Argos!
Our lucky altercation that first night,
the blows exchanged, the long love that we won
from such short anger. O great Tydeus! Why?
You should have killed me on the royal threshold.
You even went to Thebes for me and knew
my brother's household, his impieties.
No other could have come back, yet you went
as if your crown and honors were at stake.
Fame has already ceased to speak of Theseus
and pious Telamon, for you matched these.
Now you lie dead! Which wound should I search first?
Which blood is yours? Which is your enemies'?
What battle line, what countless company—
if I am not mistaken—laid you low?
The father of the gods himself felt envy,
and Mars unleashed his spear with all his strength."

And so he spoke and mourned and cleaned the man's 73
face with his tears and wiped him with his hand.
"Did you so hate my enemies? Do I
survive?" and then, deranged, he drew his sword
out of its sheathe, and he prepared to die.

His comrades stopped him, and his father-in-law
checked him, then calmed him. He reminded him
of fate and the uncertainties of war,
then slowly drew him from his friend's dead body,
the source of his laments and helplessness,
and, unobserved while speaking, sheathed his sword.

They led him off the way they lead a bull
who loses his yoke fellow in midfurrow;
his harness falls lopsided off his neck;
the weeping plowman lifts part, part the ox.

–♦–♦–♦–

Even as this occurred, Eteocles 86
was urging forward his best infantry,
young men whom Pallas would not scorn to face
in war, or Mars contend with spear to spear.

Against them tall Hippomedon held fast 89
behind his shield, his spear extended forward,
just as a rock opposes waves, afraid
of nothing in the heavens and unmoved,
despite the breaking waters, while at sea
sad sailors recognize a prodigy.

Then spoke Aonian Eteocles, 95
even as he selected his best spear:

"Have you no sense of shame, that you should guard,
while all the gods and heavens watch, this ghost,
this corpse that brings our warfare ill-repute?
No doubt the burial of such a beast
makes worthwhile this enormous task,
this unforgettable display of strength,
lest he should go to Argos to be mourned
and drip corrupted blood from his soft bier!
But do not worry; he will not be eaten
by godless monsters, birds, or pious flames—
should we allow him flames."

No more was said.
His weapon drove two layers through the bronze
shield that was wielded by Hippomedon.
Pheres and Lycus followed: Pheres' shaft
bounded, while subtle Lycus cut in half
his waving crest, the terror on his casque.

But they could not displace Hippomedon 110
nor did he move to meet opposing arms.
He stood against them all and fought, but his
sole purpose was to guard the corpse he loved,
just as a jealous cow protects her calf—
her fragile firstborn—from a hostile wolf,
anticipating him with circling horns,
fearful of nothing. She forgets her sex
lacks strength; she foams and imitates strong bulls.

At last the cloud of flying missiles thinned, 120
and he could hurl their weapons back again.
Then Alcon came with help from Sicyon
and nimble Idas's Pisan troops filled in.
Hippomedon was pleased by this and flung
a Lernaean spear against his enemies
that quickly thrust Polites through the waist
and then the shield of Mopsus, his close friend.
♦ He pierced the Phocian Cydon and Tanagraean 127
Phalanthus, also Eryx, who was turning,
searching for weapons, not expecting death
to enter through his long hair, while Phalanthus
spit teeth the spear dislodged and wondered why
his face but not his hollow throat felt safe:
he moaned and coughed up blood as he was dying.

Leonteus was attempting to extend 133
his right arm through the bands of fighting men
who hid him as he seized dead Tydeus's hair,
but he was spotted by Hippomedon
despite the crush of danger on all sides.
His savage sword cut through that outstretched hand,
as he yelled loudly, "Tydeus did it—Tydeus!
After this, show respect for warriors,
even when dead, and be afraid to seek
the ghosts of great ones, you who are so weak!"

Three times the Cadmean phalanx tried to take 140
the frightful corpse; three times Danaans
retrieved it, moving like an anxious ship
in mutinous Sicilian seas, which wanders,

despite the skipper's efforts, back and forth,
retracing, sails reversed, her former course.

Hippomedon would not be driven back 144
from his position by Sidonian forces.
He could withstand the force of catapults:
their weapons, which might frighten lofty towers,
uselessly struck his shield and he repelled them.

Irreverent Tisiphone, however, 148
remembering Elysium's king, the crimes
Tydeus committed in the recent past,
moved with dexterity around the field.
She hid her whip and sacrilegious torch
and made the serpents in her hair lie silent.
The armies felt her presence though she took
the shape of Halys, an Inachian;
soldiers and horses suddenly perspired.

The goddess wept and said, "You work in vain, 154
despite your greatness, to protect dead comrades
and the unburied bodies of the Greeks.
What do we fear? Why do we care for tombs?
The Tyrians have captured King Adrastus!
He lifts his voice and hands and calls your name;
he crawls through blood; his crown has been torn off,
his white hair flows behind him. Turn your gaze:
look at those soldiers; see, their dust comes closer!"

The anxious hero paused and weighed his worries. 164
Tisiphone was harsh and badgered him:
"Why wait? Are we not going? Do you cling
to this dead body? Is the living king
worth no more than a corpse?" At last Hippomedon
ordered his men to take his place, and he
abandoned his best friend, but still looked back
to see if someone called for his return.

He followed the stern goddess's wild footsteps 171
and hurried aimlessly he knew not where

until the sea-green Fury dropped her shield
and countless snakes broke through her wicked helmet.
Her shadow dissipated; he'd been duped.
He saw Adrastus' chariot, poor man,
and he could see the calm Inachians.

Now Tyrians controlled the corpse of Tydeus 177
and rising voices testified their joy,
but their victorious cries struck other ears
and other hearts, which secretly lamented.
Such was the hard severity of Fate
that the great Tydeus—he for whom of late
great spaces would be left on either side
as he pursued the Theban battle lines—
whether on foot or holding loosened reins—
was dragged on hostile soil, where no hand
or weapon was quiescent; there no man
showed pity for his features, stiff in death.
The troops rejoiced as with impunity
they stabbed the face they'd feared; the strong, the meek
shared this desire to validate their lives,
and they preserved their weapons, stained with blood,
to show their little children and their wives.
It was as when a lion has wreaked havoc
◆ in Moorish fields and forced the guardians 189
of flocks to keep them penned, to stand on watch
until the weary comrades of the shepherds
subdue the beast, and everyone rejoices:
farmers approach, shout loudly, and they pluck
the lion's mane and open massive jaws
and tell what they had suffered, even as
their victim hangs suspended from some roof
or dangles proudly in an ancient grove.

Although the fierce Hippomedon now knew 196
his help was useless, that he came too late
to battle for the body they had taken,
he nonetheless advanced, unstoppable,
and blindly swung his weapon. Nothing blocked

his progress, neither friends nor enemies.
He killed indifferently, until the ground
grew slick with recent victims, dying men,
armor, and broken chariots, despite
his left thigh, which impeded him. Eteocles
had hurt him with his spear, but he ignored it,
either because he fought away the pain
or else he had not noticed he was lame.

He found a horse when he saw mournful Hopleus, 204
great Tydeus' faithful friend and helpless squire,
who held his master's rapid-footed steed.
It seemed the horse complained; it hung its neck;
it did not understand its rider's fate,
and it disdained Hippomedon's new weight,
for it had only known one person's hand
since being broken years before. The man
controlled it, nonetheless, and he consoled it:

"Why balk, unhappy horse, at your new fate? 211
No longer will you know your proud king's burden
or exercise along Aetolian plains
or let the Achelous wash your mane!
All that remains for you is to avenge
his cherished ghost or, like him, die, lest you
be captured and offend his spirit further
when you bear some proud man who makes this boast,
that he bestrides the horse that Tydeus rode!"

That steed was so incensed that you would think 218
it understood him. Like a lightning bolt
it carried him away and less disdained
the hands, like those of Tydeus, on its reins,
just as a Centaur, half a man, half horse,
descends from airy Ossa to the plains:
its human portion makes the high groves shake;
its horse half frightens fields. Hippomedon,
thus mounted, overwhelmed the panting sons
of Labdacus with terror as he mowed

their unprotected necks and left behind
the bodies of the soldiers he had slain.

He reached the river, where Ismenos flowed 225
fuller than usual, an evil sign.
There he paused briefly, as the timid lines
directed their withdrawal from the field.
They stunned the stream, which welcomed warriors
and glistened as bright armor lit dark waves.
To their astonishment, Hippomedon
galloped on horseback through the hostile current
as if he had no time to drop his reins,
only to fix his weapons in the bank
and leave them leaning on a poplar trunk.

His terrified opponents tossed their own 236
into the stream, which carried them away.
Some threw their helmets off and tried to hide
as long as possible beneath the river,
like cowards. Others tried to swim across,
but harnesses constrained them, heavy belts
weighed down their bodies, and their water-soaked
hauberks hung heavy. They were drawn off course,
as sea-blue fishes in a swollen sea 242
flee from the terror of a searching dolphin
whom they have seen prospecting through the deep.
Fear drives them to the deepest, darkest parts,
where they are crowned by iridescent weeds
and do not reemerge until they see
the dolphin's arching back resurfacing
as he decides to chase a passing keel.
Just so, Hippomedon, with lance and steed, 248
uplifted by his horse's rowing feet,
pursued the scattered soldiers through the flood.
Its swimming hooves, accustomed to the land,
now paddled nimbly, now touched sunken sand.

Chromis killed Ion. Antiphon killed Chromis. 252
Hypseus killed Antiphon, then he attacked
Astyages, then Linus, who was leaving

the river in retreat, but fate forbade:
his thread of life cut short, he died on shore.

Hippomedon attacked the Theban lines; 255
Asopian Hypseus drove Danaans back;
both scared the river, muddied it with gore,
but neither one was destined to emerge.

Torn limbs bobbed down the river as it flowed, 259
and severed heads and arms rejoined torn trunks.
The current carried darts, light shields, slack bows.
Plumed crests kept casques from sinking. On the surface,
the stream was strewn with weapons; in its depths,
men floated, and the river pushed their breath
back in their mouths as bodies battled death.

From the swift stream young Argipus had seized 266
an elm that grew along the riverside,
but fierce Menoeceus saw his arms extend
and cut them off by sword. This was his end:
he struggled and he fell and he could see
his arms still clinging to the branching tree.

Sages was transfixed by the spear of Hypseus: 270
his blood resurfaced; Sages stayed below.
Agenor, bankside, dove to save his brother;
he held him, but the wounded man weighed down
the poor soul who embraced him: strong Agenor
could have resurfaced, but he held his brother.

A swirling whirlpool sucked Capetus under, 276
yet his right hand arose and threatened thunder.
The water hid his face first, then his hair,
then his good arm, and then his sword descended.

A thousand forms of death produced one fate 280
for all those wretched men. A Mycalesian
spearpoint was buried in Agyrtes' back.
He looked but saw no source: the current had
carried the flowing spear that caused his hurt.

Hippomedon's Aetolian horse was hit 284
through its strong shoulders, and the shock of death
made it rear up and hang and beat the air.
Hippomedon was undisturbed, but took
pity, pulled free the spear, and then complained
because he had to lay aside his reins.

He moved with greater confidence on foot, 289
surer of hand, as he resought the fray.
He killed slow-moving Nomius, the strong
♦ Mimas, the Thisbaean Lichas, and Lycetus
♦ the Anthedonian, then one of twins—
Thespiades—whose brother, named Panemus,
begged for a similar fate. To him he said:

"You will remain alive, and when you go
back to the walls of your unlucky Thebes,
your parents will no longer be deceived!
Thanks to the gods, Bellona's bloody hand
has pushed this battle to the rapid stream
that washes cowards down their native waters
where they will feed the monsters of the deep.
The ghost of Tydeus will not fly and screech
about their pyres. He for whom we weep
lies naked and unburied on the ground,
where he will stay till he returns to dust."

And so he overwhelmed his enemies 302
and made their wounds more bitter with his words.
Now he was furious and swung his sword;
now he plucked floating javelins to hurl.
He punctured Theron, chaste Diana's friend;
the rural Gyas; riverman Erginus;
Herses, whose hair was never cut, and Cretheus,
contemner of the deep, who often sailed
his tiny vessel through Euboean storms
♦ around the cloudy peak of Caphereus.
What may not fortune do? A lance transfixed
his breast, alas, and he was shipwrecked here,
carried away along the river's waves.

You too, Pharsalus, lost your horses to
a spear that knocked you over as you swam
the river in your lofty chariot
and tried to join your friends. The savage stream
swept them away; it drowned the harnessed steeds.

Now learned Sisters, grant that I may know 315
what exploit overcame Hippomedon
among the swollen waves, and why Ismenos
entered the fray himself. It is your task
to brush old age from fame, to travel back.

◆ The son of Faunus and the nymph Ismenis—
tender Crenaeus—loved to fight in war
upon his mother's waves: Crenaeus, who
first saw the light in that protective stream
whose green banks cradled him, his native river.
◆ The Sisters of Elysium, he thought,
would have no power there, and so he crossed
his welcoming grandfather, bank to bank,
now here, now there. The water lifts his steps,
whether he moves across or down the stream,
nor does the current stay him when he goes
upriver, for it then reverses flow.
The sea does not more gently touch the waist 328
of Glaucus—he of Anthedon—nor Triton
extend himself more high from summer waves,
nor does Palaemon seek his mother's kiss
with greater speed when he spurs his slow dolphin.

His shoulders shone with armor: his great scutcheon, 332
bright gold, on which his people's origins,
the stories of Aonia, were etched.
◆ Here the Sidonian maiden rode the white
back of a fawning bull, safe from the sea—
no need for her soft palms to hold his horns;
the water played around her dangling feet.
You would believe they traveled on the shield
and that the bull was slicing through the waves—
the sea, the stream, the main were proper shades.

Equally bold with weapons, proud of voice, 339
he called Hippomedon: "These waters are
not venomous, like Lerna's, nor do Hydras
of Hercules imbibe them. They are sacred—
this stream is sacred, wretch, and you will learn
the river you invade has nourished gods!"

Hippomedon said nothing, but approached him. 343
The stream swelled higher up and slowed his hand,
yet he, despite the waves, conveyed a blow
that carried to the chambers of his life.
The stream took fright at this impiety.
You wept, o woods on either shore, and cries 347
rang loudly all along the hollow banks.
The last word from his dying mouth was "Mother!"
as water overwhelmed his plaintive sounds.

His mother was encircled by a band
♦ of silvery sisters in a vitreous vale 351
when, shocked to hear the news, she leaped up madly,
her hair unbound, and beat her face and breasts
and ripped, in her despair, her sea-green dress.
She rises from the waves. She cries, she cries
again. Her trembling voice repeats, "Crenaeus!"

Nothing is seen except a shield, a sign—
it floats upon the waves—known all too well
by his despairing parent, while far off,
where Ismenos begins to change and mix
his waters with the greater sea, he lies.
Thus often Alcyone groans, abandoned, 360
over her wandering and dripping home
when savage Auster wafts away her fledglings
and envious Thetis swamps neglected nests.

The childless mother once again submerged 363
and deep beneath the hidden waters searched
down many currents for her sad son's corpse.
She wept as she pursued translucent roads.

Sometimes the bristling river blocked her way
and floating clouds of blood obscured her vision,
yet on she hurried, over swords and weapons,
reaching her hand inside of helmets, turning
prone bodies over. When she reached the sea
◆ she did not enter Doris' salty waters
but stayed until the Nereids took pity
and pushed the body, which had been possessed
by weltering waves, against the mother's breast.

She carried him as if he were alive 373
and lay him on the cushioned riverbank.
She dried his wet face with her tender hair
and mournful, she complained: "Is this the fate
your parents—demigods—and your immortal
grandfather gave? Is this how you will rule
our river? Alien, discordant lands
would be more kind, my miserable boy—
even the sea, which brought your body back,
as if expecting your bereaving parent.

"Is this my face? these your fierce father's eyes? 381
the billows of your grandsire in your hair?
You were the pride of forest and of stream;
I was a greater goddess while you lived
and far and wide known as the queen of Nymphs!
Where is the crowd of woodland deities 385
who sought to serve, who ringed your mother's doorway?
Why do I bring you here, in sad embrace,
to benefit your tomb and not myself?
I would be better in the savage deep,
Crenaeus! O cruel father, is not such
a death a shameful thing, and to be pitied?
What deep morass and mirey river bottom
hides you, where neither my laments nor news
of your dead grandson's body penetrate?
Hippomedon is raging, and he brags 393
that he controls your stream, whose waves and banks
tremble before him—he whose dolorous stroke

allowed the river to consume our blood.
You slave for fierce Pelasgians! Are you lazy?
At least, cruel man, come take a final look
at one of your own people's ashes, for
it is not just a grandson you must burn!"

Moans mingled with her words. She beat her breast 399
bloody, though guiltless, and her sea-blue sisters
echoed her lamentations, just as when
Leucothea, not yet a Nereid,
lamented, so they say, in Corinth's harbor,
as her cold infant vomited fierce seas.

–♦–♦–♦–

Father Ismenos, who resided in 404
his secret cavern where the clouds and winds
imbibe, and where he feeds rain-bearing bows,
and where the Tyrian fields' good years are grown,
could hear, despite the roarings of his own,
the distant lamentations and the groans
he knows must be his daughter's. He uplifted
his moss-grown neck, his heavy frozen hair.
His lengthy staff of pine escaped his grasp
and he ungripped his urn, which rolled away.
The forests and the minor rivers stared
from on the shore as he upraised his face,
rugged with ancient mud, and then emerged
out of the swollen stream. He lifted up
his foaming head, and from his sea-blue beard
sonorous droplets trickled down his chest.

One of his daughters met him, and the nymph 416
showed him her groaning sister and explained
his grandson's fate. She pointed out the man
who did this bloody deed and pressed his hand.

Ismenos stood up tall within his stream;
his horns were interwoven with green sedge;
he struck them with his fists and struck his cheeks;
he was disturbed; his voice was low. He spoke:

"Is this, o ruler of the gods, the wage 421
for one who often welcomed and observed
your doings? These I fear not to recall—
◆ the guilty horns you wore on your false face;
forbidding Phoebe to unyoke her cart;
the marriage pyre: deceptive lightning bolts!
I raised your firstborn sons: are they ungrateful?
◆ Tirynthius first crawled beside this stream;
I quenched, in these waves, flaming Bromius.
Observe how many dead are in the river, 429
what bodies I must bear, the constant flow
of weapons, and the heaps that cover me.
My currents are beset by constant warfare,
and every wave inhales impiety.
The old dead sink; the newly vanquished loom;
my banksides are connected by their gloom.
I am acclaimed by sacred incantations;
the tender thyrsus and the horns of Bacchus
are laved in my pure streams, but now the dead
constrict me so, I cannot reach the sea.
No such amount of blood fills impious Strymon;
Hebrus foams not so red when Mars makes war.
The stream that raised you now admonishes
you and your followers, o Liber—you
who have forgotten who your parents were!
Was India so easy to subdue?
But you, Hippomedon, so puffed by spoils, 442
proud to have spilled a guiltless young man's blood,
won't leave this river to return as victor
to mighty Inachus or fierce Mycenae,
unless *I* am the mortal one, and *you*
inherited your blood from deities!"

He spoke and ground his teeth and gave 446
signs to the madding waves, and cold Cithaeron
sent mountain reinforcements, age-old snows,
and ordered forward river-feeding frosts.
Asopos, brother of Ismenos, mixed
those currents with his unfamiliar strength,
sending his rivers up from open veins.

Meanwhile Ismenos searched throughout the depths
and hollows of the underworld to wake
desolate swamps and pools and stagnant lakes.
He raised his eager visage to the skies
and sucked the humid clouds and heavens dry.
Now he was flowing over either bank 455
with mounds of water, and Hippomedon,
who even then was towering midstream,
dry in his arms and shoulders, was impressed
to see the river swell, himself grow less.

The river flooded, and an angry storm 459
surged like the seas that tug the Pleiades
or fling Orion's night on frightened sailors.
Similarly Teumesia's water wracked
Hippomedon with oceanic streams
and bounded off the boss by his left shoulder.
Black foaming billows overwhelmed his shield,
broke into waves, grew larger, then surged back.
The mass of liquid overwhelmed the stream,
which plucked up trunks that held the crumbling banks,
rolled boulders from the depths, and swirled gnarled trees.

Human and river waged an even contest.
Much to the god's dismay, Hippomedon 470
never retreated; he ignored all threats;
he stubbornly opposed the rushing flow
and shoved his target hard against the current.
The ground gave way, but he maintained his place;
his hamstrings strained, his knees flexed, but he held
his balance on the slipping stones and slime
that undermined his feet and made them slide.

The hero cried, "Tell me, Ismenos, why 476
are you so angry? From what source have you
drawn strength? You serve a peaceful god;
your only blood comes from the women's chorus
when maddened matrons play their Bacchic pipes
three times a year and stain your festive rites!"

The god attacked as soon as he had finished. 481
His face was wet and dark with swimming sand.
His weapons were not words, but one oak trunk
with which he rammed three times and then a fourth.
Swollen with anger and divinity,
he flowed and struck. At last Hippomedon
slipped off his feet, his shield fell from his arm,
and he revolved and slowly turned around.
Waves inundated him; the joyous stream
pursued him as he groped; and Tyrians
tortured the man with stones and iron hail
that struck him and repulsed him from both banks.
What could he do, besieged by wave and war?
The poor man could not flee, or die, with glory.

Along the riverbank an ash tree grew 492
and leaned out from the turf. You could not say
if it belonged to dry land or the waves.
It overhung the river with its shade
and offered to Hippomedon a place
that he could reach, a hook for his right hand.
Where else along the river would he land?
But it could not withstand his downward pull,
the ponderous weight that overcame its hold
and ripped branched roots that clawed the arid earth.
The tree was thrown over the trembling man
and chunks of bank fell too and made a dam,
a bridge constructed from the stream's debris.
Here the waves gathered, and they formed a pit
of endless mud and hollow, swirling pools
that rose and fell around the warrior,
reaching his shoulders now, and now his neck,
until he was defeated and confessed
his time had come.

He said, "O mighty Mars! 506
Must I endure the shame of drowning? Will
this river take my soul? Shall I be choked
beneath slow-moving lakes and stagnant fens
like some custodian of sheep flocks caught

by rising waters from a sudden storm?
Don't I deserve to die on someone's sword?"

Juno, moved by his prayers, accosted Jove: 510
"How far do you intend, progenitor,
to press the poor Inachians? How far?
Pallas already hates her Tydeus! Delphi
is silent, since its seer was seized! And my
Hippomedon, whose household gods were Argive,
whose race rose in Mycenae and who worships
Juno above the other deities,
sinks in the sea, the prey of monstrous fish.
Is this how I reward my followers?
You used to give the victors mounds and pyres:
where are the flames of Theseus, the Athenian
custom of burning bodies after battle?"

Jove was not scornful. Juno's plea was just. 519
His quick eyes turned upon the towers of Cadmus.
The river saw his nod and drained away.

–♦–♦–♦–

Those weary shoulders and that battered chest 522
emerged above the waters, like a cliff
or shores long sought by sailors when a storm
tempers the fury of its winds, and seas
retreat and leave the deadly rocks revealed.
What did the riverbanks avail him now?
On every side Phoenician cohorts pressed
with clouds of weapons, and they threatened death.
He did not have a bit of armor left;
his wounds, which had been staunched beneath the stream,
flowed in the open air; frail veins released;
his steps gave way; cold water numbed his feet.

So down he fell, just as an oak tree falls 532
on Getic Haemon from the north wind's fury
or feeble age. Its branches, which stood high
and framed the heavens, now will leave a void,
and as it nods, the mountain and its groves

tremble in fear for where the oak will fall.
What copses will its great length overwhelm?

No one yet dared to touch his sword or helmet. 537
They stared in disbelief. The giant body
thrilled them as they approached with weapons drawn.
Hypseus, at last, approached the corpse. He took 540
the pommel from its grasp and then unlaced
the head gear from that awe-inspiring face.
He raised that helmet on his shining sword
and pranced as he displayed it to the Thebans:

"This is the terrible Hippomedon, 544
ruthless defender of unspeakable Tydeus,
the warrior who quelled the savage stream!"

Listening from far away, oppressed by grief, 546
greathearted Capaneus flexed his arm;
he weighed a mighty javelin and prayed:

"Unstoppable right hand, divinity,
you who have been a presence in my wars,
I call on you because I scorn the deities.
You are the only god whom I adore!"

He spoke; he stoked his prowess with his vows.
His quivering ash spear punctured Hypseus' shield;
it pierced his brazen hauberk and his massive
torso and took his life. So Hypseus fell
just as a lofty turret—that same sound—
falls after countless missiles rip a town
and conquerors invade its open walls.

Hovering above him, Capaneus boasts, 557
"We do not grudge you honor as you die.
See, Capaneus did this; turn your eyes!
Be glad you'll be admired by other ghosts!"

He took his sword and casque and tore away
the shield of Hypseus, and he held them over
the body that was once Hippomedon.

"O mighty duke," he said, "accept these spoils,
yours and your enemy's. Your shade shall know
a proper burial, your ashes find
suitable honors, but until the time
that I return with ceremonial fire
and take revenge, I'll let these rites suffice."

So even-handed Mars brought war in turn 566
with all its hardship both to Greeks and Thebans.
Here they mourned fierce Hippomedon, there Hypseus
(both were indomitable) and either side
took comfort in its enemy's laments.

–♦–♦–♦–

Meanwhile the mother from Arcadia 570
had nightmares of her arrow-bearing son.
Her hair disheveled and her feet unbound,
before the dawn she visited cold Ladon
to purge her evil visions in that stream.

Often through sleepless nights, weighed down by cares, 575
she would see trophies falling from the shrine
that she had consecrated, see herself
moving down wandering roads past unknown tombs,
an exile from her groves, pursued by groups
of Dryades. And she would often see
triumphs returning from her young son's wars,
his armor, comrades, and his well-known steed,
but never him. Her quiver would fall off
her shoulders, and simulacra would burn—
her portraits and her other effigies.
But that night in particular aroused
panic in her maternal breast, bad portents.

There was an oak, known through Arcadia, 585
the tallest in her groves, which she herself
had picked and dedicated to Diana,
the goddess Trivia, whose worship graced
this special tree with her divinity.
Here she would hang her bow and weary weapons,

curved tusks of boars, the skins of vanquished lions,
and antlers equal to the largest branches.
Its limbs were crowded thick with rural trophies,
the green shade overwhelmed by flashing steel.

One night, while dreaming, she returned, exhausted 593
from fierce hunts in the mountains, carrying
an Erymanthean bear's head in her grasp
and thought she saw her oak, its crown cut down,
its branches dripping blood, dead on the ground.
A nymph, when questioned, said her enemy
◆ Lyaeus and his bloody Maenads raged.
While she lamented and—with unfelt blows—
pounded her chest, night vanished, and she leaped
off her sad bed and wiped away false tears.
She purged her own impiety by dipping 602
her hair in Ladon three times and recited
words that can soothe the worries of a mother;
then, through the morning dew, she hurried to
the shrine of armed Diana and rejoiced
to see her oak and well-known grove intact.
She prayed before the goddess, and she said:

"O powerful lady of the forests, whose harsh paths 608
and militant example I repeat—
I scorn my sex in ways not known to Greeks
◆ (nor do the Amazons or Colchian
barbarians revere you more than I)—
if I have never joined the Bacchic dance
or bands of nighttime revelers, although
I am polluted by a hated husband;
if I have never rubbed the Bacchic staff
or spun soft wool; if in my heart I am
a hunter and unmarried and unwilling
◆ to hide my moral fault in secret caves,
then save my son, the child whom I disclosed,
the trembling boy I placed before your feet.
He showed that he was worthy of his blood
by crawling to, and calling for, my weapons
as soon as he had learned to weep and speak.
What do my trembling nights and dreams portend?

Let me see him victorious in the war
where bold vows and excessive trust in you
have led the boy. Or if I ask too much,
bring him back here and let him bear your weapons.
You must attend these dreadful signs of evil!
Why should the hostile Maenads and the Theban
deity rule our forest, Delian goddess?
Oh, me! if I'm an augur, let me be
ignorant of the future. Why should I
feel certain there's an omen in the oak?
What if sleep sends me truthful messages? 631
◆ By your maternal labors, mild Dictynna,
and by the honor of your brother, let
your arrows hit my grieving womb, and let
Parthenopaeus learn about my death
before I hear of his!" She spoke and saw
white-robed Diana's altar moist with tears.

The fierce divinity left Atalanta 637
stretched on her sacred threshold where she swept
the cold stones with her tresses while the goddess
flew through the stars then past Maenalian forests
to reach the walls of Cadmus by the road
that shines in heaven, the divine abode.

The goddess had reached halfway past the peaks 643
of green Parnassus when she saw her brother.
Although his cloud shone brightly, he seemed cheerless.
He was returning from the Theban war,
sad and in mourning for his prophet's death.
Then, earth had opened; now, the sun and moon
made heaven glow, a sacred confluence.
Their bows commingled, and their quivers echoed.

Apollo spoke first: "Sister, I'm aware 650
you seek among Labdacian troops to find
a young Arcadian, one who overreaches!
His loving mother has petitioned you,
and I wish Fate would let us grant her wishes.
To my embarrassment, I saw the arms
and sacred chaplet of my prophet fall

to Tartarus while he was facing me.
I could not stop his chariot or close
the gaping earth. Thus cruel, should I be worshiped?
You see my caves lament, my shrines fall silent—
the only gifts I gave my pious prophet.
Sister, desist from vain and mournful toil;
do not enlist assistance that must perish.
The young man's time is here; fate will not change;
your brother's oracles do not deceive you."

The virgin was perplexed, and she replied, 664
"Should not this poor man's end be glorious?
May not he seek the solace of hard death?
Whatever person of ill will shall stain
his right hand with this young man's innocence,
should he escape my punishment? Should not
my arrows be permitted just revenge?"
She spoke and moved her steps. She let her brother
take a small kiss, then sought infected Thebes.

—♦—♦—♦—

After the double deaths, the fight grew cruel. 670
Desire for vengeance moved both sides to fury.
Here was the squad of Hypseus—lines that lacked
their leader; there, deserted followers
of slain Hippomedon, who darkly murmured.
The straining bodies faced each other's swords.
They yearned with similar insanity
to drink the others' blood or pour their own.
They watched their cruel opponents face-to-face;
not one man would retreat a single pace.

Now swift Latona glided through the air
and stopped on Dirce's heights. The hills saluted;
glades recognized the goddess, and they trembled,
for she once wearied bow and savage arrows
in killing Niobe and seven children.

A hunter unaccustomed to the fray— 683
a horse that was enduring its first bridle—

bore Parthenopaeus proudly through the squadrons
wrapped in a tiger's double-colored hide
whose gilded talons tapped across his shoulders.
Its neck lay flat and knotted, and its mane
was chaste and bound, while on its breast there beat
a rural, crescent necklace—ivory teeth.
The young man wore a cloak, twice purple dyed, 690
a tunic bright with gold, the only work
his mother ever wove. A slender sash
was wrapped around his waist, and he had slung
a shield from his left shoulder, where it hung.
His sword was much too heavy, but he loved
the gold pin with the polished clasp that tied
the hanging belt that circled his left side,
the sound his scabbard made, the trembling noise
he heard his quiver give, the helmet chains
that fell behind his head. He shook, for joy,
his glittering, jeweled helmet and his plumes,
but when his panting casque grew hot from fighting,
he doffed it, and, bareheaded, let his locks 700
shimmer with splendid rays that seemed to glow
and match his youthful cheeks, where no red down
had yet appeared: he mourned his beard's delay
and was displeased to hear his features praised. 704
He wore a stern expression on his face,
yet anger flattered him. It made him handsome.

Mindful that he was young, the Theban bands 706
retreated and relaxed their bows, but he
pursued, despite their pity, and attacked.
His fearsome javelins and dust and sweat
won admiration from the nymphs of Sidon
along Teumesian summits; they admired
his prowess but breathed silent prayers and sighs.

A gentle sadness struck Diana's heart 712
as she observed this; teardrops stained her cheeks.

"What means of cheating your approaching death
can I, your faithful goddess, find for you?

Fierce and lamented boy, is this the war
you hurry to? Your strength is immature,
impatient, yet your spirit urges you
to seek a glorious death! Too narrow were
Maenalian forests for impulsive years
when you were young, my little one, although
without your mother you could not have moved
safely through caves of savage animals;
you hardly had the strength to bend a bow
or wield the weapons suited to a hunt,
and now your mother wearies my deaf doorposts
and sills, makes loud laments before my altars.
Happy to die, to leave a parent miserable,
you revel in war's horns and calls to battle!"

Diana did not want the boy to perish 726
ingloriously, so she descended, wrapped
in red mist, to the battle, and she stole
his slender arrows from the bold boy's back
and changed them for a set of heavenly shafts
that would not fail to wound when he attacked.
She sprayed his limbs with her ambrosial liquid
and drenched his horse so both might die unblemished.
She also murmured magic spells and charms
that Colchian women learn in secret caverns
where she instructs them in the power of herbs.

Pathenopaeus rode like dancing flames 736
and shot his naked, undirected bow,
forgetful of his mother and his country,
and of himself. He put too great a trust
in his celestial weapons—like a lion
whose mother in Gaetulia delivers
freshly slain food to him when he is little,
but when he feels his neck produce a mane
and sees his new-grown claws, then he feels savage,
refuses to be fed and loves to roam
free in the open fields. He does not know
the path back to his cave. He can't find home.

Whom did you slay with your Parrhasian bow, 744
unbridled boy? *Coroebus the Tanagrean.*
Your arrow found the narrow path between
the margin of his target and his helmet.
His jaws poured blood, and sacred venom made
his face glow red with fire. More savagely,
Eurytion. With a three-pointed barb
a skillful arrow entered his left eye.
He pulled the shaft out with his fallen orb
and tried to charge its owner, but what weapons
are stronger than the weapons of the gods?
An arrow in his other eye, its twin,
left him in darkness, but from memory
he was still able to pursue the Thebans
until he tripped on Idas, who lay prostrate.
He groped among the bodies that had fallen
in savage fighting, and he begged his friends
and enemies to help him end his life.

He slew the sons of Abas, long-haired Argus, 758
and Cydon, whose sad sister was his lover.
An oblique arrow transfixed Cydon's temples:
the point emerged; the rapid feathers stuck;
both wounds poured blood. His bitter arrows offered
pardon from death to no one: not to Lamus
for looks, or Lygdus for prophetic ribbons,
nor was Aeolus saved by adolescence.
Parthenopaeus shot the face of Lamus,
pierced Lygdus through the groin, and you, Aeolus,
groaned when his arrow punctured your white forehead.
Euboea, on its mountain rocks, bore one;
and Thisbae, white with pigeons, mourned the second;
the third will not return to green Amyclae.

Parthenopaeus never came up empty. 770
None of his missiles lacked divinity.
His right hand never rested; his shafts flew
before preceding arrows struck their mark.
Who would believe one person shot so many
or that a single hand could do such damage?

Sometimes he aimed; sometimes he changed his hands;
sometimes he chased; sometimes he feigned and ran.

–♦–♦–♦–

By now the sons of Labdacus had turned 776
and reassembled, both amazed and scornful.
The first among them was Amphion, he
of Jove's own famous blood, who up till now
was unaware of what the boy had done,
the bodies in the field. "How long can you
enjoy this respite from your fate, o son?
Your death will greatly grieve deserving parents!
Although you feed your pride and swell your mind,
nobody stoops to such a minor duel! The fight
is worth too little; it's beneath contempt!
Go back to Arcady and mix with equals, 784
play battle games at home, while angry Mars
rages in dust for real. . . . But if you want
the mournful fame that comes from valiant death,
I am prepared to kill you like a man!"

The fearsome son of Atalanta and 788
the soldiers were engaged in trading insults.
Before Amphion finished, he responded:

"Is this Thebes' army? Then I must be late! 790
What boy would keep himself from such a war?
The one you see before you is no Theban.
My race is savage: I'm Arcadian!
No Thyiad mother bore me while a slave
to Echionian Lyaeus. I
♦ have never wielded spears of infamy
or worn an odious turban on my head!
Early on I was taught to crawl along
tight rivers, enter great beasts' frightening caves,
and—why should I say more?—my mother gave
me swords and bows: your fathers pounded drums!"

Amphion could not tolerate his words 800
and threw his mighty ash spear at his head.

The deadly flash of iron spooked his horse,
which circled with its rider, turned aside,
and knocked the looming javelin off course.
This made Amphion angrier. He charged
Parthenopaeus with his outdrawn sword,
just as Latona hurried to the field
and stood before their eyes so they could see her.

There was a youth named Dorceus, a Maenalian, 808
whom Atalanta had enlisted for
her son to calm her fears and keep a watch.
He too was young and daring. This friend clung
beside the boy he loved with due regard.
Diana counterfeited him and said,
"Parthenopeaus, you have done enough
to these Ogygian armies—done enough!
Take care for your sad mother and the gods,
whomever they protect!"

But he was fearless:
"Just let me kill this one who copies me, 815
whose weapon imitates my own, whose dress
is similar, whose bridle sounds with bells!
O loyal Dorceus, I ask nothing else!
I will assume his reins and hang his armor
over Diana's door and please my mother
by capturing his quiver just for her!"
Latona heard. Her smile was mixed with tears.

—♦—♦—♦—

For some time Venus had been watching her 821
from heaven, far away, while she embraced
Gradivus and reminded him of Thebes,
for which she worried, and the dear descendants
of Cadmus and Harmonia. She hid
her sorrow in her silent heart but seized
a proper opportunity to speak:

"Isn't that woman impudent, Gradivus, 825
to interfere in battles fought by men,

arranging lines, disposing martial signs?
She chooses who will die and who will live,
even among our people! Who is she
to show such prowess, such insanity?
You will be left impaling country deer!"

The god of war was moved by her complaints 831
to leap into the battle. As he dropped
down through the empty skies, his only aide
was Anger, for the other Furies were
sweating already on the battlefield.
At once he landed next to Leto's daughter
and sternly warned her: "You have not been granted
this battle by the father of the gods!
Get off this field of men who carry arms,
you shameless woman! Do it now, or you
will learn not even Pallas matches me!"

What could she do against him? First, the spear 838
of Mars was pressing her. Next, Parthenopaeus,
your thread of life had filled its fatal distaff.
Finally, the face of Jupiter was threatening.
The goddess left at last; she had been shamed.

–♦–♦–♦–

But father Mars observed Ogygian lines 841
and moved horrendous Dryas, he whose race
inherited a hatred of Diana
from dark Orion, their progenitor.
So Dryas raged, and the Arcadians
panicked as he pursued them with his sword
and overcame their leader. Then long lines
of people from Cyllene were destroyed,
inhabitants of shadowy Tegea,
Aepytis's leaders, and Telphusian soldiers.
Although his arm grew heavy, he saved strength,
for he was certain he could slay their leader
Parthenopaeus, who arranged his troops
and felt his own fatigue: a thousand portents
and darkling clouds of death presaged his end.

And then he saw the real, the human Dorceus, 852
and worried that he had so few companions;
he sensed his failing strength, and noticed that
his empty quiver weighed less on his shoulder.
His anger drove him less and less. He seemed
only a boy, as fearful Dryas turned
the gleam of his fierce shield in his direction.
His jaws shook suddenly; his stomach tensed,
and the Arcadian felt like a swan
who sees an eagle just about to strike
and wishing Strymon's banks would open wide
tries to take shelter under trembling feathers.

Anger no longer gripped Parthenopaeus 861
once he had seen the bulk of fearsome Dryas;
instead, he felt a chill presaging death.
In vain he called Diana and the gods,
resumed his weapons (even as he paled),
and rushed to draw his unresponsive bow.
His body was oblique, about to shoot—
the arrow touched the horn, the string his chest—
when the Aonian chieftain hurled his spear
with swift and whirling motion at such speed
it cut the angled cords that tuned his string.
His hands released the shaft; the bow relaxed;
his weapons fell as his drawn string went slack.

Stung by the pain and wounded in his shoulder 871
where his thin skin was cut beneath his armor,
he slipped his reins and let his weapons drop.
After the first, a second javelin
severed the hamstrings of his horse, which stopped . . .
then Dryas fell—a miracle! He never
knew who had struck, but time will tell, hereafter.

The boy was borne across the field by comrades— 877
so young, so simple. Even as he died,
he mourned his fallen horse. Unhelmeted,
the young man's head hung limp, but dying grace
breathed from his trembling face. Men seized his hair
three or four times to lift his neck, but failed.

The sight would be unspeakably bereaving,
even in Thebes, for red blood overflowed
his white skin, and he said, as he was choking:

"I'm dying, Dorceus! Go console my mother
in her affliction. She, indeed—if worrying
can make one prophesy what's real—has seen
this sad truth in a vision or a dream.
But use a pious fraud to ease her fears;
beguile her; do not suddenly appear
or come upon her when she holds a spear.
Then, when she has invited you to speak,
say 'Mother, I deserve the punishment
you never meant to give. When I was young,
I took your weapons, and despite your efforts,
I never stopped, nor did I ever spare
your feelings; you were worried by my warfare.
Now you may live in peace and rest your fears;
no longer will my boldness be your care.
You will hear no more sounds or see the dust
my troops raise; I lie naked on the earth
where you may find me close to Mount Lycaeus.
You are not near enough to hold my head
or feel my final breath. So here, sad mother'—
he cut some strands of hair and held them out—
'accept this lock! In place of my whole body
accept the tresses that you brushed in vain,
despite my indignation. Bury them,
and as you make my obsequies, remember,
let only someone with experience
handle my armaments, and my best hounds
never again should hunt inside a cavern.
Let these unlucky weapons, from my first
campaign, be burned, or hang them as a sign
to say I was not favored by Diana.' "

—♦—♦—♦—

BOOK 10 Sacrifices

Eteocles directs the city's guards. In Argos the women pray. The House of Sleep. Thebans slaughtered. Hopleus and Dymas die retrieving the bodies of Tydeus and Parthenopaeus. Thebes assaulted. Tiresias calls for a sacrifice. Descent of Virtue. Suicide of Menoeceus, Creon's son. His mother's despair and madness. Capaneus challenges the gods. Jove's thunderbolt.

A wet night, moved by Jupiter's behest,
dimmed Phoebus in Hesperia—the west—
not out of pity for the Tyrians
or Argives but to save the innocents
who, unaligned, did not deserve to perish.

Enormous carnage marred the open field— 5
weapons and horses ridden by proud warriors
who now left scattered limbs and unburned corpses.
Inglorious platoons with tattered standards
abandoned that sick army, and the gates
that seemed so narrow when men went to war
were broad enough to handle their retreat.

Both sides knew sorrow, but the Tyrians 11
found consolation in the fact that four
Danaan armies wandered with no leaders
just as, her helmsman lost, a ship is driven
by tempests, gods, and chance through swollen seas.
So they were unconcerned to guard their city
but sought to stem their enemies from flight
lest they, in full retreat, should reach Mycenae.

A password went by tablet to the watch; 17
positions were assigned; and by the lot
Meges received command and also Lycus,
who joined him in these movements through the dark.
They had their orders issued, were equipped

with weapons, food, and torches, when their king,
Eteocles, addressed them at their parting:

"Tomorrow's light is not far off. These shadows 21
will not protect those cowards any longer,
and you will have defeated the Danaans.
Gather your courage and take heart. The gods
favor us. You have overthrown the pride
of Lerna and her foremost armies. Tydeus
has gone to Tartarus for punishment;
the augur's living ghost amazes Death;
the remnants of Hippomedon upswell
Ismenos in his pride. (It would be shameful
to count, among the conquered, the Arcadian.)
We hold our destiny in our own hands.
Never again will seven generals
with their tall crests appear above those armies,
although, of course, Adrastus has his years,
my brother youth, and Capaneus madness—
a man to fear in war. Go forward, then,
circle their camp with your unsleeping flames!
Fear not the enemy. Be vigilant,
and their supplies and treasure will be yours!"

Thus he harangued the fierce Labdacians, 35
who turned around, prepared to do again
what had exhausted them, still covered in
dust, sweat, and blood. They had no patience for
good-byes or conversations; they ignored
embraces and the friends who shook their hands.
They ringed the valley with unquiet fires
and shared the duties and the different posts,
as when a pack of rabid wolves, whom long
hunger has made dare anything, unites
under the veil of night from various fields.
The sheepfold strains and spoiled hope twists their jaws;
flocks bleat in fear; the barnyard wafts rich scents
until they break their claws on hardened grates,
press with their chests, blunt unfed teeth on gates.

—♦—♦—♦—

Now far away the Peloponnesian women
circled, as suppliants, the Argive temples
and thronged the altars of the fatherland,
praying to scepter-bearing Juno that
their men come home. They pressed their faces to
the painted doors and cold stones of the temple
and taught their little children how to kneel.
They filled the day with prayers—night added cares—
and kept the altars' fires burning high.
They offered Juno's statue cloaks of state,
a miracle of weaving that no woman
either divorced or sterile helped to sew.
They brought robes, in a wicker basket, woven
in purple with embroidery and gold,
a fit gift for a goddess of decorum:
these pictured her, great Jupiter's betrothed,
still hesitant to cease her role as sister,
with no experience of marriage, giving
young Jove a simple kiss, her eyes downcast,
not yet offended by her husband's trysts.

The Argive matrons veiled the ivory idol,
wept and lamented, and then they implored:

"O queen of heaven, look where Semele,
the Cadmean concubine, resided in
impiety and bore the rebel Bacchus!
Destroy Thebes with your lightning. You are able!"

What could she do? She knew the Fates opposed—
and Jove had set his mind against—her Greeks.
She did not want these prayers and gifts to perish,
but Chance might find a way Time might assist.
From heaven she surveyed the bolted gates,
the valley that the sleepless guards surrounded.
Anger aroused her, and her hair was wild,
and she upset what must be feared—her crown.
She felt more bitter than when she had been
scornful in heaven's emptiness and seen

♦ Alcmene and the Thunderer asleep
for two straight nights, engendering Hercules.
She therefore ordered the Aonians 79
be put to death when they were fast asleep.
She summoned Iris and commanded her
to gird herself with multicolored rings.
The crystalline divinity obeyed,
and she dropped down from heaven, following
a long, suspended arc that curved toward earth.

–♦–♦–♦–

There is a silent grove no star can pierce 84
beyond the shaded couch of setting night
(the other home of Aethiopians)
and under it, a steep and awesome cave
runs through a hollow mountain to the place
that careless Nature saves for lazy Sleep,
a household atrium, secure and safe.
Dark Rest and slack Forgetting tend the gate
with languid Sloth, who has a sleepy face.
Leisure and Silence, folding feathered wings,
sit mutely in the vestibule and chase
winds that intrude along the roof away
and let no songbirds sing or branches sway.

Although the oceans roar, the shore is silent,
nor is there any thunder from the sky.
Even the river flowing by the cave
that drops from heights among the cliffs and rocks
makes no noise by the dark, reclining flocks
and herds along the fields. New flowers wither,
and earth exhales a breath that stunts the grass.

A thousand simulations of the god 100
had been engraved by shining Mulciber
inside the cave: here, leaning on Sleep's side,
wearing a wreathe, is Pleasure; there, reclining
in rest is his companion, Labor. Here

lies Bacchus, there lies Love, the child of Mars,
sharing his common couch. Sleep also lies,
in secret chambers, deep interiors,
with Death, but these are somber images,
unseen by anyone: mere semblances.

The god himself reclines in dripping caverns 106
on blankets strewn with sleep-inducing flowers.
His clothes exude a vapor. His lethargic
corpulence warms his cushions. Dark, dank mists,
caused by his exhalations, cloud his couch.
His left hand brushes hair back from his brow;
◆ his right hand tries to grip his slipping horn.
The legions of the night, unsettled Dreams,
false flatteries inmixed with sorry truths,
appearances innumerable, were gathered
on beams and posts or scattered on the floor.
The hall was dimly lit, a feeble sheen
inviting sleep, as when a languid light
falls from a fading flame and then expires.

Here hung the multicolored virgin in 118
the blue cerulean. She lit the groves,
as shaded valleys smiled upon the goddess.
Struck by her glittering zone, the house awoke
but neither bright lamps, noises, nor the goddess,
who shouted, could arouse the God of Sleep.
He lay in his accustomed way until
Iris unveiled the full force of her lights
to penetrate his deep, unmoving eyes.

The golden source of cloud forms then began: 125
"O Sleep, the mildest god, you have been ordered
by Juno to restrain the generals
from Sidon and the people of fierce Cadmus!
They in the aftermath of battle, proudly
circle, unsleeping, the Achaean camp,
refusing to conform to your decrees.
Grant this unusual request, a rare
occasion when you may please Jupiter
and still not lose the favor of his queen!"

She spoke. She shook his lazy frame lest he 132
ignore her, then repeated what she said.
He answered with a nod, the same he gives
when dropping off to sleep, and Iris left
the darkness of his caverns, feeling heavy
till rains restored her brightness, which had dimmed.

Sleep shook his feathered feet and windy brow 137
and wrapped up in a mantle from whose folds
dark breezes exhaled cold, and he was borne
in silence through the ether till his presence
confounded the Aonians in camp.
His influence drove birds down, beasts and flocks, 141
and everywhere flat seas fell back from rocks.
As he moved through the world, slow-moving clouds
seemed stuck together, tall trees bent their tops,
and pliant skies let constellations drop.

The army felt the presence of the god
when gloom came suddenly as noises stopped—
innumerable voices, murmurings of men—
as hovering for real on humid wings
Sleep overwhelmed the camp and cast a shade—
no shade had ever been so dense, so black—
that made men roll their eyes. Their necks relaxed.
They left the words they utter cut in half.
Their hands released fierce spears and shields of light. 152
Weary heads fell on chests, and all was silence.
Even their horses would not stand upright,
and ashes suddenly consumed their fires.

Now Sleep did not extend to anxious Greeks 156
a similar repose; he drew his cloud
back from the nearby camp. That deity,
who wanders through the night, did not entice them.
They all remained in armor and disdained
the darkness and those insolent patrolmen.

A sudden shaking gripped Thiodamas— 160
the fury of the gods, a fierce disturbance—
that ordered him to prophesy their fate.

Either Saturnian Juno moved his mind
or great Apollo urged his augurer.

The man was gripped by some divinity
and leaped into the middle of the camp, 163
fearful to see and terrible to hear,
unable to contain what he conceived.
His torment overwhelmed him. Madness sat
nakedly in his face. Blood came and went
through trembling cheeks, which withered, then distended.
His eyes moved sideways, and his flowing hair,
entwined with scattered garlands, whipped his neck,
◆ as when the mother goddess of Mount Ida
incites a bloody priest of hers in Phrygia
to lacerate his arms, deep in her shrine,
then pound his breast with sticks of sacred pine
and fling his blood-stained hair—when she removes
his consciousness—and run to numb his wounds.
Fields and the sacred pine tree smeared with blood
panic. Spooked lions lift her chariot.

He entered the most deep interiors 176
and council chambers, where Adrastus wondered
how to continue or to end and sought
advice, for all the slaughter sickened him.
He was surrounded by his new commanders,
those men who had replaced the fallen chiefs
whose absence was conspicuous in council.
There was no happiness in their promotions,
just grief, as when a ship has lost its pilot
and someone must assume the empty post,
whether he be lieutenant of the midships
or one who feels the sea spray on the prow.
The new commander finds the vessel sluggish,
the rigging unresponsive, as if both
refuse submission to a minor lord.

The rapid-moving augurer inspired 187
the Argives, who felt peril and confusion:

"We bring the mighty mandates of the gods,
and warnings to be feared, my commandants.
These words are not my own: *Apollo* chants!
The deity confirms the confidence
you showed by choosing me to be his servant
and wear his sacred fillets. By the god
who oversees the auguries, this night
is ripe for exploits—and for fraudulence,
if well conceived. Our ready manliness
demands and Fortune asks our intervention.
The legions of Aonians are dull
and wrapped in sleep; we have the opportunity,
now, to avenge our leaders who are slain
and make up for the losses of these days.
Batter obstructing gates and seize your weapons.
Take up the torches for your comrades' pyres.
Now you can bury them! I saw these things,
even as we retreated, beaten, scattered
during our daylight battle. By the tripods,
and by the novel passing of my master,
I swear the birds applauded in approval.
But now what I envisioned is confirmed.
Amphiaraus came to me himself,
here, in the silent night. He rose—*himself*—
freed from the earth, again as he had been.
Only his horses showed a touch of shadow.
It was his presence, not some prodigy
of silent emptiness, nor was it something
created from a dream of which I speak.

" 'Give me my gods again,' he said. 'Return 206
the fillets of Parnassus, you false prophet!
How can you let the slow Inachians
lose such a night? Is this why I myself
taught you the flights of birds and heaven's secrets?
Proceed! Proceed! At least avenge *my* death!'
So he spoke, and it seemed he raised his spear
and drove his chariot to push me here.
Go then! Use what the gods have given you.

You will not meet the enemy; they sleep
while you receive this opportunity
that Fate permits you for a massacre.
Let those who do not fear great fame come forward.
The birds that fly at night are favorable.
Apollo joins as well; he waves his reins!"

He discomposed the night with his harangue. 219
It was not that the best men were on fire
so much as, by a single god, inspired—
provoked to join with him and follow fortune.
Thiodamas himself selected thirty,
a strong force, while the other soldiers fumed
with indignation that they must do nothing
and stay behind in camp. Some argued for
their noble birth, some their ancestors' deeds,
and some their own. Some urged a lottery,
a drawing to ensure a fair selection.

Adrastus's spirits lifted; he rejoiced, 227
despite adversity, like one who breeds
◆ swift horses on the heights of Pholoë
when he sees herds renew themselves in spring.
It pleases him that some prefer the summits,
some swim in streams, and some contend with parents.
He idly wonders which will bear the yoke
without complaining, which ones carry loads,
which ones are born for trumpets and for warfare,
and which may win the palm in the Olympics.

Thus, too, the aging Greek, the army's leader— 235
nor was he absent from this operation.
"What is the reason heaven serves our cause,
after so long, so suddenly? Do you
return, divinities, to crumbling Argos?
Is it misfortune that provokes our courage,
the remnants of our ancient blood, the seeds
of bravery that endure in suffering souls?
Noble young men, I offer you my praise.
I am enjoying your delicious mutiny,
but this encounter is deceitful, hidden,

done under cover, and unsuitable
for many men, since fraud needs secrecy.
Conserve your spirit. Take your vengeance on
the enemy when day comes, when we all
will arm ourselves, when all will enter battle!"

The courage of the men was bridled, calmed,
just as when father Aeolus maintains
control of the commotion in his cavern.
He sternly orders every exit closed
and blocks the entry with another stone
to shutter winds that seek to rouse the seas.

Agylleus, who's the son of Hercules, 249
and Actor are included by the seer.
Actor is apt to lead and issue orders;
the other has not lost his father's strength.
Each of the three has ten in his command,
and they would frighten the Aonians
even if they should meet them in the open.

Because Thiodamas had not before 253
engaged in the deceptiveness of war,
he laid aside the wreathe that he adored,
the emblem of Apollo, and allowed
Adrastus to receive what graced his brow.
A hauberk and his helm were welcome gifts
from Polynices, and he put them on.

Actor received a sword from Capaneus,
who would not go himself because he scorned
all frauds, nor did he countenance the gods.

Agylleus and rough Nomus traded weapons:
what could a bow or Herculean arrows
do with deceptive shadows in this skirmish?

The soldiers scrambled up and leaped steep walls 262
to minimize the groans of bronze-hinged portals.
Not far away they found their sleeping prey
stretched on the ground as if already slain—

work for their swords. "O comrades, go, I pray,
and fill whatever need you have for slaughter.
The gods have favored us. We have their plenty!"
Then, in a strident voice, the priest continued:
"Do you observe the drunkenness, the shame,
that blemishes these unprotected cohorts?
Did such as these dare circle Argive gates
or keep guard over us?" He spoke and drew
his bright sword; he proceeded through the ranks.
His hand moved quickly: who could count the dead,
who has the power to list these troops by name?
He stabbed their backs and chests in random order
and left their moans enclosed inside their helmets.
They poured their blood for ghosts to wander over.

One was a careless man sprawled on a couch; 277
another tripped and could not hold his spear.
Others were lying heaped in wine and weapons,
while some reclined on shields. A final cloud
of darkness settled over those whom Sleep
had overcome and left to their misfortune.

Nor was a holy power absent. Juno, 282
who wore her armor, waved a lunar torch
and cleared a path with her extended arm.
She showed the Argives bodies and inspired them.
Thiodamas could feel the goddess present,
but he said nothing. He concealed his pleasure.

But now his hand was weary, his sword weak, 286
and his success had made him feel less malice.
Not otherwise a Caspian tiger grieves
that he has lost his hunger when he sees
what he has done, the slaughter of a herd
whose ample blood has pacified his rage,
tired his jaws, and stained his spots with gore.
Just so, the weary prophet wove his way
through hundreds of Aonians; no wonder
he soon grew tired of executing shades
and wished that his opponents were awake.

Elsewhere the son of mighty Hercules 296
slaughtered the unaroused Sidonians,
and Actor did the same. Their companies
followed on gruesome paths. Blood formed black lakes.
Its streams swayed tents. Earth smoked—as death and sleep
mixed in a single vapor—and not one
of those who slumbered lifted up his face.
Over those wretched men the winged god
cast a great shadow, and they raised their eyes
only when they were just about to die.

Singing Sidonian paeans, Ialmenus 304
had seen the late stars setting as he played
his lute for fun, but would not see them rise.
The God of Sleep relaxed his languid neck;
his head lay leftward, on his instrument,
and when Agylleus stabbed him through the chest,
his practiced fingers struck the turtle shell
and his excited fingers plucked its strings.

The tables flowed with filth, as wine and blood 311
trickled and intermingled, till the Bacchic
portion sought refuge back in cups and bowls.

Wild Actor murdered Thamyris, whose limbs
were mingled with his brother's. Tagus stabbed
Echechlus, a crowned monarch, in the back,
and Danaus cut away the head of Hebrus,
who never knew what happened, so his life
went to the land of shadows still in bliss,
saved from the sadness that harsh death inflicts.

On the cold ground Calpetus lay outstretched 318
beneath his trusty yoke pole and his wheels.
His horses were Aonian, and they
grazed gently in the grass, despite his snores,
which frightened them. His wet mouth drooled. His sleep
grew heated from the warmness of his wine.
Now the Inachian prophet slit his throat,
and it emitted floods of must and gore,

a flow of blood that stopped his final snore.
He may have glimpsed his death as he was sleeping—
noticed Thiodamas, or seen black Thebes.

The fourth division of the sleeping night 326
had come, the clouds had emptied, and the stars
no longer radiated equal light.
A faster wagon breathed on Ursa Major.

Their task was ending, when prophetic Actor
called to Thiodamas: "This should suffice;
an unexpected joy for us Pelasgians.
I think that hardly any have escaped
a brutal death, unless they hide like cowards
under this mass of dead to save their lives.
Let's end while we are winning: even Thebes,
despite her known impieties, has gods;
our own, who look with favor, may recede."

Thiodamas complied and raised his palms, 336
still dripping, to the stars. "Although my hands
are not yet washed with water, I must make
this sacrifice, Apollo! I bring offerings:
I, loyal priest and fierce guard of your tripods,
bring you the nighttime spoils that you foresaw.
If I have not dishonored your commands,
if I have borne your promptings, do not scorn
to visit me, to penetrate my mind.
For now your monuments are gruesome, gore
of men and broken limbs, but if your favor
grants us our homeland and our sought-for temples,
◆ demand rich gifts from us, o Lycian Paean!
Recall our promises and order bulls
be brought before your portals!" So he spoke,
then called his joyous comrades from their weapons.

—◆—◆—◆—

◆ Among them came a Calydonian, Hopleus, 347
◆ and a Maenalian, Dymas. Tydeus and
Parthenopaeus had been their companions

and loved this fated pair, who mourned for them
and so scorned life, but Hopleus had a plan
and spoke with Dymas, the Arcadian.

"Dear Dymas, do you care for our dead princes, 351
whom birds and dogs from Thebes may now be eating?
What will Arcadians carry to your country
when his fierce mother will demand his body?
The thought of Tydeus tombless rends my heart,
although my friend was more mature than yours
and his years less lamentable to lose.
We have a chance to scrutinize the field,
go anywhere, even inside of Thebes."

Then Dymas spoke: "I swear by these quick stars 360
and by the wandering shadow of my prince—
to me a god—I too am moved by sorrow.
I have been seeking one to share my grief,
but now I'll take the lead." Before he started
he stared at heaven with a humble face
and he intoned this prayer: "O Cynthia,
queen of the secret mysteries of night,
if your divinity, as people say,
can take on threefold features and descend
into the forests as Diana, then
the boy for whom we search was your companion,
a glorious alumnus of your groves,
and you should favor us."

The goddess hears, 372
and her declining chariot makes bright
the moon, whose horns illuminate his body.
The field appears, and Thebes, and high Cithaeron,
as when destructive Jupiter ignites
the night air with his thunder. Clouds divide
and stars reveal themselves in flashing light
and earth is suddenly open to their eyes.

The same light that gave Dymas his success 375
thrilled Hopleus when he suddenly saw Tydeus.
Through the dark distance he and Dymas signaled

their mutual excitement, and each carried
the burden that he cared for on his shoulders
as if it had been brought to life again
and saved from savage death. They did not speak
or even dare to weep as they proceeded.
Impending signs of daylight threatened them
with danger, as they moved through mournful silence
with long steps and kept quiet, worried that
dim light would overcome exhausted shadows.

Fate envies pieties. Luck is a rare 384
companion for the great deeds one may dare.

They saw their camp and felt their burdens lessen 385
as they drew nearer, when at once they listened
to sounds behind them. There were clouds of dust,
for fierce Amphion led a troop of horse
Eteocles had ordered to explore
the night, to keep a vigil on the camp.
Daylight had not yet melted every shadow
when he was first to note a doubtful sight,
not too far off, across the pathless plains—
something uncertain, like bent bodies moving.
As soon as he discovered these two men,
he challenged them, "Whoever! Halt your steps!"
but they proceeded, carrying their burdens.
Amphion threatened them and hurled his spear
a fighting distance at those frightened soldiers.
Nonetheless he pretended his hand slipped;
the spear flew harmlessly before the eyes
of Dymas, who by chance preceded Hopleus.

Aepytus, though, was not magnanimous 399
and did not want to waste his javelin.
His weapon pierced through Hopleus and went on
to nick the shoulder blade of hanging Tydeus.
Hopleus collapsed, although he never dropped
his celebrated prince. He died as he
maintained his grip, but he was fortunate:
he never knew the body had been lost
and, ignorant, descended to the shades.

Dymas had turned and witnessed this. He felt
soldiers converging, and he was uncertain
whether to stand and fight or to submit
and try persuasion. Anger said to fight,
but Fortune said use prayer, do not be daring.
He had no confidence in either choice,
yet rage would not permit him to entreat.
He lay the mournful corpse before his feet
and wrapped a heavy tiger skin that he
by chance was wearing draped across his back
over his left arm, and he took his stance.
He held his sword extended, braced to meet
all of their weapons, and to live or die,
just as a lioness defends her young
whom she has lately borne when she confronts
Numidian hunters in her savage lair:
she is uncertain—as she roars with rage
and misery and stands before her cubs—
whether to bite their spears and scatter them
or let love overcome her savage heart
and glare with anger from among her young.

But now, although Amphion had forbidden
brutality, they severed his left hand.
They dragged Parthenopaeus by the hair
and Dymas prayed too late for his young friend.
He dropped his sword and begged them, "By the cradle
of Bacchus, born of lightning; by the flight
of Ino; by the youth of your Palaemon,
carry the body gently; hear my prayer!
I beg you, if by any chance you know
the joys of children, if there is a father
among you, give the boy a little fire
and a small bit of dust. His look implores,
implores you as he lies there. I will sate
the evil birds. Expose me to the beasts:
I was the one who made him go to war."

Amphion answered, "You who so desired
to bury your commander, tell us what
the cowardly Pelasgians plan to do:

they seem inactive and dispirited.
Reveal their plans and I will give you life
and guarantee your leader his last rites."

Dymas was horrified. He thrust his sword 435
through his own heart. "Was this dishonor missing
among the Argive's sorrows, that I turn
traitor? I will not pay that price, nor would
this young man want entombment on such terms."
He spoke. He tore a large gash through his chest,
fell on the boy, and with his last gasp cried:
"You shall be buried underneath my body."

Thus the illustrious Arcadian 442
and that Aetolian of equal merit,
who clung to those commanders whom they loved,
exhaled their famous souls and cherished death.

◆ *You will be long remembered, though the song*
that rises from my lyre be not as strong
as Virgil's. Possibly Euryalus
will not disdain to welcome you among
the shades, nor Phrygian Nisus share his glory.

–◆–◆–◆–

Fearsome Amphion sent some messengers 449
to bring the captive corpses to his king
and tell Eteocles what he had done.
He had the severed heads upraised
to mock and show the Argives his defiance.

At the same time, those on the Grecian walls 453
could see Thiodamas as he returned,
and they did not conceal their joyous pride.
They could discern men's sword blades—still unsheathed—
and see their armor glow from recent killing.
A new and greater roar leaped through the air
as soldiers strained and hung along stockades
to recognize companions, like a flock
of newborn baby birds who see their mother

returning in the distance through the air:
they gape and want to meet her; they hang from
the margins of their nest, and they would fall
if she did not forestall them with her breast
and stop them with her fluttering, soft wings.

While the night's deeds, the quiet work of Mars, 463
was subject to discussion, and men seized
their relatives in glad embraces, they
asked after Hopleus, looked for tardy Dymas.
Just then Amphion with his Dircean soldiers
came near the camp, and he was much displeased.
The earth was fevered from the recent slaughter;
the massacre had mounded heaps of soldiers.
He shook as if a lightning bolt had struck him;
he shuddered, could not speak, felt blind, lost strength,
and wheeled his steed around as he lamented.
A cloud of dust upswirled as his troops fled.

They had not yet enclosed themselves in Thebes 474
when swarms of Argive cohorts took the field.
Spurred by the night's success, they ran their wheels
over the limbs and steel of fallen men,
half-living gore in one foul-smelling heap.
Rivers of blood impeded chariots
as heavy horse hooves trampled broken bodies.
The troops thought this road sweet since they believed
they breeched Sidonian roofs, the blood of Thebes.

"Pelasgians!" urged Capaneus now, 482
"your prowess has been hidden far too long!
Because I can be seen, my victory
will give some satisfaction. Forward, men!
Raise up the dust and shout your battle cries.
Attack them in the open. My right hand
is ominous; my fierce, drawn sword prophetic!"

He shouted, and Adrastus was on fire, 487
as eager as his Theban son-in-law.
Thiodamas, the brooding prophet, followed.

Argives approached the walls, just as Amphion 489
was narrating the story of the slaughter.
They would have entered the despairing city
if Megareus had not responded quickly
and called down from his watchtower, "Sentinel,
the enemy is coming; close the portals!"

Sometimes excessive fear gives strength. The doors 493
shut quickly, but Echion moved too late
to bar Ogyges. Spartans stormed the gate.

The first to fall upon the threshold were 496
Panopeus, dweller in Laconia's hills;
and Oebalus, who swam the harsh Eurotas;
and you, Alcidamas, the marvel of
every gymnasium, who recently
had won the Nemean games, whose strong hands Pollux
first fastened with lead-weighted leather gloves.
You saw your master's bright orb as you died,
just as the god allowed his star to hide.
You will be mourned by the Oebalian groves, 503
the slick banks of the Spartan maiden, Leda,
and waters where her false swan made his song.
The Amyclaean nymphs of Trivia
will grieve, as will your mother, who will mourn
because you learned too well the manly arts
and laws of war in which you were instructed.
Such was the battle at the gate of Thebes.

Then Acron, leaning with his shoulders, and 509
Ialmenides, who pushed with all his weight,
forced closed the heavy portal barred with bronze,
just as a pair of oxen bend their necks
◆ to break Pangaea's long unfurrowed slopes.
The losses of their effort matched their gains
since they excluded Thebans but retained
some of the enemy: inside the walls
the Greek Ormenus fell; Amyntor stretched
his upturned hands and begged, but words and head
fell on the hostile earth, as did his necklace.

The Argives smashed the palisades, where guards 519
were powerless to stop them, and the first
cohorts of infantry approached the walls.
The horses of the cavalry, however,
refused to leap the broad expanse of ditch;
they stalled and shook before that deep abyss
and wondered why their riders pressed them forward.
Their riders urged them to the outer verge
but could not force reluctant chargers further.

Meanwhile some men ripped ramparts from the ground
while others chopped apart the gates' defenses
and heated iron bolts to make them soft.
They drove out stones with rams and ringing bronze,
rejoiced when torches landed on the roofs,
◆ and delved below the walls where, under turtles,
they undermined the bases of Thebes' turrets.

Tyrians thronged the towers on the walls, 531
their only means of safety, and they hurled
burned firebrands and steel-bright javelins,
lead missiles that caught fire as they flew,
and stones, torn from the ramparts, at their foes.
The rooftops sent a shower of savage rain.
Barred windows spit out streams of screaming arrows.
◆ It was as when the clouds that top Malea 537
◆ or high Ceraunia, which long lie still,
unmoving on the shadows of the hills,
leap down and batter ships with sudden storms.
In this way was the Argive army swamped
by Agenorean defenses, but
the deadly rain made no man turn around.
They did not look to die, yet they directed
their faces to the walls and aimed their weapons.

The heavy stroke of an Ogygian spear 544
struck Antheus as he drove his chariot,
armored with scythes, around the walls of Thebes.
His reins dropped from his hands, and he fell back;
his half-dead body dangled by his greaves—

one of the awful spectacles of war.
His armor dragged; his spear and smoking wheels
plowed three ruts in the earth; his head was jerked
from side to side and raised long plumes of dust;
his trailing tresses swept an ample path.

–♦–♦–♦–

The frightening pulse of trumpets rang through town; 552
barred doors could not keep out these fearful sounds.
Entrances were divided. In each threshold
a savage standard signaled joy or harm.
Inside, the sight was bleak, and Mars himself
would not rejoice to see it. Mourning, Madness,
Anxiety, and Cringing, wrapped in shadows,
brought horrible insanity within
the self-divided and distracted city.

You can be sure the war had entered town:
the rooftops were alive with running people;
loud cries were intermingling in the streets;
the citizens imagined swords and flames
and in their minds accepted slavery's chains.
They gave up hope; they crowded homes and temples;
they mourned and grouped around ungrateful altars.
All ages felt one fear inside the city;
old people prayed for death; the young turned pale
or burned with ardor. Ringing atria
echoed the sounds of women's lamentations.
The children wept, in shock; they did not know 568
why they were crying, but they felt the fright
arising from their mothers' mournful cries.

Love drove the women to be unashamed— 569
in this extremity—of public work,
to arm their men, enflame them, give them courage,
exhort them, even join them as they mustered,
nor did they cease to point out little children
or their ancestral doorways while they wept,
like bees in caverns of volcanic stone

who, armed with stings, resound (a nasty cloud)
and urge each other on by murmuring
and flying in the face of their opponent:
a herdsman who disturbs them when he steals.
Their weary wings soon clasp their golden home
and mourn its captured honey as they press
the combs they have constructed to their chests.

The judgment of the people was divided, 580
and no one tried to hide discordant views:
some said to let the brother have his realm—
nor did they whisper, but spoke openly,
in loud mobs—they would give it to the brother!
Terror caused loss of reverence for the king.

"Let us permit the exile to complete 584
the yearly term agreed upon, to see
his Cadmean home, to feel pain when he greets
the shadows where his father dwells. Indeed,
why should my blood atone for this deceit,
the crimes and lies of our injurious king?"
But others said, "It is too late for trust.
Now Polynices wants to conquer us!"

Others approached Tiresias in a group 589
of weeping suppliants and begged to know
the future: they sought comfort for their grief.
He would not tell them heaven's destiny,
but kept it hidden. "Do you come to me
because our ruler asked me for advice,
despite my admonition, when I counseled
against the warfare his bad faith has caused?
Nevertheless," he says, "unhappy Thebes,
if I am silent, you will be destroyed!
I am a wretched man. I cannot bear
to listen to your fall or let the flames
the Argives kindle scorch my empty eyes.
Piety overwhelms me. Daughter, pile
the altar; let us find the will of heaven."

His daughter Manto did; with practiced eyes 598
she taught her father; she described twin flames,
two peaks of blood-red fires on the altar.
Between them burned a high, translucent blaze,
and then a double upsurge formed a serpent,
a ghostly image carved against the redness
that offered meaning to her father's darkness
and answered his uncertainties at once.

He held his arms around the rings of flame; 604
his glowing face absorbed prophetic vapors;
his hair stood stiff with horror; his wild locks
lifted his trembling fillets. You would think
his eyes' lost glow restored, his sight renewed.
He finally gave expression to his frenzy:

"Attend, polluted sons of Labdacus! 610
The gods demand the greatest sacrifice.
Salvation comes, but on a stony path.
The dragon that belongs to Mars demands
propitiation, fearsome recompense.
The youngest member of the serpent's seed
must fall to guarantee our victory.
Blessed is he who dies for this reward."

Creon was standing at the savage altar 616
beside the prudent prophet. He lamented
his homeland's public destiny, but he
was startled by this sudden stroke, no less
than if a twisting spear had pierced his chest.
He listened and he knew Tiresias
called for Menoeceus, his son. His fear
persuaded him; the anxious father stood,
amazed, and felt a cold dread in his heart,
just as Sicilian seashores must endure
the whiplash of the Libyan ocean's swells.
Apollo filled the seer, who called for speed,
even as humble Creon grasped his knees
or tried to stop his mouth and silence him,
but Rumor was already carrying
the echoes of his prophecy through Thebes.

Begin, then, Clio, and recount the spur 628
that gives the youth delight in dying well
(for absent some divinity, the thought
would not occur to any). You preserve
our ancient past; you organize the ages!

Virtue, companion to the throne of Jove, 632
from where she rarely ventures to the earth,
departed, joyfully, from heaven's shores.

Either all-powerful Jove commanded her
to do so or she'd found a willing subject.
The stars of heaven, including those whose fires
she once raised to the poles, provided light
as she proceeded. Soon she touched the earth. 638

She never took her gaze from heaven's ether,
but she assumed a different form, that of
foresightful Manto. She employed deception
to change her features so that what Tiresias
had said would be believed. The god subdued
her vigor and her terror and assumed
a softer grace, a little more adornment.
She set her sword aside and donned the clothes
that prophets wear. She let her dress descend
in loose folds and twined fillets through her hair
instead of laurel. Still, her lengthy stride,
her look of dignity, revealed the goddess,
◆ as when Omphale laughed at Hercules
when he had laid aside his lion's skin:
he broke his timbrels, fumbled with his distaff,
and tried to wrap his shoulders in a mantle
made of Sidonian purple for a woman.

When she discovered you, Menoeceus, standing 650
before the Dircean turret, you were slaying
Greeks by the open portals of your city,
ready for veneration and instruction.
You looked like Haemon fighting, but although
both are consanguineous, in all things brothers,
you were the greater man. Great heaps of dead
surrounded you, your every blow brought death,

even before the goddess had arrived.
Your hands and weapons never paused; your mind
was busy, and the sphinx that topped your helmet
seemed to go crazy at the sight of blood.
It glittered, and your splattered bronze arms shone,
just as the goddess stopped your fighting hand
and held your sword hilt. "O magnanimous
youth, than whom Mars knows no one mightier
descended from the fighting seeds of Cadmus!
Leave these unworthy battles, for your strength
is meant for something other. Stars are calling.
Think higher; send your essence to the sky!
My father is excited. He runs wildly
around the altars, where the fires and fibers
confirm the message that Apollo sends—
one earthborn man must sacrifice for all.
Rumor sings this pronouncement, and the Cadmean
people believe in you, and they rejoice.
Attend the gods, and seize your noble fate.
Hurry, I pray, before you lose to Haemon!"

She spoke, and he delayed, but meanwhile she 672
softly assuaged his heart and intertwined
herself in silence through his inner being.
No cypress struck by lightning ever drank
infernal flames as quickly, root and branch,
as this young man absorbed divine possession:
he grew in passion and in love with death.

He watched in awe as Virtue left the earth: 678
he recognized her by her walk and dress
and knew it was a goddess who ascended.

"We will perform all things the gods command,
and not be slow," he said, yet even in
retreat he stabbed a Pylian named Agreus
who scaled the ramparts, then walked on, and people
proclaimed him savior—king of peace, a god;
rejoicing, they filled him with noble fire
that overcame his weariness. Attendants
followed him breathless as he rushed to town 686

and tried to miss his apprehensive parents
when suddenly his father . . . and they both
stood still, their eyes downcast, and neither one
could speak, until the elder man began:

"What new occasion brings you from the field 690
where you were fighting? Is there something more
important you prepare? Tell me, my son,
why do your eyes avoid me? I implore you,
why is your gaze so wild, your face so stern
and pale? It's clear you've heard the oracle.

"I'm begging you, my son, by all my years 694
and by the breasts of your long-suffering mother,
do not believe Tiresias. Do deities
reveal the truth to old and wicked men
whose eyes are blind, whose punishment resembles
that of decrepit Oedipus? What if
the desperate king has instigated this?
What if it's treachery and wicked fraud?
He envies our nobility, your virtue,
which we know passes that of other princes.
What we think heaven's words may well be his. 702
This is the king's idea! Do not release
the reins of your hot soul; allow some time;
be hesitant! Haste handles all things badly.
Grant this concession to your parent, please,
or when you are a father, when gray hair
and age have streaked your temples, may you feel
the fear your unrestraint is causing me.
Do not deprive my household of its gods.

"Do you feel sympathy for strangers' children,
for other fathers? Pity, first, your own
family if you have any sense of honor.
This is true dignity, true piety.
The other brings small glory, light acclaim,
a reputation death will overshadow.
But do not think a father's fear constrains you. 713
Enter the battle; face Danaan lines;
surround yourself with their opposing swords.

I will not keep you; it will be enough
if sadly I may wash your trembling wounds
and cauterize your flowing blood with tears
and send you back—and send you back again—
to savage battle. Thebes would rather *this!*"

He held Menoeceus, grasped his hands and shoulders, 718
but neither words nor weeping moved the youth's
devotion to the gods, who showed him how
to use a small deceit to calm his father
and turn aside his fears: "You are mistaken, 722
good father, and uselessly afraid; no warnings
or raving prophet's words or empty dreams
solicit me. Let shrewd Tiresias
chant to his daughter and himself; his songs
cause no anxiety, no more than would
the presence of Apollo, should he rise
from some deep shrine to seize me with his frenzy.
It is the serious condition of
my brother, whom I love, that causes me
so suddenly to come back to the city.
Haemon is wounded. An Inachian spear
makes him cry out for me. . . . Hardly managed . . .
between two lines . . . there in the dust of battle . . .
Argives already dragging him . . . but I . . .
am late. Be satisfied. Go and revive
his spirits . . . and tell those who carry him
to take care, bear him lightly. I must now
find skillful Aetion, who can sew wounds closed
and tend the deadly gashes where blood flows."

He left his words unfinished, and he fled. 734
A dark cloud seized the mind and heart of Creon.
His piety was torn, his fears discordant.
The Fates—the Parcae—forced him to believe.

–♦–♦–♦–

But meanwhile armies that had earlier 738
poured from the broken portals—cavalry,
platoons of infantry, and chariots

whose wheels and horses overran the dead—
were turned back by the strength of Capaneus.
He was the one who made high towers fall
by pounding them with whirling slings and stones;
he battered battle lines; he smoked in blood;
he opened ugly wounds with flying missiles.
His twisting arm upwhirled his javelins,
and there were no high gables on the roofs
where his spears did not penetrate their targets
and fall back to the ground perfused with gore.

The Peloponnesians now no longer thought 748
Parthenopaeus, Amphiaraus,
Hippomedon, or Tydeus was deceased;
they thought those souls had joined inside one body,
that of their comrade, who was everywhere.
Not age or form or beauty roused his mercy.
He killed those who surrendered or who fought.
No one opposed him; no one tried his fortune.
They shuddered at the madman's distant weapons,
his helmet's visor, and his awful crest.

–♦–♦–♦–

Pious Menoeceus, though, stood on the walls, 756
in a selected spot. His face seemed holy,
his presence more august than usual,
as if he had been suddenly sent down
from heaven to earth. He took his helmet off,
so he was manifest, so he was known,
and gazed at this disharmony of men.
He drew attention from the noise of war
and then commanded silence on the field:

"You warrior divinities and Phoebus 762
Apollo, you who let me die with glory!
Make Thebes, for which I sacrifice, rejoice
that I shall pay her ransom with my blood,
for I am prodigal! Reverse the war!
Dash coward fugitives on captive Lerna!
Let Father Inachus spurn shameful sons

who run away with spears stuck in their backs,
but let my death restore our Tyrian temples, 768
our children, houses, countrysides, and wives!
If I, your sacrificial victim, please you;
if I have heard, with calm ears, your seer's words;
take me as payment for the debts of Thebes
and pacify the father I deceived!"

He spoke. With one blow of his shining sword 774
he summoned his long-sought, distinguished soul,
which languished in its narrow, mournful prison.
Blood stained the towers and sanctified the walls.
He hurled himself, still with his sword imbedded,
into the armies, and he tried to fall
over the savage Argives, but while his
soul sought the highest stars and stood before
Jove to receive a crown, his body was
borne slowly down by Piety and Virtue.

The Tantalids retreated in respect. 783
The others soon recovered and rejoiced
to bear the man's remains inside their walls.
Long lines of young men raised him on their shoulders
and praised him more than Cadmus and Amphion,
the city's founders. After they sang hymns
they draped spring flowers and wreathes around his limbs
and placed his body in his family tomb
where they adored it, then resumed the war
as soon as their devotions were completed.

No longer angry, Creon now lamented
his sadness, and his wife lamented too:

"O noble son, was it for this appeasement— 793
to sacrifice yourself for savage Thebes—
that I, like some poor mother, bore and raised you?
Am I oppressed by some impiety?
Who else is so detested by the gods?
The sons I bore did not reenter me
in monstrous copulation, nor do I
mourn that I gave my son sons. But then, so?

Look at Jocasta! She has seen her children
be princes—kings!—while we must sacrifice
our pledges to the war, so that the sons
of Oedipus can alternate their rule.
Father of Lightning, are you pleased? But why
do I complain of gods and men? It's you,
savage Menoeceus, you who most of all
hurry me, in my wretchedness, toward death.
What made you want to die? What sacred frenzy 804
entered your mind? What child did I conceive?
What evil, so unlike me, did I bear?
You are descended from the war god's dragon—
from those sad souls, whose hearts knew Mars too well,
who grew up from the ground—not from *my* people!
Unbidden, on your own, you killed yourself
despite the opposition of the Fates.
You interrupt the shadows that lament.
We were alarmed by armored Capaneus
and fierce Danaans, but it was your sword—
which in a fit of madness I once gave you—
and this, your hand, that should have caused concern.
See how his blade is buried in his throat?
No Greek can push a weapon in so deep."

Her moans accompanied her words, as she 815
voiced her unhappiness and turned away
servants who would console her. Her companions
took her inside her chamber, where she sat,
her face torn by her fingernails, ignoring
daylight or anyone who spoke, and she
stared at the ground and never moved her face.
She had no power of speech—her mind was lost—
like a fierce tigress when her cubs are captured
who lies down in a cave in Scythia
alone and licks the warm stones where they lay;
her rage abates; her fierce and hungry face
holds still when flocks and cattle pass before her.
Why should she feed to nurse? for where are they
who look for her, to whom she brings such prey?

—♦—♦—♦—

So far—arms, trumpets, swords, and wounds. But now 827
comes Capaneus, seeking heavens' stars.
Dare with me, goddesses. My task demands
a greater fury from Aonian groves.

Did deepest night inflict that rage of his, 831
and did the Stygian sisters join his ranks
and give him the idea of fighting Jove?
Or was it his excessive strength, desire
for glory and the fame of dying well,
the fact that good beginnings make bad endings,
or godlike anger, which attracts us mortals?

Now Capaneus scorns the world's affairs, 836
and he grows weary of the constant slaughter.
His missiles and the weapons of the Greeks
have long since been exhausted. His right hand
is heavy, and he turns his face to heaven,
measuring lofty roofs with his fierce gaze.

He finds a road that leads him through the air, 841
a set of countless steps that twin trees flank.
He waves a branching torch of brilliant flame
that makes him seem a terror from afar;
his armor glows, and one light bathes his shield.

"This ladder will conduct my strength to Thebes, 845
my means to climb the tower Menoeceus stained.
I will discover if Apollo's false, 847
and I will learn the truth of prophecies."

He spoke, then climbed with alternating steps 848
and bragged about the wall that he had captured,
just like the Titans, when the heavens saw
those twin sons of Aloeus as they piled
earth with impiety to view the gods,
and Ossa touched the trembling Thunderer
even before huge Pelion had been added.

Then, on the brink of doom, the stunned defenders—
as if Bellona brought her bloody torch

to raze the city's towers to the ground,
or in some final rite of expiation—
hurled mighty rocks from every building's roof,
◆ threw beams, whirled thongs and Balearic slings. 857
What use are flying javelins or spears?
They rotate siege machines, work catapults,
but no barrage of weapons, front or back,
slows him. He hangs above thin air and takes
deliberate steps as if on level ground,
just as a river's constant flood and current
presses the strong points of an aging bridge
until it wears its stones and moves its stakes,
and—sensing that—resurges even harder,
with greater waves that agitate and tug
the ailing structure, till the rapid stream
tears away every fastening and breathes
openly, the victor, unimpeded.

When he is silhouetted high above 870
the turrets he so long has sought, he towers
over the trembling city and surveys
the Thebans, whom his giant shadow frightens.
He then proclaims, to their astonishment:

"Are these the worthless walls Amphion built—
the walls that followed his unwarlike chants
according to the ancient Theban fable
told shamelessly for simpletons? How hard
a task to ruin walls built by a lyre?"

He shouts his insults and with hand and foot 877
fiercely destroys the mortar work and layers
of masonry that block him. Stone supports
slip under trembling houses. Bridges crumble.
He redeploys the pieces he dislodges,
hurls broken fragments down on homes and temples
and breaks its own high walls to wreck the city.

Argive and Tyrian divinities 883
by now had circled Jupiter, complaining.
The Father, fair to each, observed their anger

and zeal increase before him. Meanwhile others'
presence restrained them. Bacchus moaned that his
mother-in-law was watching, and he glanced
sideways to catch his father's eye, then said,
"Where is that savage hand, the flaming cradle
where I was born and, lo! the lightning bolts,
the lightning bolts!" Apollo groaned for those
homes he himself had prophesied. Unhappy
Hercules valued Thebes and Argos too:
he strung his bow, but he remained uncertain.
Swift Perseus bewailed his mother's Argos.
Venus mourned for the people of Harmonia.
She stood far from her husband, whom she feared,
and looked at Mars with silent irritation.
Tritonia boldly blamed the Theban gods.
Unspeaking Juno writhed in frenzied silence.

None of this yet disturbed the peace of Jove, 897
and then their quarrel quieted because
bold Capaneus clamored from the heights:

"Where are you deities of frightened Thebes?
Where are the lazy sons of this cursed earth,
Bacchus and Hercules? I would not bother
to challenge lesser gods. Who is more worthy
than you are to descend and fight with me?
The ashes and the tomb of Semele
are in my power. Do something! Let me feel
the force of all your lightning, Jupiter!
Or is your thunder only strong enough
to frighten little girls and burn the towers
of Cadmus, whom you made your son-in-law?"

His words provoked resentment in the gods, 907
but Jove laughed at the madman, and he shook
his mass of holy hair. "What hope," he asked,
♦ "can men have when proud giants fought at Phlegra?
Must you too be destroyed?" The madding crowd
pressured the slowly moving god, demanding
weapons of vengeance. His unhappy wife
did not obstruct him now. She did not dare.

No signal had been given, but the royal 913
castle in heaven thundered. Rain clouds gathered,
although there was no wind, and darkness fell.
◆ You would have thought that Iapetus released
◆ his Stygian chains or captive Ischia
or Aetna rose to heaven's convex vaults.
The gods were too ashamed to show their fear,
but when they saw the warrior bestride
the dizzy height and madly call for battle,
they wondered if Jove's lightning would suffice.

They watched in admiration. High above
the gables of Ogygian battlements
strange sounds were heard in heaven. Skies grew dark.
Unseeing Capaneus gripped the walls
and said, as often as the clashing clouds
caused lightning, "These are fires to use in Thebes!
These will renew my oak torch, which grows weak!"

Jove's lightning hit him full strength as he spoke. 927
The clouds absorbed his crest; his shield's boss dropped;
his limbs ignited; those who watched retreated:
his burning corpse might fall on any spot.
Nevertheless he stayed and breathed his last
while facing toward the stars and leaned his smoking
body against the walls that he detested.
His earthly members fell. His soul departed.

Had Capaneus lost his strength more slowly, 938
he might have hoped to feel a second bolt.

–◆–◆–◆–

BOOK 11 Piety

Capaneus lies dead. Thebans counterattack. Megaera assists Tisiphone. Argia's effigy prompts Polynices. Eteocles sacrifices, rebukes Creon. Jocasta berates Eteocles. Antigone addresses Polynices from the walls. Adrastus departs. Piety descends, in vain. The brothers die. Oedipus emerges. Creon, named king of Thebes, forbids burial for the enemy. Antigone intervenes to save Oedipus from exile.

After the evil strength and mighty heart
of Capaneus failed, and he expired;
after he felt that lightning bolt, as fires
of vengeance blazed beside him, and he fell
earthward and carved a path that scarred the walls,
Jove's conquering right hand calmed the roiling world;
his nod brought earth and heaven back to order.

The gods congratulated his achievement,
as when he stopped the weary fight in Phlegra
or topped Enceladus with smoking Aetna.
The dead man lay on earth. He clung to fragments
of broken turret, scowling as he left
the world the memory of his great prowess
and deeds the Thunderer himself admired.
As far as Tityos (the ravisher
of Phoebus's mother) stretches in Avernus—
where vultures bristle when those birds emerge
from his deep chest and watch his members lying
huge and his liver grow to make their food—
so, where he landed, he encumbered earth
and seared the hostile field, which smelled of sulphur.
Thebans relaxed at last. The hidden masses
surged from the temples, having ceased their vows
and final lamentations. Mothers now
felt brave enough to set their children down.

The pale Achaeans, in disorganized 21
retreat, saw something scarier than hostile
armies or deadly swords. Before their eyes
they saw the wrath of Jove. They felt their armor
burn and their helmets thunder. In their fear
and trembling, they believe that Jupiter
himself pursued them, blocking flight with fire.

To take advantage of the heavens' tumult,
the army of Agenor was deployed, 26
as when a lion snaps his heavy jaws
on undefeated leaders of the herds
along Massylian plains, then turns away
contented. Growling bears come forward; greedy
wolves show their presence and ignobly—tamely—
suck on the wounds of someone else's prey.

Eurymedon, a rustic, ventured forward; 32
his armor bristled; he bore country weapons.
A son of Pan, he had inherited
his aptness to promote disturbances.
Alatreus was his boy and mirrored him,
but his exertions overpassed his years,
despite his tender youth. Both men were blessed,
but he who had begotten was the happier.
It was not easy to distinguish whose
armor rang louder or whose spear flew faster.

The palisades were packed by fleeing soldiers. 39
O Mars, what alterations you produce!
The Thebans, who once scaled their city's walls,
were now attacking to defend the town.
Like south winds blowing, like the clouds returning,
first this field then the other surged like tides
whose white swirls strip then bury oceansides.
The young Tirynthians, whose armor copied 45
that of their kinsman Hercules, were dying
everywhere, while in heaven he was mourning
to see their clubs and quivers, which matched his.
He watched blood stain their Nemean lion skins.

The herald Enyeus held a slender trumpet 49
and manned an Argive watchtower's iron summit.
He was exposed to view, and as he signaled
his suffering companions to retreat
(persuading them to seek their camp's protection),
an arrow flew obliquely through the sky
and pinned the player's left hand to his ear,
and there it hung. His soul fled through thin air.
His cold lips hushed. Only his trumpet blared.

–♦–♦–♦–

Tisiphone had done her wicked deeds 57
and now was growing weary of both armies.
She wished to end the war, to kill both brothers,
but would not trust herself with such a task
unless she could convince Megaera, her
beloved sister and her sister's serpents
to instigate the pair to join in battle.
She therefore hastened to a distant valley 62
and stuck her Stygian sword blade in the soil.
She murmured to the earth the name of her
not present, and—an unmistakable
sign to the Stygian kingdom—lifted up
the king snake on her forehead. It—the prince
of her cerulean tresses—gave long hisses
whose sound brought instant horror to the land,
to seas and skies, and made the Father reach
yet once again to seize his Aetnean fires.

Megaera heard the summons. She, by chance, 69
stood by her parent and by all in Dis
who honored Capaneus and gave his
distinguished shade some water from the Styx.
The ponderous earth broke open. Ghosts rejoiced. 72
Megaera all at once stood under heaven,
and daylight lessened to the same extent
as shadows in the underworld grew dim.

Her hideous sister seized upon her hand, 76
clasped her, and told her, "Sister, up till now

I have worked unassisted to perform
our Stygian father's mad and fearful orders
while you, as I succeeded in this world,
restrained weak spirits in Elysium.
My efforts were not wasted. I collected 81
a fierce toll in that interval. Blood soaks
the fields; it smokes in lakes. The banks of Lethe
rejoice with countless dead: a satisfying
sign of my force. But what is this to me?
Let Mars be satisfied. Let Enyo take
credit for what she tells the world. You saw—
he surely makes a show in Stygian shadows—
the prince who is insatiable, who gnaws
the miserable head I gave him, he whose jaws
blood stains and fouls, whose face drips thick, black gore.
The horror of the thunder that descended
from heaven even now, you know about.

"But I disdain the wars where deities 90
engage the mad assaults of mortal beings,
whose anger is so vast it causes lightning.
So—I confess it, sister—my long effort
leaves my heart weary, and my hand is slow.
This air dims my infernal torch. My serpents,
unused to so much starlight, fall asleep.
You, though, have been protected till this moment.
Your tresses, fresh from washing in Cocytos,
stand elevated, strong. Join forces with me,
not to prepare the usual encounter
or war for Mars, but so that brothers—*brothers!*—
will draw their swords and meet. If Piety
and Faith (the nurturer) resist, they will
be overcome. Although our task is great,
we two will raise discordant arms and hate.
Select the one—why should you hesitate?—
whose standard you will carry. Both should be
easy for us, but I am most concerned
that our resolve not be retarded by
the wavering multitudes, a mother's pleas,
or smooth persuasions from Antigone.

♦ "Moreover, he whose prayers were wearying, 105
who called the Furies to avenge his eyes,
who keeps—they say—from all society,
now feels himself a father, mourns his children.
I have resisted, but I'll enter Thebes
and face the household I have come to know.
The godless outcast must obey your orders.
Impel the Argive to impiety
but take care that Adrastus not prevail
or that Lernaean plebes promote delay.
Join, as my enemy, the mutual fray!"

With that, the sisters went their separate ways, 113
as Boreas and Notus leave the poles
on heaven's separate hinges and then meet
after one wind has fed on Rhipaean snows,
the other Libyan quicksand. Rivers, forests,
and clouds collide and clamor. Soon destruction
is everywhere apparent. Farmers weep
their damages. Tired sailors wail at sea.

–♦–♦–♦–

When the high Father saw them from Olympus 119
defile the light of day and cast a pall
across the shimmering orbit of the sun,
he turned aside his eyes and sternly spoke:

"Heavenly dwellers, we have seen armed madness 122
taken as far as decency allows.
♦ The wars were lawful till a single man
contrived impieties and dared to hurl
♦ himself against my right hand. Now a pair
of criminals begins a duel that Earth
in all her miseries has never known.
Let it be distant from divinities,
unknown to Jupiter! Avert your eyes!
It was enough we saw the deadly meal
of Tantalus, Lycaon's wicked altars,
Mycenae rush the rapid stars through heaven.
The orbit of the sun is once again

about to be disturbed. Accept, o Earth,
these evil clouds, and let the skies recede.
I must protect my world of deities
◆ and not permit Astraea's constellation
◆ or Leda's brothers to behold such things."

Thus the omnipotent father spoke and turned
his gaze from evil fields and let the world
no longer know his sweet serenity.

–◆–◆–◆–

◆ The virgin daughter of the god of darkness 136
by now had followed Polynices' path
through Argive battle lines. She found the man
under a portal, wondering if he
should end this tragedy by flight, or die.
While walking on the walls in nighttime dimness, 139
uncertain, weighing worries and solutions,
he saw an effigy that he believed
must be a portent. It was carrying
nuptial tapers. He discerned his wife,
Argia, hair disheveled, who was bearing
a dismal lamp, and when he asked her why
she walked in mourning, what her sad signs meant,
she wept and turned away her silent flame.
He knew he saw a product of his mind.
How could she leave Mycenae and approach
the palisades, and no one see her coming?
He felt Fate's warning, his impending doom,
and feared what he perceived, when suddenly
the Fury for whom Acheron had opened
tapped on his breastplate three times with her flail.
He burned, he lost his reason, he forgot
his realm; his only thought, impending slaughter,
his misery, his wish to meet his death
in blood that poured from stab wounds on his brother.

At once he told Adrastus, "I am late 154
indeed, the last of our fraternity,
survivor of the Argives, but in this

time of distress I must make my decision.
I will engage in battle on my own.
I should have fought when Argive blood was whole,
before we lost our leaders' reverend souls
and all the best Danaan youth were gone.
I could have placed upon my head the crown
that caused such sorrow in so many towns.

"The time for such an offer has been lost, 161
but let me now at least repay my debt.
As my wife's father, you repress your grief;
you care about your son-in-law's dishonor.
But I am he who, when you ruled in peace
and pious government, led you to leave
your realm and country. How I wish my troubles
had found a welcome in some other city!
Punish me this way—why draw back? It is
decreed! My destiny is fixed—I'll challenge
my brother to a final duel. . . . Don't try
to hinder me. You do not have the power.
Not if my dismal mother or sad sisters
stepped in to stop the fighting, not if my
father himself delayed my rush to battle
or drew a helmet over his dead eyes,
would I desist. Should I not drink Thebes' blood
and take advantage of your men who died?

"I saw earth gaping, but I did not move— 175
saw Tydeus dying for a crime I caused.
◆ Defenseless Tegea demands her lord,
whose childless mother in Parrhasian caves
makes moans against me. When Hippomedon
poured blood into the waters of Ismenos,
I could not scale its banks, nor climb the towers
of Thebes as thunder rumbled. How can I
live in such fear? But I will pay my debt.
Let everyone assemble: aging fathers,
Pelasgian mothers, and the younger women,
all those whose joys I've stolen and whose homes
I've emptied: I will fight my brother! What
more can I do? Let them observe, and let them

pray that Eteocles will win. For now,
farewell, my wife. And farewell sweet Mycenae!

"Father-in-law and friend, not all the guilt 188
and evils are my fault, for I was helped
by the injurious Parcae and the gods.
Be careful with my ashes. Save me from
flesh-eating birds. Conceal me from my brother.
Carry my urn back. This is all I ask—
then find a better husband for your daughter!"

They walked in tears, as when the spring returns 193
and Thracian snows melt, when high Haemus shrinks
and Rhodope descends in narrow streams.
The elder man was starting to assuage
his violence with genial advice,
when the cruel Fury cut off his address
and brought new terror. She assumed the features
of an Inachian named Pherclus: she
quickly gave Polynices fatal arms,
a swift, wing-footed stallion, and his casque,
which dimmed Adrastus' words. She put it on
his head, then told him: "Hurry! Cease delaying!
They say Eteocles has reached the gates!"
She seized the man and set him on his steed. 202
The pallid rider turned and caught a last
glimpse of the flitting shadow of the goddess.

–♦–♦–♦–

In vain the Tyrian king made offerings 205
to Jupiter as payment for his lightning;
he also hoped that he'd disarm the Argives.
Neither the heavenly father nor another
divinity was present at his altars,
but mischievous Tisiphone attended
among his trembling servants, redirecting
his prayers to the Thunderer—of hell:

"Greatest of gods, although unreverential 210
Argos and bitter Juno may be jealous,

the origins of Thebes are owed to you,
for you disturbed the Bacchic dance in Sidon
by ravishing Europa, our ancestress,
whom you allowed to ride your back while you
murmured false vows as you swam peaceful seas.
Nor were you unsuccessful in possessing 215
another Cadmean woman, Semele,
whose Tyrian hearth and home you overpowered.
By now, I think, you look with gratitude 217
on these beloved walls and us, your kinsmen.
You use your thunder to defend us, just
as if your realm in heaven were assaulted.
We saw you massing clouds around our towers,
and we rejoiced to be recipients
of your benignant lightning and to know
the thunder that old generations heard.
Accept our flocks, our mounds of frankincense, 222
our sacrificial bull. But it is not for mortals
to make sufficient offerings. Our Bacchus
and Hercules contend to pay your due.
Defend these walls for them." He spoke these words,
but then a burst of black flame struck his face;
it tore his hair and burned away his crown.

A fierce bull started bleeding on the shrine 228
before it had been sacrificed; it raised
the altar on its mad horns then escaped
despite the crowds of those who blocked its way.
◆ Attendants scattered while the haruspex
consoled the king, who lost his strength but ordered
the sacrifice continued and completed.
He hid great fears behind his false expression,
◆ not unlike Hercules when he felt flames
run through his bones: though the Oetaean garment
clung to his members, nonetheless he finished
his vows and carried offerings of incense
until the torment was so great, he screamed.
He had been hard before, enured to pain,
but Nessus burned his victim's inner organs.

—◆—◆—◆—

Aepytus left his station at the gates 239
and half-dead, breathing hard from running, brought
a garbled message to the anxious king:

"Break off your pious rituals, o leader!—
your ill-timed, sacred sacrifice. Your brother
stands at the city walls, and he defies
your barricading gates with spear and bridle,
repeats your name, and calls for you to duel!"

Mournful once more, the king's companions wept; 246
they groaned to hear that message, and their soldiers
caused a commotion as they struck their weapons.
The king prayed, "Great progenitor of gods,
now is the time for lightning! What offense
made Capaneus special?" He was wary,
raging with hate, but also took delight
to be so angry, like a ruling bull
after the leisure of his rival's exile:
he hears a hostile lowing with sharp ears
and recognizes threats. He stands before
his herd, hot, full of anger, and exhales
humid and burning breath. His savage feet
paw at the ground; his horns slice through the air.
Earth quakes; the trembling vales expect a battle.

Advisers to the king were never lacking: 257
"He's harmless. Let him pound the walls." "Can he
make such a challenge with his broken army?"
"It's misery and madness, courting danger,
not to weigh fear, to scoff and scorn at safety."
"Stand firm against this onslaught on your throne.
Let us repulse the enemy. Give us
the order to attack!" Thus his attendants,
but Creon came, and he was hot with grief
because his heart was burning for Menoeceus.
Creon could find no peace, and he felt free
to speak against the war. He thought he reached
and grasped his son; he thought he saw blood spilling
in rivers down his breast, and always, always
he saw Menoeceus fall from that cruel tower.

He knew Eteocles was hesitant 269
to fight and told him, "Miserable man!
Your power derives from citizens who die,
from war and Fate and tears! So why should we
endure you any longer? Seek your vengeance!
We have atoned for your impieties
for long enough before unfavorable gods.
You have exhausted Thebes, which had been crowded
with citizens and filled with arms and wealth.
You cast long shadows on this emptiness,
like heaven's plague or earth's malignancy.
We cannot keep our commoners in service:
their bodies lie unburnt along the ground;
their country's river wafts them to the sea;
some seek their limbs; some tend their anxious wounds.

"Restore the state its brothers, sons, and fathers. 279
Restore men to the fields and to their homes.
Where is great Hypseus? neighboring Dryas?
sonorous Phocis's arms? Euboean leaders?
The equal chance of war has made them ghosts,
but you, my son, lie dead! My source of shame,
your city's sacrifice! A sacrifice!—
like a mute yearling from a common herd
embellished with the first fruits of the field,
condemned to die in some nefarious rite.
Ay, me! And does this man still hesitate
when called to meet opposing Mars? Does he
yet stand? Does impious Tiresias
order another soul to fight, or issue
more prophecies designed for my destruction?
I, in my misery, have only Haemon!
Will you send him to war while you remain
safely inside the walls where you can watch?
Why do you snort and glance at servant soldiers?
Your men want you to go, to pay the price.
Your mother and your sisters each detest you.
Your brother threatens you with death. He rages
and threatens with his sword. Do you not hear?
He's battering the fierce bars on your gates!"

So spoke the father as he rolled in waves 297
of misery and ground his angry teeth.
The king replied, "You don't fool anyone,
nor are you moved by your son's public fate.
It fits a father so to speak and boast,
but your tears hide ambition, secret hopes.
You use his death to veil your foolish vows.
You press me—uselessly—as if you were
the heir presumptive to my vacant throne,
but Fortune will not let the scepter fall
to one like you, unworthy of his son—
not in a city that derives from Sidon!
I could have easy vengeance, even now—
but let me have my arms first. Servants, arms!
The brothers are about to meet in battle!
Creon wants something to assuage his wounds:
let him enjoy my madness. When I win,
he will repay his debt!" So he postponed
their disagreement and replaced his sword,
which he had drawn in anger, in its scabbard.
He bristled like a serpent whom some shepherd
has struck by chance: it draws its poison forward
through its long body to its mouth but when
the stranger changes paths and deviates,
and the threat lessens, it relaxes its
pointless defense and drinks its angry venom.

–◆–◆–◆–

Now when Jocasta, their distracted mother, 315
first heard reports that her two sons might die,
she credited the news. She was not slow
to bare her breast, to tear her face and hair
until blood flowed. Unmindful of her sex
and what was inappropriate, she went in public
◆ just like Agave, Pentheus' mother, when
she climbed the summit of the frantic mountain
to bring his promised head to fierce Lyaeus.
Neither her pious daughters nor companions 321
could move as fast as she did, for her latest

grief made her strong; her lamentations stirred
fierce sentiments in her declining age.

The king by then had donned his glorious helmet 324
and bound his deadly javelins with thongs.
He was examining his horse, which thrilled
to horns and grew intrepid hearing trumpets,
when suddenly his mother loomed before him.
The king and all his servants paled with fear;
his squire withdrew the offer of his spear.

"What is this madness? Has the Fury risen 329
again—still undiminished—to our kingdom?
Will you two duel . . . you—after everything,
after you led twin armies, ordered horrors?
Where will the victor go? To seek my lap?
You've made my dreadful husband's darkness happy,
but my eyes punish me: they let me see
this day of destiny! O savage man,
whom do you think you threaten with your stare?
Why do you blanche and blush and change expressions,
murmur and gnash your teeth? I feel great grief
that you might win, but you will fight this duel
at home, where I may stand beside the threshold,
before the gates, an inauspicious sign,
to make you conscious of your awful crime!
You will see these gray hairs, these breasts you trample,
this womb your horse must tread! Degenerate,
why do you push your shield and pommel—stop this!—
when I oppose you? I have sworn no vows
against you by the deities of Styx,
nor called upon the Furies with blind prayers!
Pity a miserable woman, I implore you!
I am your mother, not your father! Sinful man,
delay your guilt! Consider what you hear!
What if your brother pounds the walls and stirs
a war of great impiety against you?
That is because his mother and his sisters
do not deter his movements. We are busy
petitioning and begging you: he has
only Adrastus to dissuade him, who

perhaps has ordered him to fight! Will you
leave your ancestral portals, household gods,
and our embrace to duel against your brother?"

–♦–♦–♦–

Elsewhere Antigone with silent steps 354
stole through obstructing crowds and madly scaled
the high Ogygian walls. She did not let
her maidenhood and innocence deter her.
Actor, her old companion, followed after
but did not have the strength to climb the towers.
She paused as she surveyed the distant army 359
and recognized her brother, who assailed
their city with proud words and javelins,
a shameful sight. At once she filled the air
with heartfelt lamentations, and she spoke
like one prepared to hurtle from the wall:

"Constrain your weapons, brother! Pause to look, 363
here, at this tower! Let my eyes behold
your bristling crest! Are we the enemy?
Is this how we demand our yearly turn?
Is this good faith? complaints appropriate
to virtuous exile and a valid cause?
If there is any sweetness in your home life,
then by your Argive hearth (for you have lost
your fame among the Tyrians), my brother,
subdue your rage! Both of the cities and
both armies beg you. So do I, who am
devoted to you both and now suspected
of evil by the king. O dire one, listen!
Soften your warlike face and let me see
the features that I love for what may be
the last time; let me see if these laments
have made you weep. They say our mother's groans
and prayers have stopped Eteocles already.
He has replaced the sword he had withdrawn!
Do you resist me, one who night and day
weeps for your wandering exile—I, who placate
the father you so frequently enrage?

Why do you free your brother of his guilt?
He did you injury, and he mistreats
his people. Look, you call him, but he stays!"

His wrath was just beginning to abate, 382
because of what she said, despite the Fury
who shouted and obstructed him. His hand
had dropped already, he had slowly turned
his reins, and he was silent. Then he groaned,
tears filtered through his casque, his rage grew dull;
he felt an equal shame for having come—
being the guilty party—and for leaving.
But then Tisiphone repulsed his mother
and through the broken gates she shoved his brother,
who suddenly was clamoring, "I'm here,
though envious that you were first to challenge!
Do not accuse me of delay. Our mother
encumbered me as I prepared my weapons.
O Thebes, you are uncertain who will rule.
For sure it will be he who wins this duel!"

The other was no milder. He exclaimed, 392
"Barbarian, do you keep faith at last?
Do you emerge to fight a fair encounter?
After so long, o brother, we engage!
Our covenant, our contract, still remains!"

His mood was hostile as he viewed the man: 396
he envied his innumerable attendants,
his royal casque, his horse's purple drapery,
his shield that gleamed with gold, though he himself
bore honorable weapons and a brilliant cloak.
Argia made his fine, uncommon garment
◆ in the Maeonian mode, and with her skillful
fingers wove purple threads through webs of gold.

The brothers charged together through the dust. 403
The Furies who'd prepared their shining weapons,
who'd woven serpents through their horse's manes
controlled their champions and gave them guidance.

Fraternal strife unfolded on that field; 406
similar faces clashed beneath those casques.
A single womb made war against itself:
flags trembled; trumpets ceased; war horns were silent.
Three times from hell's black shores its vast king thundered;
three times he shook the bottom of the world.
Pallas and Mars—the gods of war—departed:
he drove his frightened chariot far off;
Minerva hid behind a Gorgon's visor.
Glorious Virtue left. Bellona snuffed
her flames. In turn the Stygian sisters blushed.
The miserable people peeped from towering roofs;
groans came from every turret; tears wet towers.
The old complained that they had lived too long;
mothers laid bare their breasts, kept their small children
from witnessing the battle; and the king
of Tartarus himself commanded his
gates opened that Ogygian ghosts might see
their relatives at war. These took their seats
on native hills, where they bedimmed the daylight
and marveled that their own crimes were surpassed.

After Adrastus heard the pair had been 424
goaded to open combat, and no sin
sufficed to rouse in them a sense of shame,
he rode between them, indiscriminate—
himself a king and venerable with age.
But what did they, who scorned their own relations,
care what a foreign sovereign might say?

Nonetheless he implored: "Must Tyrians 428
and Argives too watch these impieties?
Where is your sense of justice, of the gods,
the rules of war? Do not maintain this anger!
You are my enemy, Eteocles,
although if rage permitted, you would see
in blood we are not distant: I implore you!
And you, my son-in-law! Here is my offer:
if you have such desire to hold a scepter,
I will remove my royal livery.

Govern, alone, in Argos and in Lerna!"
His speech no more convinced the pair to stop 435
their raging battle than tall Black Sea breakers
♦ keep the Cyanean islands' cliffs apart.

As his words faded, he could see their steeds 439
driven to battle through twin clouds of dust,
could see mad fingers testing thongs for throwing.
He raced away from everything: the camp,
his army, son-in-law, and Thebes, and he
propelled Arion forward, though that steed
turned in its yoke and uttered prophecies.
♦ Just so, the king of shadows left his cart
and turned pale when he entered Tartarus,
the portion he inherited, when he
fell to misfortune, lost the lottery.

Fortune, however, intervened, stopped battle, 447
delayed a little, hesitated, waited
as this impiety, this crime, took shape.
Two times they charged in vain. Two times their horses
were spurred but spared by inadvertent errors.
Their spears, untainted yet by sacred blood,
were blocked and pushed aside. Hands strained at reins.
Fierce goads put unfair pressure on fierce steeds.
But there was more: the awesome prodigies
of heaven moved the armies to contend,
to interfere in that fraternal strife;
a silent murmur ran through either side.

–♦–♦–♦–

♦ Piety had been sitting by herself, 458
separate in heaven, for a long time now,
offended by both deities and humans.
She did not wear her customary garb
or shining face. Her hair had shed its ribbons,
and she wept over this fraternal strife
like the sad sister and uneasy mother
of those who fought. She also reprimanded

Jove and the Parcae for their injuries
and wondered if she should leave heaven's light
and enter Erebus, the halls of Styx.

She cried, "Queen Nature, why did you conceive
me as an obstacle to men and gods
in their fierce rages? I am nothing now
among the nations, nor am I revered.
O, madness—men and dire Promethean arts!
Behold the race of mortals! Things were better
when sea and land were vacant, after Pyrrha!"

She spoke, and looked for some way she could help.
"At least I am permitted to attempt;
even if unsuccessful, I will try!"

She flew down from the poles, a streak of white
through dark clouds. Though the goddess was distressed,
as soon as she had settled on the ground
peace calmed the battle lines. Men felt their crimes.
Tears streaked their faces and ran down their breasts.
A silent horror overcame the brothers.
Piety wore feigned weapons, virile arms,
and called to these and those, "Now stop this! Cease!
Who has no brothers, sons, loved ones at home?
Is it not clear that heaven shows you pity?
Chance herself swerves, steeds stall, and weapons tumble!"

She would have made them hesitate, had not 482
savage Tisiphone observed her fraud
and, swift as heaven's lightning, reappeared.
"Why do you interfere with those who dare
to fight," she clamored, "you who dedicate
yourself to peace? You idle goddess, this
field is our field! The day is ours! You come
too late here to defend destructive Thebes!
Where did you hide when Bacchus called for war,
when orgies made the mothers rage in arms?
Where were you idling when the snake of Mars
drank foul streams, Cadmus plowed, the beaten Sphinx

expired, when Oedipus met Laius, when
he wed Jocasta by my torch and fire?"

With hissing hydras and her outstretched flame 492
the Fury drove her back, and Piety
avoided her and hid her eyes, ashamed.
She drew her drooping cloak around her face
and fled, but would complain to Jove the Great.

–♦–♦–♦–

Anger grew hotter, provocation stronger. 497
Arms pleased and armies turned. They wished to watch.
Foul deeds commenced. Eteocles, the king,
was faithless. He prepared his weapons,
worried a deadly spear would strike him first,
but failed to land his blow. The golden shield
of Polynices caught along its rim
the spear that he had tried to aim dead center.

It was the exile's turn. His deadly prayer 503
rang clear, "O gods whom blinded Oedipus
successfully petitioned to ignite
crimes and impieties, the gift I ask
is not improper: let me expiate
my violence by using this same sword
to rend my breast, as long as I can grasp
the scepter he'll abandon when he leaves
and bears away his grief, a lesser ghost!"

His fast spear flew between the rider's thigh 510
and his steed's spine—it could have killed them both—
but disappointed Polynices' prayer:
the rider was unhurt—his flexed knee spared
him injury—although the spear point sliced
a slanting wound across his charger's side.
The swift steed fled, scorned his tight reins, and drew
an arc of blood along the reddening field.
The exiled one rejoiced, for he believed—
as did the terrified Eteocles—

the blood spores were his brother's; he released
his reins and blindly struck the wounded charger.
Reins, hands, and weapons mingled. Both steeds stumbled
and fell; their legs were tangled up and jumbled,
like ships the cloudy south wind blows together
that break their oars and intertwine their stays;
they fight against the dark, the storm, themselves,
and then they sink, together, in the deep.

Such was their duel. They strove without design; 524
they showed no art, so mighty was their anger.
They saw candescent hatred through their helmets
and scrutinized each other, steely-eyed.
There was no space between them; their swords meshed,
theirs hand conjoined, and they were fiercely driven
by one another's pantings, just as if
they heard shrill bugles and the sound of horns.
As when rash anger drives two thrashing boars 530
together, and their backs upsurge with bristles,
flames tremble in their eyes and their hooked teeth
and crescent tusks resound. A hunter watches
the battle from a nearby rock and blanches;
he silences his hounds. The boars clash madly.
Their wounds are not yet deadly, but blood flows.

Impiety, but no need—yet—for Furies, 536
who stood, instead, and watched in admiration,
jealous of men whose rage surpassed their own.
Each brother sought—and loved—the other's blood,
and each ignored his own. At last the exile,
whose rage was stronger and who thought his cause
had greater justice, rushed, and he struck deep:
he shoved his sword inside his brother's body
where tapered links of steel exposed his groin.
Pain did not triumph, but the king knew fear,
felt cold steel, and withdrew behind his shield.
Soon his limbs weakened; soon he understood
his wound's extent and, feeling ill, breathed hard.
His enemy, however, did not spare him,
even as he drew back, but loudly taunted:

"Where are you going, brother? Are you leaving?
Your reign has left you languid, full of sleep,
worn out from too much quiet. You have ruled
under long shadows. But observe my limbs,
hardened by scarcity and lean from exile.
Learn not to trust in fortune but to fight!"

And so those wretches dueled. A little life 552
was yet remaining in the evil king, but he
was weary; he could not stand up much longer,
yet even as he died, he planned a final
fraud—so he fell. Cithaeron heard the roar.
His brother, thinking he had won, upraised
his palms to heaven: "All is well! My vows
are heard! His eyes are heavy and I see
death swimming in his face. Somebody, quickly,
while he has vision, take away his scepter.
Remove the signs of rank that crown his hair."
He spoke, and he moved forward, and his armor—
he even wished to strip his brother's armor,
as if to ornament his homeland's altars.
Eteocles, however, still had strength— 562
enough to satisfy his rage and vengeance—
and when he felt the other lean above him,
he raised his sword in secret, supplemented
his failing force with hate and—pleased by his
destiny—stabbed his brother through the heart.

Then Polynices: "Are you living? Does 568
your hatred still survive? O, treacherous!
Can you not find a quiet place to rest?
◆ Then come with me to shadows! If judge Minos
still guards the Cnosian urn and punishes
kings, I will claim my contract!" Nothing further.
He fell. His heavy armor smote his brother.

Go, gruesome souls! Pollute funereal 574
Tartarus with your deaths and consummate
your punishment in hell. You Stygian goddesses,
spare men from evil. May this single day
have seen sufficient horrors for all ages

and for all countries. May its memory
of criminality not reach the future.
May kings alone be conscious of this strife!

–◆–◆–◆–

The father of this infamy emerged, 580
the battle done, from deep and gloomy shadows.
He stood half dead before his dreadful door,
his hair and beard begrimed with ancient gore.
Stiff tresses veiled his head, which Furies haunted.
Filth marked the traces of his sunken sockets.
His left side was uplifted by his daughter,
his right leaned on his staff. It was as if
◆ the sailor of the stagnant stream Avernus,
weary of ghosts, should seek the upper regions
and agitate the pale stars and the sun.
His strength would weaken in the air of heaven
and many shadows would remain on shore,
since no one ferries them. In just this manner
Oedipus sought the field when he emerged.

He told his mournful daughter, "Lead me to 594
my sons, I pray, and lay their father's hands
on their remains!" Antigone delayed,
uncertain what would happen. Chariots,
dead carrion, and weapons blocked their way
and slowed them as they clung to one another.
Old steps move slow. The guide—poor woman!—struggled.

She shouted out to tell him she had found 599
the objects of their search; he hurled himself—
an old man, speechless—over cold limbs, corpses.
He wallowed, moaning, on their bloody wounds
and took some time to find the words that followed.
He drew off helmets, sought their hidden faces.
His sighs, at long last, ceased. The old man spoke:

"My mind takes pity. Is this piety, 605
after so long, that strikes me? Does my heart
feel clemency? You, Nature, have defeated

a saddened parent. Dried wounds bathe in tears.
My hands, which knew impiety, strike flesh,
and I lament. Accept due offerings
for your unholy dyings—and my cruelties.
It is not given me to recognize
my sons, to frame fit speeches. Tell me, woman,
which am I holding? How can one as savage
as I conduct their funerals and rites?
I wish I had my eyes to wrack once more, 614
to tear my visage, as I did before.
Too sad, too just, that evil prayers, a parent's
curses against his children, should be heard.
Which of the gods attended me and caught
my words and passed them over to the Fates?
Madness herself and War were moving forces:
my father and my mother and my kingdom,
my fallen eyes! But I myself did nothing—
I swear it by dark hell, which comforts me,
and by my daughter's undeserved despair!
O, may I die and enter Dis with honor!
May Laius not be angry, not avoid me.
Aye, me! What tangled brothers do I trace?
What wounds? I pray, unclasp your hands. Divide
your hostile grips, my sons. Embrace your father!"

A death wish seized the old man as he mourned.
He sought the means in secret, but his daughter
had cautiously removed her brothers' weapons.
Oedipus raved. "Where are the instruments
of death? Are they encased inside the bodies?
Alas, the Furies!" As he spoke, his feeble
companion lifted him, and she suppressed
her sorrow while rejoicing that he wept.

–♦–♦–♦–

Meanwhile, the queen, Jocasta—when the duel 634
between her sons raised clamor and brought terror—
removed a sad memorial, the sword
of scepter-bearing Laius, from its shrine.
Cursing the gods, her bed of infamy,

the ghost of her first husband, her son's madness,
she struggled but she summoned up her strength
and pushed the sword blade through her leaning breast.
The blow burst her old veins, and her sad bed 640
was cleansed of its impieties by blood.
Ismene fell and covered her thin body.
Where the wound spurted, she let down her hair,
she wept, and she attended, like Erigone,
sad daughter of Icarius, who mourned
her father in the woods of Marathon
where he was slaughtered: when that daughter cried
sufficiently, she started to untie
her girdle, picked a strong bough, looked to die.

–◆–◆–◆–

Now Fortune, happy to have foiled the hopes 648
of those two princes, with malignant hand
transferred the scepter and Amphion's realm
elsewhere—to Creon, who held rights from Cadmus.
This was the outcome of that useless war:
the brothers fought for *him*. Those who descended
from Mars proclaimed him, while the debt Menoeceus
paid for the city reconciled the people.

Creon then took the throne that kills its kings 654
in sad Aonia, where power entices,
where love of rule seduces. Will new rulers
never be taught by previous examples?
Look!—he is pleased to hold his foul position,
to rule his kingdom and become a tyrant.

What more, improving Fortune, can you do? 659
Creon forgot his fatherhood, the kingdom
he had inherited, his son Menoeceus.
Pursuing savage customs of the court
(a gauge and indication of his feelings)
he ordered that Danaans be denied
their final flames, that those unfortunate
in war be left unburied under heaven,
their sad ghosts homeless. But when Oedipus

met him before the portal of Ogygia,
fear made him pause a moment. In his heart
he knew his rank was less. He held his temper,
but he assumed a regal countenance
and dared to chide his blind antagonist:
"Go far away! You are a hated omen
to us, the victors. Turn aside the Furies.
Let your departure unpollute our city.
What you have long desired has come to pass.
Your sons are dead. What vows do you have left?"

Oedipus shook, enraged. His trembling sockets 673
stared, as if they could see. Dismissing age,
he dropped his staff. He shoved aside his daughter—
his rage was his support, and pride erupted:

"Have you the leisure, Creon, to be cruel?
You only now assumed our wicked kingdom,
the place of our past fortune, you poor man,
yet you take time to trample fallen kings.
Already you drive victims from their tombs
and comrades from our walls. It seems you are
well able to protect our Theban scepter
on your first day. But why do you restrict
your new authority? Why measure out
so narrowly such honors? You say, 'Exile!'
This is a timid mercy for a king!
Why not be greedy? Stain your savage sword.
Believe me, you may do it. Your attendants
are ready to comply, and brave enough
to slice a neck that offers no resistance.
Begin! Do you expect that I will grovel
prone at the feet of my unruly master?
What if I tried? Would you respond? Would you
threaten to punish me? Do you think any
fears can defeat me? Order me from Thebes?
I would leave earth and heaven willingly
and without urging turn my vengeful hand
cruelly against myself! What more can you,
my king, my enemy, command? I leave—
I flee—this seat of criminality.

What does it matter where I take my blindness,
my drawn-out death? Not everyone denies
a man who knows misfortune, who requires
only a place to sleep. But Thebes is pleasant.
My origins are known here, and the stars
are gentle to my eyes. I have my wife
and children. You own Thebes. You rule the walls
that Cadmus, Laius, and, in God's name, I
also once governed. Now you must marry and
breed loyal sons, although I hope you lack
the strength and purpose to evade misfortune
with your own hand. May *you* love life when ruined.
There, I have said enough about your future.
Daughter, take me away, and far. But why
should I hurt you? Great king, choose me a guide!"

Afraid of being left, Antigone 707
petitioned Creon, in her misery,
for something else: "O reverend Creon, by
Menoeceus's sacred ghost and your just rule,
assist a man afflicted. Disregard
his arrogance, for years of suffering
alter his discourse, make him rude to others.
How he insults the deities and Fates!
Mourning has hardened him. He is not easy,
even for me. He is indomitable.
A wretched liberty and savage hope
for senseless death have long lived in his heart.
See how expertly he provokes your anger.
He welcomes punishment. But you, I pray,
will occupy your reign with charity,
help the unfortunate, and venerate
the fate of former kings. He once was high—
unexiled, on his throne—surrounded by
armed men, but helped the lowly, doling equal
laws to the poor and powerful. He now,
from all those servants, has a single woman.
Is he a hindrance to your happiness?
Do you bring hate, pose your realm's strength against him,
repulse him from your city? Is it that
he moans too loudly here before your portals

or bothers you with inconvenient vows?
Rest easy. He will weep far from your palace.
I will subdue his pride, teach him submission,
lead him away from men, and settle him
in his accustomed dwelling as an exile.

"What foreign walls will open to a wanderer? 730
Should he proceed to Argos, crawl in filth
to cold Mycenae, or report the deaths
of Grecians at the gates of dashed Adrastus?
Should he, a Theban king, seek charity?
Would you have him expose impieties
committed by our family or reveal
embarrassing occurrences? I pray,
whatever we have done, conceal us, Creon!
This service we request will not last long.
Pity old age, I beg you. Let the sad
ghost of my father find a place to sleep.
Surely he may be buried here in Thebes."

So she petitioned him and bowed down low, 739
but Oedipus withdrew her, threatening
wrath and disdaining mercy, like a lion
deep in his cave, whom woods and mountains feared
when he was young—but now he stretches, indolent,
deprived of strength and full of years, and yet
his face is lordly, his maturity
unwelcoming, and if his flaccid ears
should hear a roar, he rises and remembers
who he is. He bemoans his former strength
and envies lions who now rule the plains.

The king was moved by her request, but he 748
would not grant everything she asked. He kept
part of his favor back. "You will not be
stopped at our country's borders as you wander,
but do not stain our homes or sacred temples.
Cithaeron and the bogs are fit enough,
and this land suits your darkness to inhabit:
two peoples lie here, bloody, from the battles!"
He spoke. The groaning people and his courtiers

feigned approbation as he sought the gates.
He moved with royal dignity and pride.

Meanwhile the Argives secretly
left their encampment, which had proved so fatal.
No standards and no generals remained,
nor any man, as they returned in silence,
choosing, instead of death with glory, lives
of infamy, embarrassing retreat.
Night favored them. Kind shadows veiled defeat.

–♦–♦–♦–

BOOK 12 Clemency

The aftermath of battle. The funeral pyre of Menoeceus. Creon's decree. From Argos the mourning women travel toward Thebes. Ornytus warns them away, suggesting they ask Theseus and the Athenians for assistance. Argia finds her husband's body, meets Antigone. The fiery strife of Polynices and Eteocles. Argia and Antigone arrested. Juno leads the Argive women to Athens. The Altar of Clemency. Theseus defeats Creon.

Dawn was awake. Not all the stars had set.
The slim horns of the moon saw day approach.
◆ Tithonia dispersed the timid clouds
and readied heaven for returning Phoebus
when, from the Theban households, Dirce's army
started, and men complained of night's delay.

Even though they might sleep—their first reprieve
since conflict ended—still the sickly peace
dispelled their quiet, and their victory
could not undo the savagery of war.
They hardly dared to sally, to demolish
fortifications, to unbar their portals.
Former fears stood before them, and the horrors
of vacant fields, just as earth totters for
sailors long used to waves when they first land.
So they gazed, stupefied, but moved no closer,
afraid the sprawling bodies might arise.
Just so, if doves of Ida see a serpent
ascend the entrance to an outcropped tower,
they chase their nestlings in. They use their talons
to guard their teeming nursery and unfurl
their passive feathers to prepare for battle.
Although the golden fellow glides away,
the white ones fear void skies, and when they fly
at last, they quake and gaze from stars on high.

People moved past the lifeless and the fallen 22
remnants of war, wherever Grief and Mourning—
those blood-stained leaders—took them. Some saw corpses;
some looked at weapons; others stared at gashes
and saw dead friends beside dead enemies.
Some mourned a car or calmed, as best they could,
untended horses. Some kissed wounds or praised
those who showed valor. Some inspected cold
mounds of dead men. Sword hilts and javelins
lay openly in severed hands, and arrows stood
upright in eyeballs, but of many deaths,
no trace. So people wandered, their laments
held in abeyance, ready for the worst.

–♦–♦–♦–

Among the mangled bodies there arose 33
a senseless competition. People strove
to lead a funeral, conduct a rite,
but fortune mocked them. Often they lamented
their enemies, for it was difficult
to know whom to avoid, whose blood to tread.
Those with no cause to grieve, whose homes were whole,
wandered and searched the Greeks' deserted tents
and put them to the torch, or, as occurs
after a battle, scoured the scattered dust
to find where Tydeus lay or see the chasm
that opened when the augurer was seized
or find the gods' opponent and observe
whether those limbs that lightning struck still burned.

Day waned, but tears continued, nor did evening 44
and the late hour disperse them. Those in pain
loved lamentation. They enjoyed their sorrow.
No one went home; instead, they kept their vigil
nightlong beside the bodies; they made moans
and chased off beasts with flames as well as groans.

–♦–♦–♦–

Lucifer, star of morning, and the Dawn 50
were wrestling for the third time, and the hills
had yielded up the honor of their woods.
Great beams had come from Teumesus, and logs
friendly to flames were hewn on Mount Cithaeron.
On high pyres burned the viscera of men.
Ogygian shades rejoiced at this last gift,
but sad souls of uncovered Greeks made gyres
and raised laments around forbidden fires.

The spirit of impiety—that is, 57
savage Eteocles—did not receive
the honors of a king, yet found a pyre.
His brother, by command, was held an Argive
and driven from the flames—his ghost, an exile.

The king (his father) and the Thebans put 60
Menoeceus on no ordinary pile,
no common mound constructed from hard logs.
His pyre was martial, made from chariots
and shields and other weapons of the Greeks.
He lay, as victor, on this hostile heap,
his brow bound by the laurel leaves of peace
♦ and woolen fillets, just as Hercules
lay down on burning Oeta when the stars
delighted him by calling for his presence.

The father butchered victims still alive— 68
captured Pelasgians and bridled horses—
a solace for his fortunes in the war.
The high flames flickered over them until
Creon spoke words expected from a father:

"Had your desire for fame not been so great, 72
my son, you would be worshiped here in Thebes,
where you would be the future king. But you
have spoiled impending pleasures and made bitter
my public service, which I never sought.

"Although I think your virtue raises you 76
to heaven's vaults to dwell among immortals

where you are deified, yet I must grieve.
Let them build temples and high shrines in Thebes.
A parent may be left alone to mourn.
What larger sacrifice, what solemn rites
might I still give? None, not if I—whose life
a son's blood has preserved (there lies the crime)—
were to mix fatal Argos and myself
and beaten-down Mycenae on your pyre.

"Does one same day, and one same war, send you 84
to Tartarus, my son, together with
those ill-starred brothers? Is my fate the same
as mournful Oedipus? Good Jupiter,
how similar the shadows we lament.
Accept, my son, what your success achieved:
my right-hand's scepter, and my brow's proud crown—
your gifts, which bring your father little joy.
At least the sad ghost of Eteocles will see
you king . . . will see you king." As he was speaking,
he stripped away his crown and dropped his staff,
then violent, enraged, began again:

"Let Argives call me savage and unkind
to bar their dead from burning, but not you.
I wish I could preserve their corpses whole
and chase their souls from heaven and from hell.
I would find savage beasts and taloned birds
and lead them to those princes' impious members.
But they will be resolved into a dew, 99
there where they lie, by time and Mother Earth.
So I repeat, and say it once again:
let no one dare give fire or final rites
to these Pelasgians, for the punishment
is death. That person will increase their number.
I swear this by the gods and great Menoeceus."
He spoke, then comrades took him to his palace.

–♦–♦–♦–

Meanwhile, drawn on by rumors, a sad band 105
♦ of miserable women—widows, grieving mothers—

left empty Argos. These Inachians
behaved like captive slaves. Each had her own
disfigurements, but all looked desolate.
Their hair hung down their breasts; their gowns were girded;
their faces lacerated by their nails;
their soft arms swollen by lamenting blows.

The queen of this black crew of maddened women 111
was widowed Argia, whom her sad retainers
helped to resume her journey when she stumbled.
She did not seek her father or a kingdom.
Her sole fidelity, the only name
she called, was Polynices, her beloved,
for whom she left Mycenae to inhabit
Cadmus's ill-starred city on the Dirce.

Deipyle, not yielding to her sister,
came next and led a muster of Lernaean
and Calydonian women to attend
the funeral of Tydeus. She had heard,
poor girl, the news of his impiety,
his wicked mouthfuls, but ignored it all.
Dead was her husband, and her love misspent.
After her, bitter—also pitiable— 121
Nealce duly mourned Hippomedon;
then came Amphiaraus's evil wife,
who had to build, alas, an empty pyre.
The final line of mourners walked behind
the comrade of Manaelian Diana—
Parthenopaeus' mother—now bereft,
and sad Evadne, wife of Capaneus.
The former grieved and mourned her bold son's deeds.
The latter, mindful of her mighty husband,
wept fiercely, and she blamed the stars in heaven.

Hecate observed them from Lycaean groves 129
and followed them, lamenting. Ino (now
◆ the Theban mother called Leucothea)
wept as they made their way past either sea.
Although she also mourned Proserpina,
◆ the Eleüsin Ceres mourned the wanderers

who moved at night. She showed them secret fires,
and Juno, Saturn's daughter, guided them
but veiled their travels lest her people block
their movements and their enterprise be stopped,
which promised so much glory. She, moreover,
bid Iris tend the princes' lifeless bodies
and soak their rotting limbs with secret dews
and medicines ambrosial to preserve
their quality, to keep them undiminished
as they awaited flames and funeral pyres.

Behold, Ornytus, filthy in his face, 140
pale from a gaping gash (his friends had gone,
and he was burdened by that recent wound),
timid and furtive, made his struggling way
on secret paths, upheld by half a spear.
He did not need to ask; the cause was clear
why he now found his solitude disturbed.
The sole Lernaeans now who still remained
were anxious women. He spoke words of warning:

"What pathways do you follow, wretched ladies? 149
Do you seek bones and ashes of dead husbands?
A sentinel of shades stands vigilant
and counts unburied bodies for the king.
Those who approach to weep are driven back.
Only wild beasts and birds may venture closer.
Will even-handed Creon sympathize
with your lamentings? You may sooner pray
◆ before the evil altars of Busiris,
◆ the famished horses of the Odrysae,
or the divinities of Sicily!
I know him: he will seize you, suppliants,
and have you killed, not on your husband's bodies,
but far away from dear departed shades.
You should proceed now, while the road is safe: 160
return to Lerna. There fix empty names
on vacant sepulchers. Call missing ghosts
to hollow tombs. Or you may go implore
Athenian assistance. They say Theseus
is coming back from Thrace, a conqueror,

favored by fortune. Creon must be forced
by war and arms to follow human customs!"

And so he spoke. Tears welled among the women. 166
Their zeal and forward impetus was halted.
A single paleness froze in all their faces,
as when the Hyrcanian tigress' hungry roar
floats over gentle heifers, and the herd
agitates at the sound. Each feels great terror.
Whom will she seize? Whose backs will feed her hunger?

Instantly disagreements of opinion 173
flared up for different reasons. Some
wished to confront proud Creon there in Thebes;
some wished to test Athenian clemency.
The last choice, that for cowards, was retreat.

A sudden and unusual desire 177
for action took Argia at this moment.
Her plan was difficult, most dangerous,
but great need made her disregard her sex.
She would confront the kingdom's wicked law,
something no Thracian woman would attempt
◆ nor any daughter from the snows of Phasis,
even surrounded by unmarried cohorts.
She skillfully constructed a deceit
to separate herself from faithful friends.
She was contemptuous of life, made bold
by long laments as she prepared to face
the bloody king and cruel divinities.
Her Polynices stood before her eyes, 187
no other than himself in every guise:
now as a guest before a trembling girl;
now promising her wedlock at the altar;
now a kind husband; now a warrior,
sadly embracing her; now gazing back
from the last portal's threshold. But no image
captured her mind more frequently than that
of him, bewildered, on the field of blood,
stripped of his armor, searching for his pyre.

Her mind was driven mad by her distress,
and her chaste passion made her court her death.

She turned to her Pelasgian companions
and said, "Solicit the Athenians;
go seek the ones who arm at Marathon. 196
May Fortune grant your pious labors favor.
But let me, who alone has caused our ruin,
penetrate the Ogygian city-state
and be the first to feel the tyrant's thunder.
I will not strike—unheard—the fierce town's gates.
My husband's sisters live there, and their mother.
I will not go unrecognized through Thebes.
So do not stay my steps, for something powerful,
some heartfelt omen, draws me toward that town."

She spoke no further, and she chose Menoetes 204
(her guardian, who once instructed her
on modesty and maidenhood) to walk
with her, alone. Though inexperienced,
ignorant of the countryside, she hurried
along the path on which Ornytus traveled,
away from her companions in distress.
When she was far enough away, she cried,
"How could I wait for Theseus to make
his slow decision while in hostile fields
you waste away so sadly? Will his captains
or righteous haruspex accede to war?
Meanwhile your body rots! Is it not better
that my own limbs should feel hooked claws of birds?
My loyal husband, if among the shadows 214
you still have feelings, you must be complaining
to Stygian gods that I am late, uncaring.
Whether by chance you lie exposed or buried,
the blame is mine. Is there no strength in sorrow?
Is there no death? Is Creon not unkind?
Ornytus, give me strength to carry on!"

She spoke, then sped across Megarian fields. 219
Those she encountered pointed out the way

and shivered at her misery, afraid.
Her face was fierce, her heart calm, as she passed.
No sounds upset her. Overwhelming danger
soothed her who frightened others whom she met,
◆ as when the mountain Dindyma resounds
in Phrygia, at night, with lamentations,
as she herself, the goddess, drives a woman,
the raving leader of the celebrations
among the pines where Simois begins,
to mutilate herself—gives her the knife
◆ and marks her with a crown of woolen twists.

Titan—the sun, the father—had by now 228
hidden his chariot of fire in
Hesperian waters, to emerge again
from other oceans, yet Argia's grief
made her oblivious of heavy hardships
and unaware of evening. Gloomy fields
were nothing terrible, nor did she stop
her search past fallen trees, on pathless rocks,
through secret forests that are dark by day,
across new plowlands drained by hidden ditches,
and over rivers. She moved on, unharmed,
past sleeping beasts, foul caves of bristling monsters.

Menoetes felt ashamed to walk more slowly,
and he admired the pace of his frail pupil,
so forceful were her courage and her grief.
What homes of men and animals did she 239
not rattle with her sighs? How often did
she lose her way or wander from the solace
of her companion's torch, as freezing shadows
muffled its flame? But now the ridge of Pentheus
arose before the weary travelers.
It sides stretched broadly when Menoetes, panting,
nearly exhausted, thus began to speak:

"If hope is not deceived by what we've done, 246
I think, Argia, we cannot be far
from the Ogygian dwellings and the bodies
that lie unburied, for the air is foul.

It moves in fetid waves from somewhere near,
and birds of prey are circling in the skies.
The soil is bloody, and the walls not distant.
See their long shadows stretch across the field,
the dying lights that flicker from the watchtowers?
The town is close." The night itself was silent.
The sole lights in the dark and gloom were stars.

Argia raised her hand toward town and shivered: 255
"O Thebes, which I once longed for, now so hostile—
and yet, if you return my husband's corpse
undamaged, you may also be my solace.
See how I am arrayed, how I am bruised
on my first visitation to your precincts—
wife of the son of mighty Oedipus.
My prayers are not impertinent: I want
only to mourn and burn my husband's body.
Give him to me, I beg you—he who was
an exile and defeated in this war,
whom you deny his own paternal soil.
O Polynices, come to me, I pray—
if ghosts may take on form and spirits
wander when they abandon carnal substance,
show me the way to reach you! Guide me to
yourself, if I am worthy!" So she spoke,
and, entering a nearby country cottage,
renewed the dying fires of her torch
and wildly ran again through grisly fields
like childless Ceres on the stones of Aetna,
who shone her brilliant torchlight on the slopes
of Sicily and through Ausonia
♦ and traced the furrows of that dark conveyor
whose carriage left wide wheel ruts in the dust:
♦ Enceladus himself reechoed her
mad lamentations; he emitted flames
to light her way; the rivers, forests, seas,
and clouds called out "Persephone"; only
her Stygian husband's hall maintained its silence.

Argia's faithful mentor must remind her, 278
in her excitement, to remember Creon,

to dip her torch, to move more furtively.
The queen—who even now through all the towns
of Argos was revered, the lofty goal
of suitors, and the great hope of her race—
moved through the deadly night, alone, unguided,
among her enemies. She made her way
through heaps of armor, over blood-slick grass,
and she was not afraid of flying groups
of ghosts or shades or spirits that bemoaned
their missing limbs. Her sightless steps ignored
weapons and swords she walked on. Her sole care
was not to tread dead bodies, any one
of which might be, she thought, her husband's corpse.
The faint stars gave her light enough to see
the faces of prone bodies she upturned.
She studied and she scrutinized the dead.

—♦—♦—♦—

Juno, by chance, had slipped from Jove's embrace 291
and traveled secretly through sleepy shades
to Theseus' walls in order to persuade
Pallas to listen to the supplicants
and give them easy entrance into Athens.
She grieved as she beheld from heaven's pole
guiltless Argia wandering through the fields,
laboring vainly. So she found the Moon,
driving her lunar horses, and approached.

Discoursing in a pleasant way, she said,
"Do me a little favor, Cynthia. 299
You know that you owe Juno some respect,
since you, maliciously, at Jove's request,
combined three nights for Hercules—but let
me set aside old quarrels. Here's the task:
Argia, my faithful priestess—daughter of
our Inachus—as you can see, is seeking
her husband through thick shadows, sick at heart.
Clouds dull your brightness. I would like
for you to show your horns and move your orbit
closer than usual to earth. Send Sleep

(he who controls your dripping reins and leans
before you) to the watchmen of Aonia."

These things were barely uttered, when the goddess 309
rent clouds, revealed her sphere in all its might,
frightened the shadows, stripped the stars of light.
Juno herself could hardly bear her sight.

As soon as brilliance bathed the fields, Argia 312
discerned her husband's cloak. She knew the pattern
that she herself had woven, miserable woman.
It had been hidden, since the purple cloth
was bloody, dark, and mournful. She was sure
that she had found her husband—she invoked
the gods—then saw him lying in the dust,
practically trampled. She felt faint; her sight
and hearing failed; great grief obstructed tears.
She lay across his face and searched for breath:
none issued from his mouth. The woman pressed
his hair and clothes for blood and gathered flecks.

As soon as she could speak, "My husband, is 321
this you I see, who marched to war to win
the country you were owed, the son-in-law
of King Adrastus? Is this how I greet
your triumph? I lift sightless eyes and cheeks!
I am Argia: I have come to Thebes!
Lead me inside your city: let me see
the dwelling of your father; offer me
what you were given—hospitality!
Alas, what am I saying? All the native
earth that you own, you lie on—outstretched, naked.
Why quarrel now? Your brother has no power.
Have you no other relatives who mourn?
Where is your mother and Antigone,
your famous sister? You were overthrown
for me; indeed you died for me alone!
I said, as I recall, 'Where are you going?
What scepter do you seek that is denied you?
Argos is yours, your wife's own father's court
is yours to rule—continuous succession

and unapportioned sway.' But why do I
complain? I pressured you to fight. I asked
my sorrowful father for what I now hold—
you in my arms. The gods have done me well,
and I thank Fortune that my hopes were met,
the purpose of my traveling fulfilled.
I find your body whole, but, ay me! how
deeply your wounds gape! Could a brother do this?
Tell me, where does that foul thief lie? I would—
could I approach—fend birds, drive back fierce beasts.
Has he been given flames? a funeral pyre?
May your land see you not deprived of fire!
You shall be burned, and tears—to kings denied—
shall drop for you. Our loyal love shall last
forever, and your tomb will be attended.
Our son will be our grief's memorial—
a little Polynices for my couch."

—♦—♦—♦—

Behold, another torch, and other moans.
Antigone approached in misery.
She sought her brother's body after she
had found a way to leave her walled-in city.
She had been tended closely all this while:
the king himself had ordered vigilance,
more watch fires, frequent changes of her guards.
The woman made excuses for delay
to both her brother and the gods when she
burst wildly through the walls as soon as sleep
had overcome the standing sentinels.
Her passion tore the countryside, as when
a little lion roars to find its mother.
She had not traveled long; she knew the field—
its dangers and just where her brother died.
Menoetes, who was idle, saw her coming,
and he restrained the groans of his dear charge.
But when her straining ears first heard those sounds
and by the light of stars she saw dark clothing,
caked hair, a face that blood had stained, she asked,

"Whom do you seek? And who are you, bold woman?
Do you not know this night belongs to me?"

Argia did not speak but threw her veil 367
over her own and Polynices' face,
and sudden fear made her forget her sorrow.
Her silence made Antigone suspicious;
she watched this woman and her guardian
but neither moved. They stared, and they said nothing
until at last Argia raised her veil
and spoke as she embraced her husband's body:

"I can reveal myself and join with you, 374
if Creon's harsh commands have caused you terror,
or you have come, like me, to search among
these old and bloody remnants of the war.
If you are wretched, as your sighs and tears
indicate, join me. Let us trust each other.
I am Adrastus's daughter. But who comes?
The laws forbid a pyre for Polynices . . ."

Her words dismayed the Cadmean. She trembled, 380
then interrupted her: "Unseeing Fortune!
Did you fear me, your partner in distress?
You hold my limbs, and you bewail my body.
I came here after you—I'm so ashamed.
A sister's cowardly impiety . . .
she first . . ." They fell together over him,
avid, in joined embrace, their hair and tears
mingling. They shared his limbs, alternately
leaning upon his face; each one in turn
solaced herself along his precious neck.

Then one recalled her brother, one her husband, 389
and one told tales of Thebes, and one of Argos.
Argia took more time to tell sad deeds:

"I swear by our communal rituals
of secret sorrow, by our common ghosts,
and by the conscious stars that Polynices—

even in wandering exile—never missed
his stolen honors, precious mother's love,
or native soil. He only cared for you,
and night and day would cry, 'Antigone!'
I was less loved, more easily abandoned.
Perhaps before this tragedy you watched
from some high tower as he issued banners
among Greek legions, and he looked at you
from his position and saluted you
with sword or by a nod of his tall crest
while we were far away. What god was it
that made his anger run to this extreme?
Why were your prayers no use? Did he deny
what you requested?"

Then Antigone
began to tell what happened, his sad fate,
until both women heard Menoetes' warning:
"Enough! Do what you started. Starlight wanes.
The day draws near, and you must end your task.
When you have lit the flames, then you may weep."

Not far away Ismenos roared in flood, 409
turbulent in its banks and stained with blood.
Here the frail women bore the battered body.
They formed a team; their friend lent equal effort.
So was the smoking corpse of Phaëthon
washed by his sisters, daughters of the sun,
when they bestowed his corpse beside the Po.
As soon as he was buried, weeping trees
stood by that stream: his sisters turned to poplars.

After they washed the body to restore 416
honor to those dead limbs, when they had given
their final kisses, those two wretched women
searched for some fire, but every spark was cold.
Pits held extinguished ashes. Piles were silent.

Whether by chance or godly intervention, 420
the fierce limbs of Eteocles were lying
upon a funeral pyre that smoked nearby,

just as if Fortune had prepared a spot
for wondrous scenes. Perhaps Eumenides—
the Furies—saved that place for flames to strive.
Both women made an effort to revive 424
a faint flame in the burned logs they had spied.
They wept for happiness and hoped whoever's
body they found was mild and would allow
himself a partner in the final rites
those last coals granted, where the shades united.

The brothers lay together. Then the pyre 429
shook as the first corpse fed the hungry fires
and drove the stranger back. A wave of flame
◆ split at its peak and gleamed, a double top
of cloven light, as if pale death combined
the torches of the Furies. Each round blaze
was menacing and strove to be the higher.
The very timbers settled, driven by
the weight of their commotion, and the virgin—
Antigone—was terrified. She cried:

"We have aroused old hatreds; we shall die! 437
That must have been his brother! Who would drive
a stranger's shade away? I recognize
a fragment of his shield, a half-burned belt.
Do you see flames recede then clash again?
The war changed nothing; their foul hate survives!
O bitter men, while you fight, Creon thrives!
Your realm is lost! What good is this mad passion?
Control your tempers! You, deprived of justice,
an exile everywhere, desist! Your wife
implores this, and your sister! Or shall we
enter the savage flames to intervene?"

These things were hardly said when suddenly 447
a tremor shook the field and towers of Thebes.
Now the discordant pyre had formed a chasm;
now watchmen, to whom sleep had given dreams
of evil doings, found their quiet shattered:
soldiers rushed out and scoured the countryside.
Only Menoetes feared them. Those two women

who stood before the pyre expressed their spite
for Creon's beastly law, and they confessed
their misdeeds openly, and they were fearless,
for they could see the corpses were consumed.
Now pain of death enticed them and they burned
with hope to perish boldly, each competing
to claim responsibility for stealing
the body of a husband and a brother.
One claimed she found the corpse, and one the flames.
One loved, and one was loyal. Each craved pain 459
and sought to slip her hands in cuffs and chains.
They showed no reverence. Their angry words
and hate replaced all awe, or so you'd think.
They raised discordant voices, clamoring
to make their captors take them to the king.

–♦–♦–♦–

Juno, meanwhile, had led the Argive women 464
to distant Athens where they were astonished—
herself no less—by Pallas and her kindness.
The people gave the mourning women welcome
and recognized their need for lamentation.
The goddess Juno offered olive branches
and garlands those petitioners adopted;
she taught the women how to veil their eyes
and move in muffled cloaks and carry urns,
now empty, for the ashes of their men.

People of every age poured from their homes 471
in Athens, and they lined the streets and rooftops.
Why such a multitude, such sympathy?
They moaned before they even knew the reason
or what was wrong, because the goddess merged
among both populations and explained
the mystery of who these women were,
the dead whom they are mourning, what they wished,
while they themselves, in random conversations,
complained about the cruelty of Creon
and the harsh laws of Thebes. The birds of Thrace,
whose words are mangled, do not chatter longer

♦ about the crimes and wickedness of Tereus,
his bridal couches, his duplicities.

An altar once stood in the city center 481
unoccupied by any god of power.
♦ There gentle Clemency had found her seat,
made sacred by the misery of men.
The goddess never lacked for supplicants;
no prayer was ever censured or denied.
Whoever asked was heard, and night and day
one might approach and, merely by lamenting,
enlist the goddess. Rituals were few:
no flames or bloody rites or frankincense.
Tears soaked the altar, and above it hung
sad offerings of women's severed hair
and clothing left behind when Fortune changed.
Within its sacred, reverential grove
were laurels twined with wool and humble olives,
but effigies were lacking—no medallions,
no image of the deity who dwells
in human minds and animates men's hearts.
She welcomes those in peril, and the poor
flock to a shrine the fortunate ignore.

♦ The story is that sons of Hercules 498
founded this altar when the deity
(their father) died and they were saved in battle.
But fame falls short of truth; the facts are these:
the gods themselves, to whom the land of Athens
had always given hospitality,
hallowed a common forum as a refuge
for needy souls—just as they once gave laws,
a new man, sacred rites, and seeds that fall
on empty fields—so that the wrath and threats
of tyrants be kept distant and the altars
of justice be uninfluenced by Fortune.

Now countless nations worshiped at this shrine: 506
those who lost wars, exiles from native lands,
those dispossessed of rule or charged with crimes
although they lacked intention. Such came there

to seek asylum, an abode of welcome.
◆ It sheltered Oedipus from Furies once,
◆ protected the besieged Olynthians,
◆ and hid distraught Orestes from his mother.

Directed by the commoners, the band 512
of Argive women anxiously approached,
and those unfortunates already there
yielded their places. Instantly their hearts
found rest and moderation for their cares,
just as the cranes that flee their native winds
◆ fill southern airs with joy when they see Pharos:
they love the gentle weather, taunt the snows,
and let the Nile assimilate their cold.

—◆—◆—◆—

◆ After his bitter wars in Scythia, 519
Theseus drove his laureled chariot
back to his native country. Joyful shouts
rang out; the peoples' voices reached the stars.
Before him came the spoils of war and cars—
the image of the cruelty of Mars—
that women drove, and there were wagons heaped
with crests drawn by sad steeds and broken axes
the Amazons employed to cut down forests
◆ and chop Maeotis' ice. They also bore
light quivers, fiery baldrics pocked with gems,
and blood-stained, half-moon shields the women used.
They did not tremble or admit their sex
or moan like rabble; they refused to beg
and only sought unspoused Minerva's altar.

The leading passion of the people was 532
to see the victor driving snow-white steeds:
nor did Hippolyta draw less attention,
as she, with kind regard, endured the bonds
of marriage. The Athenian women marveled—
they murmured and exchanged oblique regards—
to see her break her country's rigid custom
by covering her bosom with her cloak.

She hid her breasts, and she had trimmed her hair.
Although barbarian, she graced great Athens
and came to bear her warlike husband children.

The mournful Argives moved back from the shrine 540
on which they had been seated to admire
the long line of the triumph and its riches
while thoughts of fallen husbands filled their minds.

When Theseus slowed his chariot enough
to lend an ear and ask them to explain
◆ what caused their prayers, the wife of Capaneus
responded boldly to his invitation:

"O warlike son of Aegeus, Fortune gives 546
you unsought paths to glory through our fall.
We are no foreign race; no common guilt
infects us. Home is Argos, and our husbands
were princes—also fighters, to our sorrow.
What was the point of raising seven armies
to castigate the city of Agenor?
But deaths are not the cause of our complaint;
such things occur; it is the law of war,
yet those who fell in battle were not monsters
from caves in Sicily or biformed Centaurs
from Ossa. I will spare you family names,
but they were men, and born of men, great Theseus!
They took their being under these same stars,
suffered your common destiny, and ate
the food you eat. Now Creon outlaws flames
and bans their passage through the gates of Styx
as if he were the Lethean ferryman
or father of the Furies. He suspends
their ghosts between the poles of hell and heaven.

"O Nature, source and origin! Where is 561
the godhead, he who hurls judicial lightning?
And where are you, Athena? The seventh dawn
has risen, but your shy steeds shun the slain.
The brilliance of the bright celestial spheres
diminishes. Rays flicker. Savage beasts

and birds of prey avoid the noxious fare.
Fields waft fouled air that weighs the winds and skies.
Help us to gather bare bones, putrid flesh:
I do not think that very much survives.

"Athenians—good sons of Cecrops—hurry! 570
Lay down the law—your cause is just—before
Emathians and Thracians come to grief,
as well as any others who believe
in final rites and flames for those deceased.
We fought, but rage must end. Death blunts grim hatred.
We know your reputation for great deeds:
who else will limit Creon's savagery?
You do not leave your dead—foul Cercyon
and Sinis—to wild beasts, for you decreed
that even wicked Sciron be cremated.
Here you return with bands of Amazons
whose tombs, no doubt, still smoke along the Don—
so you enhance your triumph. Do this deed
for earth and hell and heaven. As you freed
from fear your homelands—Marathon and Crete—
do not distress old Hecale, who saved you.
So may Athena aid you in your wars
and sacred Hercules not envy your
actions, which equal his. And may your mother
see you triumphant in your chariot,
always and always, and may none of Athens
suffer defeat and beg, as I am doing."

She spoke, and all the women raised their hands 587
in supplication and began to clamor,
moving Neptunian Theseus to tears.
In righteous indignation he exclaimed:

"What Fury caused this custom in that kingdom?
No one was so inclined when I left Greece
to seek the Euxine snows and Scythia.
What moved such madness? Ill-abiding Creon,
did you think Theseus beaten? I am here,
and do not think that I am sick of killing!

My spear still thirsts for blood that should be spilled.
Let there be no delay! My faithful Phegeus,
turn your horn-footed steed and ride to Thebes.
Don't hesitate! Say they must give the Greeks
their funerals and pyres or hear from me."

He spoke these words, nor did he let the wars 599
or rigor of his travels interfere.
He spurred his men, and he renewed the weary,
just as a bull reclaims his fields and females
after a battle, but if forests echo
the chance arrival of some challenger,
he will prepare for battle, bellow, paw
the ground, and cover wounds with dust and dirt
because his head and neck drip from his hurts.

–◆–◆–◆–

Athena struck the image of Medusa, 606
the Libyan terror pictured on her shield—
she who protects her heart. Her serpents rose
at once and as a unit gazed at Thebes.
Even before the Attic army marched,
unhappy Dirce feared their trumpets' cries.
Fresh from the Caucasus, the troops rearmed, 611
and farming districts sent rude sons to war.
◆ They gathered—those who furrowed freezing Brauron,
◆ Monychia's fields, or Marathon (not yet
◆ famed for her Persian conquest), or Piraeus,
where swaying sailors stand on solid ground.
These ranked themselves behind their leaders' banners.

True to their native gods—hospitable— 618
◆ Icarius and Celeus armed their squadrons,
◆ as did the rich groves of Aegaleos;
◆ verdant Melaenae; Parnes, fit for vines;
◆ and Lycabessos, best for brimming olives.
Frightful Alaeus marched, and he who plowed
◆ fragrant Hymettus and, Acharnae, you
whose ivy twists around ill-figured thyrsi.

♦ Soldiers left Sounion, seen from far away 625
by eastern sailors, there where Aegeus fell
into the wandering sea that took his name
when he was, by his ship's false sails, deceived.

♦ Salamis sent her people, and Eleusis, 627
the town of Ceres. They hung up their plows
♦ and went to war. Callirhoë sent those
whom her nine winding rivers circumscribe,
so too Ilissos, who watched Boreas,
♦ the Thracian rapist, snatch Orithyia,
but nonetheless concealed him on her shores.
♦ That hillside sent its people to the wars
where once the gods contended, till a tree
grew from the cliffs and cast its long, new shadow
over the ebbing seas. Hippolyta
would have gone too and led her northern troops
but the sure hope of her expectant womb
restrained her, and her husband recommended
that she retire from war and sacrifice
her well-worn quiver for a bride's attire.

When Theseus saw his eager army shine 639
with pleasing weapons, snatching kisses from
children who love them, and their brief embraces,
he stood in his high chariot to say:

"You who defend the universal rights
and laws of men, prepare your worthy hearts
for this our enterprise, since it is clear
that Nature leads us, that we have the favor
of gods, men, and the silent ghosts of hell.
For their part, they enlist a band of Furies:
serpent-haired sisters lead the Theban banners.
March joyously, I pray, and trust our cause."

He spoke, then hurled his spear to start the march 649
like cloudy Jupiter when he draws nigh
the north pole and, at winter's first approach,
makes the stars tremble and sets Aeolus
at liberty. Then winter, whom long quiet

has left indignant, whistles Arctic winds.
Then waves and mountains welter. Darkling clouds
battle. Mad lightning celebrates with thunder.

Beaten, earth groaned. Strong hooves upturned green
meadows. 656
Trampled fields died beneath the countless waves
of men and horses, and their armor shone
through clinging clouds of dust, and from afar
it glistened and their lances gleamed through clouds.
Men added night's soft shadows to their labors 661
and vied to keep the army up to speed,
to see who, from some hill, would first spy Thebes,
whose lance would first attack Ogygian walls.
But far away Neptunian Theseus dwarfed
◆ his army with his great shield. It displayed 665
the hundred cities and the hundred walls
of Crete—the origins of his renown—
where in the windings of a monstrous cave,
he twists a bull's rough neck with both his hands.
His muscled arms constrain the animal;
he keeps his head withdrawn to dodge its horns.
Terror takes hold of men when Theseus,
armed with that fearsome image, goes to war,
for they see double hands, twice drenched in gore.
He broods upon his former deeds himself,
his band of comrades, the once fearful threshold,
◆ the clue he followed, Ariadne's pallor.

–◆–◆–◆–

Meanwhile that ruffian Creon had commanded 677
the widowed daughter of Adrastus and
Antigone to die. He chained their hands
behind their backs, but both of them rejoiced.
Proud, and in love with death, they stretched their necks
for execution, just as Phegeus brought
an embassy from Theseus. He extended
an olive branch in peace but his demand
was bellicose. He threatened and repeated
the words of his commander, making clear

that Theseus approached and that his cohorts
already covered intervening fields.

The Theban Creon wavered in some doubt; 688
his menaces diminished; anger cooled;
but then he steeled himself and grimly smiled,
pretending: "Was our warning insufficient
notice to beaten Argos? Once again
an enemy arrives to breach our walls.
Fine, let them come. But following the war,
let there be no complaints when those who fall
suffer our law." He spoke, but he could see
dust cloud the sky and hide the peaks of Tyre.
He grew pale, discomposed, yet ordered men
to arm and he himself demanded weapons.
Nevertheless, he saw Menoeceus weeping
and Furies crowd his courtyard and the Greeks
rejoicing to ascend their funeral pyres.
Why should he go on living? Why should Thebes
now lose the peace that cost her so much blood?

Infantry seized the weapons they had hung
as trophies for their household gods; their breasts
were covered by cracked shields; their casques lacked crests;
their spears were still not clean of human gore;
steeds were disheveled; ramparts insecure.
The walls had fallen on each side of town;
the Thebans had exhausted their defenses.
Not much remained where Capaneus fought.
The soldiers were too pale and sick to kiss
their wives or children one last time, nor did
their shattered parents offer any prayers.

But Theseus, the leader of the Greeks, 709
saw brilliant sunlight shine through broken clouds
and armor glinting in the dawn's first rays.
He swooped along the field and raced beneath
the walls where bodies lay, while deep inside
his helmet he breathed dust and pestilence,
foul vapors from the corpses he deplored,
yet felt the flames of righteous wrath for war.

Creon refused to let his army wage
war on the fallen bodies of Danaans
a second time. Was his choice virtuous
or did he so desire to drink fresh blood
that he preferred new fields for mangled slaughter?

Bellona led each army differently.
The Theban side was soundless; trumpets silent;
their swords hung low; the army seemed fatigued;
their right hands loosed the looped ends of their slings,
and men whose gashes still poured blood gave ground.
Then the Cecropian princes lost their ardor:
their threats grew timid; their just rage declined,
just as winds weaken if their fury finds
no hindering trees. Waves die without a shore.

Theseus, the sea-born hero, raised his spear
of Marathonian oak; its gruesome shadow
fell on the enemy; its bright tip flashed
and filled the field, as when the god of war
◆ drives his Edonian chariot along
the slopes of Haemus, bearing Death and Rout
on his swift axle. Just so, pallid Terror
harried Agenor's sons; they fled in panic,
but Theseus scorned to follow fugitives;
his sword did not find dignity in slaughter,
though other great men gorge themselves
by killing common soldiers, just as dogs
and wolves who have no honor take delight
in fearful, prostrate prey. Yet, anger stokes
great lions: Theseus killed Olenius
and Lamyrus—the first as he plucked arrows
up from his quiver and the second as
he raised the vicious burden of a boulder.
Three spears destroyed the three sons of Alcetus
from far off. They had trusted in their prowess,
but Phyleus took a spear point through the chest,
then Helops's teeth bit iron, then the shoulder
of Iapyx felt the third. Next Theseus sought
Haemon, who towered above his chariot,
drawn by four horses. He released his fierce

weapon of war, and it made Haemon swerve.
It struck two steeds from far and would have pierced
another but the cart's pole interfered.

Thereafter Creon was the only one 752
Theseus pursued. He shouted out a vow
and saw him in the frontlines of the battle
urging his soldiers, prodding them in vain.
All of his comrades fled as Creon sought
to turn them back; by contrast Theseus
ordered his men to halt, to trust the gods
and his right hand. Finally Creon realized
everyone hated him. He paused, prepared
for one last fit of rage and lethal fury:
he took heart from the thought that he would die.

"You do not fight the half-moon shields of women," 761
he cried, "nor face a band of virgins. Men
battle in blood here. We slew mighty Tydeus,
furious Hippomedon, and sent the soul
of Capaneus hellward. What rash fury
makes you do battle here and intervene?
Those you avenge are dead. Have you not seen?"

He spoke and hurled a deadly spear that fixed,
harmless, in Theseus's shield rim. Aegeus's son
laughed at his words and effort; like a nightmare,
he then prepared his great shaft, bound with iron,
for one huge thrust, but not before he cried
these proud words: "Argive ghosts, to whom I give
this victim, open Tartarus and Chaos.
Warn the Eumenides. I send you Creon!"

He spoke. His trembling weapon cleaved the wind 773
and entered where the myriad links of mail
formed Creon's hauberk. His unholy blood
poured through a thousand crevices. He died,
and when he fell, his eyes were open wide.

Theseus stood over him and solemnly 778
removed his armor, saying, "Should not corpses

receive the flames that righteousness requires?
Should not the vanquished have their burial?
Enter the place of gruesome punishments:
I swear we will perform your final rites!"

–◆–◆–◆–

The banners of the loyal armies met; 782
the soldiers intermingled; they agreed
to peace, now, on that battlefield, and Theseus
became the city's guest; men prayed that he
would dignify their homes and enter Thebes.
The victor did not scorn his enemies
but glorified their households with his presence.
Ogygian maids and matrons celebrated,
◆ as when the Ganges, worn by wars and Bacchus,
praises the orgies that have made her drunk.

The clamoring of women reached the stars
on Dirce's shadowy, opposing heights,
and the Pelasgian matrons hurried down
◆ like raving Thyiades who gather for
a drunken orgy. You would think they sought,
or had committed, some impiety.
They wept from happiness, shed tears of joy.
As sounds of mourning guided them along,
crowds drew them here and there, first to great Theseus,
then toward Creon, then to their deceased.

–◆–◆–◆–

So many corpses, commoners and princes;
so many moans; so many mighty deeds.
I could not count them, even should some god
open my spirit to a hundred tales:
how bold Evadne looked for signs of lightning
on mighty Capaneus and lay down,
undone, beside the fires that she loved;
how the grim spouse of Tydeus made excuses,
lying beside him, kissing his rough corpse;
how Argia tells her sister her sad vigils,

♦ and how the Erymanthian mother moaned
for Parthenopaeus, the Arcadian,
who, drained of blood, still never lost his looks:
Parthenopaeus, the Arcadian,
whom either army mourned with equal force.

Not if Apollo filled me with new furor
could I recount these things. After so long
at sea, my little vessel reaches port.

Will you, my Thebaid, *endure for ages,*
survive your author, and be read? Twelve years
I spent, preoccupied, but surely Fame
already comes to you, though young, and carves
a friendly path to guide you to the future.
Caesar, magnanimous, has deigned to know you.
Italy's schoolrooms teach you, and the young
memorize passages. So thrive, I pray,
but do not envy the divine Aeneid.
Follow well back. Always adore her traces.
If any envy clouds you, it will fade;
when I am gone due honor will be paid.

–♦–♦–♦–

Notes

Line numbers refer to the Latin text. *Met.* = Ovid, *Metamorphoses*

Book 1. Exile

1.20: *Dacians* Conquered by Domitian ("Jove" at 1.22), the emperor under whom Statius wrote, they inhabited an area roughly that of modern Romania.

1.63: *and his untruth* The untruth of Polybus was his misrepresentation of himself as Oedipus's natural father.

1.66: *the wicked Sphinx* A beast with the head of a woman and the body of a winged lion, the Sphinx terrorized Thebes at the behest of Juno by asking all travelers who approached the city the following question: what walks on four legs in the morning, two at midday, and three in the evening? All who could not correctly respond to the question were killed on the spot. Oedipus finally provided the answer to the riddle ("Man," represented in childhood, adulthood, and old age), prompting the Sphinx to throw herself from a cliff in despair. The people of Thebes made him king out of gratitude.

1.130: *companions disagree* Boccaccio adapts Statius's sentiment in describing the conflict between Palaemon and Arcite (see *Teseida* 5.13).

1.165: *savage one* Eteocles

1.184: *battle lines of brothers* The Spartoi, or sown men, who grew out of the earth when Cadmus sowed the dragon's teeth

1.221: *Phaëthon* Apollo, the god of the sun, permitted his son to drive the chariot of the sun across the sky, but the youth lost control of the horses and plummeted out of control toward the earth. Jupiter killed Phaëthon with a flash of lightning to prevent catastrophe. See *Met.* 1 and 2.

1.230: *women* A reference to the mountain revels of Theban women devoted to Bacchus (see the story of Pentheus in *Met.* 3.700–733)

1.262: *Or level Sparta?* Mycenae and Sparta, along with Argos, were cities on the Peloponnesian peninsula that Juno identifies as her favorites (see *Iliad* 4.50). Samos was an island in the Aegean Sea that housed a large temple to the goddess.

1.264: *Mareotic Copts* The Copts were devotees of the goddess Isis. Mareotis was a district in northern Egypt.

1.272: *Alpheus seeks Arethusa* Arethusa tells how she escaped underground to Sicily to avoid the attentions of Alpheus, a hunter and Peloponnesian river, who pursued her across the sea to the island of Ortygia (*Met.* 5.577ff.).

1.278: *Mount Ida, Crete* Where the nymphs raised Jupiter (cf. *Met.* 4.293; *Aeneid* 12.412)

1.297: *Lethe* The river of forgetfulness in Hades. All souls who drank from it would forget their former lives (cf. *Aeneid* 6.705).

1.303: *Atlas's grandson* Mercury

1.333: *Scironic cliffs* In Megaris, on the Isthmus of Corinth. *Scylla* was the daughter of Nisus, king of Megara. She betrayed her father by cutting off his precious lock of purple hair, the absence of which assured his death (*Met.* 8.8ff.).

1.347: *Aeolus* King of the winds, who held dominion over the lesser winds: Zephyrus, Auster, Boreas, and Eurus (cf. *Met.* 1.64ff.)

1.382: *Larissa* Fortress that dominated the skyline of Argos, whose ruins are still visible

1.402: *brother's death* Tydeus was banished from Calydon for the murder of his brother Olenias (some say his uncle); see Pausanias 1.8.5.

1.420: *Rhipaean* Mountains in northern Scythia, source of the Don

1.453: *I left the Acheloian fields* Tydeus alludes to the great hunt for the Calydonian boar. The Achelous is the largest river in Greece, bordering Acarnania and Aetolia.

1.475–77: *loyalty* The pairs mentioned are models of friendship in Roman poetry. Pylades was Orestes' cousin and companion; each young man was willing to sacrifice his life for the other (see Euripides' *Iphigenia in Tauris*). Pirithoüs was the son of Ixion and king of the Lapithae, mythical inhabitants of the mountains in Thessaly. Pirithoüs raided Attica, but King Theseus held off his attack. The two became friends and together took part in many adventures (cf. *Met.* 8.302).

1.487: *Cleonae* Another reference to Hercules' first labor. Cleonae was a town in Argolis near Nemea; Teumessus was a mountain outside of Thebes, where the young Hercules killed the lion of Cithaeron (see *Met.* 6.417).

1.490: *Calydonian boar* Tydeus's older half brother Meleager organized the hunt for the Calydonian boar. The skin of the boar was originally awarded to Atalanta (mother of Parthenopaeus), who was the first hunter to strike the boar (see *Met.* 8.426).

1.543–51: *Cast images* Medusa, the Gorgon whose looks turned all who gazed on her to stone, beheaded by Perseus. Ganymede, another misfit and victim, was a beautiful young man whom Zeus, in the form of an eagle, carried away up to Mount Olympus to serve as cupbearer to the gods.

1.561: *I'll explain* Adrastus's narrative—an explanation for the Apollonian holiday in progress—centers on the actions that the Argive hero Coroebus took in rescuing his people from a plague inflicted on them by Apollo. A delaying tactic typical of Adrastus, the story serves as a parable by which Polynices and Tydeus may learn the dangers of rushing into conflict. Statius's dramatic irony recalls Homer's, when the brilliant orator Nestor fails to persuade Agamemnon not to offend Achilles in book 1 of the *Iliad*. Here another elder statesmen fails to persuade young men to restrain themselves. In its length and complexity, Adrastus's apologue also recalls the speech of Phoenix to Achilles in the ninth book of the *Iliad*.

1.562: *The Python* The holy beast of Delphi, formerly called Pytho. Phoebus killed it on the Bay of Cirrha, on the Corinthian Gulf, south of Delphi (see *Met.* 1.438).

1.597: *Acheron* A river of the underworld whose name is used as a metonymy (the part for the whole) for the entire underworld

1.635: *dog star* The presence of the star Sirius, prominent in late summer, implies that the plague brings great heat and drought.

1.636: *Paean* An epithet meaning "healer" or "helper" (*Met.* 14.720); used ironically by Statius, if not by Adrastus. Apollo is often a troubled figure in myths, less successful than one imagines him, less morally grounded, as when he fails to score with Daphne, or loses his son Phaëthon (*Met.* 1–2), or, here, punishes innocent people. He has some of the ruthlessness of a king's son as early as the first book of the *Iliad.*

1.643: *Thymbra* City in the region of Troas famous for its temple to Apollo (cf. *Aeneid* 3.85)

1.687: *Syrtes'* Two dangerous sandbanks on the northern shores of Africa (the Greater and Lesser Syrtes of modern Libya)

1.696: *Patara's* Site, in Lycia, of an oracle of Apollo that only spoke in the winter

1.709: *Marsyas* A satyr who was skilled at playing the flute. He challenged Apollo to a musical contest and lost; he was flayed alive and transformed into a river. The examples of Apollo's victories (1.709–15) are ironic, since the objects of the god's wrath were helpless to defend themselves. See *Met.* 6, where other subaltern figures suffer at the hands of the gods.

1.720: *Mithras* The sun god of the Persians. Roman Mithraism was one of the mystery cults, confined to men, with secret rites and stages for devotees to pass. Statius alludes to the tauroctony: represented in art, Mithras kneels on the back of a bull and looks away as he kills it. The cult spread through the Roman Empire, starting in the second half of the first century. It included a form of baptism, a ceremonial meal, and ordeals.

Book 2. Ambush

2.71: *That day* The Bacchanalia, or Dionysia, were festivals held in honor of Bacchus at various times of the year. They provided an opportunity for drunkenness and frivolity in the form of dances and plays; but by Statius's day, they had a reputation of promoting criminal behavior and sexual deviance. This celebration contrasts with the Argive festival in honor of Apollo in book 1.

2.82: *Bistonians* A Thracian tribe

2.85: *Iacchus* One of the mystical names for Bacchus (cf. *Met.* 4.15); poetic for wine

2.163: *Pharaeans* Pharae was a town in Thessaly.

2.166: *the Pisan father's chariot* An allusion to the chariot race between Pelops and Oenomaus, king of Pisa and father of Hippodamia. After Oenomaus heard a prophecy that he would be killed by his son-in-law, he tried to prevent his daughter's marriage. When many suitors approached him, he declared that he would hold a contest whereby any man who could defeat him in a race would win Hippodamia (the losers would be beheaded). Pelops bribed Oenomaus's charioteer, who removed a pin from the chariot so it would break down in the midst of the race. Oenomaus was thrown from the chariot and died. Adrastus seems oblivious to the baleful significance of his allusion.

2.179: *in Sicyon* Adrastus himself had been an exile in Sicyon, where he became king before being readmitted to Argos; according to Lactantius, the Argives asked him to rule because his lenient nature would tame their barbaric customs.

2.184: *Mycenae's crimes* That is, misbehavior that occurred in Mycenae, one of the oldest Greek cities. According to Greek myths, Thyestes slept with Atreus's wife and deceived his brother into killing his own son; Atreus (the father of Agamemnon and Menelaus) murdered Thyestes' sons and served their flesh to him in a banquet. Atreus then forced Thyestes into exile. Seneca's *Thyestes,* a Roman play, was a favorite source of revenge plays like *Hamlet.*

2.185: *Elis* The western portion of the Peloponnesus (cf. *Met.* 2.679)

2.217–22: *so skillfully was it conceived* The following ecphrasis (the literary convention of describing a painting or sculpture) consists of a sketchy genealogy of the kings of Argos. Inachus is depicted with his son Phoroneus and grandson Iasius. Danaus was made king after taking refuge in Argos with his fifty daughters; he ordered the women to kill their husbands, his nephews, who had ousted him from his kingdom in Libya. Abas, Danaus's grandson, was the twelfth king of Argos. His son Acrisius was the father of Danaë, whom Jupiter raped when he appeared to her as a shower of gold. See *Met.* 4.604. Coroebus may refer to the hero whose story is told in book 1.

2.237: *fierce sister* Diana, goddess of the moon and the hunt, patroness of virginity, who is identified with the Greek Artemis

2.239: from *Cynthus and from Aracynthus* Cynthus is a mountain of Delos, birthplace of Apollo and Diana (see *Met.* 2.221); Aracynthus is a mountain in Aetolia, south of Thessaly, between Boeotia and Attica.

2.268–96: *this gift* The necklace of Harmonia, a symbol of treachery, brought misfortune to all who owned it. The striking description of this piece of jewelry includes various references to harbingers of doom (such as Medusa and the Golden Fleece). Statius's digression gives him the opportunity to allude to the miseries of the Theban women who were cursed by the ornament. *Lemnos* is the island where Vulcan kept his forge. The *Telchines* were members of a race descended from Neptune; they excelled in brass work; see *Met.* 7.365. The *mournful fruit* refers to the golden apples of the Hesperides, which were guarded for Juno by a hundred-headed serpent. The *cestus* was the girdle of Venus, imbued with her powers of seduction. The passage describes the effects of the necklace on several of its owners. Harmonia and Cadmus were turned into snakes, though not apparently as a direct result of the necklace (see *Met.* 4.582). Their daughter Semele (mother of Bacchus) died when, at Juno's urging, she asked to see Jupiter in his full glory (see *Met.* 3.259–315). Jocasta's misfortunes continue through the epic.

2.299: *The wife* Eriphyle, Amphiaraus's wife, coveted Argia's necklace and devised a plot to obtain it (see 4.190–212). Amphiaraus reluctantly participated in the war on Thebes, losing his life in the bargain; Alcmaeon, his son, eventually avenged his death by killing Eriphyle. Like Orestes, Alcmaeon was driven mad by the Furies because of his impiety. See *Met.* 9.403–17, where Themis mentions the war against Thebes.

2.421: *Geloni* A northern Scythian tribe, from modern Ukraine

2.563–64: *Pholus . . . Lapiths* The Centaurs and Lapithae, both races descended from Ixion, were mortal enemies due to a dispute over rights to their progenitor's kingdom. The simile seems to refer to the drunken brawl that started up at the wedding of Pirithoüs (Ixion's son and leader of the Lapithae) and Hippodamia (see *Met.* 12.210ff.). The centaur Pholus derives from a story tangential to the fourth labor of Hercules (see Apollodorus, *Library* 2.5.4).

2.574–75: *Halys/and Phaedimus* These characters appear to be Statius's creation.

2.596: *Briareus* Briareus, also called Aegaeon, was one of the three Uranidae, sons of Uranus (Heaven) and Gaea (Earth). They were hundred-armed giants who tried to overthrow the Olympian gods in a war waged in Thrace (Phlegra). Homer mentions the battle in the first book of the *Iliad* (see also *Aeneid* 6.287 and *Met.* 2.10).

2:598: *Pelethronium* A district in Thessaly inhabited by the Lapiths and Centaurs

2:599: *Pyracmon* One of the Cyclopes (see *Aeneid* 8.425)

2.629–43: *Thespiadae* The brothers, from the town of Thespiae in Boeotia, at the southeastern foot of Helicon, die in each other's arms, an emblem of fraternal piety; the scene ironically foreshadows and contrasts the deaths of Polynices and Eteocles at each other's hands.

2.666: *Celenaean* Celaenae was a town in Phrygia where Marsyas competed with Apollo on the flute.

2.684: *Tritonian maiden* Triton was a river and lake in African near the Lesser Syrtes where, according to some myths, Minerva was born. The goddess of handiwork, Minerva was identified with the Greek goddess of wisdom, Pallas Athena. The places Tydeus mentions when he prays to her after the battle were sacred to Minerva. Itone, a town in Boeotia, had a sanctuary to her.

2.693: *Maeon* Homer depicts Maeon as grateful for having been spared by Tydeus (*Iliad* 4); that tradition indicates that Maeon later buried Tydeus out of respect (Pausanias, *Description of Greece* 9.18).

Book 3. Omens

3.34–35: *Tethys drove Hyperion* Tethys was goddess of the sea and mother of the sea nymphs and river gods (see *Met.* 2.509). She and Hyperion, father of the Sun (*Met.* 4.192), but here identified with the sun, were children of Gaea (Earth), according to an early tradition recorded by Hesiod, *Theogony.*

3.88: *he thrust* Statius invented Maeon's suicide; the eulogy that follows has no source.

3.106: *Dodona's sacred grove/and Cirrha's prophetess* Dodona, a city of Epirus, where the oracle delivered prophecies interpreted from the rustling of leaves (see *Met.* 13.716). Cirrha is a town in Phocis devoted to Apollo; Cirrha's prophetess is probably a figure of speech for the Delphic oracle.

3.134: *twins* The Thespians whom Tydeus killed (2.629)

3.168: *mingle your precious ashes in one urn* Ide's prayer anticipates the mutual funeral pyre of Polynices and Eteocles in book 12. The translation reflects a possible pun on *urna* and *una* (one).

3.178–213: *Aletes* recounts the misfortunes of the house of Cadmus; Ovid relates the stories of Cadmus, Semele, Athamas, Pentheus, Niobe, and Actaeon in the *Met.* 3, 4, and 6. Statius has alluded to all these myths at least once prior to Aletes' narrative.

3.205: *queen* According to later commentators (cf. Apollodorus, *Library* 3.5.5), Dirce, the wife of the Theban prince Lycus, was either thrown into a fountain or metamorphosed into it on account of her cruelty to Antiopa, her husband's former wife, whom she tied to the neck of a bull.

3.227: *Sarmatia* Area controlled by a Slavic people; modern Poland and Russia. This passage may allude to Domitian's recent campaign against the Dacians.

3.274–75: *Lemnos . . . Vulcan* Deceived by his wife Venus and Mars, Vulcan devised a net to catch the lovers in the act (see *Met.* 4.167–89). Vulcan was born on the island of Lemnos (cf. *Met.* 13.313).

3.319: *Othrys . . . Ossa* Mountains in Thessaly, according to Virgil (*Aeneid* 7.675), but Statius locates Othrys in Thrace (4.655).

3.353: *Bebrycian woods* In Bithynia, a district in Asia Minor

3.381: *by which he tried their hearts* Polynices' manipulative behavior puts him on a par with the rabble-rousers in Thebes and implies that, despite the wrong he has suffered, he is not morally superior to Eteocles.

3.410: *Nereus . . . Hours* Nereus was an ancient sea god, one of the Titans. The Hours were three daughters of Zeus and Thetis; they were associated with the passing of the seasons and other divisions of time.

3.422: *Therapnae* Taenarus, Nemea, and Therapnae (the birthplace of Helen and her brothers Castor and Pollux, in Laconia; cf. 7.793) were towns and regions surrounding Argos.

3.438: *Cyclades* Islands including Myconos and Gyaros near Delos in the Aegean Sea. Delos had been a floating island until Neptune fixed it to the neighboring islands so that Leto could safely give birth to her twins Apollo and Diana.

3.462: *Aphesas* A mountain near Nemea. After his successes in northern Africa, Perseus returns to Argos and uses the Gorgon to defeat Proetus (see *Met.* 5.236ff.). Perseus's mother was Danaë.

3.474–76: *Cirrha . . . Chaonian* See note to 3.106. Chaonia is another name for Epirus and the Molossi were people who lived in the eastern part of Epirus. Amphiaraus refers to various means of prophecy; he prefers augury, the study of the flights of birds.

3.481: *Dictaean* Poetic for Cretan, from a mountain named Dicte, where Jupiter was concealed in a cave to save him from his father Saturn

3.476–80: Amphiaraus lists a number of famous oracles of various gods. *Ammon,* in Africa, held an oracle near a temple where Jupiter was worshiped. *Lycia,* a region of Asia Minor, housed an oracle of Apollo at Patara. The *sacred ox* refers to the Egyptian Apis, represented as a bull, who had a shrine at Memphis, in Egypt. Branchidae, on the coast of Ionia, housed the oracle of Apollo Didymeus, established by Apollo's son *Branchus,* according to Lactantius (gloss to *Thebaid* 8.199–200). Mount *Lycaon,* in Arcadia, was sacred to Pan (cf. *Met.* 1.217; *Aeneid* 8.344). This list acts as an invocation of sorts.

3.513: *god of Thymbra* Apollo, who had a temple in Troas at Thymbra (cf. *Aeneid* 3.85)

3.547: *know all too well* Amphiaraus sees an omen of his own death.

3.557–59: *entrails . . . horrors in Thessaly* Statius refers to various means of prophecy: haruspices (the reading of entrails of sacrificial animals), augury, astrology, and witchcraft.

3.595–96: *Enceladus . . . Pelorus* Enceladus was a giant who attempted to overthrow the gods; Jupiter killed him and buried him under Mount Aetna (cf. *Aeneid* 3.578). Pelorus is the northeast corner of Sicily.

3.598: *Excited Capaneus moved* Capaneus takes on the role of rabble-rouser in this passage, as the crowd's response to his speeches implies. His disdain for the gods assures his death.

3.683: *Thessander* The son of Polynices went on to lead the sons (the Epigoni) of the seven leaders of the Argive army on a second siege of Thebes. Their venture was successful; the citizens of Thebes fled, and Thessander gained the throne. He later died en route to Troy with Agamemnon, according to Pausanias (*Description of Greece* 9.5.14). Virgil includes a Thessander among the Greeks hiding in the Trojan horse (*Aeneid* 2.261).

Book 4. Thirst

4.6: *Bellona* Goddess of war and sister of Mars, who is more personification than deity at this point in the narrative. She represents the spirit of warfare that grips the city of Argos in the wake of Capaneus's call to arms.

4.32–186: What follows is a catalog of arms, a standard epic device. Statius describes the troops of the seven heroes. Each leader of the Argive army is singled out for recognition; each has some distinctive (and often symbolic) insignia or armor. Ovid gives a somewhat similar catalog of Theban allies (*Met.* 6.412–20).

4.43: *Arion* Fabled offspring of Neptune and Ceres, a war horse known for his swiftness. He leads Polynices' chariot in the funeral games in book 6 and helps Adrastus escape Thebes at the end of the war; he also talks, like the steed of Achilles at the end of *Iliad* 19, an example of what Aristotle in the *Poetics* called an acceptable marvel, a probable impossibility.

4.44–48: *Prosymna . . . Thyrea* Statius identifies neighboring towns in Argolis that enlist to fight the war. The Spartans had captured Thyrea (a town on the border between Argolis and Laconia) from Argos in the seventh century b.c., but they were eventually overthrown by the Thebans (who were supported by the Argives and Arcadians) in a siege led by Epaminondas in the fourth century. As a result of this conflict, the Spartans lost supremacy over Greece, and Thebes became the dominant force of Greece for a brief time.

4.50: *Sicyon* Town in northern Argolis where Adrastus was king, known for its olive oil. See note to 2.179.

4.53–58: *they say* The story appears to be Statius's invention. He once again alludes to the crimes of various families: the houses of Atreus (Mycenae) and Cadmus (Thebes), and the Thracian people under King Lycurgus, who was cursed by Bacchus for his insolence; the god put him into a Bacchic frenzy during which he inadvertently killed his own son (Apollodorus, *Library* 3.5.1).

4.60: *the river that inspires poets* A reference to the Pirene, a spring in the citadel of Corinth that bubbled up when Pegasus struck his foot on a rock. Corinth's Mount Helicon, near the harbor, was sacred to the gods, particularly the muses, who were responsible for poetic inspiration.

4.69: *some great bull* Statius uses an apt simile to describe the old warlord.

4.80: *Adrastus gave/his son-in-law* Because Polynices wages war against his own homeland, he has no cities from which he can tap soldiers. Adrastus gives him command of troops from these cities. Troezen, in southeast Argolis, was the birthplace of Theseus; it was named after one of the sons of Pelops.

4.87: *a sphinx* The figure on the handle of Polynices' sword calls to mind the plague on Thebes before Oedipus's arrival; the image does not appear to portend victory.

4.101ff.: *Aetolia* Tydeus's home province, north of the Gulf of Corinth. *Pleuron* has special significance as the place where Meleager's sisters were turned into guinea hens as they grieved their brother's death (*Met.* 8.526ff.). The *grim-visaged river* is the Achelous, where Hercules wrestled the river god in its manifestation as a bull. The hero removed one of Achelous's horns, which the Naiads turned into the Cornucopia. Statius imitates Ovid's description of Achelous's dejection (*Met.* 9.81–88).

4.118: *Achaean rivers* The numerous references to rivers in the catalog of Hippomedon's troops foreshadow the means of his death. The rivers Lyrcius, Inachus, Asterion, and Erasinos are all in Argolis.

4.124: *Enna* Town in central Sicily where Proserpina was picking flowers when Pluto carried her off: "that fair field / of *Enna*, where *Proserpin* gath'ring flow'rs / Herself a fairer Flow'r by gloomy *Dis* / Was gather'd" (Milton, *Paradise Lost* 4.268–270; cf. *Met.* 5.385).

4.127: *Nestor* The old warrior who counseled the Greeks in the *Iliad.* Neleus refused to purify Hercules for a murder the hero had committed, and Hercules took vengeance by killing all his sons but Nestor.

4.133: *the night of Danaus* Hippomedon's shield depicts the story of the Danaïds (see note to 2.217); the image suggests the guilt that still hangs over Argos due to the massacre.

4.137: *War terrified his steed* According to the ancient glossator Lactantius, the steed is terrified because it is new to war.

4.140: *Hylaeus* A centaur who tried to rape Atalanta (cf. *Aeneid* 8.294). According to Lactantius, the phrase "both his chests" refers to his human and his equine chests.

4.158: *Oete* Mount Oete, the site of Hercules' death and apotheosis (see *Met.* 9.159–272)

4.160: *Molorchus* A poor tender of vines, at whose home outside of Nemea (in Cleonae) Hercules stayed prior to completing his first labor (cf. Statius's *Silvae* 3.1.29)

4.169: *Hydra* The ecphrastic representation of the Lernaean Hydra, one of Hercules's labors, makes for a daunting introduction of the fierce Capaneus.

4.178–82: *the troops assigned* Messenia was the southwest province of the Peloponnesian peninsula; Messene, at the foot of Mount Ithome, was its capital. Amphigenia, Helos, Pteleon, Dorion, Thyron, and Aepy are all towns mentioned in Homer's catalog of Nestor's troops in the second book of the *Iliad.*

4.183–86: *Thamyris . . . Marsyas* Statius provides two examples of impiety toward the gods. Thamyris, a Thracian singer, challenged the Muses to a contest. He lost, and for his impertinence, the Muses blinded him and deprived him of his musical skills; see Ovid's *Ars Amatoria* 3.399. Marsyas, a skilled flute player, challenged Apollo to a contest between his flute and the god's lyre. The Muses judged in favor of Apollo, who flayed Marsyas alive; the tears shed for him by the satyrs and nymphs collected into a river which took his name (*Met.* 6.382–400). See also the note to 1.709.

4.190: *The ruses of his wife* Eriphyle. See 2.268 for references to those cursed by the necklace.

4.223: *Amyclae* The Laconian town where the beautiful Hyacinthus, loved by Apollo, was accidentally killed by a discus thrown by the god. The remorseful Apollo turned the young man into a flower (*Met.* 10.162–66) The myth foreshadows the honor that Apollo will bestow on Amphiaraus.

4.236: *swan feathers* The Latin *Ledaeus apex* (swan crest) alludes to Leda, mother of Castor and Pollux, who were buried in Lacedaemon, the capital of Laconia. The flourish on the armor pays tribute to the twins.

4.249: *His mother* Statius follows the Arcadian version of the myth of Atalanta. As an infant, she had been left to die in an Arcadian forest, where she was nursed by a bear, raised by hunters, and herself became a great huntress, devoted to her virginity. Milanion eventually wooed her, and by him she gave birth to Parthenopaeus. Because the boy was so beautiful, Diana (virgin goddess and patron of the hunt to whom Atalanta had dedicated herself before marriage) forgave Atalanta for giving up her virginity (see Apollodorus, *Library* 3.9.2ff.)

4.267: *Calydonia* Atalanta was the first to hit the Calydonian boar in Meleager's great hunt in Ovid's version of her story (*Met.* 10.560ff.).

4.269: *Cydonean* Cydon was a town on the north coast of Crete (cf. Virgil's *Eclogues* 10.59).

4.286–91: *Rhipe . . . Pheneos* The catalog of Agapenor's troops in the second book of the *Iliad* names the first five of Statius's Arcadian towns. *Cyllene* was the fabled birthplace of Mercury and home of his temple. *Pheneos* was a town at the foot of Mount Cyllene; its lake fed the waters of the infernal rivers.

4.292: *Azan* A district of Arcadia named after Azan, one of the sons of King Arcas and the nymph Erato (see Pausanias, *Description of Greece* 8.4.2–3). Further names of Arcadian towns follow in this passage.

4.297: *Hercules* The hero defeated the Erymanthean boar, his third labor, and used bronze rattles to disperse the ill-omened birds of Stymphalos.

4.308: *two other brothers* Underscoring the betrayal theme, Statius makes another disparaging reference to Mycenae, referring to the strife of Atreus (father of Agamemnon and Menelaus) and Thyestes; see note to 2.184.

4.373: *Plataea* A city on Mount Cithaeron

4.383: *Nysaean father* Bacchus, after Nysa, the village on Mount Helicon that was home to the god. His cult had spread far from Boeotia by Statius's time— hence the references to Thrace, India (Ganges), and Ethiopia (Red Sea), all of which had towns called Nysus.

4.389: *Hermus* A river in Asia Minor

4.393: *Caucasus* Mountain range between the Black Sea and the Caspian Sea; home of the mythical Amazons

4.414: *grim Death* Tiresias prefers oracles of the dead as a method of prophecy over augury (used by Amphiaraus in book 3) and haruspicy. Therefore, the ghost of Laius once again plays an important role in the epic; ironically, he is now doling out the kind of obscure prophecies that he could not comprehend when he was alive.

4.494: *Gaetulia* A province in northwestern Africa

4.514: *afraid/to say* According to Lactantius, this god, whose name cannot be pronounced, was the demiurge, which became, by a scribal errors, the Demogorgone of Renaissance poets like Boiardo and Spenser. See C. S. Lewis, *The Discarded Image* (Cambridge: Cambridge University Press, 1964), pp. 39–40.

4.530: *Minos* King of Crete, known for his wisdom and justice—hence, he was appointed judge of the dead in the underworld (cf. *Aeneid* 6.432 and *Met.* 9.436)

4.536–40: *there is no need/to tell of these* In this passage, Tiresias alludes to punishments doled out in Tartarus, the part of the underworld reserved for the damned. Sisyphus, a wicked king of Corinth, was condemned eternally to push a rock up a hill. Tantalus tested the omniscience of the gods by serving them his son Pelops in a pie; he was placed in a lake whose waters receded when he attempted to drink from it. Tityos was killed and punished for impiety toward Diana; vultures continually fed on his flesh (*Met.* 4.457–58). Ixion was punished for failing to honor Jupiter after the god had shown mercy toward him; he was consequently strapped to a wheel that turned perpetually. Versions of these figures can be found in the *Odyssey, Aeneid,* and *Metamorphoses.*

4.551: *Medea . . . Circe* Two enchantresses. Medea, subject of a play by Euripides, took vengeance on her husband Jason for his infidelity by killing their children and his mistress. Circe, who appears in Homer's *Odyssey,* turned Odysseus's companions into swine.

4.553–78: *Cadmus is first* The following passage provides a genealogy of the house of Cadmus; Statius has already alluded to most of these figures earlier in the epic. All the ghosts of the family are described in their most miserable states.

4.561–78: *group of daughters* Daughters of Cadmus and Harmonia. *Autonoë* was the mother of Actaeon. *Ino* jumped into the sea with her infant son when her husband Athamas attempted to kill them (he did kill their older son, Learchus). *Semele* died before giving birth to Bacchus. *Agave,* in a Bacchic frenzy, killed her son Pentheus. According to Fulgentius, the daughters represent the various stages of drunkenness, a moral appropriate to a city dedicated to the god of wine.

4.652: *Start from the dim beginnings of their fame* Statius calls attention to his own digression, suggesting that its subject matter is relevant, particularly because nothing else remains of the Theban narrative but the inevitable loss of life in the war.

4.653: *Liber* Bacchus

4.658: *unbridled lynxes* The lynx was sacred to Bacchus; they are unbridled because the god of wine is unrestrained.

4.662: *the members of his sect* Statius lists personifications of moods associated with drunkenness.

[4.716–23]: This translation leaves out these lines, generally considered spurious. Line numbers, however, continue as if the passage were included.

4.745: *Syene* A city on the east bank of the Nile in southern Egypt; source of a reddish granite (Statius, *Silvae* 4.2.27).

4.789: *the Berecynthian mother* From the mountain Berecentus in Phrygia, sacred to Cybele, mother of Jupiter

4.801: *So did* Statius refers to escapades of the young gods to dignify Opheltes, renamed Archemorus (first to die), who will undergo apotheosis upon his death.

4.815: *Leucas* An island off the northwest coast of Greece in the Ionian Sea, which housed a temple dedicated to Apollo. Ambracia was a town on the coast.

4.834: *the raging lion's shaggy mane* Another allusion to Hercules' defeat of the Nemean lion

4.844–46: *Ladon* A river that flowed in Arcadia. *Xanthus* flowed in Lycia; *Spercheos* in Thessaly; and *Lycormas* in Aetolia.

Book 5. The story of Lemnos

5.12: *Paraetonian Nile* Paraetonium was a city on the northern coast of Africa between Egypt and the Syrtes; the adjectival form means "Egyptian." Pharus was an island off the coast of Egypt.

5.20: *then spoke* Adrastus takes advantage of the opportunity for delay by asking Hypsipyle to tell her story to the troops. Hypsipyle's narrative not only prevents the army from continuing but also provides an example of filial piety that underscores the sinfulness of the Argive campaign.

5.51: *Mulciber* A surname of Vulcan, meaning one who softens things

5.61: *Paphos* A city on Cyprus that housed a temple of Venus

5.70: *Amores* Little loves, cupids, or *putti*

5.71: *Hymen* The god of marriage—here a metaphor for conjugal relations. Apollodorus says that Venus cursed the Lemnian women with a foul body odor that scared their husbands away (*Library* 1.9.17). Apollonius says that the men were more interested in their Thracian lovers (*Argonautica* 1.609ff.).

5.90: *Polyxo* In the *Argonautica* (1.667ff.), Polyxo is Hypsipyle's nurse; she convinces the Lemnian women to admit the Argonauts, reasoning that Lemnos will eventually need men to sustain itself. Statius rewrites her as an agitator.

5.92: *Teumesian* Theban. A thyad (from thiasus, a riotous group of revelers) is a Bacchante.

5.120: *while we stand here idly* Polyxo refers to the Danaids; see note to 2.217.

5.122: *she avenged her bed, her marriage* Tereus, king of Thrace, raped his sister-in-law Philomela; he then imprisoned her and cut out her tongue to prevent her from speaking of the crime. She communicated the story to her sister Procne through a tapestry she wove. The two women avenged themselves on Tereus by killing his son and serving the boy's flesh to him at a banquet. See *Met.* 6.420–674.

5.176: *No vigorous god* An ill portent, signifying that the gods have withdrawn from the island

5.182–83: *Paros . . . Cyclades . . . Thasos* Neighboring islands

5.184: *shadowed Lemnos* Mount Athos, west of Lemnos on the Strymonian Gulf in Macedonia. The mountain casts a long shadow on Lemnos at sunset.

5.189–91: *They had leisure* The Lemnian men tell stories of their northern conquests. The Strymon was a river in Macedonia.

5.207: *Let me consider!* A brief catalog of the dead follows; Hypsipyle calls attention to the various impieties committed by mothers, sisters, and wives against the men and boys.

5.227: *her twin* These twins are the only brother-sister pair in the epic (not counting Antigone, Ismene, Polynices, and Eteocles, and if we assume Statius suppressed the fact that Eriphyle was Adrastus's sister, for which see Lewis and Short's entry on Talaus, their father). Lycaste's unwillingness to harm her brother, and her subsequent despair at his death, suggests Statius's ideal of a natural piety between siblings.

5.263: *cloud-born gods* The Centaurs (see note to 2.562)

5.265: *Thyoneus* Thyone is the name Bacchus bestowed on his mother Semele when he raised her from the dead; Thyoneus, or son of Thyone, is one of the various names Ovid lists for the god of wine (*Met.* 4.13).

5.332: *Massylian* The Massyli were a tribe of Numidia, in northern Africa; here, poetic for African (cf. *Aeneid* 4.132).

5.337: *Minyans* A name for the Argonauts, from Minyas, a king in Thessaly (cf. *Met.* 7.1)

5.347: *Symplegades* The Cyaneae, in Statius's Latin, also called Symplegades according to Lewis and Short, were two small rocky islands at the entrance to the Black Sea at the Strait of Bosporus.

5.398: *We saw the sons* A catalog of Argonauts follows; these warriors all appear in the first book of Apollonius's *Argonautica*. Telamon and Peleus were both banished from their father's kingdom after having conspired in the murder of their brother Phocus (*Argonautica* 1.90–94).

5.405: *Meleager, Idas, and Talaus* Meleager was the son of King Oeneus and hunted the Calydonian boar (*Met.* 8.299ff.). Talaus was Adrastus's father, although Statius does not indicate this. Idas and his brother Lynceus, who are mentioned together in the *Argonautica* (1.151–55), were cousins of Castor and Pollux and died at their hands (see Apollodorus, *Library* 3.11.2).

5.407: *Tyndareus's son* Castor or Pollux

5.413: *Tiphys* The first helmsman of the Argos (cf. Virgil, *Eclogues,* 4.34). Because he died before the Argonauts reached Colchis, Ancaeus took over steering the ship (*Argonautica* 2.851ff.).

5.428: *Aethiopia's Red Sea shores* See *Iliad* 1.420ff.

5.431: *Marathon* The Cretan bull (object of the seventh labor of Hercules) had terrorized the countryside of Marathon until Theseus captured it. Ovid refers to the incident (*Met.* 7.433–34).

5.432: *brothers from Thrace* Boreas's sons, Calais (mentioned at line 411) and Zetes (cf. *Met.* 6.716). Apollonius describes them as having wings with golden scales (*Argonautica* 1.211ff.). They were the heroes responsible for chasing the Harpies away from Phineus (*Met.* 7.3).

5.435: *Admetus* The Pheraean king for whom Apollo served as a shepherd to atone for killing the Cyclops (cf. Virgil's *Georgics* 3.9 and *Aeneid* 7.761; also Apollodorus, *Library* 3.10.4)

5.436: *son of Calydon* Meleager.

5.437: *Oebalidae* The epithet refers to Oebalus, king of Sparta, who was the paternal grandfather of Castor and Pollux. Since at least one of the two was already mentioned at line 407, this allusion completes the pair.

5.443: *Young Hylas* Friend and quiver bearer to Hercules (*Argonautica* 1.131–32). The boy was famous for his beauty, which brought about his demise; while filling a pitcher at a spring, Hylas was pulled under water by a nymph or nymphs who wanted to kiss him. Hercules was devastated by the loss and left the Argonautic expedition as a result. Cf. Virgil, *Eclogues* 6.44.

5.458: *In Colchis* When the Argonauts reached Colchis, where King Aeëtes guarded the golden fleece, Jason seduced Medea, the king's daughter (cf. *Met.* 7.1ff.).

5.487: *Chios* An island southeast of Lemnos near the Ionian coast

5.506: *a dragon born of earth* The Inachian serpent, like the Delphic Python that Adrastus describes in book 1, is sacred to a god—in this case Jupiter, the Thunderer (line 511).

Statius derives his description of the beast from Ovid's account of the dragon of Cadmus (sacred to Mars) in *Met.* 3.30–34.

5.529: *His size recalled the dragon* Statius refers to the large constellation Draco, the tail of which circles Ursa Major and Ursa Minor (cf. *Met.* 3.45).

5.609: *Archemorus* "First to die." Hypsipyle renames Opheltes to honor him as the first casualty of the Theban war; see line 739 for Amphiaraus's public renaming of the boy.

5.640: *Perseus's mountain* Mount Aphesas, the same place where Amphiaraus and Melampus conduct their augury (cf. note to 3.462)

5.707: *two-formed Triton* The son of Neptune, represented as a man with a dolphin's tail (cf. *Met.* 2.8)

5.709: *Thetis* A sea nymph, mother of Achilles by Peleus

Book 6. Funeral Games

6.5: *Such contests* Statius refers to the origins of the games of Olympia, Delphi, and the Isthmus of Corinth; this book relates the establishment of the Nemean games. Hercules held funeral games at Olympia (in the district of Pisatis) in honor of Pelops. The Delphic games celebrated Apollo's slaying of the Python. The Isthmian festival originated from funeral games held in honor of Melicertes, the infant son of Ino; both were deified (as Palaemon and Leucothea) after they jumped off the Isthmus of Corinth into the Mediterranean (see *Met.* 4.519–30).

6.7: *wild olive leaves* The winners in the festival were crowned with wreaths of olive branches.

6.54: *young cypress* Cypress was associated with funerals.

6.64: *Linus* Apollo's son, the baby whose death Adrastus describes in book 1. The child's story is ominously depicted on Opheltes' baby blanket.

6.87: *ill-fated war* The scene of warriors attempting to expiate their crime of having killed a sacred snake recalls Apollo's situation after his destruction of the Python at Delphi. Like Apollo, the Argives commit further impieties in their efforts to appease the deities.

[6.88–89]: Lines probably spurious, omitted in translation

6.93–103: *Sacred it stood* The sacred forest is an epic trope (cf. *Met.* 3.28). Statius presents a catalog of Nemean trees in this passage; the list closely resembles the catalog of trees in Virgil's *Culex*, 123–45. Boccaccio includes a close imitation of Statius's lines in *Teseida* 11.

6.108: *Ismara* A Thracian town (cf. *Aeneid* 10.351)

6.111: *Pales* The Italian goddess of shepherds and pastures

6.111: *Silvanus* Roman god of forests, sometimes identified with Pan and Faunus, linked by Virgil with the cypress (*Georgics* 1.20)

6.124: *two quivers had undone her* Niobe lost all her children—twelve according to Homer (*Iliad* 24.603), fourteen in later sources—to the arrows of Apollo and Diana. Pelops was Niobe's brother; Sipylus was her home and the place where she metamorphosed into stone (*Met.* 6.310–12).

6.227–33: Many editors believe these verses are spurious. Hill surrounds them by brackets.

6.238: *Nine times* Nine days was the time allotted for mourning in Roman practice; the same number of days passes between the funeral rites for Anchises and the commencement of the games in his honor (*Aeneid* 5.104–5).

6.249: *the unarmed contests* The rest of book 6 describes the games played in honor of Opheltes (now Archemorus). Statius employs the epic convention of funeral games (cf. *Iliad* 23, *Aeneid* 5) to depict the seven Argive heroes in their glory before they go on to meet their doom at Thebes. Each hero participates in a game that is appropriate to his physical strength, age, and temperament; for example Parthenopaeus is perfectly suited to footraces ("This sport suits agile men," lines 550–51) because he is young and lean, and because his mother, Atalanta, was a runner.

6.269: *effigies* Statius describes a Roman funeral rite. Noble families kept masks (*imagines*) of their ancestors that they used in funeral processions. Tacitus describes one such procession in honor of Junia, Cato's niece (*Annals* 3.74). The ancestors listed here are Argives rather than Nemeans, perhaps because the procession is introducing the games rather than accompanying the funeral of Opheltes. As with previous catalogs of Argives, Statius calls attention to unflattering details of the kingdom's history.

6.277: *Argus* The hundred-eyed creature that Juno commanded to watch over Io (*Met.* 1.625)

6.285: *Myrtilos* King Oenomaus's charioteer, whom Pelops bribed to throw the race (see note to 2.166). Rather than rewarding Myrtilos for his treachery, Pelops killed him.

6.286: *Acrisius* Danaë's father, who suffered for refusing to recognize Bacchus as a god (*Met.* 4.607–11)

6.288: *Amymone* A daughter of Danaus identified with a river in Argos

6.291: *sons of Belus* Danaus and Aegyptus, whose truce was broken when Danaus ordered his daughters to kill their husbands, Aegyptus's sons (see note to 2.217)

6.311: *King Eurystheus's toils* That is, the twelve labors of Hercules, assigned by Eurystheus, king of Mycenae (Nemean lion, Lernaean hydra, rapid stag with golden horns, Erymanthian boar, stables of Augeas, Stymphalian birds, Cretan bull, mares of Diomede, girdle of Hippolyte, Geryon and his oxen, apples of the Hesperides, Cerberus; see *Met.* 9.184–96).

6.321: *his happy son* Phaëthon (see note to 1.221).

6.328: *Cyllarus* One of the centaurs killed at the wedding of Pirithoüs (see note to 2.563). Because he was so beautiful, many female centaurs vied for his attention (*Met.* 12.393–403).

6.329: *Amyclean* Amyclae, a town in Laconia, home of Castor and Pollux

6.358: *Phlegra* The location of the battle between the Olympians and the Giants (see note to 2.596)

6.360: *his brothers' deeds* Apollo's brothers—other sons of Jove—could refer to Mars, Bacchus, Hercules, and Perseus, among others.

6.381: *Admetus will receive old age* Apollo arranged for Admetus to win immortality if someone would agree to die in his place; Alcestis, his wife, sacrificed herself. The story is the subject of Euripides' *Alcestis*.

6.383: *sad birds* The translation transfers the epithet "sad" from Amphiaraus to the birds (hypallage).

6.419: *white rain* Horse foam

6.434–35: *Though each desired to win, they never clashed* Hypsipyle's sons are models of fraternal piety.

6.596: *Cydonian* Cydon, a city in Crete, known for its expert archers

6.598: *Hyrcanian* Hyrcania was a Persian province near Parthia (the northeastern part of modern Iran) on the southern coast of the Caspian Sea.

6.608: *Diana (Trivia)* The goddess is called Trivia because of her threefold nature: Diana (the virgin huntress), Selene (the moon), and Hecate (the underworld).

6.632: *Tegaean* From Tegea, a town in Arcadia; here, Parthenopaeus

6.652: *Ephyreians* Corinthians, named after the nymph Ephyre (cf. *Met.* 2.240)

6.652: *Acarnanians* Acarnania was most western province of Greece, on the Ionian Sea.

6.666: *Mount Pangaea* A mountain in Thrace, on the border of Macedonia, near Philippi

6.725: *Cnosian* After Cnosis (Gnosus), former capital of Crete and home of Minos

6.742: *He'd grown up in the god's gymnasium* Homer identifies Pollux as a champion boxer (*Iliad* 3.237; *Odyssey* 11.300).

6.837: *Cleonae* A town in Argolis near Nemea (*Met.* 6.417)

6.894: *the earthborn Libyan* Antaeus, the giant who derived his strength from the earth. Hercules defeated him by holding him up in the air and strangling him (*Met.* 9.184).

6.927: *Lyctian* Cretan (after Lyctus, a town in eastern Crete; cf. *Met.* 7.490)

Book 7. Earth Opens

7.8: *Parrhasian dipper* The constellation Ursa Major, which is the metamorphosed Callisto (*Met.* 2.401ff.). Parrhasia is a district in Arcadia.

7.40: *Here he saw lifeless trees and shrines to Mars* The following passage describes the horrors of the temple of Mars. Boccaccio (*Teseida* 7.29–37), Chaucer (*Knight's Tale* 3.1967–2050), and Spenser (*Faerie Queene* 4.1.20–24) all imitate this passage, paying particular attention to Statius's personifications.

7.66: *Hebrus* The main river in Thrace, which starts in Mount Haemus

7.162–63: *Danaë's . . . Amyclae* Danaë, Callisto, and Leda were the mothers, respectively, of Perseus, Arcas, and Castor and Pollux. Bacchus certainly should have had precedence over these lesser sons of Jupiter.

7.182: *My brother* Apollo, who was born on Delos

7.184: *Pallas saved the citadel* Refers to the contest between Minerva and Neptune over which of them would become patron god of Athens (*Met.* 6.70ff.)

7.186: *Epaphus* Another son of Jupiter, by Io, Epaphus founded Egyptian city of Memphis (*Met.* 1.748)

7.191: *whose bull fared better* Bacchus reminds Jove of Alcmena, Antiope, and Europa. The late classical authority Lactantius applied the epithet *felicior* (more fortunate) to Europa instead of Jove, who, transformed into a bull, carried her to sea, because she did not die in flames, like Bacchus's mother Semele.

7.204: *ancient Calydonians* Diana sent a fierce boar to Calydon as retribution for the Calydonians' failure to honor her at harvest time (see *Met.* 8.272).

7.207: *Labdacus* Father of Laius

7.255: *There—look!* A catalog of heroes, towns, and rivers of Boeotia, Phocis, and Euboea follows. Most of the towns are mentioned in Homer's catalog of Greek ships (see *Iliad* 2.494–545).

7.255–56: *gold bolt of lightning/ and trident* Orion was the son of both Jupiter and Neptune (see Ovid, *Fasti* 5.493–544); his grandson can therefore rightly lay claim to the insignia of both gods. Several versions of the myth relate different reasons for Diana's anger, but Statius might be alluding to her thwarted plan to marry Orion (see Hyginus, *De Astrologia* 2.34).

7.271: *Neptune's progeny* Mycalessos, Melas, and Gargaphie are Boeotian rivers.

7.273: *Gargaphie* Diana (one of Hecate's identities) killed Actaeon in this river valley (*Met.* 3.138ff.).

7.283–84: *Permesse, and pleasant Olmius* Rivers of Mount Helicon

7.287: *Strymon's stream* A river in the north dividing Macedonia and Thrace

7.307: *Glisantan* Pausanias identifies Glisas as the location of the Epigoni's battle against the Thebans (9.5.13).

7.315: *Asopos* The god of an Achaean river. It was also the name of a river in Boeotia. The details about Asopos's defiance of Jove are appropriate to a description of the hero Hypseus, who dies at the hands of the impious Capaneus in book 9.

7.334: *Euripus* The strait that separates Euboea from Boeotia

7.335: *Glaucus* A fisherman who turned into a merman after eating a magic plant (*Met.* 13.898–968)

7.349: *Cephisus* A Boeotian river (father of Narcissus, see *Met.* 3.341–46)

7.352: *the god's mass killings* The Phocians wear armor that depicts two of Apollo's victories. He defeated the giant Tityus, who had assaulted his mother (*Odyssey* 11.576–81), and he killed the Python at Delos.

7.397: *he carries suckling youngsters to their mothers* This simile casts a more flattering light on Eteocles than any previous description, again calling to question whether either brother is ultimately more blameworthy.

7.412: *Sparta* The site of worship of the Gemini (Castor and Pollux)

7.414: *Lycaon's frenzied ghost* Lycaon was an Arcadian king who was changed into a wolf for testing Jupiter's godhead (see *Met.* 1.197–239).

7.422: *The Peloponnesian phalanx* This fearless group is the part of the army led by Capaneus (see note to 4.178).

7.476: *an olive branch with black wool twists* A traditional sign of supplication

7.566: *Erythraean shores* Erythras was a mythical king of Asia or Arabia after whom the Red Sea, Arabian Gulf, and Indian Gulf were named; here Statius refers to the Indian Ocean, according to Lewis and Short.

7.685–86: *Ismara . . . Tmolos* Again, Statius lists places associated with the worship of Bacchus (see note to 4.383). Ismara was a town in Thrace, near Maronea, the place from which Odysseus acquired the sweet wine he uses to inebriate Polyphemus (*Odyssey* 9.193ff.). Tmolos was a mountain in Asia Minor.

7.718: *Carystos* A town on the southern shore of Euboea

7.792: *Castor and Pollux let their sister shine* The Gemini and their sister Helen were patron deities of sailors (see Horace, *Odes* 1.3).

Book 8. Savage Hunger

8.15: *Elysium* The part of the underworld reserved for the virtuous

8.18: *the pallid furrower of waters* Charon, the ferryman who carries souls across the river Styx

8.26: *turn thumbs* In contests at the Forum, spectators would vote on the fate of a defeated gladiator by signaling with their thumbs (thumbs up was actually the sign of condemnation). See Juvenal, *Satires* 3.36.

8.38: *third encounter* The Olympian brothers Jupiter, Neptune, and Pluto drew lots for their kingdoms; Pluto received "the world of harmful things" after losing the heavens and seas to his brothers (see *Iliad* 15.185–92).

8.42: *the rattling chains* After the Olympians defeated the Titans (among them Saturn, Jupiter's father), Jupiter had them imprisoned in Tartarus (see Hesiod, *Theogony* 717ff.).

8.50: *both sons/of Tyndareus* That is, Castor and Pollux. Because their mother Leda was impregnated by both Jupiter and her husband Tyndareus, only Pollux (Jupiter's son) was granted access to Olympus after death. The brothers therefore shared this honor by taking turns each day between Olympus and the underworld. See *Odyssey* 11.298–304.

8.50: *Ixion* See note to 4.536.

8.53–56: *Pirithoüs* Pirithous and Theseus tried to kidnap Pluto's queen, Proserpina; Hercules carried Cerberus to the surface. This passage echoes *Aeneid* 6.392–94, in which Charon complains to Aeneas of his difficulties.

8.57: *Thracian bard* Odrysian in the original, from Odrysae, a people of Thrace (cf. *Met.* 6.490); here, Orpheus, who, by charming Pluto with his music, convinced the god to release Eurydice's shade from the underworld (*Met.* 10.1–85)

8.62: *Sicily* Pluto ascended to the island of Sicily to carry off Proserpina (*Met.* 5.341ff.).

8.197: *Tenedos and Chryse* Tenedos was an island in the Aegean near the coast of Troy; Chryse was a town on the mainland near Troy. Both places were sites of worship of Apollo, whose priest Chryses invokes the names of these towns when he calls down Apollo's curse on the Greeks (*Iliad* 1.35–42).

8.198: *Branchus* A priest (some say a son) of Apollo. The following names are sites of Apollonian oracles; see note to 3.474, note to 3.476–80, and note to 3.513.

8.199: *Clarius* A name for Apollo, after Claros, a town on the coast of Ionia celebrated for its temple to the god

8.212: *Tiphys' sudden death* See note to 5.413.

8.237: *Hydaspes River* A tributary of the Indus River in northern India

8.305: *Promethean man, the stones of Pyrrha* Prometheus is credited with creating the first humans (*Met.* 1.78–88). Pyrrha and Deucalion repopulated the earth after a great flood by throwing over their shoulders stones that grew into humans (*Met.* 1.400–402).

8.311: *Two chariots* The sun and the moon

8.352: *seven gates* Thebes was famous for its seven gates; the Greek epithet for Thebes is *Heptapulos*, "seven-gated."

8.364–65: *the Eleans, the Spartans,/and Pylians* These men had been under Amphiaraus's charge; see 4.238.

8.426: *Aquilo* The north wind, the Roman version of Boreas (see *Aeneid* 1.102)

8.437: *Taÿgetus* A mountain range between Laconia and Messenia

8.466: *Onchestian* Onchestus was a town in Boeotia that was sacred to Neptune (*Iliad* 2.506).

8.477: *Maera* A Nereid impregnated by Jupiter. She and Eriphyle are mentioned together in the list of women whom Odysseus sees in the underworld (*Odyssey* 11.326).

8.482–84: *Calydonians* Calydon, Pylene, Pleuron, and Olenus are towns mentioned in Homer's catalog of Aetolian warriors (*Iliad* 2.638–40).

8.509: *Amphitryon* The husband of Alcmene, Hercules' father (*Met.* 6.112)

8.518: *the snakes that bristled on her breast* These are the snakes on the head of Medusa, which decorates the aegis, Minerva's breastplate or shield.

8.532: *Lucania* An ancient district of southern Italy, roughly equivalent to modern Basilicata

8.545: *Mount Gaurus* A mountain on the eastern coast of Italy, near Naples

8.551: *Urania* The muse of astronomy

8.616: *nightingale and swallow* See note to 5.122.

8.675: *the bird/that carries lightning* Literally, the flame carrier— that is, the eagle, the bird sacred to Jupiter

8.758: *Tritonian Pallas* "Tritonian" is an epithet for Minerva, perhaps in reference to Libya's Lake Triton. Homer calls her "Tritogeneia" (*Iliad* 4.515, *Odyssey* 3.378).

Book 9. Tide and Time

9.127: *Tanagraean* Tanagraea was a district in Boeotia that housed a temple to Bacchus.

9.189: *Moorish* Mauritanian, North African

9.290–91: *Thisbaean Lichas, and Lycetus/the Anthedonian* Anthedon and Thisbae were Boeotian towns; both are mentioned in Homer's catalog of Boeotia (see note to 7.255).

9.307: *Caphereus* A cape on the east coast of Euboea

9.319: *Faunus and the nymph Ismenis* Faunus was the Roman god of the forest; Ismenis was the daughter of the river god Ismenos.

9.323: *Sisters of Elysium* The Fates

9.334: *Sidonian maiden* Europa

9.351: *silvery sisters* Nereids

9.371: *Doris'* The sea, in general; Doris was the mother of the Nereids (*Met.* 2.11).

9.423: *the guilty horns* Ismenos refers to some of Jupiter's indiscretions (with Europa, Alcmena, and Semele).

9.427: *Tirynthius* Hercules (after Tiryns, the city from which his mother came)

9.598: *Maenads* Bacchantes

9.611: *Colchian/barbarians* The Argonauts (after Colchis, the island that held the golden fleece)

9.617: *to hide my moral fault in secret caves* See note to 4.249.

9.632: *Dictynna* Another name for Diana (*Met.* 2.441)

9.796: *spears of infamy* That is, thyrsi, the staffs carried by Bacchantes. Parthenopaeus distinguishes himself from the Thebans, who he implies are to blame for their devotion to Bacchus.

Book 10. Sacrifices

10.56: *They offered Juno's statue cloaks of state* In their effort to placate Juno, the Argive women present the goddess's statue with a *peplus,* an intricately embroidered robe depicting, in this case, Juno as a young bride (cf. *Aeneid* 1.479–82). Suppliant women of Troy similarly appeal to Athena (*Iliad* 6.286ff.).

10.77: *Alcmene* Disguising himself as her husband, Jupiter spent two nights with Alcmene engendering Hercules (*Met.* 6.111).

10.111: *slipping horn* Somnus poured sleep over his victims from a horn.

10.170: *the mother goddess of Mount Ida* Cybele (see note to 4.789). Her ecstatic priests, Corybantes (or Curetes), mutilated themselves when celebrating the festival that honored Attis (see Ovid, *Fasti* 4.179ff.).

10.228: *Pholoë* A mountain between Arcadia and Elis, where Centaurs lived (Apollodorus, *Library* 2.5.4)

10.343: *Paean* See note to 1.636.

10.347–48: *a Calydonian, Hopleus, and a Maenalian, Dymas* Dymas and Hopleus are modeled after Virgil's Nisus and Euryalus (*Aeneid* 9.176ff.). The relationship of the younger and older man replicates the bond each had with his captain, Parthenopaeus (an Arcadian, like Dymas) and Tydeus (whose half brother Meleager killed the Calydonian boar).

10.445: *You will be long remembered* A eulogy reminiscent of that for Maeon (see 3.88ff.)

10.512: *Pangaea* A Macedonian mountain range, site of King Lycurgus's death (cf. note to 4.53).

10.530: *turtles* Either a sort of covering shed beneath which sappers could undermine a tower or a close formation of soldiers holding shields together over their heads while besieging the walls of a city.

10.537: *Malea/or high Ceraunia* The cape between the Laconian and Argolic gulfs on the Peloponnesus mountain range on the coast of Epirus, known to be dangerous to ships (see *Aeneid* 3.506)

10.646: *as when Omphale laughed at Hercules* The simile refers to Hercules' affair with Omphale, the Lydian queen who made him wear her clothes (see Ovid, *Heroides* 9).

10.857: *Balearic* The Baleares (inhabitants of modern Majorca and Minorca, islands east of Spain) were skilled slingers (see Caesar, *Gallic War* 2.7).

10.909: *when proud giants fought at Phlegra* See note to 2.596.

10.916: *Iapetus* One of the Titans, imprisoned in Tartarus for defying Jupiter (*Iliad* 8.479)

10.917: *Ischia* Modern name of ancient Inarime

Book 11. Piety

11.8: *Enceledus* See note to 3.595.

11.84: *Enyo* The Greek equivalent of Bellona (see note to 4.6)

11.105: *he whose prayers* Oedipus

11.124: *a single man* Capaneus

11.125: *a pair* Polynices and Eteocles

11.132–33: *Astraea's constellation/or Leda's brothers* Virgo and Gemini. Astraea was the daughter of Jupiter and Themis, goddess of justice. She fled earth due to the depravity of humankind (*Met.* 1.150).

11.136: *The virgin daughter of the god of darkness* Megaera

11.177: *her lord* Parthenopaeus

11.231: *haruspex* See note to 3.557.

11.234: *Hercules* Hercules burned to death after donning a cloak poisoned by his rival Nessus (*Met.* 9.134–88).

11.318: *Agave* See note to 4.561.

11.401: *Maeonian* Lydian, that is, exotically Eastern

11.438: *Cyanean islands' cliffs* The Cyaneae, also known as the Symplegades, were islands at the opening of the Black Sea that reputedly crashed together whenever ships tried to pass among them (see Homer, *Odyssey* 12.59–72).

11.445: *king of shadows* Pluto

11.458: *Piety* Pietas—the personified deity of loyalty, duty, and filial love—was central to the Romans' conception of themselves. Piety has been absent from Thebes throughout the poem; therefore, Tisiphone's response to the goddess is warranted.

11.571: *Minos* See note to 4.530.

11.588: *sailor of the stagnant stream Avernus* Charon

11.645: *Erigone* Subject of an etiological myth accounting for the constellation Virgo (cf. note to 11.132), Erigone committed suicide after discovering that her father had been killed by drunken shepherds (Apollodorus, *Library* 3.14.7).

Book 12. Clemency

12.3: *Tithonia* The dawn, or Aurora. The name is transferred from her husband Tithonus, a mortal to whom the gods granted eternal life but not eternal youth. As he aged, he withered until he metamorphosed into a grasshopper.

12.67: *just as Hercules* See note to 4.158.

12.106: *miserable women* The mourning and pilgrimage of the Argive women is central to many analogous works of literature; see, for example, Aeschylus' *Seven against Thebes,* Boccaccio's *Teseida,* Chaucer's *Knight's Tale,* and Shakespeare's *The Two Noble Kinsmen.*

12.131: *Leucothea* See note to 6.5.

12.132: *Eleüsin* Eleusis was a city in Attica where rites were held in honor of Ceres.

12.155: *Busiris* An Egyptian king who sacrificed a human every year to appease Jupiter (see Apollodorus, *Library* 2.5.11). Both Busiris and Odrysius were overcome by Hercules.

12.156: *Odrysiae* A Thracian people. King Diomedes of Thrace owned the horses, which ate the flesh of humans (Apollodorus, *Library* 2.5.8).

12.181–82: *nor any daughter from the snows of Phasis* That is, Medea, who was called Phasias (*Met.* 7.298).

12.225: *Dindyma* A Phrygian mountain sacred to Cybele

12.273–74: *dark conveyer* Pluto (see note to 4.124)

12.275: *Enceladus* See note to 3.595.

12.431: *a double top* The dueling flames motif inspired one of Dante's punishments in hell: that of Ulysses and Diomedes (the son of Tydeus); see *Inferno,* canto 26.

12.480: *the crimes and wickedness of Tereus* See note to 5.122.

12.482: *Clemency* Clementia was seen as a prototype of the Christian god, since she had no form and no set rites. Dante regarded Statius as a Christian (*Purgatorio* 21 and 22), partly because this description of the god's altar seemed to supply Christian overtones.

12.498: *sons of Hercules* The Heraclidae. Euripides tells of how they appealed to Theseus for clemency after having been pursued by King Eurystheus (see *Met.* 9.273–75).

12.510: *It sheltered Oedipus* An anachronistic reference. Oedipus took refuge north of Athens, in the town of Colonus, just before his death. See Sophocles, *Oedipus at Colonus.*

12.510: *Olynthians* Olynthus was a Macedonian town that appealed to Athens for military assistance when it was under attack by King Philippus (see Demosthenes, *Olynthia* 1, 2, and 3). Statius might here be using Clemency as a metonym for Athens.

12.511: *Orestes* Tried and acquitted in Athens for the murder of his mother, Clytemnestra (see Aeschylus, *Eumenides)*

12.516: *Pharos* An island off of the Egyptian coast

12.519: *After his bitter wars in Scythia* Theseus has just returned from his recent victory over the Amazons, whose queen (Hippolyta) he married.

12.526: *Maeotis'* A sea in Scythia (the modern Sea of Azov), connected to the Black Sea by the Cimmerian Strait

12.545: *wife of Capaneus* In Euripides's *Suppliants,* Adrastus petitions Theseus for help in burying the dead.

12.570: *Cecrops* The founder and civilizer of Athens

12.571: *Emathians* The Macedonians

12.576–77: Statius lists several criminals whom Theseus defeated; each was known to be a threat to travelers. *Cercyon* challenged travelers to wrestling contests and killed them after he won; *Sinis* catapulted them to their deaths with bent pine trees; and *Sciron* threw them into the sea (see *Met.* 7.439–47).

12.588: *Neptunian* An epithet for Theseus ("Neptunius heros," *Met.* 9.1), derived from the legend that he was the son of Neptune (see Plutarch, *Theseus*)

12.615–17: *Brauron,/Monychia . . . Marathon* Attic districts. *Piraeus* is the primary harbor of Athens.

12.619–24: *Icarius and Celeus* Prominent men of Attica. Icarius, who lived in Athens, was Erigone's father; Celeus was the king of Eleusis, northwest of Athens. Statius provides a catalog of Attic mountain, valley, and river towns that supply Theseus with troops. *Aegaleos, Parnes, Lycabessos,* and *Hymettus* are all mountains, the last of which was known for its honey (hence "fragrant"). *Melaenae* was an Attic village; *Acharnae* was a district at the base of Mount Parnes.

12.625: *Sounion* A cape in southern Attica on which a temple to Minerva stood. After receiving a ship's signal that led him to believe his son had been devoured by the Minotaur, Aegeus (Theseus's father) threw himself into the sea from this promontory.

12.627: *Salamis* An island southwest of the Attic coast

12.629: *Callirhoë* A spring in Athens with nine water heads that provided the water source for wells throughout the city (see Pausanias 1.14.1)

12.630: *Orithyia* The mother of Calais and Zetes by Boreas, the north wind (see *Met.* 6.712)

12.632: *hillside* The Acropolis, the site where Neptune and Minerva contended for patronage of Athens. The tree that decided the contest was the olive, Minerva's gift to the Athenians (see *Met.* 6.81).

12.665–66: *his great shield* The shield of Theseus depicts his own previous conquests—in particular, his victory over the Minotaur.

12.676: *Ariadne's* The daughter of King Minos, who helped Theseus escape from the labyrinth by means of a trail of thread (*Met.* 8.172)

12.733: *Edonian* Thracian

12.788: *Ganges* See note to 4.383.

12.793: *Thyiades* Followers of Bacchus (cf. *Aeneid* 4.302)

12.805: *Erymanthian* Atalanta (after Erymanthus, the Arcadian mountain)

Selected Proper Names

Achaea: Northern Peloponnesus or southeast Thessaly; used by Homer to refer to all of Greece; Achaean means Greek.

Achelous: A river (and, by association, its god) in the western mainland of Greece that forms the border between Archania and Aetolia. Achelous wrestled with Hercules in a contest for the hand of Deianira (Ovid, *Metamorphoses* 9.1–97).

Adrastus: King of Argos and sole survivor of the seven against Thebes

Agenor: Father of Cadmus

Amores: Literally, loves; little cupids or putti

Amphiaraus: One of the seven against Thebes; a prophet of Apollo, swallowed alive by the earth

Amphion: King who erected a wall around Thebes. He borrowed Apollo's lyre and charmed the stones into place with his song.

Antigone: Daughter of Oedipus

Aonia: District that contains Thebes; part of Boeotia, from Aon, son of Neptune

Arcadia: Region in Greece in the central Peloponnesus. The Arcadian is sometimes Mercury, sometimes Parthenopaeus.

Arcturus: Star whose presence in autumn indicates foul weather (hence, the moon perhaps dimmed by clouds at 2.58)

Arethusa: Spring in Syracuse, Sicily

Argive: From the city of Argos

Asopos: River in Boeotia

Atropos: One of the Moirae, or Fates, sister of Clotho, who spins the thread of life, and Lachesis, who measures the thread. Atropos cuts the thread; her name means "not turnable."

Bacchus: Son of Cadmus's daughter Semele and Zeus; god of wine, the patron god of Thebes; a name of Dionysius

Boötes: Constellation known today as the Big Dipper, formerly the Wagon or Wain. The word means "oxen-driver."

Boreas: North wind

Bromius: Name for Bacchus, deriving from a Greek epithet for the god that referred to shouting and uproar

Capaneus: One of the seven against Thebes; killed by lightning

Cerberus: Doglike, triple-headed guardian of the entrance to the underworld

Cirrha: Site of Apollo's oracle; city in Phocis near Delphi

Cithaeron: Mountain in Boeotia, sacred to Bacchus

Clio: Muse of History

Cocytos: Mythic river in the Lower World

Coroebus: Citizen of Argos who killed Apollo's monster and shamed the god

Creon: Father of Haemon and Menoeceus who assumes control of Thebes after the deaths of Polynices and Eteocles

Cyclops: Plural, in this translation, for those who forge Jove's lightning bolts (related to but not the same as the group of shepherds to which belonged the one-eyed monster Polyphemus, met by Odysseus)

Cyllene: Mountain where Maia gave birth to Mercury

Danaë: Seduced by Jupiter, who appeared as a shower of gold in her lap; the mother of Perseus.

Danaus: Founder of Argos and father of fifty daughters who murdered their husbands at his command. Like Homer,

Statius uses Danai (Danaans in this translation) to refer to Greeks.

Dione: Mother of Venus

Dirae: Sister Furies

Dirce: Stream in Boeotia; the region around it

Echion: One of the survivors of those born when Cadmus sowed the dragon's teeth; a synonym for Theban. "Echion's miserable son" is Polynices.

Erasinus: River in Argolis

Erymanthos: Mountain chain in Arcadia; home of the Erymanthian boar, killed by Hercules

Eriphyle: Wife of Amphiaraus, who convinced her husband to join in the war against Thebes, which he knew was doomed

Eteocles: Son of Oedipus and Jocasta, brother of Polynices, Antigone, and Ismene, who refuses to relinquish control of Thebes

Euhius: Bacchus, god of wine

Eumenides: Polite name (the "good ones") for the avenging Furies

Eurotas: East wind; also, a river in Laconia on which Sparta stood

Gradivus: Mars; from *gradior,* he who marches forth

Haemon: Son of Creon

Haemus: Mountain range in Thrace, one of the regions mentioned by the Bacchante as a place of worship for the god

Hippomedon: One of the seven against Thebes; drowned

Ilissos: River in Athens, sacred to Minerva

Inachus: Former king of Argos and the name of the local river. Inachian youth are Greeks (see 8.363).

Io: Jupiter turned Io into a heifer to hide her from Juno, then had Mercury put to sleep the thousand-eyed Argus, who guarded her. According to Ovid, she became the Egyptian goddess Isis (*Metamorphoses* 1.588ff.).

Ismene: Daughter of Oedipus

Ismenos: River of Boeotia, near Thebes. The Ismenian hero is Polynices (see 2.307; cf. *Metamorphoses* 2.244).

Isthmos: Isthmus of Corinth

Jove: Ruler of the gods. "Infernal Jove," literally, black Jove, is Pluto, the god of underworld, who gained his realm when he drew lots with Jupiter (another name for Jove) and Neptune (cf. *Aeneid* 4.638: Juppiter Stygius).

Laconia: Land of the Spartans

Laius: Father of Oedipus, whose sword killed him at the crossroads in Phocis

Lerna: Marsh in Argolis; home of the Hydra, the nine-headed monster that Hercules killed in his second labor

Lethe: Infernal stream of forgetfulness

Linus: Infant son of Apollo and the daughter of Crotopus, elsewhere named Psamanthe. A festival of lamentation commemorated his death after he was eaten by dogs.

Lucifer: Morning star (from Latin for "light bearer")

Lucina: Goddess of childbirth, identified with both Juno and Diana, so named because she brings to light

Lyaeus: Name for Bacchus, from a word meaning to "loosen"

Maenalos: Range of mountains in Arcadia, sacred to Pan and Bacchus, whose orgies were celebrated there. Mercury was born in Arcadia (see 7.65).

Maia: Oldest of the Pleiades, the Arcadian seven sisters, who were daughters of Atlas; mother of Mercury

Malea: Promontory in Laconia, at the southwestern tip of the Peloponnesus

Megaera: One of the three Furies or Erinyes who imprisoned Phlegyas, son of Mars, king of the Lapithae and father of Ixion (cf. *Aeneid* 12.846)

Melanippus: Slayer of Tydeus. Dante's Menalippo

Menoeceus: Son of Creon, who jumped off a tower to save Thebes

Mopsus: Famous seer who traveled with the Argonauts

Nemea: Valley in the Argolis, southwest of Corinth, where Hercules performed the first of his twelve labors by killing the Nemean lion

Neptune: Roman god of the oceans, like the Greek Poseidon; brother of Jupiter

Niobe: Apollo killed the seven sons and seven daughters of Niobe (the "Theban mother") because her ability to give birth dishonored Latona. Lactantius notes that Homer says she had twelve children (*Iliad* 24.603); Sophocles says fourteen. She was turned to stone on Mount Sipylus.

Oenomaus: King who required a chariot race against whoever sought the hand of his daughter Hippodamia. Those who lost were fed to his man-eating horses, which Juno compares with the Thracian steeds of Diomedes (Hercules eighth labor).

Oete: Mountain range of Thessaly

Ogyges: First ruler of Thebes; hence, Ogygian is a synonym for Theban.

Olenian: From the town in Achaia named after Olenos, the husband of Lethaea, who changed into a stone (see *Metamorphoses* 10.69)

Osiris: Egyptian deity

Palaemon: Sea god, the immortalized manifestation of Melicertes, son of Ino (one of the daughters of Cadmus); god of harbors and patron of sailors (see *Metamorphoses* 4.542)

Parnassus: Range of mountains west of Boeotia. Delphi, Apollo's birthplace, is located at its southern end.

Parcae: Roman version of the Moirae, the Fates: Clotho, Lachesis, and Atropos

Parrhasis: Town of Arcadia, home of Callisto, who was turned into a bear and became the constellation Ursa Major, a constellation that never sets below the horizon

Parthenopaeus: Son of Atalanta, youngest of the seven against Thebes

Phocis: Site of the crossroads where Oedipus killed his father Laius

Phoroneus: Son of Inachus, king of Argos; brother of Io; husband of Niobe

Phrygian: Apollo helped build Troy, in Phrygia.

Pieros: King of an area on the border of Thrace and Macedonia who gave his nine daughters the names of the muses (cf. *Metamorphoses* 5.302)

Polybus: King of Corinth, adoptive father of Oedipus. His untruth was his misrepresentation of himself as Oedipus's natural father.

Proserpina: Daughter of Jupiter and Ceres, married to Pluto (Dis); queen of the underworld

Semele: Daughter of Cadmus, mother of Bacchus. Juno tricked her into asking to see Jupiter in all his power. The experience destroyed her when he appeared as thunder and lightning.

Strymon: River in Macedonia; also the name of Chromis's horse (see 6.464)

Styx: River in the underworld

Taenaros: Promontory and town of Laconia; fabled entrance to the underworld and site of a temple to Poseidon (Neptune)

Tantalus: King of Phrygia, who boiled his son Pelops and served him at a banquet for the gods; punished in the underworld by being unable to reach a fruit tree or water

Tartarus: Abyss of the underworld (Statius uses the plural form, Tartara)

Thessaly: District of northern Greece famous for witches and magic

Theseus: Ruler of Athens

Tityos: Giant whom Jove condemned to lie in a field of the underworld where vultures eternally fed on his entrails

Tydeus: One of the seven against Thebes, son of Oeneus and father of Diomedes, who gnawed the head of Menalippus

Tyre: Town in Phoenicia; another name for Thebes, because Cadmus came from Tyre

Selected Annotated Bibliography

Ahl, F. M. "Statius' *Thebaid:* A Reconsideration." *Aufstieg und Niedergang der römischen Welt,* II, 32.5 (1986): 2803–2912.

A good look at the Greek tradition from which Statius drew, including the family connection between Amphiaraus and Adrastus that Statius does not mention. "Statius constantly undermines fixed boundaries and definitions. Virtually every character and every action is subjected to constantly changing perspectives and frames of reference. . . . In even the tiniest details of his epic Statius shows how events are misconstrued" (p. 2898).

Anderson, David. *Before the Knight's Tale.* Philadelphia: University of Pennsylvania Press, 1988.

A detailed study of how Boccaccio and Chaucer rewrote the *Thebaid.* Chaucer may have picked up the hint that Polynices had a son with Antigone and that the son is Palamon, "a kynges brother son, pardee" because Eteocles suspects her love for Polynices (*Thebaid* 11.371) and Lactantius says the siblings slept together.

Barthes, Roland. *On Racine.* New York: Hill and Wang, 1964.

Fraternal hatred is not the work of an hour, Barthes argues. As Eteocles says of Polynices in Racine's *La Thébaïde:* "Ce n'est pas son orgueil, c'est lui seul que je hais."

Boiardo, Matteo Maria. *Orlando Innamorato* (Orlando in Love). Translated with an introduction and notes by Charles Stanley Ross. West Lafayette, Ind.: Parlor Press, 2004.

Chance, Jane. *Medieval Mythography: From Roman North Africa to the School of Chartres, A.D. 433–1177.* Gainesville: University of Florida Press, 1994.

This volume provides a detailed summary of scholarship identifying *Thebaid* commentators like Fulgentius and Lactantius (p. 543) and the manuscript tradition of the poem (p. 169).

Coleman, Kathleen M. "Recent Scholarship on the *Thebaid* and *Achilleid*: An Overview." In *Statius II: Thebaid. Books 1–7,* ed. and trans. D. R. Shackleton Bailey, pp. 9–37. Loeb Classical Library. Cambridge, Mass.: Harvard University Press, 2003.

Contains a good account of recent work by text editors.

Dominick, William J. *The Mythic Voice of Statius: Power and Politics in the* Thebaid. Leiden: E. J. Brill, 1994.

Correlates the *Thebaid* to the struggle for power in Rome.

Edwards, Robert, R., ed., John Lydgate, *The Siege of Thebes.* Kalamazoo, Mich.: Medieval Institute Publications, 2001.

Edwards reviews the prose redactions of *Le roman de Thèbes* and the symbolism of "desire, confusion, and catastrophe" of Chaucer's "broche of Thebes." In giving the history of Lydgate's addition to the *Canterbury Tales,* he mentions also that John Gower's *Confessio Amantis* retells the story of Capaneus's defiance of Zeus.

Feeney, D. C. *The Gods in Epic: Poets and Critics of the Classical Tradition.* New York: Oxford University Press, 1991.

Feeney notices that Statius's principle motif is divagation and delay, and that even Opheltes' new name, which means "Beginner of Doom" (Môros [Gk.]) also means "originator of delay" (*mora*). "Criticism of the poem's episodic progress evaporates before the evidence that the poet calls our attention again and again to his dilatory manner of narrating" (p. 340). Feeney also reads the silence of Apollo's oracles in book 9 as "an image of the sun-god going into eclipse" (p. 373).

Fulgentius, Fabius Planciades. "On the *Thebaid.*" In *Fulgentius the Mythographer,* trans. Leslie George Whitbread. Columbus: Ohio University Press, 1971.

Gossage, A. J. "Virgil and the Flavian Epic." In *Virgil,* ed. D. R. Dudley, pp. 67–93. New York: Basic Books, 1969.

A good comparison of the *Aeneid* and the *Thebaid,* as well as the *Argonautica* of Valerius Flaccus and the *Punica* of Diodorus Siculus.

Henderson, John. *Fighting for Rome: Poets and Caesars, History, and Civil War.* Cambridge: Cambridge University Press, 1998.

This book and Henderson's other essays on Statius define the outer limits of classical scholarship. Henderson is nearly always difficult and inspiring. "Expect miles of post-Homeric machinery: Olympian inserts, twin catalogues and teichoscopy, necromancy and underworld scenography, funeral games and *aristeiai,* prayer-sequences and prophecy, tragical included narrative and etiological hymn, developed formal similes, battle-*Sturm und Drang,* mountain vastnesses tipping out torrential volumes of surging verse by the dozen, the whole works" (p. 215).

Hutchinson, G. O. *Latin Literature from Seneca to Juvenal: A Critical Study.* Oxford: Clarendon Press, 1993.

Hutchinson reads Statius's style closely, commenting on the poet's use of epigram, his lightness of touch, and his ability to prepare an effect and still surprise, which Hutchinson compares to Boiardo's art (p. 94). Also Boiardan is Statius's "inexhaustible imagination and fancy." Hutchinson adds that the contrast between the giant serpent that kills Opheltes and the toddling infant illustrates how Statius's "use of language, searchingly vivid and refined, gives a constant sense of subtlety in the midst of extremity; his brilliant wit removes us from any simple immersion in narrative with a singular audacity and sharpness" (p. 121). Hutchinson also considers how Statius connects the two halves of his poem more closely than Virgil does. For example, Tydeus's defeat of fifty Thebans foreshadows the battles that make up the latter part of the poem. An exception is Hypsipyle's story of Lemnos. Although modeled on Aeneas's account of the fall of Troy, its tenuous connection the main narrative recalls the conscious mannerism of Ovid's *Metamorphoses* (p. 179).

Lactantius. *Lactantii Placidi: In Statii Thebaida Commentum.* Ed. Robert Dale Sweeney. Stuttgart: Teubner, 1997.

An edition of the commentary by Lactantius Placidus.

Laistner, M. L. W. *Thought and Letters in Western Europe, A.D. 500 to 900.* Ithaca: Cornell University Press, 1957.

A good account of how the Roman literary heritage was preserved.

Lewis, C. S. "Dante's Statius." In *Studies in Medieval and Renaissance Literature*, pp. 94–102. Cambridge: Cambridge University Press, 1966.

Lewis argues that the horrors of Statius are a "sincere reaction to the terrible period" in which he lived and that Dante would have read him as he would read a "medieval moral theologian." Lewis also treats Statius in *The Allegory of Love* (Oxford, 1936), where he argues that the *Thebaid* reflects a shift in imaginative power from the ancient gods to personifications like Piety and Clemency. A third work, *The Discarded Image* (Cambridge: Cambridge University Press, 1964), comments on the figure of Nature and the scholia of Lactantius that created the figure Demogorgone.

Lewis, Charlton T. *A Latin Dictionary.* Oxford: At the Clarendon Press, 1996.

This dictionary, which first appeared in 1879, is a revision of a work edited by E. A. Andrews and is based on the work of German philologists and Charles Short. It is commonly referred to as Lewis and Short. It contains extensive annotations on Statius's *Thebaid.*

Mackay, I. A. "Statius in Purgatory." *Classica et Mediaevalia* 26 (1965): 293–305.

Mackay mentions Statius's trope of alternative explanations; for example, the possible reasons for earthquakes (*Thebaid* 7.809–17).

Martinez, Ronald. "Dante and the Two Canons: Statius in Virgil's Footsteps (*Purgatorio* 21–30)." *Comparative Literature Studies* 32 (1995): 151–75.

Martinez shows how Dante used Statius to conceive his own relation to Virgil. He notes the influence of Statius's final lines (they were copied as a model formula for closure by Petrarch's *Africa,* Joseph of Exeter, Walter of Chatillon, Alain de Lille's *Anticlaudianus,* and Boccaccio's *Filocolo*). Martinez also points out that the repetition of Parthenopaeus, the Arcadian, at the end of the *Thebaid* imitates the triple invocation of Orpheus for Eurydice at the end of Virgil's *Georgics.*

Patterson, Lee. *Chaucer and the Subject of History.* Madison: University of Wisconsin Press, 1991.

Patterson argues that the classics gave Chaucer a form that allowed meaning and interpretability without allegorical exegesis; and "a prospect upon life that is capacious and synoptic but not dismissively transcendental—in other words, a historiography" (p. 61). He contrasts the recursive violence that Chaucer associated with Thebes (as when the incest of Oedipus replays the fate of Cadmus's earthborn soldiers) with the linear but limited plot of Christian causality, which obscures the role of chance and is finally grounded in human will. Patterson also argues that the "broche of Thebes" is a "sign of illicit sexuality," made by Vulcan for Harmonia, daughter of Mars and Venus, when she marries Cadmus, causing their exile from the city and transformation to serpents. Next it belongs to Semele, struck by Jove's lightning; then Agave, driven mad by the Furies; then Argia, who gives it to Euripyle if she will reveal the hiding place of her husband Amphiaraus, an act of betrayal that leads to his engulfment in the earth. The brooch rouses erotic emotions with deadly consequences, puts love and war at odds in mutual subversion, and operates as a metonym for "the primal polymorphousness of Theban emotions and the self-destructive regressiveness that results from submitting to a self unknown" (p. 76).

Putnam, Michael C. J. *Virgil's Aeneid: Interpretation and Influence.* Chapel Hill: University of North Carolina Press, 1995.

One of several excellent modern readings of the *Aeneid* that stresses the moral ambiguity of Aeneas.

Rajna, Pio. *Le fonti dell'*Orlando furioso. Florence: Sansoni, 1900.

Rajna relates Statius's Hopleus and Dymas to Argia and Antigone as well as to Ariosto's Medoro. The death of Parthenopaeus is the model for that of Dardinello, son of Almonte, whom Rinaldo slays in canto 18 of the *Furioso.*

Ross, Charles. "Alternating Reigns: Seven against Thebes. A New Translation of the *Thebaid.*" *Two Lines: A Journal of Translation* (Spring 1998): 152–77.

I list this publication of a version of my introduction and the first 150 lines of this translation as evidence that much of my thinking about Statius dates from about this period.

Sanok, Catherine. "Criseyde, Cassandre, and the *Thebaid:* Women and the Theban Subtext of Chaucer's *Troilus and Criseyde.*" *Studies in the Age of Chaucer* 20 (1998): 41–71.

A strong feminist appreciation of the *Thebaid* as well as a scholarly analysis of the relationship of Chaucer to Statius.

Schwartz, Regina. *The Curse of Cain.* Chicago: University of Chicago Press, 1997.

An intriguing reading of the Old Testament that relates fraternal strife, homosexuality, and scarcity to monotheism.

Snijder, H. *Thebaid: A Commentary on Book III.* Amsterdam: Adolf M. Hakkert, 1968.

The poem is a work of horror and cruelty that shows "to what depths of degradation man can sink when impiety, hatred and jealousy" overcome him.

Togail na Tebe: The Thebaid of Statius. With introduction, translation, vocabulary, and notes by George Calder. Cambridge: At the University Press, 1922.

The Irish text edited from two manuscripts.

Vessey, David. *Statius and the* Thebaid. Cambridge: Cambridge University Press, 1973.

"It would be wrong to see in the *Thebaid* any subtle political allegory" (p. 63). A full-length study of the poem.

Wetherbee, Winthrop. "'*Per te poeta fui, per te Cristiano*': Dante, Statius, and the Narrator of Chaucer's *Troilus.*" In *Vernacular Poetics in the Middle Ages,* ed. Lois Ebin. Kalamazoo, Mich.: Medieval Institute Publications, 1984.

In arguing that Chaucer found hints of transcendence in the *Thebaid,* just as Dante did, Wetherbee offers an uplifting reading of Statius's poem, despite the darkness of Statius's vision. Evil dominates the lives of most of the characters. Even Theseus must kill, but Amphiaraus and Menoeceus embody *pietas* because they are heroic despite knowing they are doomed. Pathenopaeus's physical appearance signals the absence of "any debasing passion" or worldly awareness of fate. Antigone, too, shows *pietas,* and the aged Phorbas sees her as a source of hope, despite the crimes of Thebes. Wetherbee suggests that the infusion of *virtus* into Menoeceus is the source of Dante's having Statius explain how divine *virtù* enters the embryonic soul. Like Menoeceus, the soul lives only to die, once it feels divine fire.

Acknowledgments

My need to translate Statius was prompted by a paper on Statius's pacifism written by CoryAnne Harrigan for a Renaissance seminar. We were reading David Quint's *Epic and Empire* (Princeton University Press, 1992), which privileges Virgil and Lucan but not Statius, the third of Rome's great epic poets. The lacuna seemed obvious; moreover, confronting Statius was, for me, a way to further understand the literary taste of C. S. Lewis. Lewis's cultural stock is currently being sold short because of his religion and ideas about women (which are not my own), but he knew how to read.

For help in establishing the form of this translation I want to thank Robert Kastor and Allen Mandelbaum. For comments on either the translation or the introduction I am grateful to Emily Allen, Martha Craig, Angelica Duran, and Jennifer Tonsing. Statius (and Boiardo) gave me something to talk about while I was driving Seamus Heaney to the airport a few years ago, and Heaney—a wonderful man—put me in touch with Jonathan Galassi, who kindly gave me ten minutes to pitch Statius. "One degree of separation too much from the general public" was his verdict a week later. And so extra credit must be given to the Johns Hopkins University Press, which has supported me almost from the beginning. Ann Astell directed my attention to Southey. CoryAnne, now Professor, Harrigan drafted the notes to this volume, a huge task, and deserves far more credit than this small acknowledgment can offer.

Perhaps for political reasons that I point out in my introduction, Statius is currently enjoying a revival among scholars. I want to mention here Betty Rose Nagle's *The* Sylvae *of Statius* (Indiana University Press, 2004), which reached me when this book was in page proof. Professor Nagle's introduction adds to our picture of the poet, and the translation helps revive an author who was more than good enough for every major poet in Italy and many in England. Professor Nagle also explains some procedures of translation that I share; for example, Statius has a relatively small vocabulary, "so repeated use of the same word is not necessarily significant" (Nagle, p. 30); sometimes glosses are incorporated into the text for the convenience of the reader. Unlike her, I have chosen in general to ignore Statius's use of the historical present and have kept to the past tense in English. Another minor difference is that for the most part I retain Statius's habit of occasionally addressing people in the second person.

One of the many such recent classicists writing on Statius notices that readers of Italian Renaissance romances (like Lewis, like me) find Statius easy to appreciate. This category includes my wife Clare, who approved Statius's density after the free flow of Boiardo and gave me the go-ahead for this project. This translation is naturally dedicated to her, and to Slaney and Sam, better readers than I ever was at their age.